P9-DXI-930

PERSONAL ADJUSTMENT

AN APPROACH THROUGH THE STUDY OF HEALTHY PERSONALITY

SIDNEY M. JOURARD, Ph.D.
UNIVERSITY OF FLORIDA

PERSONAL

ADJUSTMENT

AN APPROACH THROUGH THE STUDY OF HEALTHY PERSONALITY

SECOND EDITION

THE MACMILLAN COMPANY, NEW YORK
COLLIER-MACMILLAN LTD., LONDON

Second Printing

Library of Congress catalog card number: 63–10902

The Macmillan Company, New York
Collier-Macmillan Canada, Ltd., Galt, Ontario
Divisions of The Crowell-Collier Publishing Company

Printed in the United States of America

I dedicate this book not just to those whom I love but to all who see man as an end, not as a tool or as an obstacle.

PREFACE TO THE SECOND EDITION

To be "average" in personality means to suffer from various "socially patterned defects," as Fromm calls them. That is, the typical person in our society usually shows signs of premature arrest in his growth; he may carry symptoms of neurosis which are so widely shared in his society that he does not realize he is half sick. The simple fact is that in an age when space is being explored, and when man has the nuclear power to destroy this planet, average personality *is just not good enough.* We need to learn more about man's potentials for fuller personal development, in the hope that future parents and teachers will be able to rear generations of healthier personalities.

When I wrote the first edition of this book, the concept of healthy personality, or positive mental health, was just beginning to gain currency in psychology and psychiatry. In the time that has intervened, considerably more has been written on the subject, and I have tried to incorporate relevant new material in this edition. I have also sought to write in a simpler style, so that the subject matter will be more readily communicated to the reader.

The book is primarily intended as a text for undergraduate courses in personality adjustment, or mental health. The notes and references at the end of each chapter have been included to provide the serious student with a guide to additional readings which will amplify points made in the text. Of course, these references also served the writer as source material and as documentation for many of his views.

I hope that the experience of reading this book will help many students to make decisions and to gain insights that will foster healthier personality growth. And I hope, too, that some may become so fascinated by the challenge of healthy personality that they choose it as a field of study to which they might ultimately make a professional contribution.

I have organized this edition in two broad sections. The first eight chapters deal with the person: with standards for evaluating him as a whole; with his needs, his cognition, emotion, his relation to his body, his self-structure, and his conscience. The last five chapters are devoted to man in relation to his fellow man. I discuss interpersonal behavior as it is manifested by the individual. Then, I focus on characteristics of his relations with others, with a view to highlighting factors in healthy transactions. Next, I discuss love. In the first edition, I included my discussion of sex in the earlier section. This time I decided that sex is more properly viewed as an interpersonal, not an individual, behavior pattern, and so the chapter on sex appears after the one on love. The last chapter, which deals with therapy, is an effort to help students understand better how man can help his fellow man grow toward healthier personality. Although the chapter deals with the professional therapist in relation to his patients, students will often see parallels between effective therapy and good relationships with one's friends and family.

Here and there throughout the text, as well as in the last chapter, the term *personality therapy* is employed instead of the word *psychotherapy*. This slight modification in nomenclature is introduced to provide consistency and to avoid the dualism implicit in the latter term. The terms *personality hygiene* and *personality health* are employed for the same reasons, as alternates for *mental* hygiene and *mental* health.

I want to thank some of the people with whom I have been associated over the past few years; the many conversations I had with them helped me to extend and modify many of my ideas about healthy personality. The present revision is the better, I think, because of my contacts with Dr. Hugh Davis, Dr. Ira Gordon, Dr. Milan Kolarik, Dr. Ted Landsman, Dean Dorothy M. Smith, and Dr. Carolyn Taylor, all at the University of Florida. I owe an especial debt of gratitude to Dr. Emily Stogdill, of the Ohio State University, who made a painstaking study of the first draft manuscript of this revision. And as before, I acknowledge with thanks the encouragement of my wife, Toni Jourard, and the proud deference shown me by my sons—Jeff, Marty, and Leonard—as I worked.

CONTENTS

PERSONAL ADJUSTMENT

AN APPROACH THROUGH THE STUDY OF HEALTHY PERSONALITY

CHAPTER *1*

SOME DEFINITIONS OF HEALTHY PERSONALITY

INTRODUCTION

Most of us think we know what we mean when we speak of health. Yet a little critical thinking will reveal that the meaning of the term is as complex as it is elusive. We assume we are healthy when we are not sick. Everyone knows what it means to be sick. It means that our body hurts; we have a fever, we lack energy, and we lose interest in everything except getting well. But what is this condition of health that we lose when we become sick? Doctors describe the state of health in terms of physiological indices of one kind or another: "normal" body temperature, "normal" white-cell count, "normal" heart rate and blood pressure, and so on. These are all signs that our body is functioning "well."

Health is a value, *and it refers to a mode of bodily functioning which is sought after when it has been lost. Everybody wants to be healthy, to have a body which is free from pain, has lots of energy, and which will last a long time. Perhaps here we have a general definition of health: that mode of organ-functioning which insures that the body will be pain-free, energetic, and long-lived.*[1]

But today, it has become customary to distinguish between physical and mental health. What is referred to by the term "mental health"? Does it mean the same as physical health? Can we say a healthy mind is one which is free of pain, has lots of energy, and lives a long time? Not likely, because the mind is a concept, not a thing. The body is a physical object which can be seen, dissected, felt, weighed, and measured. The mind cannot be dealt with in this fashion. Since this is so, how can we speak of mental health, or of a healthy mind?[2]

We shall speak in this book of healthy personality *instead of mental health. Personality, too, is an abstract term. It refers to characteristic ways in which a person reacts to life situations. Healthy personality refers to ways of behaving that are valued. By whom are they valued? In a strict sense we might say healthy personality refers to ways of behaving that are valued by "mental hygienists," or* personality hygienists, *as the experts who work in this field (psychiatrists and psychologists) will be called. These ways of behaving will most likely be valued by the person himself and by society as a whole, if the society is healthy.*[3]

We may well ask at this point, "Why should personality hygienists be specially qualified to pass judgment on how people ought to behave in order to become happy and healthy?" The reason lies in the fact that personality hygienists, especially practicing therapists of personality, have studied man more minutely than he has ever been studied throughout history. On the basis of their intimate knowledge of the subjective side of man, they have gradually evolved more complete knowledge of man's potentials for growth and happiness as well as for misery and regression. Further, they have learned some of the conditions under which man attains happiness and growth and some of the identifiable features of healthy personality and behavior. We shall explore some concepts of healthy personality proposed by various psychiatrists and psychologists; but before we do, it will be useful to draw a distinction between normal *personality and* healthy *personality.*

NORMAL OR MODAL PERSONALITY

There are few words that have been used with so many meanings as "normal."[4] In physical medicine, the term is used as a synonym for health. In statistics, the word means, literally, characteristic of the norm; that is, common, average, or representative of a group. In earlier works on mental hygiene, to be normal meant that a person was free from the symptoms of mental disease. In the present work, *normal* will be used in the statistical sense, referring to traits that are typical, representative, or "modal." In fact, we shall prefer the word *modal* to normal, since in the statistical sense it means roughly the same thing, yet is free of the additional connotations of normal. *Normal* or *modal personality,* then, refers to the traits which characterize an individual who is representative of or similar to a larger class of persons. We could speak of a modal, middle-class American, or a modal college professor, or a modal Okinawan. It is the modal personality which sociologists and anthropologists describe in their field studies of societies. They ignore individual differences among members of a group and strive to depict the reaction patterns which are shared by the group members. Naturally, there are many practical uses to which knowledge of modal personality can be put. If we know what reaction patterns to expect from people in general, we can influence and control their behavior to a marked degree. Thus, if we know that people like an individual who smiles and passes compliments, and that if people like you they will buy what you sell, it follows that salesmen should be trained to smile and pass compliments. The politician directs his speeches toward the modal personality. He tries to determine what most people in his audience want to hear and then speaks accordingly, hoping they will all respond favorably to his remarks.

Obviously, modal personality is not necessarily healthy personality. There may be many traits quite common to the general population which a personality hygienist would deplore. For example, it might be normal for people chronically to repress certain feelings such as anger, but the hygienist would not regard this as a healthy trait. He would regard it as unhealthy, because prolonged repression of such feelings is suspected to be a factor in the development of many ills, physical ("psychosomatic") as well as psychological. The modal personality may be regarded as a person with a twofold potential. He can "grow" in the direction of fuller functioning, or healthier personality, and he can "regress" in the direction of mental illness. One of the objectives of this book is to help increase the likelihood of healthier personality growth and to decrease the probability of outright mental illness. Now, let us look at some concepts of healthy personality.

CONCEPTS OF HEALTHY PERSONALITY

A PSYCHOANALYTIC VIEW OF HEALTHY PERSONALITY. Freud, the founder of psychoanalysis, did not make a serious effort at describing healthy personality, because he was primarily interested in neurosis. He contented himself by stating that health consisted in the ability to love and to do productive work. His theory of personality structure, however, points to factors which permit fulfillment of the capacities to love and to work.

One can portray healthy personality (ability to love and work) in psychoanalytic concepts by stating it is an outcome of *harmony among id, ego, and superego.* Another trait of healthy personality is implied by a statement Freud made about the goal of psychoanalytic therapy: "Where id was, there shall ego be."

These technical formulations will mean little to students who are not acquainted with psychoanalytic terminology, and so we shall define some of these terms in order to elucidate the meaning implied above.

According to the psychoanalysts,[5] personality can be divided into three major realms, or substructures—the *id,* the *ego,* and the *superego.* The id is the term used to refer to basic urges, impulses, or instincts that are inborn. Ego refers to the active, controlling, perceiving, learning functions of personality. Superego refers to the morals, ideas, and taboos a person acquires in the process of growing up. It is the task of the ego to scan external reality and inner experience, and then choose and direct the organism's behavior so that needs will be met without danger to the organism and without violating moral taboos. In unhealthy personalities, such as neurotic patients, the ego is deficient in strength and is unable to perform the complicated tasks of accurately appraising outer reality and inner, subjective reality and then reconciling among the conflicting demands of impulses, morals, and external reality. Neurotic patients have typically handled the conflicts generated between impulses (like sex or aggression) and morality by repression, that is, by blotting them from awareness. It is this repression which fosters the development of the incapacitating neurotic symptoms.

If a person's upbringing had been adequate (the psychoanalysts did not fully explain such adequacy), his ego would be sufficiently strong to resolve conflicts between needs, or between impulses and morals, and the healthier personality would thus be able to gratify his needs and yet remain free of guilt or of social blame. Since he would be less prone to repress many of his feelings (repression consumes energy), his energy would be available for productive work. Since he would not be afraid or ashamed of his feelings and emotions (because of a reasonable conscience), he could be freer in expressing himself in loving relationships. Hence, the relationship between ability to love and work, and the concept of harmony among id, ego, and superego, can assume greater meaning. The phrase "Where id was, there shall ego be" can be translated to mean "Where a person behaved compulsively or impulsively, he can, if healthy, substitute rational choice and control." That is, healthy personalities can *choose* between expressing feelings and withholding such expression; between pursuing gratification of needs and postponing such a quest for gratification.

We can amplify the psychoanalytic concept of healthy personality, then, by asserting that it presumes harmony among the separate components of personality. This harmony calls for an ego of optimum strength and a superego or conscience which is not unduly harsh, tyrannical, and unreasonable. Given such an ego and superego, the desired harmony within personality becomes feasible, and love and work become possible.

The theory just outlined is plausible as its stands and has great explanatory power. The main difficulty with it is that it is difficult to specify signs of a strong ego and to describe a humane superego. Later in this book (pages 152, 250) we shall attempt to overcome these deficiencies. We have mentioned the psychoanalytic concept of health, however, for historical reasons and also because it has had a profound effect on later workers, as we shall see below.

ADLER'S VIEW: SOCIAL FEELING. Alfred Adler[6] was one of the few psychiatrists who were drawn to Freud's ideas in the early part of this century. He began to work as an orthodox psychoanalyst but soon found he could not agree with some of Freud's theoretical formulations, especially Freud's view of the role played by sex in the development of neurosis. (See pages 235–236.) Adler asserted that inferiority feelings and compensatory strivings for superiority played the most crucial roles in neurotic illness and interfered with the capacity to love and to work. He saw as one important goal of personal growth and of therapy the attainment of *gemeinschaftsgefühl.* The German word *gemeinschaftsgefühl* has been translated as "social interest" or "social feeling." This term refers to a feeling of oneness, a brotherly feeling toward one's fellow man. People who have achieved *gemeinschaftsgefühl* no longer compete irrationally with others, nor do they strive to be "one-up" on them. They see their fellow men as worthy beings to be regarded as ends in themselves, not as threats or as mere tools to be used for self-advancement.

Adler thus introduced and emphasized an *interpersonal* facet to theories of healthy personality. His writings have been influential in psychiatry and in education, though perhaps less widely recognized than those of Freud. The concept of social feeling accords with the highest precepts of ethics and religion and represents a wholesome corrective to the more pathology-oriented psychoanalytic writing.

HEALTHY PERSONALITY IN JUNG'S WRITING. Carl Gustav Jung, like Adler and Otto Rank (discussed below), was an early student and collaborator of Freud's, but he too departed from Freud's views and commenced a productive career in psychotherapy, research, and writing.[7] His theories of personality structure and development do not lend themselves to succinct statement, but should be directly read by serious students. The portions of his writing that bear on healthy personality concern us most directly here. Jung saw, as goals of growth and of therapy, *the attainment of selfhood*—the integration of conflicting elements in personality into a unique, harmonious pattern. Man becomes a healthy personality when he becomes a "self"—a responsible, unique person who has found a purpose or a meaning for his existence.

Jung's emphasis upon selfhood, that is, responsible, purposive individuality as a goal for man's development is a basic tenet not only in his "analytic psychology" school of thought but also in current existentialist writings. This is not to deny that Freud, Adler, and many of the other theorists of healthy personality also illustrated existentialist viewpoints.

OTTO RANK: CREATIVITY, INDIVIDUALITY, AND AFFIRMATION OF ONE'S OWN WILL. Otto Rank[8] was another of Freud's early followers who, like Adler and Jung, later went his own way. The points in his numerous writings which bear on healthy personality have to do with "willing" and with "creativity." Rank regarded the creative artist as a pinnacle of human growth. The artist was seen as one with courage to assert his difference from the mass of men and who dared to shape reality as he wished it to be, rather than passively "adjusting" to a fixed, frozen reality. Rank saw neurotics as persons with strong wills and strong creative urges but who lacked the final courage to impose their individual stamp on the world. Instead, they "shaped" their own personalities (as a sculptor shapes his clay) *in order to please others.* Healthy personality, for Rank, implied the courage to become a separate, distinct person, the courage to express one's difference from others, and the courage to be inventive and creative in various spheres of existence.

Rank's emphasis on willing, on creativity, on individuality, and on separation of oneself from dependency on others has had an influence on many contemporary workers. Certainly, we would have to agree that healthy personality must imply some ability to assert oneself and to behave, not in slavishly conforming ways, but in more autonomous, creative fashion.

ERICH FROMM'S "PRODUCTIVE ORIENTATION." Erich Fromm is a contemporary psychoanalyst who is often classified as a "neo-Freudian." He sought to harmonize many of Freud's basic concepts with perspectives offered by sociology and humanistic ethics. Fromm's concept of the *productive orientation* may be regarded as his view of healthy personality.[9] According to Fromm, people relate to the world and to other people in certain basic ways, which he calls "orientations." He distinguishes between "non-productive" and "productive" orientations. The former include the *receptive* orientation, the *hoarding* orientation, the *exploitative* orientation, and the *marketing* orientation. People in whom these orientations predominate behave as if they had no inner resources, no "good" within themselves; they act as if everything that is worth while is possessed by other people. Their life task is to get other people to give them things (receptive characters); to hang on to what they already have, giving as little as they can to others (hoarding characters); to seize from others by force or guile (exploitative characters); or (marketing characters) they regard their own personalities as *commodities* whose worth is determined by their "market value." That is, marketing personalities strive to mold their behavior so as to be pleasing to bosses, customers, friends, and they regard their personal worth primarily in terms of how others regard them and how much money they can earn.

By contrast, the person who has achieved a productive orientation is able to love himself and is able to establish truly loving relations with other persons; he is able to employ his reason to grasp and understand the world; and he is able to do productive work, in the sense of art or craftsmanship, thus bringing values into the world.

Clearly, the attainment of a productive orientation is seen by Fromm as a goal of personal development, or as an aim of effective personality therapy.

HARRY STACK SULLIVAN: ACCURATE PERCEPTION OF PEOPLE. Sullivan was a highly influential American psychiatrist.[10] He developed what is called the "interpersonal school" in psychiatry, combining Freudian concepts with those developed in American social psychology. He believed the proper study of psychiatry was not the person as such, but rather his *relationships with people.* Sullivan noted that neurotic or psychotic patients behaved toward others as if they had traits, feelings, or attitudes which in reality they did not possess. By implication then, healthy personality would be manifested by a person whose concepts about other people were realistic, not confused by past experiences. Sullivan stated that a person could achieve lasting satisfactions and security in his relations with other people only if he had a clear idea of the other person and of himself, and what was going on between them. "Satisfactions" refers to the fulfillment of bodily needs, such as the need for food, rest, sexual gratification; "security," in Sullivan's writings, refers to the emotional state that is produced in a person when he has earned affection, status, and esteem from others. It does not mean safety. Thus, Sullivan extended Adler's interpersonal emphasis (on "social feeling") by pointing to the importance of clear awareness of self *and other* in interpersonal relationships.

HEALTHY PERSONALITY: AN EXISTENTIAL VIEW. The existential philosophers—Kierkegaard and Nietzsche in the nineteenth century and Heidegger, Marcel, Sartre, Tillich, and Buber in the twentieth, to name the more important among them—have written much about the human condition, and their writings have commanded increased attention from psychologists and psychiatrists.[11] Implicit in their writings is a view of healthy personality which will doubtless become increasingly influential among scientific students of man. We will see some of this influence already in Rogers' views, which we outline below. Here we shall attempt only to spell out a brief portrait of healthy personality from an existential standpoint.

According to existential writers, man alone has the capacity to choose his behavior and hence to shape his "essence," i.e., his observable characteristics at any point in time. The healthy personality, according to this view, takes responsibility for his actions, makes decisions, and seeks to "transcend" the determining, limiting effects on his behavior of handicap, social pressures to conformity, extreme stress, and biological impulses and feelings. The healthy personality becomes aware of the pressures these impersonal forces impose on his action, but he *chooses* whether or not he will act in conformity with them or in opposition to them. Only man can thus choose and hence "make" himself.

The healthy personality displays "courage to be."[12] This term implies knowing and asserting one's feelings, opinions, beliefs, and goals and taking the consequences which follow from such assertion. It implies freedom to choose between hiding or faking one's real self and letting others know one as one is.

The healthy personality regards himself as a *person,* not as a collection of social roles[13] or an instrument of others, the state, or his impulses. In dealing with other people, he treats them as persons too, like himself, rather than as things, objects, tools, or instruments of his wishes. That is, he lives in "dialogue"[14] with his fellow men rather than deal with them impersonally.

The healthy personality becomes aware of his own "being" and sees his life and what he makes of it as his own responsibility, not the responsibility of the state, or his parents, or other people. One becomes most keenly aware of one's being when one squarely faces the fact that one will die some day. The realization that one's days are numbered and that it is up to oneself to make the most of one's life are what is meant by awakening to one's being.

From the existential point of view, average people and the mentally ill both suffer some degree of estrangement from their own being, from nature, and from their fellow men. They find the responsibility of freedom too frightening, and so they let their lives be lived for them by impulses or by social pressures to conformity. In the process, they lose their selves, or their being. Awakening to one's being, assuming responsibility for one's existence, finding the courage to be, and treating other people as persons rather than things (entering into dialogue with them) are thus among the goals of growth and of therapy for the existential psychologists and psychiatrists.

Comment. In the writings of Maslow and Rogers, considered below, we will notice clear signs of the influence of existential thinking as well as of earlier psychoanalytic theorizing. Let us turn now to Maslow.

A. H. MASLOW: "SELF-ACTUALIZING PEOPLE." A. H. Maslow is a contemporary psychologist who has devoted himself to the study of the conditions under which man develops his human capacities to their fullest degree. He believes the key to such development is in the gratification of basic needs.[15] These needs develop in an hierarchical sequence, from "lower" to "higher," and a man must meet the demands of his lower needs before those of the higher levels can emerge. This hierarchy, from lowest to highest, includes: *physical* needs, such as the need for food and water; *safety* needs, illustrated by the quest for a milieu which is relatively free from threats to life and which fosters a sense of security; *belonging and love* needs, illustrated by the felt hunger for affectionate, accepting relationships with other persons; *esteem* needs, illustrated by the desire to be respected by others for one's accomplishments and the quest for recognition and prestige. Once a person has successfully learned to cope with these needs as they arise, his energies will then be more readily freed for *self-actualization.* Actualization of self cannot be sought as a goal in its own right, however; rather, it seems to be a *by-product* of active commitment of one's talents to some cause outside the self, such as the quest for beauty, truth, or justice.[16] Without some such mission in life, a person is likely to experience boredom or a sense of stultification. Once he finds a purpose (or purposes), he can then dedicate his energies and talents to its fulfillment. As he meets the challenges of the tasks he will encounter, his growth or actualization will be fostered.

Maslow developed his ideas through study of numbers of people who met his criteria for being well along in the process of actualizing themselves.[17] Some of the traits that appeared consistently in his self-actualizing (S-A) cases were:

1. *A more adequate perception of reality and more comfortable relations with reality than occur in average people.* His S-A cases seemed to detect the spurious, the fake, and the dishonest in interpersonal relations and to be attuned to the truth and to reality in all spheres of life. They eschewed the illusory and preferred to cope with even unpleasant reality rather than retreat to pleasant fantasies.

2. *A high degree of acceptance of themselves, of others, and of the realities of human nature.* They were not ashamed of being what they were, and they were not shocked or dismayed to find foibles and shortcomings in themselves or in others.

3. *Spontaneity.* The S-A people displayed spontaneity in their thinking, emotions, and behavior to a greater extent than average people.

4. *Problem-centeredness.* Maslow's subjects seemed all to be focused on problems *outside* themselves. They were not overly self-conscious; they were not problems *to* themselves, and could hence devote their attention to a task, duty, or mission that seemed peculiarly cut out for them.

5. *A need for privacy.* The S-A people could enjoy solitude; indeed, they would even seek it out on occasion, needing it for periods of intense concentration on subjects of interest to them.

6. *A high degree of autonomy.* The S-A people seemed able to remain true to themselves in the face of rejection or unpopularity; they were able to pursue their interests and projects and maintain their integrity even when it hurt to do so.

7. *A continued freshness of appreciation.* The S-A people showed the capacity to "appreciate again and again, freshly and naïvely, the basic goods of life . . . a sunset, a flower, a baby, a person"; it was as if they avoided merely lumping experiences into categories and then dismissing them. Rather, they could see the unique in many apparently commonplace experiences.

8. *Frequent "mystic experiences."* The S-A people seemed subject to periodic experiences that are often called "mystic" or "oceanic"—feelings that one's boundaries as a person have suddenly evaporated

and one has truly become a part of all mankind and even of all nature.

9. *Gemeinschaftsgefühl.* The German word *gemeinschaftsgefühl* also means "brotherly feeling," the feeling of belongingness to all mankind (related to the mystic experiences above); the attitude was found to be characteristic of S-A people. They felt a sense of identification with mankind as a whole, such that they could become concerned not only with the lot of members of their immediate family but also with the situation of persons from different cultures.

10. *Close relationships with a few friends or loved ones.* Maslow found that his S-A subjects, while not necessarily very popular, did have the capacity to establish truly close, loving relationships with at least one or two other people.

11. *Democratic character structures.* The S-A people tended to judge people and to be friendly with them, not on the basis of race, status, religion, or other group membership traits; rather, they related to others as *individuals.*

12. *A strong ethical sense.* The S-A subjects were found to have a highly developed sense of ethics. Though their notions of right and wrong were not always wholly conventional, their behavior was always chosen with reference to its ethical meaning.

13. *Unhostile senses of humor.* The S-A people had senses of humor which made common human foibles, pretensions, and foolishness the subject of laughter, rather than sadism, smut, or rebellion against authority.

14. *Creativeness.* The S-A people were creative and inventive in some areas of their existence, not followers of the usual ways of doing or thinking.

15. *Resistance to enculturation.* The S-A subjects could detach themselves somewhat from complete absorption, or "brainwashing," or imprinting by their cultures. This would permit them to adopt critical attitudes toward cultural inconsistencies or unfairness within their own society.

Truly, this is a most impressive collection of attributes! One would like to meet or to become such a person. We have dwelt at length on Maslow's composite portrait of self-actualization because it offers a detailed conception of human potentials—a concept of man at his best. Certainly it is worth while to ponder what man might become, in the hope that more of us might learn to move toward those seemingly Utopian levels of being. In a sense, this book is devoted to further exploration of paths to self-actualization.

CARL ROGERS: "FULLY FUNCTIONING PERSONS." Carl Rogers has practiced psychotherapy for many years, and he has recently reported a description of the behavior which patients show when they have been granted freedom "to become," as occurs during the process of effective personality therapy.[18] These traits include:

1. *Aversions to façades.* The patients seek to cease struggling to be what they are not.

2. *Aversions to "oughts."* They cease guiding their conduct in terms of unreal, internalized images of what they ought to be, ought to become.

3. *Movement away from "meeting others' expectations" in slavish fashion.* They stop trying compulsively to please others.

4. *Movement toward self-direction.* The patients move toward choosing their own behavior in responsible fashion.

5. *Movement toward accepting themselves.* They accept themselves as persons in process of "becoming."

6. *Movement toward being open to their experience.* They do not blot out thoughts, feelings, perceptions, and memories which might be unpleasant.

7. *Movement toward acceptance.* They accept others and trust themselves.

Rogers summarizes his conception of persons in process of becoming healthier personalities by asserting that they seek to *be* what they *are* and take the consequences which follow therefrom. When they can do this, they feel that their external behavior expresses their real selves. This mode of existence is described as "existential living," and it implies behavior which more fully expresses what one is at any time. Existential living may be contrasted with such terms as "pretense," "phoniness," or "inauthenticity." We might comment that the "existential" modes of functioning provide the basis for "becoming what one potentially is," because "real being" yields consequences that change one from what one now is to what one will next be. Real being permits growth and learning to occur.

Another name for "real being" is *experiencing*.[19] This term, proposed by a colleague of Rogers' (Eugene Gendlin), refers to the ongoing flow of *feeling* which seems to accompany consciousness. It is not always noticed in everyday life, but in therapy it comes into sharper focus. The moments of fullest experiencing appear to be moments when personality is in process of *change* toward fuller functioning.

In summarizing Rogers' contribution to the definition of healthy personality, we have employed his terminology as much as we could. Some of these terms may be difficult for students to grasp. It would not be doing too much violence to Rogers' writing to assert that, in his view, healthy personalities present themselves to others as they truly are at that moment. They do not try to mispresent their feelings or beliefs, but instead, they say what they think, express what they feel, take the consequences of so doing, and more generally, are not ashamed to be who and what they are.

In the next sections, we will briefly outline the statements of several men about key factors in healthy personality. One of these authors (Ruesch) is concerned, not with the characteristics of healthy personality, but rather with an important function which is a *sine qua non* for wellness—namely, communication. Another contributor (Blatz) focuses upon the desirable type of response to problems, challenges, or more generally, insecurity, which is deemed indicative of the attainment of healthy personality. A third (Allport) simply lists several criteria, and a fourth (Buddhist-Taoist) emphasizes the role of "letting be."

JURGEN RUESCH: EFFECTIVE COMMUNICATION. Ruesch, a contemporary psychiatrist, proposed that competence at communication is an indicator of the health of personality.[20] He regards the mentally ill as persons who are deficient in some of the skills essential to full communication with others, e.g., inability to transmit "messages" (thoughts, feelings, and so on), inability to perceive or notice messages, or inability to decode (i.e., understand the meaning of) the messages that have been received. Healthy personality, from this point of view, entails mastery of the many problems involved in communication with others.

Ruesch's emphasis upon the importance of communication for

health represents a valuable synthesis of psychiatric concepts with concepts derived from communication-engineering theory and practice. By calling attention to the crucial role played by communication in the attainment and maintenance of healthy personality, Ruesch opened the way to numerous important researches. Moreover, as we shall see later (pages 341–354), dread of communicating certain aspects of one's experience to others can seriously impair one's health, while openness in such communication makes possible the fulfillment of love, growth, and other worth-while goals.

WILLIAM BLATZ: "INDEPENDENT SECURITY." Blatz, a prominent Canadian child psychologist, believes that self-reliance is the trait which reveals the health or lack of health of a personality. Self-reliance is manifested by a person who has attained some measure of *independent security.* By independent security Blatz means "the state of consciousness which accompanies a willingness to accept the consequences of one's own decisions and actions." He distinguishes between dependent security and independent security. In the former, "an agent (some other person) accepts the responsibility for the consequences of an individual's actions. The individual then feels free to act in accordance with his own desires and wishes because he does not have to accept the consequences of his behavior." Independent security "can be attained in only one way—by the acquisition of a skill through learning. Whenever an individual is presented with a situation for which he is inadequately prepared . . . he must make one of two choices—he must either retreat or attack. . . . The individual must, if he is to attack, emerge from the state of dependent security and accept the state of *insecurity* (my italics). This attack will, of course, result in learning. . . . The individual . . . learns that satisfaction results from overcoming the apprehension and anxiety experienced when insecure, and that he may thus reach a state of independent security through learning."[21]

Blatz's concept of independent security has been mentioned because it provides a link between the applied field of personality hygiene and the experimentally based science of learning. Blatz recognized that the freedom or courage to learn new skills, when one encounters new problems, is an indicant of full functioning in the human being, and must be regarded as a sign of healthy personality. The attainment of a broad repertoire of skills (competence, adequacy) is coming to be recognized as an important factor in the maintenance of healthy personality.

ALLPORT'S SIX CRITERIA OF HEALTHY PERSONALITY. Allport, one of America's leading psychologists, has in a long career at Harvard University made many contributions to the theory of personality. In seeking to define the healthy personality,[22] he proposed the following criteria:

1. *Ego-extension.* Ego-extension is the capacity of taking an interest in more than one's body and one's material possessions.

2. *Self-objectification.* Self-objectification is the ability to know and understand oneself, to recognize how one's present behavior and reactions are influenced by similar experiences in the past. It implies the capacity to look at oneself objectively, even to be able to laugh at oneself. A sense of humor depends upon such self-objectification.

3. *A unifying philosophy of life.* This philosophy may or may not be religious, but it needs to be, at least, a frame of meaning and of responsibility into which life's major activities fit.

4. *The capacity for a warm, profound relating of oneself to others.*

5. *The possession of realistic skills, abilities, and perceptions with which to cope with the practical problems of life.*

6. *A compassionate regard for all living creatures.* This compassion includes respect for individual persons and a disposition to participate with others in activities that will improve the human lot.

This list of criteria, quoted almost unchanged from one of Allport's publications, shows much overlap with those cited by Maslow, Fromm, and others, thus illustrating how those who have attempted to study healthy personality have influenced one another through their writings.

LIBERATION: THE ZEN BUDDHIST VERSION OF HEALTHY PERSONALITY. The quest for health and happiness has existed as long as man has been able to reflect upon his condition. In the East—India, China, and Japan, especially—Buddhist and Taoist monks and philosophers concerned themselves many centuries ago with the problem of how man could liberate himself from cramping, misery- and illness-yielding habits of thought and behavior to attain a happier, healthier, freer existence. Some of those who attained "liberation" and "enlightenment" became teachers, seeking to help others attain the same degree of emancipation from stifling habit and custom. Alan Watts, a present-day English philosopher, devoted many years to study of Eastern philosophies and religions, and in a brilliant series of highly readable books,[23] has ably interpreted the major teachings of ancient Eastern philosophers to Western audiences. He saw a marked parallel between the goal of liberation, which Buddhist monks offer their disciples, and the goal of healthy personality, which personality therapists offer their disturbed and unhappy patients. Further, he saw marked parallels between the various techniques employed by monks to elicit "enlightenment" and modern techniques of therapy practiced by present-day psychiatrists and psychologists. Finally, he called attention to parallels between descriptions of the state of enlightenment and of the state of healthy personality.

According to Watts, a spokesman for Zen Buddhists, man becomes neurotically ill or unhappy because he separates himself too radically from nature, his fellow man, and from his own organism. He equates his very identity with a concept or idea of himself *instead of with his whole being*. In the process of so separating himself from nature, his fellows, and his organism, he loses contact with the "flow" or "process" of life, which is essentially spontaneous. Man replaces spontaneity in his experience, thinking, and behavior with strong efforts to control and regulate his thoughts, memories, feelings, and actions. Liberation (and by implication, healthy personality) occurs when a person is able to adopt the attitude of "letting be," or "letting happen." That is, he "lets go" his conscious, controlling ego, or self, and experiences life in somewhat the following fashion: Instead of experiencing vision as "I am looking at the tree," he experiences it as "Looking at the tree is happening." Instead of a person's "trying" to swim, "liberated" swimming is experienced as "Swimming is permitted to happen" or "Swimming is going on." When a person *stops trying* to make things happen, when he stops trying to *make* himself behave in some desired way, it is argued that the desired events or behavior will spontaneously happen.

All of this may sound mystical and capricious at first glance. This is only because it is difficult in a brief space to paraphrase the careful interpretations of Buddhist thinking which Watts provides. The student is encouraged to consult those of Watts' books mentioned in the footnotes. For our immediate purposes, we can assert that, in the Zen Buddhist view, healthy personality entails liberation from effortful constraint on, and control over, spontaneous thinking, feeling, and action; it entails attainment of an attitude of "letting oneself be" and letting others and nature "be."

ARE THESE DEFINITIONS OF HEALTHY PERSONALITY DIFFERENT?

We have reviewed numerous concepts of healthy personality in the preceding sections. The question may properly be raised, "Are these definitions and indicators of healthy personality essentially different? Is any one more basic or valid than the others?" The more obvious similarities among these definitions probably stem from the fact that the various authors were influenced by one another; e.g., Fromm was strongly influenced by the work of Freud. Another source of overlap is the fact that the authors we cited share certain values and ideals in common, since all of them come from Western European culture. It is interesting to note, however, that ideas from Eastern philosophy have begun to appear in the writings of those who are concerned with the health of personality. Maslow is an example of such a man. It may be expected that, as more psychologists read extensively in the literature of the East, the influence of Taoism and Zen Buddhism will be more strongly evident in writings on personality.

Another question we may raise is directed at the different facets of personality that have been regarded as indices of health: Are these indices but different "surface" manifestations of some more basic, underlying factor of health? Or are they rather separate dimensions? A final answer to this question has by no means been found, but one psychologist, Marie Jahoda,[24] has pointed out that most definitions of "positive mental health" call attention to one or more of the following six aspects of man:

1. *The attitudes shown by a person toward his own self.*
2. *The style and degree of his self-actualization.*
3. *The degree of personal integration achieved by the individual.*

4. *The degree of autonomy achieved by the person.*
5. *The adequacy of the person's perception of reality.*
6. *The degree of environmental mastery achieved by the person.*

The reader can see, from review of several of the conceptions of healthy personality already cited, that this classification does justice to most of the portraits and indicants summarized in this chapter.

A GENERAL DEFINITION OF HEALTHY PERSONALITY

Any single definition clearly will be inadequate in some degree, yet it will be useful to have some succinct statement of what healthy personality is. The following is an effort at such succinct formulation:

Healthy personality is manifested by the individual who has been able to gratify his basic needs through acceptable behavior such that his own personality is no longer a problem to him. He can take himself more or less for granted and devote his energies and thoughts to socially meaningful interests and problems beyond security, or lovability, or status.

USES OF A CONCEPT OF HEALTHY PERSONALITY

A clearly stated definition of healthy personality can be useful for (a) research into personality health, (b) evaluating the results of personality therapy, (c) evaluating the effects of preventive health measures on a given population, and (d) self-evaluation purposes.

PERSONALITY-HEALTH RESEARCH. Millions of dollars annually are spent on research into ways and means of improving the personality health of the nation and of curing the mentally ill. A detailed description of the healthy personality would be invaluable to the researcher, for it would enable him to solve such problems as: How many unhealthy personalities are there?[25] What are the varying degrees of personality illness prevalent in a given group? How can we promote healthy personality?

EVALUATION OF PERSONALITY THERAPY. A neurotic or psychotic

person undergoing psychotherapy wants to know when he has become healthy, and, of course, so does his therapist. A clear concept of personality health would make it possible to devise objective means of rating the over-all health of the personality and disclose which traits have become healthy through treatment and which traits are as yet in need of improvement.

EVALUATION OF PERSONALITY-HYGIENE WORK. Mental health workers are a very industrious group who make speeches, show films, offer courses, conduct discussion groups, and so on, all with the aim of promoting personality health. The problem of evaluating the effects, if any, of these well-intended measures, is a staggering one. Clearly formulated concepts of healthy personality would make it possible for the worker to make before-and-after tests of his population in order to determine what effects he has produced.

SELF-EVALUATION. Every student certainly has asked himself the question, "Am I neurotic, or am I healthy?" Unfortunately, the criteria against which he compares himself are often unclear. A clear specification of the traits of healthy personality would permit the individual to study himself and compare his present traits with the traits deemed indicative of positive health by qualified experts.

These uses of a concept of healthy personality are clearly practical and more than justify the efforts undertaken by those men, whose work we have reviewed, to provide just such a precise definition. However, it is only fair to observe that, while there has been considerable agreement among experts in what traits characterize healthy personality, agreement is still far from perfect. This only means that more research and more efforts at definition are called for.

SOME QUESTIONS ABOUT HEALTHY PERSONALITY

IS HEALTHY PERSONALITY "HAPPINESS"? Everybody wants to be happy, though few people can define this state, and fewer still can know that they are happy when they are happy. Doubtless, one knows happiness best in retrospect—one looks back at some period that has been lived through and decides that one was happy at that time and not happy at some other time. I believe that happiness is a by-product of the fulfillment of values, including the gratification of needs. The attainment of need-gratification and the fulfillment of other values are tasks which people must tackle if life is to have meaning, zest, and purpose. Therefore, we should have to regard healthy personalities as more capable of producing happiness for themselves (and others) than unhealthy personalities would be. However, one should not regard healthy personality as a state of perpetual, grinning delight, because life always contains some tragedy, some failure, some suffering. The one who is happy when objective conditions warrant misery is not a healthy personality; more likely, he is out of touch with reality.

IS HEALTHY PERSONALITY "PEACE OF MIND"? Peace of mind implies absence of conflict, a sense of tranquility, a belief that all current problems have been solved. It implies perfect adjustment to one's social environment, such that life then becomes automatic, effortless, and unthinking. A person who was thus perpetually tranquil, whose life was so perfectly adjusted to his mileu that his behavior functioned with the precision of a well-oiled machine would not be human, and he would not be a healthy personality. Rather, he would be more akin to a robot. Healthy personality implies some ability to face and wrestle with conflicts, with value-dilemmas, plus the sensitivity to feel conflict acutely. It also implies some ability to arrive at workable solutions to dilemmas, such that life can then proceed. But these solutions are never permanent. There is a sense in which peace of mind and healthy personality are compatible; when a person has chosen some goal to work toward and sees it as worth while, he may have "peace of mind" despite trials and tribulations because he is not plagued by doubt and conflict over what he should be doing.

IS HEALTHY PERSONALITY "ADJUSTMENT"? The ability to adjust and conform, to delimit one's behavior to the bounds of legality and respectability is certainly one facet of healthy personality. However, many people see conforming adjustment as the *summum bonum,* which it is not. Guards at the Nazi death camps were adjusted conformists to their group, but we could hardly call such monsters healthy personalities. Nor could we call a person healthy who sought to suppress all thoughts, feelings, and actions which departed somewhat from social norms. Such a person would lack identity, and the enforced suppression of individuality would take a subtle toll in the form of enervation, illness, or boredom. There are times when health, morality, and progress all are served by taking a courageous stand against prevailing patterns of conformity, times when adjustment to society is absolutely unhealthy and maladjustment in the form of vigorous opposition to society's present norms is most compatible with health.

IS HEALTHY PERSONALITY "SUCCESS"? When we think of "success," we generally think of economic success. Popular literature abounds with such titles as "How to Be a Success," but perusal of such volumes shows that, in order to become successful, one must often pay such prices as foregoing sincerity and authenticity in dealing with others—one must want success enough to pay the price that is called for. Healthy personality implies a different kind of success from the economic sort. It implies success at the art of living, loving, and fulfilling one's potentials. It implies a continuous process of facing life with integrity, even in the face of economic failure.

HEALTHY PERSONALITY, MODAL PERSONALITY, AND UNHEALTHY PERSONALITY

We noted above that the modal or typical person was not necessarily a healthy personality. Indeed, we suggested that average people are "poised" between their potentials for fuller functioning on the one hand, and their capacity to become mentally ill on the other.[26] The people who develop neurotic or psychotic symptoms which prevent them from carrying on an existence that is satisfying to them and acceptable to society need expert help to work through their problems in living. It is clear, however, that if a person becomes mentally ill, his life up to the time he developed his symptoms was not adequate to forestall his illness. One of the purposes of this book is to provide some guidelines for modal personalities, to help them attain greater self-actualization, and to diminish the probability that they will develop incapacitating personality disorders.

The remainder of the present volume is devoted to discussion of selected aspects of personality. The aim is to throw light on those modes of behavior which foster healthier personality.

SUMMARY

The term "health" is difficult to define in reference to the body, and it is increasingly difficult to define in reference to the "mind." To avoid the problem of defining "mental health," we propose to speak instead of healthy personality. *This term refers to modes of behavior which are valued because they gratify needs, are appropriate to the person's age and society, his personal value-system, and the immediate situation. Such behavior, presumably, decreases the likelihood of illness and permits growth of personality to proceed.*

Healthy personality differs from normal *or* modal *personality, in that the latter term refers only to traits or behavior patterns that are typical of members of a given group. Behavior that is typical is not necessarily healthy.*

In order to provide an orientation to the field of healthy personality, various psychiatrists and psychologists have attempted to describe traits and criteria of health. Commencing with Freud and the orthodox psychoanalysts, these men include Adler, Jung, Rank, Fromm, Sullivan, the "existentialists," Maslow, Rogers, Ruesch, Blatz, Allport, and the Zen Buddhists. Parallels and overlap are clearly apparent in these writers' concepts of healthy personality. The overlap may be attrib-

uted to their common acquaintance with the values of Western man, values which have begun to be influenced by views of Eastern philosophies.

There are several practical uses to which explicit formulations of a concept of healthy personality might be put: viz., as an aid to research, evaluation of therapy and preventive work, and self-evaluation. The health of personality is relevant to happiness, peace of mind, adjustment, and success.

NOTES AND REFERENCES

Excellent supplementary reading will be provided by those references marked with an asterisk (*).

1. Efforts to define health and disease in general terms are made periodically by physicians as new knowledge is uncovered. A recent formulation is given in Engel, G. L., "A Unified Conception of Health and Disease" in *Perspectives in Biology and Medicine, 3,* 459–485 (1960).

2. See Brown, J. F., *Psychodynamics of Abnormal Behavior* (New York: McGraw, 1940), ch. 3. He explores the problem of the mind-body dualism with clarity and expounds the modern "organismic" point of view.

*3. Fromm has explored the question of whether a society as a whole can be diagnosed "sick." See Fromm, E., *The Sane Society* (New York: Rinehart, 1955), ch. 2.

*4. See Maslow, A. H., *Motivation and Personality* (New York: Harper, 1954), ch. 17, for a critical discussion of the concept of normality.

5. Freud's views of personality development and structure are succinctly stated in Freud, S., *An Outline of Psychoanalysis* (New York: Norton, 1949). The descriptions of the genital character and of health in general are to be found in: Hartmann, H., "Psychoanalysis and the Concept of Health," *Int. J. Psychoanal., 20,* Parts III and IV (1939); Abraham, K., "Character Formation on the Genital Level of the Libido" in Abraham, K., *Selected Papers on Psychoanalysis, Vol. I.,* (New York: Basic Books, 1953), pp. 407–417; Jones, E., "The Concept of a Normal Mind," *Int. J. Psychoanal., 23,* 1–8, 1942; Reich, W., *Character Analysis* (New York: Orgone Institute Press, 1949), pp. 164–170. A fine overview of psychoanalysis in relation to subsequent devel-

opments is Harper, R. A., *Psychoanalysis and Psychotherapy: 36 Systems** (New York: Prentice-Hall, 1959).

*6. The best introduction to Adler's extensive writing is provided in Ansbacher, H. L. and Ansbacher, Rowena R. (eds.), *The Individual Psychology of Alfred Adler* (New York: Basic Books, 1956).

*7. Jung has written an immense amount. The student is advised to consult a secondary source to get an overview of his many writings. See, for example, Hall, C. S. and Lindzey, G., *Theories of Personality* (New York: Wiley, 1957) pp. 76–113. Two good paperbacks to consult are Jung, C. G., *Modern Man in Search of a Soul* (New York: Harcourt [Harvest Books H B-2], 1933) and Jung, C. G., *The Undiscovered Self,* (New York: New American Library [Mentor Book], 1959).

8. See the discussion of Rank in Thompson, Clara, *Psychoanalysis: Evolution and Development* (New York: Hermitage, 1950), pp. 174–182.

*9. See Fromm, E., *Man for Himself* (New York: Rinehart, 1947), pp. 174–182. See also his book *The Sane Society* (New York: Rinehart, 1955), p. 32.

10. Sullivan's thinking is presented in Sullivan, H. S., *The Interpersonal Theory of Psychiatry* (New York: Norton, 1953). It is difficult reading for the beginning student.

*11. A good overview of the thinking of existential philosophers is presented by Blackham, H. J., *Six Existentialist Thinkers* (New York: Harper [Harper Torchbooks], 1959). For a review of the impact of existential thinking on psychology, see: May, R. (ed.), *Existential Psychology** (New York: Random, 1961); May, R., Angel, E., and Ellenberger, H. F. (eds.), *Existence. A New Dimension in Psychiatry and Psychology* (New York: Basic Books, 1958), especially Part I; also Braaten, L. J., "The Main Themes of 'Existentialism' from the Viewpoint of a Psychotherapist," *Ment. Hyg., 45,* 10–17 (1961), and Pervin, L. A., "Existentialism, Psychology, and Psychotherapy," *Amer. Psychol., 15,* 305–309 (1960). A superb account of the "human situation" is given in Fromm, E., *op. cit.,* ch. 3.

*12. *Cf.* Tillich, P., *The Courage to Be* (New Haven: Yale, 1959). Paperbound edition.

13. See Tournier, P., *The Meaning of Persons* (New York: Harper, 1957), especially chs. 2 and 3, in which the distinction between "person" and "personage" is introduced.

*14. Buber, M., *Between Man and Man* (Boston: Beacon Press, 1955), pp. 19–24.

*15. Maslow, A. H., *op. cit.,* ch. 5, "A Theory of Human Motivation."

16. Frankl is explicit on the point that self-actualization cannot be achieved through direct pursuit but is rather a *by-product* of the pursuit of one's chosen life tasks. See Frankl, V. E. "Beyond Self-Actualization and Self-Expression." *J. Existent. Psychiat., 1,* 5–20 (1960).

*17. Maslow, A. H., *op. cit.,* ch. 12, "Self-Actualizing People: A Study of Psychological Health."

*18. Rogers, C. R., *On Becoming a Person* (Boston: Houghton, 1961), pp. 163–198.

19. Gendlin, E. T. "Experiencing: A Variable in the Process of Therapeutic Change," *Amer. J. Psychotherapy, 15,* 233–245 (1961); *Experiencing and the Creation of Meaning* (New York: Free Press, 1962); *Theory of Personality Change,* unpublished, 1962).

20. Ruesch, J. and Bateson, G., *Communication, the Social Matrix of Psychiatry* (New York: Norton, 1951), especially p. 87.

*21. Blatz, W. E., *Understanding the Young Child* (New York: Morrow, 1944), pp. 165–168. A later view, similar to that of Blatz but elaborated in a different way, is in White, R. W., "Motivation Reconsidered: The Concept of Competence," *Psychol. Rev., 66,* 297–233; see also Combs, A. W. and Snygg, D., *Individual Behavior* (2nd ed.; New York: Harper, 1959) ch. 12.

22. Allport, G. W., "Personality: Normal and Abnormal," *Sociol. Rev., 6,* 167–180 (1958).

*23. The material in this section is a highly condensed paraphrase of ideas presented in the following of Watts's books: Watts, A. W., *The Way of Zen* (New York: Mentor, 1959), chs. 1 and 4; *Nature, Man, and Woman* (New York: Mentor, 1960), ch. 3; and *Psychotherapy East and West* (New York: Pantheon, 1961), especially pp. 127 ff. A readable account of Zen is provided by D. T. Suzuki, in Fromm, E., Suzuki, D. T., and de Martino, R., *Zen Buddhism and Psychoanalysis* (New York: Harper, 1960). A rather debunking but very readable account of Zen Buddhism is given in Koestler, A., *The Lotus and the Robot* (New York: Macmillan, 1961).

*24. Jahoda, Marie, *Current Concepts of Positive Mental Health* (New York: Basic Books, 1958), pp. 23–24.

25. In a recent, well-designed study, 1,660 citizens between the ages of 20 and 59 in New York City were interviewed, and their level of mental health was rated according to the following criteria: (1) ease of social interaction; (2) capacity for pursuit of realistic goals; (3) fulfillment of biological goals, such as child bearing and rearing; (4) satisfying sense of social belonging: sensitivity to the needs of others; (5) feeling of adequacy in social roles (particularly sexual); (6) optimal balance between independency-dependency, rigidity-plasticity needs; (7) capacity for utilization of essential creativity; (8) capacity to accept deprivations and individual differences; (9) conservative handling of hostilities and aggressions; (10) identification with ethical and moral values; (11) adaptability to stress (homeostasis); and (12) healthy acceptance of self (e.g., body-image and self-image). The more the subjects conformed to these criteria, the healthier they were judged to be. The results of the study are too complex to be summarized. The interested student should read the original report: Srole, L. *et al, Mental Health in the Metropolis, the Midtown Manhattan Study,* New York, McGraw, 1962).

Some studies have been made of healthier personalities, where the subjects have been selected, not by psychologists, but rather by their peers or their teachers. The subjects were nominated as persons embodying "soundness," or "normality," and they were *then* tested or interviewed by experts in order to specify their characteristics. For examples of such studies, see Barron, F., *Personal Soundness in University Graduate Students* (Berkeley: U. of Cal. Press, 1954); Bonney, M. E., "A Descriptive Study of the Normal Personality," *J. Clin. Psychol., 18,* 256–266 (1962). A good commentary on research approaches to healthy personality is Smith, M. B., "Research Strategies Toward a Conception of Positive Mental Health," *Amer. Psychol., 14,* 673–681 (1959).

26. Some psychiatrists are discontented with the very concept of mental illness, preferring to replace it with the concept of "problems in living." For an example of this view, see Szasz, T., "The Myth of Mental Illness," *Amer. Psychol., 15,* 113–118 (1960). Not all psychologists are in agreement on the value of attempting to itemize criteria of positive health. See Smith, M. B., "Mental Health Reconsidered: A Special Case of the Problem of Values in Psychology," *Amer. Psychol.,* 16, 299–306 (1961). Szasz and Smith both illustrate the "ferment" which is currently going on in the thinking about the problems of personality health and illness. Such ferment is desirable because it leads to new ways of looking at old problems.

CHAPTER 2
NEED-GRATIFICATION AND HEALTHY PERSONALITY

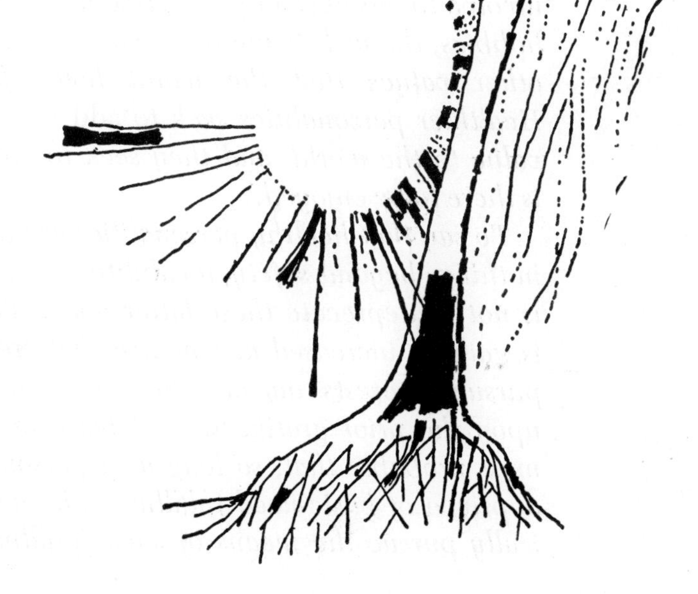

INTRODUCTION

Healthy personalities are individuals involved in and committed to interests beyond *their comfort, health, safety, lovability, or status within some group. These latter goals are important, however, and healthier persons have displayed some measure of competence in attaining them, so that such basic needs are no longer problematic to them. Rather than devote their time, thought, and energy to such questions as "How can I become better loved, or more safe, or more admired? How can I get more frequent sensual pleasure?" they involve themselves in productive work, enjoyable hobbies, the well-being of others, and the myriad other values that the world holds for man. Healthier personalities seek to* add *something of value to the world, and they seek to* enjoy *what is there to be enjoyed.*[1]

To say that healthy personalities are interested in things beyond safety, lovability, sex, or success is not to deprecate these latter goals. The thesis is gaining increased acceptance that freedom to pursue interests outside the self is dependent upon the prior gratification of basic needs. It is most probable that, so long as a person remains deprived of basic-need fulfillment, he will chronically pursue the means of such fulfillment, and his interests will be narrow because of his chronic preoccupation with self.

WHAT MAKES A NEED "BASIC"?

The term "need" is used in many ways in everyday discourse. One person says he needs rest, and another says he needs a yacht. One man says he needs praise, and another says he needs vitamins. In each case, the people are speaking of things they *want,* but more than that, they are saying that *unless* they get whatever it is they say they need, some undesirable consequence will follow.

In the context of this book, we shall regard a need as basic if its gratification or fulfillment fosters health, full functioning, and growth of personality. Maslow[2] states a need can be adjudged basic if:

1. *Its deprivation breeds illness (mental* or *physical).*
2. *Gratification of the need prevents illness.*
3. *Identification and gratification of the need restores health in a person who is presently ill.*
4. *The deprived person prefers gratification of these needs over any others, under conditions of free choice.*
5. *The need is not in a state of tension or privation in healthy persons.*
6. *A subjective feeling of yearning, lack, or desire prevails when the need is not fulfilled.*
7. *Gratification of the need feels good; gratification produces a subjective sense of healthy well-being.* There is further implied the idea that when the need is met, the person doesn't think about it until the next time it arises; he is free for other pursuits.

In the following sections, we shall review some needs which meet these criteria almost totally.

SOME BASIC NEEDS IN MAN[3]

SURVIVAL. Most basic of all human needs is the affirmation of life, the desire to continue living. When life is under threat, man usually places all other considerations in a subordinate position. The man who believes his life is in jeopardy will do almost anything, including break laws, kill others, sacrifice wealth, and so on, in order to eliminate the threat and preserve his existence. It is only on rare occasions, however, that man faces a naked threat to his very life, and so for our present purposes, it will suffice merely to remind the student that the need to survive is sometimes the most powerful determiner of action that man can know. Still more rarely, man may regard his life as less important than some other value; under these conditions, he may sacrifice his existence.

PHYSICAL NEEDS. By physical needs, we have reference to such basic matters as food, drink, relief from pain and discomfort, and adequate shelter. Modern society does a better job of satisfying these needs than was true in earlier stages of history, and so the quests for food, shelter, and comfort are not so powerful determiners of everyday behavior as are other needs which we shall mention below. However, whenever a person experiences a threat to his supplies, or his access to supplies, of food or shelter, he will do anything and everything, short of sacrificing his life, to secure these vital things.

LOVE AND SEX. Man, in order to function as a social and human being, needs to have been the recipient of love from others.[4] If he has been sufficiently loved as a child, and has learned acceptable ways of behaving among others, the probability is high that some other person will choose him to love. Of course, as we shall see in a later chapter, one of the most powerful determiners of one's lovability is one's willingness to love first, or at least reciprocally. When a person feels he is insufficiently loved, his quest for love from others may become a chronic mission, and many other values may be sacrificed in order to elicit loving behavior from others.[5] A *healthy* personality may sacrifice his career, wealth, pride, or dignity in order to be with the person he loves, but this is different from a lifelong quest for tokens of love from others undertaken by an unhealthy personality who is not able to love in return.

The quest for sexual gratification is frequently confused with the search for love. Sexual "hunger" is often one of the most powerful determiners of action, on a par with other basic needs, and highly deprived individuals may pay any price to obtain the pleasures of sexual release. However, in human society, sexual behavior is surrounded by many taboos, customs, and conditions in order to insure that children, if conceived, will be born within a family that can responsibly care for and rear them. One of the developmental tasks which confronts individuals who aspire to healthy personality is the problem of reconciling their sexual needs with such other values as a clear conscience, the integrity of others, and their reputation and status within society.

STATUS, SUCCESS, AND SELF-ESTEEM. Man needs to feel that he is recognized, respected, and approved by other members of the groups within which he carries out his existence. Without such recognition or status, he tends to feel inferior, worthless, isolated, and resentful. The quest for wealth, power, prestige, and other symbols of status is universal in all societies, although the means of attaining such status and the symbols of its attainment differ widely from society to society.[6] Men do many things, not for the satisfaction that may be intrinsic to their activity, but rather for "badges" of status. Thus, a man may work nearly to the point of exhaustion, neglecting his physical health and the needs and wishes of his family for his companionship in order to be able to afford a Cadillac motor car. The status symbolized by a Cadillac seems worth the cost in effort and time to obtain it. He may not enjoy his work, he may not enjoy seeing his family suffer from neglect, the Cadillac may not transport him any better than a less costly vehicle, but so urgent is his quest for status, he is willing to pay the price.[7]

Let us not underrate the strength of the status drive in modern man. The puzzling thing is, how does it become so powerful a determiner of action? Healthy personalities are able to attain a status which satisfies them, and they do not make such attainment the sole purpose of their existence, to which all other values are subordinated. How do they transcend the fanatic commitment to high status? No convenient answer can be offered, but perhaps in the discussion provided by the remainder of the book, leads to answers may be provided.

One hypothesis that has some evidence to support it is that the fanatic quest for status is in reality a substitute, or compensation, for lack of gratification of the needs for love and for physical deprivations associated with an economically impoverished childhood. It is as if the "success-starved" person is trying to make up in his adult years for privations of childhood and can never "get enough."

PHYSICAL AND MENTAL HEALTH. When a person cannot carry out his customary way of life because of incapacitating symptoms—pain, fever, or weakness in the case of physical diseases, and crippling anxiety, depression, or other psychiatric symptoms in the case of "mental illness," he generally ignores all other interests and needs in order to regain his health. However, illness is a very complex reaction to life, and there is reason to suspect that for some, it may be a welcome event, providing socially acceptable respite from a life that has been too burdensome or stressing up to that point. Yet, for most people, illness of any kind is so unpleasant an event, that they do all that is necessary in order to overcome the limitations on existence that it imposes. It is meaningful, then, to speak of "health needs" as powerful determiners of action, even though illness likely arises *because* other basic needs have *not* been met. Much of a person's everyday behavior is modified or selected for its relevance to the maintenance of his health. He takes precautions, consults doctors, and chooses his surroundings with care.[8] When a person makes a fetish of health and devotes undue thought, time, and expense to its protection—even when he is ostensibly in good condition—he is described by psychiatrists as a hypochondriac. The implication is that chronic preoccupation with health is itself a symptom of a type of personality maladjustment, one which calls for specialized therapeutic measures.

FREEDOM. Man needs varying degrees of freedom to conduct his life according to his own decisions, wishes, and plans. That freedom is a powerful value is amply attested to by the many wars that have been fought in its name. We can distinguish between objective freedom, which refers to the relative absence of real physical or social restrictions on one's behavior, and subjective freedom. The latter term may be designated the *feeling of freedom.*[9] It refers to subjective estimates of how free one is to move about, experiment, perform, venture, and otherwise express oneself. Healthy personalities are effective at securing for themselves an environment within which there is the greatest possible amount of objective freedom, and they welcome the feeling of freedom. Less healthy personalities may be ineffective at finding desirable amounts of freedom; they may seek more than they can adequately and fruitfully deal with, or they may not have struggled effectively enough to win the amount that they might need. They may not see the extent of objective freedom that is available to them. Indeed, unhealthy personalities may dread freedom, both objective freedom and the subjective feeling of freedom. They find it anxiety-producing, or even terrifying, and can only carry out their daily lives so long as they feel under compulsion or restraint from external sources, e.g., laws or orders.[10]

We have included freedom as a basic need because it seems apparent that man cannot fully develop to his potentials when this freedom is denied him, and because, when it has been withdrawn—through dictatorship or other means—man may subordinate all other values, even his own life, to attain it.

CHALLENGE. Another basic human need may be called the need for challenge. Deprivation of challenge is experienced variously as boredom, stultification, or emptiness in existence.[11] The need for challenge manifests itself most keenly when a person has made a "successful adjustment" to his life, when he has been able to fulfill his needs for food and shelter, status, love, sex, and so on, and finds the sameness of his existence palling. Under these conditions, the boredom serves as an inner goad, prodding the man to seek novelty, the unknown, the exciting, perhaps even the dangerous.

Healthier personalities respond to challenge with full mobilization of their energies and resources, and they grapple with it in ways that result in new learning and new directions and values for their lives. Less healthy persons may avoid challenge and seek to preserve sameness in their existence.

Challenge may be provided by another person, by catastrophes[12] or problems, or by one's religious orientation. It has the effect of helping bring about growth and desirable change in persons, and so may be regarded as a basic need together with the others mentioned above.

COGNITIVE CLARITY. Evidence has been gathered to show that man cannot long endure ambiguity or contradictions in his knowledge. In the face of uncertainty, man seems impelled to construct answers or interpretations of the situation, presumably because he can get on with action *only* when he has made a satisfactory interpretation of the situation. His interpretation may not be valid, but it seems true that man prefers even false interpretations to none at all. Thus, a person may hear noises in the sky which he cannot at first identify. The experience of not knowing may fill him with anxiety, and until he can assign some interpretation to the noise, he may be virtually paralyzed. Once he interprets the noise, he can then behave in some way that will be most compatible with his values. For example, he may interpret the sound as the noise made by a jet aircraft which has just crashed through the sound barrier. This satisfies him, and he gets on with whatever he was doing. Or, he may construe the noise in some bizarre way—perhaps he regards it as the sound of a missile carrying an atomic warhead, and he promptly runs to find shelter. He may be wrong, of course, but at least his interpretation permits him to *do* something.

In addition to the need for *some* interpretation of situations and stimuli, man has been found to need consistency among his presently held beliefs. When new "cognitions"—perceptions and beliefs—are not consonant or compatible with presently held beliefs, the state of "cognitive dissonance" is said to exist. A considerable body of evidence has been gathered to show that the state of cognitive dissonance influences behavior very much like any other basic need or drive.[13] Under the instigation of a conflict between presently held knowledge and new information, persons will frequently even distort evidence or blind themselves to logical implications in order to eliminate the state of dissonance. Parenthetically, it may be stated that healthier personalities will be better able to tolerate ambiguity than unhealthy personalities, and they will resolve the tensions brought about by cognitive dissonance in ways that do the most justice to logic and evidence (see Chapter 3, for the discussion of reality-contact).

VARIED EXPERIENCE. Another basic need that has been recognized is for varied experience—new stimulation of all kinds. Man needs variety in stimulation, not just to avoid boredom, but actually to preserve his ability to perceive the world and to function adequately.

When a person is radically deprived of the customary variety of sights, sounds, smells, conversation, and so on—as sometimes happens in solitary confinement—he begins to feel strange, and he may show signs of deteriorating as a person. Recently, a number of experiments in "sensory deprivation" have been conducted, showing that when volunteer subjects are placed in a special room that is soundless, when their vision is closed off by special goggles, and when they have been immersed in warm water kept at body temperature (to reduce the experience of tactile stimulaion), they begin to hallucinate and go through other psychotic-like experiences.[14]

Variety in "stimulus input," then, may be regarded as a basic need, even though deprivation as extreme as that produced in the laboratory seldom occurs in everyday life.

IDIOSYNCRATIC NEED-HIERARCHIES

Maslow states that man's basic needs are hierarchically arranged, from lowest, or most basic, up to the highest (see page 12). He states further that higher-level needs will not become effective determiners of a man's action until needs at the lower level have been gratified. In the preceding sections, we did not arrange the needs in any ladderlike sequence, because it seems most probable that they are *all* essential to human life. If a person has been able to meet these needs, then such matters as the pursuit of goals outside the self indeed becomes possible or likely; but in any given person, the relative importance of any given *basic* need is an idiosyncratic matter. Thus, for one, sex may be the most important basic need, while for another, status or cognitive clarity may be paramount.

We make this observation because we cannot know what will move or motivate a man unless we know precisely which of his basic needs is the most urgent at a given time. Man pursues gratification, and if other people possess the means for satisfying his basic needs, they acquire a considerable measure of control over his action. They can give him the rewards when his behavior complies with their wishes and withhold the means of satisfaction when he ignores these wishes or commands. This vulnerability to control may make man appear like a readily controlled and manipulated being. Indeed, many people seek to capitalize on man's susceptibility to such control, e.g., advertisers, politicians, and others with a vested interest in reducing man's autonomy and freedom of choice. Fortunately, man can *choose* from among his basic needs, even under conditions of privation, and so he retains some measure of freedom to decide when he will comply with the wishes of those who would control him and when he will choose freedom and suffer the consequences of privation.

BASIC-NEED PRIVATION

SIGNS OF BASIC-NEED PRIVATION

If a person has been able to cope effectively with the needs listed above, the probability is high that he will be relatively happy, he will fall ill seldom, and he will find his life meaningful, challenging, and satisfying. If, on the other hand, he has experienced prolonged privation or frustration of these needs, it can be expected that various symptoms of deprivation or frustration will arise. The nature and subjective "feel" of these symptoms will vary depending upon which need has been thwarted. If the man's life or other values have been placed under threat, then he will experience *anxiety*. If various physical needs have not been met, he will experience chronic hunger or perhaps discomfort. If a man has lacked love, or affectionate friendship, he may feel *lonely* or perhaps *depressed*. If he has been sexually thwarted, he may experience unremitting sexual fantasies. If he has not been getting the status and recognition which he longs for, he may suffer *feelings of inferiority*. If his physical health has been below optimum, he may feel *weak* or in a state of recurrent or *chronic malaise*. If a person has been deprived of freedom, he may feel *driven* or *compelled*, neither state being very welcome. And if a person has not been able to find meaning, purpose, and challenge in his life, he may suffer *boredom*. Anxiety may betoken lack of cognitive clarity, and an impoverished mental life may betoken relative sensory deprivation. Let us now explore several reasons for failure to meet basic needs. We will discuss problems in diagnosis of one's own needs; impoverished environments; and lack of "helpers."

FACTORS IN NEED-PRIVATION AND GRATIFICATION

PROBLEMS IN THE DIAGNOSIS OF NEEDS. It is not always possible for a person correctly to identify the symptoms of his unfulfilled needs. One reason lies in the fact that people differ in degree of sensitivity to their own inner experience. Some individuals are quite interested in and cognizant of their flow of experience, while others are incapable of detecting any but the most powerful of inner feelings or emotions. One factor which influences the degree to which a person can correctly label his changing wants and feelings is the degree to which he is *self-alienated.* Self-alienation, a term discussed more fully below (see pages 157–160), refers to a learned tendency to ignore or misperceive one's subjective experience because of fear or shame relating to the nature of one's spontaneous being. Since needs cannot be met unless the person is able to identify them, it follows that any factors that promote self-alienation, that is, which interfere with the person's willingness and ability to examine his subjective experience, will diminish his competence at meeting needs. Such factors include an overly strict conscience and anxiety (see Chapters 6, 8).

Factors which contribute to the ability to acknowledge and recognize one's own needs include self-honesty, insight, and a conscience which does not condemn a person for being human, that is, for having the needs, feelings, and wishes that seem inevitably linked to the human situation. Another factor is the availability of friends, loved ones, or confidants. With these persons available, one can report one's unhappiness to them and enlist their help in the effort to determine the causes of the misery.

IMPOVERISHED ENVIRONMENTS. We cannot fully understand the behavior or condition of any man without paying due attention to the environment in which he grew up and in which he presently lives. By "environment" we mean more than the physical world;

more especially, we are referring to his social and interpersonal environment—the individual people with whom he lived and presently lives and his society with its customs, taboos, and incentives.

Some individuals, presently suffering many of the symptoms of unfulfilled needs, grew up in an environment devoid of basic-need fulfillment. Their parents may have been unaffectionate, cold, critical, and rejecting. Their social world may have been excessively narrow, conservative, lacking in stimulation and interesting activities. They may have been subjected to dictatorial upbringing, both at home and in the schools. At the present time, they may be living in a similar network of relationships with others. Under these conditions, it is not difficult to understand why such persons may find their lives characterized by chronic psychological suffering, e.g., anxiety, depression, boredom, hopelessness, or other evidences of frustration of their basic needs.

A healthier and more satisfying existence can be attained by such persons if they change environments—move to a new locale, meet new people, and so on. However, such mobility is seldom without complications; too, changes in one's life are usually accompanied and even prevented by anxiety concerning the unknown. Many persons seem willing to continue a familiar though unsatisfying existence rather than risk changing to a life that only *might* be better. It is only when suffering is so intense as to render continued existence unbearable that one will face the anxiety of the unknown and take a chance at changing milieux.

LACK OF HELPERS. A *helper* may be defined as a "therapeutic person," one in relationship with whom a person derives a heightened sense of his own worth, competence, and over-all well-being (see Chapter 13). Researchers have just begun to seek out persons in the population at large who produce these effects upon others, through their interaction with them. One hypothesis about the characteristics of helpers has been provided by Rogers.[15] He was trying to describe the behavior of professional personality therapists when they were effective at helping patients become healthier personalities. The characteristics of a good professional therapist (and of a "helper") included:

1. *Trustworthiness.* He is of good will and can be depended on to keep his word.

2. *Openness.* He communicates his feelings and reactions fully to the other person.

3. *Not afraid to like.* He permits himself to experience and express positive feelings for the other person.

4. *Respect for differences.* He shows the courage to recognize his differences in opinion and attitude from those of the other person.

5. *"Letting be."* He shows willingness to permit the other person to be himself.

6. *Empathy.* He has the ability and willingness to see the world from the other person's point of view.

7. *Positive regard.* He displays honest acceptance of the other person, in all his difference.

8. *Tact.* He has enough sensitivity to avoid threatening the other person.

9. *Permissiveness.* He avoids judging or evaluating the conduct or experience of the other person.

10. *Faith in man's potentials.* He is profoundly committed to the belief that people can change and grow.

If a person has, as friend, spouse, parent, or teacher, someone who has characteristics such as these, he will feel free to reveal his inner experience to him whenever he is troubled,[16] and can be sure that he will receive some clarification, acceptance, and support. On the other hand, if the person cannot trust others deeply enough to find out if they *can* be helpers, or if there simply are none such persons available, then he will lack one of the conditions which contributes to need-recognition and -fulfillment.

LACK OF COURAGE. Courage implies a willingness to face the unknown and to make one's way in spite of the presence of strong anxiety. People differ in their degree of self-confidence and in their willingness to undertake novel, untested behavior in new situations. The kinds of experiences which seem to impair the development of courage include frequent traumatic episodes and minimal opportunity to learn skills. "Traumatic episodes" are experiences of being hurt at a time when one was helpless and unable to cope with the situation. Such traumas seem to foster a firm resolve to avoid any possible recurrence of fear and anxiety and lead to the development of a life hemmed in with precautions.

It is clear that the fulfillment of needs will often call for large measures of courage, and wherever the person cannot find this faith in himself, he will tend to remain in unsatisfying situations rather than risk the unknown. One of the factors which fosters courage is the presence of an "encourager"—some person who does have faith or confidence in the *potential* courage that lies latent in all timorous people. The deeply religious person can sometimes draw upon his reserves of courage through prayer. In prayer, it is as if the person experiences God encouraging him to proceed, in spite of the fear.

FRUSTRATION AND HEALTHY PERSONALITY

Satisfaction of needs seldom can be attained without some measure of struggle and delay, and there are often strong barriers which stand between a person and the goals he is pursuing. When delay and interference are prolonged, and when the need is one of some urgency, psychological tension increases. When the tension mounts to an extreme degree (the precise amount will vary from person to person, and in the same person at different times), disorganization of behavior may occur.

We shall reserve the word *frustration* to refer to the level of tension which produces irrational, disorganized conduct. This meaning of the word corresponds roughly to the usage adopted by Maier.[17] Maier distinguishes between motivated behavior and frustration-instigated behavior. The former refers to flexible, voluntary behavior in pursuit of some goal. Frustration-produced behavior has as its sole aim the reduction of frustration tension. Consequently, it may not be very well adapted to the requirements of the environment. A frustrated person is one who cannot reason and who cannot behave in his usually effective ways. All he can do is "blow off steam."

Frustration of this degree is undesirable from a personality-hygiene point of view. Delay in gratification is not a bad thing for personality hygiene, however. As long as the level of tension permits effective instrumental action, delay can actually promote personality health, for it makes sure a person will feel his tensions acutely enough to get into action. In addition, experience with delay helps to build up "frustration resistance," or *ego-strength*—a desirable consequence for personality health.

The desirable reaction to tension-increase brought on by gratification delay or interference is one which involves: (1) increased persistence in efforts to reach the goal; (2) increased flexibility or variability in the methods adopted to reach the goal; (3) if the goals cannot be reached by these procedures, the healthy search for a substitute.

An example will illustrate the healthy reactions to delay in gratification. A person may want very badly to obtain a date with a certain girl. She refuses him. Her refusal may spur him to greater effort. He then modifies his approach; he changes his behavior so that it is more pleasing to her, he showers her with attention, and so on. If she accedes, fine. If she does not, the man is wise to give her up and pursue some other girl. Naturally, this is not always easy to do—yet it must be done if the individual is to remain healthy.

If the young man's need-tensions increase beyond his frustration-threshold, then we may expect to find any of a wide variety of frustration-produced behavior patterns, none of which will attain the objective: a date with the girl. He may explode into anger; he may cry; he may withdraw from the situation before he has really tried; he may retreat into fantasies about conquest, and so on.

FRUSTRATION-THRESHOLDS. We pointed out there is a level of tension below which the person can think rationally and behave effectively. When the tension increases above this point, efficiency breaks down, and irrational thinking and expressive behavior take the place of rational thinking and effective action. This hypothetical point on the tension continuum is called the *frustration-threshold.* If we had some way of quantifying tension of all kinds—need-tensions and emotional tensions, irrespective of quality and source—it could be demonstrated that the frustration-threshold varies from person to person on a given need, and within the person for the same need at different times or for different needs.

A mother "needs" her house to be very neat, orderly, and clean.

In the forenoon, her three-year-old son might spill a glass of milk, leave his toys in disarray, and scatter magazines all over the newly-cleaned living room. Her reaction at the time is one of mild anger, followed by efficient attempts to set things straight. At five-thirty in the afternoon, the child repeats his efforts at messing up the house. This time the mother "explodes"—she spanks the child, hurls some chinaware herself, and is unable to begin preparations for supper until she has vented all the tension the mess has provoked.

We do not know why frustration-thresholds vary within the person or between persons. We can agree that frustration-produced behavior is unhealthy, since it prevents a person from keeping his wits in order to find satisfactions. There is personality-hygiene value in high frustration-thresholds. A good deal of basic psychological research is required in order to discover: (a) a means of quantifying tension, independent of the need in question; (b) the amount of tension which produces disorganization; and (c) the correlates of frustration-thresholds as these vary between persons and within the person. When this research has been successfully accomplished, it will be possible to discover means for increasing frustration-thresholds in the general population, as a project in public personality hygiene.

Even without benefit of the fruits of systematic research, we can make a few observations about correlates of frustration-thresholds. It can easily be demonstrated that *optimum physical health* produces high frustration-thresholds. When a person is run-down, weak, fatigued, he is less able to pursue goals effectively in the face of interference and even minor stress. He frustrates easily.

A *broad repertoire of skills* will decrease the frequency of frustrating experiences, even if it doesn't affect the frustration-thresholds. The more skills a person has acquired, the less frequently he will be blocked in his quest for satisfactions. The unskilled person is more likely to experience frustration than the competent person. The young child has many wants and few skills, and will generally experience frequent frustration unless adults intervene to make sure he enjoys a reasonable number of satisfactions.

People who managed to survive the extremely stressing conditions of wartime concentration camps in Germany—so-called "death camps"—have pointed out that a strong commitment to life, a sense of a mission to fulfill, and a *strong sense of meaning and purpose in one's life* were definite factors in survival.[18] There is the further implication that individuals who had such a sense of mission or dedication were less readily frustrated by the deprivations, stresses, and pressure of extremely hostile environments.

CONFLICTING NEEDS

It is common for a person to experience conflict between needs or wishes associated with them. He may want to study and also to go out to the movies. He may want to marry one girl, and at the same time he loves another. He may want to have fun but also be good.

The healthy thing to do with conflict is to admit its existence, study all the alternatives as rationally as one can in the light of one's value-system, make a decision, act on it, and accept all the consequences which follow. Among the consequences to be accepted are regrets over what one has lost in connection with the abandoned alternatives. No decision can ever be made without some fear that it is the wrong decision. There is nothing inconsistent with personality health in the idea that a decision, once made, will still leave the person uncertain that it is the best or "rightest" one.

"Existential" conflicts frequently arise where each choice has positive values and negative implications associated with it. Any alternative, if chosen, will affect one's life profoundly. Examples are, to marry or not to marry, to take this job or that. To make such decisions calls for courage, and the ability to decide in such conflicts is truly an attribute of healthy personality. Such courage seems to grow out of experience at decision-making.

UNCONSCIOUS NEEDS

To be conscious of a need means to experience the tension produced by privation, to identify this tension, and then to experience a wish or desire to ameliorate the situation. Thus, one may be sexually deprived, identify the signs of such deprivation in oneself, and set about the task of obtaining sexual gratification. But suppose that one regards such sexual wishes as forbidden? Under these conditions, acknowledgment of one's real feelings and wishes might give rise to powerful guilt or anxiety. The guilt or anxiety will then motivate the person to rid his mind of the offending thoughts. The effort at riddance is called repression (see Chapter 7), and it may or may not be wholly successful. Nevertheless, if a person does repress his thoughts or his awareness of some needs or wishes, he has not eliminated the causes that brought the wishes about. The causes continue to operate. We then have a state of affairs where conditions foster awareness of a type of tension—in this case, sexual desire—but the person cannot or will not acknowledge the existence of such desire. Instead, he pursues other goals and interests in spite of the continuous presence of the *causes* of erotic thoughts. We might expect that goals other than sex will become less attractive for the person, because he does not want them wholeheartedly. Furthermore, we might expect that his efforts to attain the substitute goals would be somewhat more fatiguing than they would be if the tensions of sexual privation were not present. We can speak with meaning of *unconscious* needs or motives, if by "unconscious" we mean (a) the conditions for conscious awareness of some need are present, and (b) the person is not aware of, or will not acknowledge the existence of, the relevant tensions.

Freud was the first psychologist to devote systematic attention to the role of unconscious need-tensions in behavior, and since his first writings a good deal of attention has been devoted to the subject by other psychologists.[19] A convincing experimental demonstration of unconscious motivation was published by Erickson.[20] He showed how persons could carry out posthypnotic suggestions without knowing the real reasons. The real reasons were the hypnotist's commands. The experimental subject would make up reasons or rationalizations for his actions.

We may assume that need-tensions will influence a person's overt behavior, his thoughts, and his feelings whether or not he recognizes them and labels them accurately.

Why would any need-tensions become unconscious? Perhaps

Freud was correct in assuming that the more appropriate question was rather, why will any needs become conscious?

We shall assert that a need-tension will be conscious and accurately labeled by the person unless: (a) the individual's conscience comprises values which strongly condemn the very fact of having such needs, much less acting upon them; (b) the person has had experiences in the past where behavior instigated by the need-tensions resulted in extreme pain, loss of parental love, or punishment; in this case, the need-tension becomes a cue which triggers off anxiety; or (c) in the past, the longings for need-objects have met with frustration. In our culture, the kinds of needs or feelings most likely to be repressed, hence unconscious, are sex, anger, the desire to be dependent and taken care of, positive feelings of affection, and the feeling of freedom.

In these circumstances, the need-tensions will not be recognized or acted on with appropriate goal-seeking behavior. In the past, when they were recognized they led to guilt, anxiety, or the anticipation of frustration. In order to reduce these painful tensions, the person stopped thinking about the longings in question and occupied his thoughts and awareness with other, less painful need-tensions. Repression is the name given to the response of "stopping thinking,"[21] of not allowing oneself to think about, remember, evaluate, or fanstasy painful subject matter.

But the need-tensions, or at least their physiological substratum, will persist in spite of repression and continue to influence the behavior of the individual. The difference between conscious and unconscious needs lies in the fact that a person cannot control behavior provoked by unconscious determiners, and he cannot satisfy needs of whose nature he is unaware.

THE INFERENCE OF MOTIVES—CONSCIOUS AND UNCONSCIOUS

We continuously read or try to read the motives of the other person. The most common bases that are employed for inferring the intentions, feelings, and needs of the other person are: (a) observations of his facial expression, tone of voice, and gestures, which generally disclose what the person is feeling; and (b) observations of the person's action and its consequences; from the actions and consequences, the observer formulates hypotheses as to the need-tensions of the behavior—his aims, intentions, wishes, and so on.

Ordinarily, we are able to check our inferences about the motives of the other person by asking him. His verbal report is generally used to validate our hypotheses. He will correct us, agree with us, or disagree with our formulations of his motives.

When are we justified in assuming that the motives of the other person are unconscious? We can never be absolutely certain, but we can entertain the hypothesis of unconscious motivation (a) when the person acts in ways that produce consequences he *denies* intending to produce; (b) when he manifests many expressive signs of emotional tensions, feelings, and so on, without acknowledging to the observer he feels any of these things; and (c) when there are obvious *inconsistencies* in behavior at different times, e.g., kindness and brutality, intelligent and stupid behavior.

In addition to these general "signs" of unconscious motivation, there are many other more subtle indicators that unconscious need-tensions may be present and operative. These include:

1. *Dream-content which seems bizarre and incomprehensible to the dreamer.*
2. *Fantasy-content which surprises and shocks the daydreamer.*
3. *Errors and slips in speech, writing, and gestures.*
4. *Body postures and evidence of bodily tensions.*
5. *The forgetting of intentions, names, and so on.*
6. *Accidents of all kinds.*
7. *Performance on certain projective tests of personality.*

ILLUSTRATIONS OF LIKELY INSTANCES OF UNCONSCIOUS MOTIVATION

The author, influenced by Freud's monumental books *The Psychopathology of Everyday Life* and *The Interpretation of Dreams*[22] has collected some examples from his experience that seem to disclose unconscious motivation.

1. *An example from dreams.* A nine-year-old child was judged by all who knew him to be very "good." He was extremely obedient to

his parents and affirmed his love for his father in almost every conversation with anybody. He related this dream to the author:

"I dreamed that I was a soldier, and we had a very mean and cruel officer. One day, when nobody was around, he was beating up a very nice lady. I took my machine gun and shot him a million times. He fell into a lot of little pieces when I was finished."

One does not have to be a professional interpreter of dreams to suspect that the officer was a symbolic version of his father, toward whom the boy had strong but repressed hostility, while the "nice lady" was his mother, to whom he was very attached.

2. *An example from fantasy.* A student preparing for the ministry related with embarrassment and guilt that he was afraid to be alone or without some busywork to perform. When asked why, he said that as soon as he was idle, his mind filled with the most "sinful and voluptuous images of sex." He couldn't understand why this should be, as he was ordinarily a very upright and "clean-thinking" young man.

3. *Slips of the tongue and pen.* The following item came from a local newspaper: A minister had spent some time in Hollywood, and was interviewed by a local reporter with respect to his impressions. The article related how the minister deplored the moral turpitude of many of Hollywood's citizens. The article ended with this sentence (the italics are mine): "It is a shame the way our nation's best entertainers, in their lives offstage, are forever making *pubic* spectacles of themselves." The author does not know who was responsible for omitting the crucial *l* in the italicized word—the minister, the reporter, the copyreader, or the linotypist.

4. *Examples from body posturing and tensions.* Fromm,[23] Reich,[24] and other psychoanalysts have suggested that variations in the muscle tonus of parts of a person's body may reflect repressed emotions and need-tensions. Fromm mentions that the person with a "receptive" character-orientation may have a very soft, almost suckling, mouth. Everyone has had the experience of a flaccid handshake from a person who denies that he is insincere. A female student complained that men were forever "making passes" at her, yet she denied having any erotic interest in males. Observation revealed she was extremely coquettish in her bodily movements. She

wiggled her hips when walking, pushed her chest high; when talking with a man, she glued her eyes, alternately opened and narrowed, to his. Repressed hostility may be manifested by excessive muscular tension in the forehead, neck, or shoulders, often resulting in headaches, a "pain in the neck," and back pain.[25]

5. *Forgetting of intentions, names.* The author forgot to write a letter of recommendation for a graduate student whom he disliked for personal reasons that had nothing to do with the student's ability. Fortunately the student, who was competent, received the position without benefit of the letter.

6. *Accidents.* Accidents may result in disadvantage either to the person himself or to others, depending upon the unconscious motivation—guilt in the former, hostility in the latter. A woman spilled ink on the manuscript her husband was working on (neglecting her as he did the work) as she cleaned his study. A man made a mistake which cost him his position. He had won the position in competition with a friend, about whom he had secretly conveyed damaging information to the prospective employer.

7. *Examples from projective tests.* A 22-year-old undergraduate student consulted with the author for help with vague guilt feelings; inability to study; and fierce headaches which occurred whenever he went home or was obliged to spend any time with the Dean, one or two of his professors, or with the boss at a job where he worked regularly during the summer. He appeared to be extremely polite and deferential to authority. (He used the word *sir* in almost every sentence when talking to the author.) In the Thematic Apperception Test (TAT), many of his stories included some expression of violence and hatred toward the authority figures which were seen or imagined. The student told this story about TAT Card 12M, which shows an old man stretching his hand toward the reclining figure of a younger man:

"This boy is having a nap. The old man, his father, is coming in to get him out of bed so he'll get back to his studies. His father has been nagging him for ages about how lazy he is. The boy has been putting up with this for a long time. This is the last straw. When he wakes up, he'll be so mad he'll start beating on his father. He'll grab a chair and start mashing in his head. When he finishes, his old man will be a bloody pulp. The boy will get the electric chair, but he won't care, it was worth it."

It is not too farfetched to infer there is at least some unconscious hostility toward authority figures in this young man.

There is no discovered way, as yet, to prove that an inference of unconscious motivation is warranted. Nevertheless, it can be shown that the motives a person will consider as possible determiners of his behavior will change under special circumstances. A patient entering psychotherapy may behave in ways that hurt or humiliate his wife; yet at the outset, he may vigorously deny having any hostile feelings toward her. As the therapy proceeds, he may gradually entertain the hypothesis he has hostile feelings toward her. Finally he can admit having hostile feelings, without any guilt or anxiety whatsoever. In addition, his hostility, if rational and warranted, may come to be expressed much more openly than was the case before. And it very often happens that recognition and understanding of irrational hostility will reduce or eliminate it.

UNCONSCIOUS NEEDS AND HEALTHY PERSONALITY

The personality hygienist generally regards repression as an unhealthy mechanism and unconscious motives as unhealthy motives. The reason for this condemnation lies in the fact that it is only when one's own needs are accurately diagnosed that one can find effective ways of gratifying them. Repressed needs must remain chronically unfulfilled needs. Their influence on behavior is chronic, they interfere with other activity which is in progress, and they prevent emergence into consciousness of other, higher needs.

In addition to the above reasons, the personality hygienist condemns unconscious needs as unhealthy because the mechanism of repression is usually an undesirable or unhealthy way of solving problems. Repression is sometimes undertaken because of an overly strict conscience—it is regarded as healthier to attempt to change the conscience or to accept the fact that one is not as "good" as one would like to believe. Repression is undertaken as a means of warding off anxiety; there are more effective and healthier ways of handling anxiety. Repression is undertaken to ward off the possibility of painful frustration; there are healthier ways of avoiding frustration, including learning more effective skills. It is only in instances where repression is temporary and permits important action to be completed, or where it forestalls serious psychosis, that a personality hygienist would regard it as desirable.

HEALTHY FEATURES OF THE UNCONSCIOUS[26]

CREATIVITY. It is true that in many persons, especially those who are afraid or ashamed of their needs, the unconscious will indeed be a source of unacceptable wishes and feelings. However, healthier personalities have been more successful in acknowledging and gratifying needs for affection, sex, status, and so on. Consequently, their unconscious will be less a dread, repressed aspect of personality and more a fount of innovation, self-integration, and creativity. Creative individuals show less fear of their own experiencing and functioning, less fear of the free play of their fantasy, and so they are able to "unrepress" to a considerable degree. In so freeing their unconscious from its customary bonds of inhibition and repression, they experience the welcome and sometimes surprising admission to consciousness of new ideas, solutions to problems, insights into themselves, and other valued creations.

CONSCIENCE AND GUILT. Sexuality or unacceptable drives like aggression are not the only aspects of personality which are typically repressed. Mowrer has been able to show with many examples that individuals frequently repress their consciences and the guilt which should be experienced when a person violates this unconscious conscience. If a man has acquired a conscience which could guide him in the direction of the fullest growth and personal integration, then repression of such a conscience could truly be regarded as a repression of the individual's healthiest potentials. In common parlance, the individual who is said to have a "hardened heart," like Scrooge in Dickens' classic *Christmas Carol,* is one who has likely repressed his conscience and the guilt to which it might give rise. The awakening or unrepression of conscience in such individuals would likely produce acute guilt. The guilt, if acknowledged, could motivate the person to change his usual ways of behavior from self-centered pursuit of satisfaction to more loving concern for others.

GOALS BEYOND BASIC-NEED FULFILLMENT

If a person has coped adequately with his basic needs, such that they are being fulfilled under the conditions of his present life-circumstances, his energy and thoughts are freed for other interests. The exact nature of these interests will differ widely from person to person, but the intensity of involvement and the diversity of interests in matters outside the self can serve as a rough index of the degree of health of the over-all personality.[27] When a man ceases to be a problem to himself, in virtue of the successful attainment of security, love, status, and other basic needs, he can actually begin to *see* the world in a manner which differs from the way "deficiency-motivated" persons see it.

A healthy personality is able to find fascination and challenge in the beauties and problems which life poses and provides. His perception and energies are not bound to the problem of quieting unease, pain, loneliness, boredom, or other subjective symptoms of basic-need privation. These needs have been successfully coped with, or at the least, the healthy personality feels confident that whenever such basic needs arise, he will be competent to cope with them. Consequently, he can afford to "forget" himself and become involved in work, play, other persons' problems, and perhaps the well-being of mankind as a whole. It is difficult to become concerned about the hunger or slavery of another person when one is in the midst of such privation oneself. When one has experienced and then transcended these conditions, one can "empathize" (that is, imagine with vividness) the experience of others, and one can then hurl one's energies and talents into the service of their well-being.

One useful index of the degree to which a person has coped with his basic needs is a *relative absence of self-consciousness* (see also Chapter 6, pages 182–184). Self-consciousness means that one is keenly and usually painfully aware of one's own behavior and experience. Since it is difficult, if not impossible, for man to attend to two different things simultaneously, the man who is watching himself is less able to watch events in the external world. Hence, the unfulfilled person, ridden with ungratified needs, is less likely to notice anything in the world that is irrelevant to his need. The person who is anxious about his status, or his acceptance by others, will pay careful attention to how he is appearing to others, striving to make sure he will do nothing that would jeopardize his likability. All the time he is watching himself, he is paying less attention to other people, for example, or to the beauty of a sunset—in short, he will see less of what there is to be seen in the world.

Many interests and values grow out of a person's earlier quest for the means of gratifying basic needs. Thus, a man may become a physician as a means of assuring for himself an income which will satisfy a need for economic security. However, once the man has become trained and is earning the money he was seeking, he may (indeed, he *should*) find intrinsic fascination in the challenges posed by illness. His motivation for the practice of medicine changes then from a quest for money to a quest for new knowledge of ways and means of relieving suffering. Whenever an interest in some form of activity comes into being as a means of satisfying basic needs and then changes into a spontaneous fascination, the motive is said to be *functionally autonomous* of its more basic origins.[28] We do not fully understand the mechanisms by which functional autonomy of motives occurs, but it is true that human motives do follow such a transformation. Indeed, the presence of functionally autonomous motives in a person may be regarded as a further indicant of the health of his personality, while the chronic presence of basic need-tensions betokens less than adequate and healthy personality.

SUMMARY

Healthy personality is manifested by a relative absence of anxious self-consciousness and by lively interest in and pursuit of goals beyond security, love, status, or recognition. However, the freedom to become attentive to and involved in the world outside oneself is an outgrowth of prior gratification of basic needs. Various authors, such as Maslow and Fromm, have attempted to spell out lists of man's basic needs. Maslow has proposed that man needs physical gratifications (food, drink, and so on), safety, love, and recognition before he can freely address himself to problems outside himself. Fromm has stated that man needs (a) a sense of relatedness *to his fellow man, in order to overcome a sense of loneliness and isolation; (b) a sense of* transcendence, *which means the felt capacity to create and to be the master of nature rather than a passive victim of capricious natural forces; (c) a sense of* rootedness, *or the feeling of belonging to some group or society; (d) a sense of* identity, *experienced as the feeling that one is not just a cipher or an indistinguishable group member, but rather a distinct, recognized, and appreciated individual; (e) a* frame of orientation and devotion: *a philosophy of life or a religion which provides direction, meaning, and purpose to one's existence.*

In modification of the views of these two men it is suggested that man's basic needs include survival, physical gratification, love and affiliation, status, success and self-esteem, physical and mental health, freedom, challenge, cognitive clarity and variety in experience. If he meets these needs, he is freed to pursue other values outside the well-being of the self. Symptoms of basic-need privation include anxiety, loneliness, depression, feel-

ings of inferiority, weakness, driven feelings, and boredom.

Factors contributing to chronic privation of basic needs include impoverished environments, inability to diagnose one's own needs, and the lack of "helpers"—people whom one trusts, to whom one can confide one's difficulties and expect helpful responses in return.

Frustration is defined as the tension that arises when one is blocked from attainment of goals which would satisfy basic needs. Frustration gives rise to disorganized behavior. Frustration of this intensity can be forestalled by good health, a wide repertoire of skills, and a strong sense of purpose. Conflicts in need must be met with decision, if healthy personality is to be promoted, though it is recognized that many conflicts are acute.

Needs are likely to be unconscious when recognition of them would be embarrassing, guilt-provoking, or anxiety-producing. When a person will not acknowledge his needs, these needs give rise to unconscious motives. Unconscious motives manifest themselves in disguised ways, e.g., in dreams, accidents, slips of the tongue, and so on. In healthier personalities, the unconscious features of personality function as a welcome source of creativity, and the unconscious may also harbor the individual's conscience.

Many interests and fascinations which characterize healthier personalities originate in the quest for gratification of basic needs. Motives that come into being as a desire for basic-need gratification become transformed into interests in things "for themselves." The mechanisms by which such transformation comes about are not known, but the motives themselves are then said to become "functionally autonomous" of their origins.

NOTES AND REFERENCES

Excellent supplementary reading will be provided by those references marked with an asterisk (*).

*1. In this connection, Frankl speaks of "creative" and "experiential" values. See, for example, Frankl, V. E., *From Death Camp to Existentialism* (Boston: Beacon, 1959), pp. 97–111. Creative values refers to the actual production of anything new through work, while experiential values refers to the more passive enjoyment of the good things in life.

*2. See Maslow, A. H., *Motivation and Personality* (New York: Harper, 1954), chs. 5, 6, 7. Also his book, *Toward a Psychology of Being* (Princeton, N.J.: Van Nostrand, 1962), ch. 3.

3. The discussion of need is adapted from Maslow, A. H., *op. cit.* For a different view of man's needs, see Combs, A. W. and Snygg, D., *Individual Behavior* (2nd ed.; New York: Harper, 1959), ch. 3.

4. *Cf.* Bowlby, J., *Child Care and the Growth of Love* (London: Pelican, 1953), pp. 11–17; Halmos, P., *Towards a Measure of Man* (London: Routledge and Kegan Paul, 1957), pp. 60–81.

*5. *Cf.* Horney, K., *Neurosis and Human Growth* (New York: Norton, 1950), ch. 9; see also Schachter, S., *The Psychology of Affiliation* (Stanford, Cal., Stanford U. P., 1959), for an experimental analysis of factors in the quest for closeness.

6. *Cf.* McClelland, D., *The Achieving Society* (New York: Van Nostrand, 1961).

*7. *Cf.* Packard, V., *The Status Seekers* (New York: McKay, 1959), for a nontechnical account of the human cost of status.

8. Two sociologists have reported some data on "illness behavior"—the action undertaken by persons to get well when they perceive themselves as sick. See Mechanic, D. and Volkart, E. H., "Illness Behavior and Medical Diagnosis," *J. Health & Hum. Beh., 1,* 86–94 (1960). An interesting analysis of the quest for "hygienic" work-environments in contrast with the quest for fascination and challenge in work is given in Herzberg, F. and Hamlin, R. M.,

"A Motivation-Hygiene Concept of Mental Health," *Ment. Hyg., 45,* 394–401 (1961).

*9. *Cf.* Barron, F., "Freedom As Feeling," *J. Humanistic Psychol., 1,* 91–100 (1961).

*10. Fromm, E., *Escape from Freedom* (New York: Rinehart, 1941), pp. 3–23.

11. *Cf.* Shaw, F. J., "Reconciliation, An Integrating Concept in Psychology," ch. 1 in Shaw, F. J., *Reconciliation* (posthumous volume collated by Jourard, S. M.); to be published.

12. See Fritz, C., "Disaster," in Merton, R. K. and Nisbet, R. A., *Social Problems and Disorganization* (New York: Harcourt, 1961).

13. See Frenkel-Brunswik, Else, "Intolerance of Ambiguity As an Emotional and Perceptual Personality Variable," *J. Pers., 18,* 108–143 (1949); Rokeach, M., *The Open and Closed Mind* (New York, Basic Books, 1960); Festinger, L., *A Theory of Cognitive Dissonance* (Evanston, Ill.: Row, 1957); Kelley, G. A., *The Psychology of Personal Constructs, I., A Theory of Personality* (New York: Norton, 1955), ch. 2; Shaw, F. J., "Transitional Experiences and Psychological Growth," *ETC, 15,* 39–45 (1957).

14. Fiske, D. W., "Effects of Monotonous and Restricted Stimulation," in Fiske, D. W. and Maddi, S. R., *Functions of Varied Experience* (Homewood, Ill.: Dorsey, 1961), ch. 5. Good reviews in technical journals are Thorpe, J. G., "Sensory Deprivation," *J. Ment. Sci., 107,* 1047–1059 (1961); Solomon, P., Liederman, P. H., Mendelson, J., and Wexler, D., "Sensory Deprivation. A Review," *Amer. J. Psychiat., 114,* 357–363 (1957).

*15. Rogers, C. R., *On Becoming a Person* (New York: Houghton, 1961), pp. 39–58.

*16. See Jourard, S. M., "Healthy Personality and Self-Disclosure," *Ment. Hyg., 43,* 499–507 (1959).

17. See Maier, N. R. F., *Frustration. The Study of Behavior Without a Goal* (New York: McGraw, 1949).

18. *Cf.* Frankl, V. E., *op. cit.*

19. See Herron, W. G., "The Evidence for the Unconscious," *Psychoanal. and Psychoanal. Rev., 49,* 93–99 (1962).

20. Erickson, M. G., "Experimental Demonstrations of the Psychopathology of Everyday Life," *Psychoanal. Quart., 8,* 338–353 (1939).

21. *Cf.* Dollard, J. and Miller, N. E., *Personality and Psychotherapy* (New York: McGraw, 1950), p. 220.

22. In Brill, A. A., *op. cit.*

23. Fromm, E., *Man for Himself* (New York: Rinehart, 1947).

24. Reich, W., *Character Analysis* (New York: Orgone Institute Press, 1949).

25. See Moloney, J. C., *The Magic Cloak: A Contribution to the Psychology of Authoritarianism* (Wakefield, Mass.: Montrose Press, 1949), pp. 99–101. See also ch. 13 for a discussion of diverse psychosomatic symptoms which Moloney found to be associated with repressed hostility in persons who lived

in authoritarian social settings. The entire book is an excellent treatise on authoritarianism. For experimental demonstrations of muscular tension, see Malmo, R. B., Shagass, C., and Davis, J. F., "Electromyographic Studies of Muscular Tension in Psychiatric Patients under Stress," *J. Clin. Exper. Psychopath., 12,* 45–66 (1951).

*26. See Maslow, A. H., *Toward a Psychology of Being* (Princeton, N.J.: Van Nostrand, 1962), pp. 19–41, for a discussion of the creative aspects of the unconscious. The account of repressed conscience and guilt is adapted from Mowrer, O. H., *The Crisis in Psychiatry and Religion* (Princeton, N.J.: Van Nostrand, 1961), ch. 2. Jung earlier noted the capacity of the unconscious to foster selfhood and creativity. See Jung, C. G., *Two Essays on Analytic Psychology* (New York: Meridian, 1956), pp. 182–197.

27. Maslow, A. H., *op. cit.,* pp. 132–133, 194–195.

28. *Cf.* Allport, G. W., *Pattern and Growth in Personality* (New York: Holt, 1961), pp. 226–229.

CHAPTER *3*

REALITY-CONTACT AND HEALTHY PERSONALITY

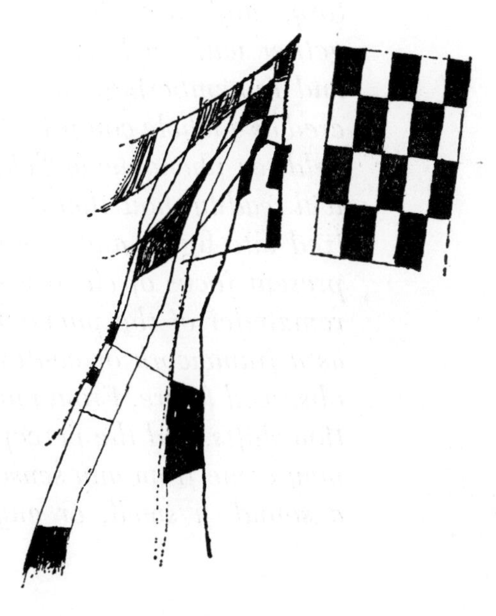

INTRODUCTION

We live in the world, not as it is, but as we perceive and assume it to be. Our behavior is guided by our experience, or, to use a more technical word, by our perceptual-cognitive field. *This term stands for the total of our sensory and cognitive activity at any given time. Other words that may be employed to refer to the same referent are* phenomenal field, field of awareness, *or* assumptive world. *If the reader will examine his consciousness for a moment, he will notice that it includes visual, auditory, tactile, olfactory, gustatory, and organic-kinesthetic perceptions, together with such processes as thinking, fantasy, and remembering. All these phenomena considered as a whole comprise the perceptual-cognitive field, or phenomenal field. Further introspection will readily show that this "field" is always organized into* figure *and* ground. Figure *refers to the present focus of clearest attention;* ground *is the remainder of the phenomenal field which serves as a framework or context for the more directly observed figure. From moment to moment, attention shifts, and the percept which becomes figure may come from any sense modality: viz., a sight, a sound, a smell, or any combination of these* that has most meaning to the person at that instant; or the person may "tune out" his perception of external reality and attend to his own thoughts, memories, or fantasies.

This technical introduction to the phenomenological point of view in psychology[1] is offered to provide the student with a convenient frame of reference for a discussion of reality-contact. Our behavior is always undertaken with reference to the perceived world, the assumptive world.[2] We can hardly make sense out of anybody's behavior unless we somehow learn from him how the world appears to him—what he is paying attention to, how he interprets the things which he sees and hears, and what his predictions and expectations are regarding the human, animal, natural, and artificial things about him. If we see a man run in terror from a kitten, we will doubtless be puzzled by such strange behavior, because to us the kitten looks cute, furry, and harmless. An interview with the terrified man may reveal that he believes the kitten is rabid or is a carrier of some other disease. Once we learn how the man perceives this kitten, what the kitten means to him, his behavior then makes sense to us. However, we can always raise the question, "How accurate is the man's perception or belief about this particular kitten?" Another way of posing this question is to ask, "How efficient or adequate is this man's contact with reality?"

We always behave in accordance with our be-

liefs about the world, but the accuracy of these beliefs certainly will affect the adequacy of our behavior. Since healthy personality calls for competence in identifying and gratifying needs, it should be obvious that any individual whose beliefs about the world, himself, and other people are accurate will have more chances of attaining healthy personality than one whose perceptions and beliefs are false. More succinctly, we can assert that reality-contact is a basic condition for the attainment in maintenance of healthy personality.

When we say that a person has good or efficient reality-contact, we are saying that his perceptions and beliefs—the content of his perceptual-cognitive field, which helps determine his behavior—are veridical. Veridicality *means that other competent observers or thinkers, confronted by the same data, would see or interpret things as this person does and would arrive at similar conclusions.* Reality-contact *means that one's beliefs about the world are compatible with evidence, logic, and the opinion of competent authorities.*

A person's perceptions and beliefs about any aspect of the world, including himself, will be inaccurate or distorted unless the person takes active steps to verify his cognition.[3] *Reality-contact is not a given, it is an achievement! Efficient contact with reality must be worked for, because there are powerful psychological forces at work at all times tending to distort our percep-*

tion, our thinking and reasoning, and our remembering. These forces are generated by our emotions and by unfulfilled needs of all kinds.

THE INFLUENCES OF NEEDS AND EMOTIONS ON COGNITION

In the first place, the content of our perceptual-cognitive field is necessarily selective; it cannot include all inner and outer reality that exists at a given moment. Only part of the ongoing flow or process of feelings, thoughts, and external events are detected by our sense organs and represented in our phenomenal field. Our sense organs are similar to TV or radio receivers; they are differentially sensitive to stimuli of different intensities and qualities. But even within the receptive range of our senses, we still notice only a fraction of all the sensory information which reaches our brain. One of the important determiners of figure, that is, of our interested attention, is emotion and unfulfilled needs. Our feelings and our needs "steer" cognitive activities like perception, thinking, remembering, and fantasy, so that the figure will be that cognition—percept, thought, or memory—which is most relevant to our needs of the moment. Our cognitive processes are thus "servants" of our needs. When we are hungry, we think and dream about food, we search for it, and we tend to ignore everything in the world which is inedible or which will not help us to get food. If we are sexually deprived, we tend to have fantasies with erotic themes, we find it difficult to think about other things, and we look at the world from the standpoint of the sexual gratifications and frustrations it is likely to afford. If a person is anxious because of some threat to his security, he is unlikely to notice the beauties of nature; he is too busy seeking the source of danger so that he might escape from it. There have been many experiments conducted[4] to demonstrate how needs determine our attention and the content of our thinking, remembering, and fantasy, and so we need not dwell further upon this point. More germane to our discussion is the manner in which emotions and unfulfilled needs operate so as to *distort* our perception and beliefs. Let us introduce the theory of *autism* to serve as a framework to our discussion.

AUTISM AND COGNITION

Autism refers to the tendency of persons to perceive, remember, imagine, and believe in ways that are more determined by needs and emotions than by evidence or logic. Freud referred to this tendency as the "pleasure principle," and he saw it as a factor which constantly opposed the "reality principle"—the effort to learn the truth, no matter how unpleasant or painful it might be. Freud's hypothesis of the pleasure principle[5] is not so general as the theory of autism, since it proposes only that we perceive and believe what will yield pleasure and deny painful aspects of reality. The theory of autism makes allowance for beliefs which are unpleasant and at the same time untrue.

Autism is evident whenever we jump to some conclusion without checking it for its congruence with available data or other, tested truths. Thus, a thirst-ridden prospector on a desert may conclude that the shimmering he sees in the distance is an oasis where he will be able to drink, and he exhausts himself running toward it, only to find that it recedes into the distance with each step he takes. A woman starved for affection may conclude that a man who places a hand on her shoulder is expressing thereby his undying love. In fact, he may only be propping himself up to avoid stumbling. A student, unsure of his ability to complete his studies, gets a note from his professor that reads "Please come to see me." He feels certain his professor is going to fail him. In fact, the teacher may be intending to invite the student to his house for dinner. A person, needing to bolster his self-esteem, may "remember" his past in a way that is inaccurate but flattering.

The probability of forming autistic beliefs is highest when needs or emotions are most intense and when the available information is incomplete or ambiguous.[6]

The passenger with little faith in the safety of airplanes will conclude that the engines are on fire if he should look out the window on a night flight; actually, he is likely noticing only the normal exhaust flames. His anxiety is strong, and the amount of information available to him is limited. Consequently, he jumps to a conclusion based upon his emotions, rather than postponing his judgment until he has considered other hypotheses.

Our needs and emotions not only make us believe things that are untrue and see or hear inaccurately, they can also blind us to truth. If a perception, belief, or memory were to give rise to devastating depression or hopelessness, there might be a strong tendency for people simply to ignore or deny the disquieting truth. Anyone who has suffered the death of a loved one will know how difficult it is to realize that the deceased will not be seen any more. People tend to forget, or more accurately, to repress or blot out the memory of events that were painful or humiliating.

TWO COMMON SOURCES OF AUTISTIC BELIEFS: SELF AND OTHERS

We have stated that autistic beliefs are most likely to be formed in relation to phenomena that pertain to our needs and feelings and where access to information that is essential for accurate beliefs is hard to obtain. Both these conditions exist in our observations of ourselves and of other people.

BELIEFS ABOUT THE SELF. We are far from indifferent when it comes to believing things about our own personalities. To maintain our self-esteem, we need to believe some things about ourselves, e.g., that we are morally good, truthful, consistent, hard-working, and so on, and to deny some other aspects of our experience and behavior. If we were to believe, for example, that we lie and cheat and are immoral and dishonest, the likelihood is strong that we would experience considerable guilt and self-hate. To avoid these feelings, we tend to believe we are good, and the belief is accompanied by a warm glow of self-righteousness and heightened self-esteem. Coupled with the presence of a strong need for self-esteem is the fact that it is difficult for many people to obtain the information which would serve as a basis for a detailed and accurate concept of themselves. Introspection and fully detailed recollection of the past (reality-contact with one's personal past) are not easy to carry out;

yet, in the absence of such self-observation, the data for constructing an accurate self-concept are simply not available. Consequently, it may be expected that people will entertain many autistic beliefs about their own personalities (see Chapter 3).

BELIEFS ABOUT OTHER PEOPLE. Many of our most important needs can only be gratified through relationships with other people. This means that strong emotions and need-tensions are likely to be mobilized in our interpersonal relationships. Reliable information about another person is difficult to obtain, since much of his behavior goes on at times when we cannot see it. Furthermore, his inner experience—*his* phenomenal field—is not accessible to our direct vision. We can only learn the subjective side of another person if he confides in us, and he may not be willing to entrust us with personal information.[7] Often, we are obliged to form our concept of another person on the basis of his overt behavior alone. Hence, it should be no surprise that our concepts of other people in our lives are frequently inaccurate and that we often make mistakes in predicting their reactions. In Chapter 10, we will examine more fully the process of forming accurate concepts of others' personalities.

REALITY-TESTING

Our chances of behaving effectively are increased if we perceive accurately and construct beliefs about the world that are valid. But we know that unfulfilled needs and strong emotions can distort our cognition, so that we often misinterpret facts, arrive at erroneous conclusions, and, indeed, frequently fail to see and hear what is there. How does a person go about increasing the efficiency of his cognition? How does a person carry out reality-testing? Indeed, why would a person seek the truth when unreality is often more pleasant in the short run?

Reality-testing means applying the rules of scientific inquiry to everyday life. When we engage in reality-testing, we are systematically doubting our own initial perceptions and beliefs until we have scrutinized them more carefully and checked them against further evidence. We do this when we have learned that truth, ultimately, is the best servant of our other needs and is a value or end in itself.

AN EXAMPLE OF REALITY-TESTING

A nineteen-year-old girl once consulted with me, seeking help with a problem that was bothering her. She believed her roommate was stealing her money, jewelry, and even stationery. She had noticed various items missing from her dresser from time to time, and she concluded that her roommate was the guilty party. However, she could not bring herself to accuse the other girl to her face. Instead, she felt distrust and resentment and struggled to conceal these feelings from the roommate. Their relationship gradually deteriorated to one of formality, forced politeness, and false expressions of friendship.

I asked the girl why she didn't bring the whole issue out into the open. She stated that if she did this, the other girl would hate her, and she couldn't stand this. I asked if there was any other possible way of interpreting the loss of her money and jewelry. She replied that she hadn't thought of any. Rather, she had concluded that if her things were missing, they must have been stolen by the person closest to her. When I suggested that her roommate might be saddened at the way their friendship had deteriorated and that she might welcome some frank talk to settle things, the girl admitted that this might be possible, but she was afraid to talk to her about the problem. However, she agreed to broach the subject. Next time I saw the girl, she was happy to report that she had discussed the whole affair; she learned that her roommate was puzzled by the way their relationship had changed. Moreover, she was glad to discuss the loss of the articles with her and she was able to clear herself of any blame. In fact, it was learned that the roommate too had been missing some money, and investigation by the dormitory counselor brought forth the fact that other girls had been robbed and that the guilty party was a cleaning woman, who was promptly discharged.

This example illustrates how some initial, untested beliefs that one person forms about some aspect of the world—in this case, about another person—can lead to misunderstandings in interpersonal relationships and to considerable unhappiness. At first, the girl was afraid to carry out any efforts at reality-testing, to see if her assumption of the guilt of her roommate was warranted. This illustrates another aspect of reality-testing; frequently, people may be reluctant or afraid to go after the information which is crucial to the formation of accurate beliefs. Yet, if a person gives in to his fear of getting at the truth, he is almost sure to become increasingly out of touch with reality; this almost guarantees deterioration of over-all personality health.

RULES FOR REALITY-TESTING

Everyone can learn to become more effective at reality-testing if he will follow these rules:

1. *State the belief clearly.*
2. *Ask, "What evidence is there to support this belief?"*
3. *Ask, "Is there any other way of interpreting this evidence?"*
4. *Try to determine how consistent the belief is with other beliefs that are known to be valid.*

Now, we shall illustrate. A student believes his teacher dislikes him. Let us put words in his mouth and arrange an imaginary monologue.

"My teacher hates me. What evidence do I have for this belief? Why, the fact that he gave me a very low grade, plus the fact that yesterday when I greeted him in the hall, he didn't turn my way to acknowledge the greeting. But let me see. Is there any other way of interpreting this evidence? Well, what factors can produce low grades? One of them is insufficient study and faulty understanding of the course. As it happens, I haven't cracked a book all quarter, and I cut half my lectures to play billiards and go to the burlesque. Maybe that's why I flunked. But what about the fact that I greeted the professor and he didn't even nod? Well, maybe he didn't hear me. I must admit I spoke very low, and the hall was noisy. Finally, this professor is widely believed to be extremely fair and impartial in his dealings with students, and so my belief about his hating me isn't consistent wih his reputation."

Systematic application of this set of rules will help the reader to make sure his beliefs come closer to accuracy than would be the case if he ignored the activity of reality-testing.

A BARRIER TO REALITY-TESTING: FEAR

Fear and anxiety are the most basic barriers to reality-testing. It takes courage to face the truth, and frequently this courage may be lacking. Our security and self-esteem are frequently grounded on a set of fixed beliefs, and whenever we encounter evidence which is dissonant with these, we may undergo an attack of anxiety. Healthier personalities will proceed to go after the truth in spite of their anxiety, while those who are less healthy may seek to reduce their anxiety by denying or distorting the evidence which is in conflict with their beliefs.

New information which results in the revision of one's beliefs about reality seems to be crucial to ongoing personality growth. When persons fear the unknown or the unfamiliar, it is as if they are also afraid to grow toward fuller self-actualization.[8] Thus, it can be concluded that those persons who fear reality-testing are less likely to fulfill their potentialities than the more secure and courageous, who seek the truth.

PROMOTING THE REALITY-TESTING HABIT

Since reality-testing appears to be so important a factor in healthy personality, we may well ask, "How can it be encouraged?"

Education and personality therapy are two means by which a respect for reality and a desire for truth can be fostered.

EDUCATION AND REALITY-CONTACT. Public education is believed to be the most important means by which a person can arrive at a broad grasp of basic truths and accurate beliefs about the world. Education is thought to consist of the dispensing of facts, the teaching of skills basic to the acquisition of new facts, and the critical testing of old ones. Any teacher knows that students at all levels do not come into the classroom in a state of cognitive emptiness. Every student from kindergarten up to graduate school holds many beliefs

—some accurate and many inaccurate—which serve as a barrier to the acquisition of newer, more tested ones. Part of the skill in teaching consists in drawing out a student's present beliefs and encouraging him to test these against more reliable information. When classes are large, it is difficult for a teacher to find out what a student thinks or believes or knows.

PERSONALITY THERAPY AND REALITY-CONTACT. One of the most widely held aims of personality therapists, irrespective of theoretical orientation, is to increase reality-contact and promote the reality-testing habit. In taking measures designed to "strengthen the ego" of the patient, the psychoanalyst is hoping to help the patient gain enough courage and strength to test present erroneous beliefs and to face painful aspects of reality, including the realities of the patient's own past behavior.

MEASURING REALITY-CONTACT

The most basic means for measuring reality-contact is to compare what a person believes with "the facts." This involves getting some explicit statement of what a person believes and having at hand some criterion against which to compare it. The criterion may be observable facts, or it may be the opinion of qualified experts.

Thus, we can ask a person what he believes about engines, the causes of rain, how babies are born, or why people contract colds. The more that a person's beliefs depart from reality, the more deviant, ineffective, and unhealthy we might expect his behavior to be.

Psychologists have devised some sophisticated but still crude means for the actual measurement of reality-contact. One of these is an adaptation of the Rorschach Test. Norms have been assembled, based on the responses of thousands of unhospitalized (i.e., normal) people to the ink blots. These responses serve as a crude standard of what is accurate, or realistic.[9] When a person interprets some aspect of a blot in a way that differs from these norms, and does this repeatedly, he is deemed to suffer from some impairment in reality-contact. It is assumed that if he perceives ink blots in a deviant manner from most other people, he will also perceive and believe other things in a deviant manner.

There is a great advantage to objective means of measuring the extent to which a person is in contact with reality, but almost anyone can approximate an objective test by simply asserting his beliefs clearly and comparing them with some criterion. The criteria against which beliefs might be compared include facts, the opinions of others deemed to be competent, and, in some instances, logic. Often, a person might believe something against the opinion of the majority and yet be right in his belief. Many scientific discoveries which threatened man's pride met with considerable opposition from laymen and scientific colleagues alike, though later the unpopular beliefs came to be affirmed more widely. Thus, the work of Copernicus, Galileo, Freud, and Darwin all met both learned and ignorant opposition. All those workers were undoubtedly viewed by many of their contemporaries as being "crazy" and "unrealistic."

In a personality-hygiene program, the measurement of reality-contact will come to be a very urgent problem, as will the problem of improving the reality-contact of the broad mass of people. One might say that all measures aimed at increasing education, knowledge, and the habit of reality-testing among large numbers of people are personality-hygiene measures. The facts about life and the world may not be pleasant for some people, but since we live in a world of facts, there is considerable advantage to be gained from knowing them.

LIVING IN THE "RAW WORLD"

It is probably the lot of the human being that once he has learned speech, his perception of reality is always filtered through, and guided by, his *concepts* of reality. For example, if you learn the concept *gun* and then look at a gun, you probably see something entirely different from what a primitive savage might; guns have no place, nor even a word to describe them, in his culture.[10]

Words, concepts, or symbols may be said to *limit* what a person will actually observe in a concrete situation. Once a concept has been learned, a person will look at a given object only long enough to place it in its proper category or to assign an appropriate name to it. He may then ignore, or fail to observe, much of what is actually there before him. We are all familiar with the bigoted person who, once he has determined that a person is a Jew or a Negro, never looks further at the person. He "knows" the properties of "all" members who fall into those classes. In reality, the bigot fails to observe the enormous amount of variation among members of a class of any sort.[11]

The ability to break down broad categories and classes and to discern the individual, the particular, the unique, is a valuable one from the personality-hygiene point of view. This is not to say that "rubricizing" is a bad thing.[12] On the contrary, it appears to be inescapable. But the ability to see what is there, to transcend labels and classes and apprehend the thing before one's view, is a means of enriching one's knowledge of the world and of deepening one's contact with reality. To be able to see the "raw world" involves the ability to abandon presently held concepts and categories. Something of this ability is possessed by the productive scientist who deliberately ignores the orthodoxies and looks ever afresh at the raw data which prompted the formation of present-day concepts and categories.

The artist probably possesses the ability to apprehend the unique, the individual object, to a marked degree.

The ability to set conventional categories and concepts aside and to look fully at the world with minimal preconceptions seems to be a trait which facilitates scientific discovery, art, human relations, and more generally, an enrichment of the sensory experiences of living.

The capacity to let oneself see or perceive what is there seems to entail *the temporary cessation of an active, searching or critical attitude.* Need-directed perception is like a highly focused searchlight darting here and there, seeking the objects which will satisfy needs and ignoring everything which is irrelevant to the need. "Being-cognition," as Maslow has called it, refers to a more passive mode of perceiving. It involves *letting* oneself be reached, touched, or affected by what is there so that the perception is richer. In Maslow's own words, "The most efficient way to perceive the intrinsic nature of the world is to be more passive than active, determined as much as possible by the intrinsic organization of that which is perceived and as little as possible by nature of the perceiver. This kind of detached, Taoist [a Chinese philosophy], passive, non-interfering awareness of all the simultaneously existing aspects of the concrete, has much in common with some descriptions of the aesthetic experience and of the mystic experience. The stress is the same. Do we see the real, concrete world, or do we see our own system of rubrics, motives, expectations and abstractions which we have projected onto the real world. Or, to put it very bluntly, do we see or are we blind?"[13]

This mode of cognition, however, seems to be possible only at those times when a person has adequately coped with his basic needs, so that they are not pressing for fulfillment. When a person is anxious, or sexually deprived, or hungry, it is as if his organs of perceiving and of knowing have been "commandeered" to find the means for gratification. The perceptual-cognitive apparatus seems most free to play, to be most receptive to new impressions, when the urgency of needs is diminished. The implication is clear—if a person wants to know hitherto unnoticed features of the world which confronts him, his chances of so doing are increased at those times when his basic needs are temporarily satisfied.

The direction of our cognition by needs certainly has adaptive value, because it increases our chances of finding the things that will satisfy our needs, and it permits us to locate and then avoid dangers in our environment.[14] However, if persons are *always* perceiving the world under the instigation of their needs, the likelihood is strong that they will simply not see, smell, hear, and feel much that exists. The aesthetic, appreciative contemplation of reality, with no purpose other than the delight of looking at it, or experiencing it, lends a dimension of richness to an existence that is ordinarily characterized by the search for satisfaction. Competence at gratifying one's needs frees one from time to time of the necessity to be forever struggling and permits one the luxury (or necessity) of aesthetic gazing.

SUMMARY

People behave under the direction of their perceptual-cognitive fields; that is, they behave in the world as they see it and assume it to be. Our perceptions and assumptions about the world are frequently distorted because of the influence of unfulfilled needs and emotion. The tendency of perception and cognition to be distorted by emotion and need-tensions is described as autism. *One can counteract the autistic influence of emotion by reality-testing, which means adopting the attitude that one's present impressions of reality are hypotheses which need to be tested before they are fully believed and acted upon. Reality-testing frequently calls for courage, because at times the truth may be painful. However, efficient contact with reality is a necessary condition for healthy personality.*

Our view of the world at times when we are seeking gratification of basic needs, such as hunger, sex, or status, is different from the view we can have when our needs have temporarily been fulfilled. When we are in a state of satisfaction, our cognitive "apparatus" is free to play, to receive impressions without picking and choosing them for their relevance to our immediate needs. The term aesthetic cognition is appropriate to describe this passive, receiving, enjoying, contemplative type of perception and thinking. The capacity for aesthetic cognition can be regarded as a sign of healthy personality. Inability to perceive in this manner probably signifies that a person is still struggling to gratify various needs. Aesthetic, playful cognition not only enriches our existence; it appears to be one of the conditions for making new discoveries in reality, and so it has value for us beyond its status as a sign of healthy personality.

NOTES AND REFERENCES

Excellent supplementary reading will be provided by those references marked with an asterisk (*).

*1. A more detailed and systematic statement of the phenomenological point of view is provided by Combs, A. and Snygg, D., *Individual Behavior* (2nd ed.; New York: Harper, 1959), especially chapter 2.

*2. See Cantril, H., *The Why of Man's Experience* (New York: Macmillan, 1950), pp. 87–104, for a fuller discussion of the concept of the "assumptive world."

*3. *Cf.* Murphy, G., *Personality, A Biosocial Approach to Origins and Structure* (New York: Harper, 1947), especially chs. 14, 15. See also Solley, C. M. and Murphy, G., *Development of the Perceptual World* (New York: Basic Books, 1960), ch. 4.

4. Reviews of research dealing with the influence of needs and emotions, "set," interests, and other "central" factors on the cognitive processes are *Contemporary Approaches to Cognition: A Symposium Held at the University of Colorado;* Bruner, J. S. and others, contributors, (Cambridge: Harvard U. P., 1957); Murphy, G., *op. cit.;* Krech, D. and Crutchfield, R. S., *Theory and Problems in Social Psychology* (New York: McGraw, 1948), chs. 3, 4, 5, 6; Scheerer, M., "Cognitive Theory," in Lindzey, G., *Handbook of Social Psychology,* I, (Cambridge, Mass.: Addison-Wesley, 1954), ch. 3; Rapaport, D., *Emotions and Memory* (New York: International Universities Press, 1950).

5. See Freud, S., "Formulations Regarding the Two Principles in Mental Functioning," in Freud, S., *Collected Papers,* IV (London; Hogarth, 1953), ch. 1.

6. Murphy, G., *op. cit.,* ch. 15.

7. See Jourard, S. M., "Healthy Personality and Self-Disclosure," *Ment. Hyg.,* *43,* 499–507 (1959).

*8. Maslow, A. H., *Toward a Psychology of Being* (New York: Van Nostrand, 1962), ch. 5.

9. *Cf.* Hertz, Marguerite, *Frequency Tables for Scoring Responses to the Rorschach Inkblot Test* (3rd ed., Cleveland, Ohio: Western Reserve, 1951).

10. The field of semantics is devoted to study of how our concepts both facilitate and interfere with accurate cognition. See Hayakawa, S. I., *Language in Action* (New York: Harcourt, 1941), for a readable introduction to this field of study.

*11. See Allport, G., *The Nature of Prejudice* (Cambridge, Mass.: Addison-Wesley, 1954), ch. 2, for an excellent discussion of the way categorization is related to prejudice and bigotry.

12. See Maslow, A. H., *Motivation and Personality* (New York: Harper, 1954), ch. 14; also Maslow, A. H., *op. cit.*, ch. 9.

*13. Maslow, A. H., reference 8, p. 38. Maslow's two books (references 8 and 12) are basic and required reading for any student who wishes to be properly introduced to the "positive approach" in psychology. Fuller description of the unsearching, aesthetic mode of cognition may be found in Watts, A. W., *The Way of Zen* (New York: Mentor, 1959), pp. 152–153; and Schachtel, E. G., *Metamorphosis. On the Development of Affect, Perception, Attention, and Memory* (New York: Basic Books, 1959), especially pp. 220 ff.

14. Maslow, A. H., *op. cit.* (reference 8), ch. 8, "Some Dangers of Being-Cognition."

CHAPTER *4*
EMOTION
AND HEALTHY PERSONALITY

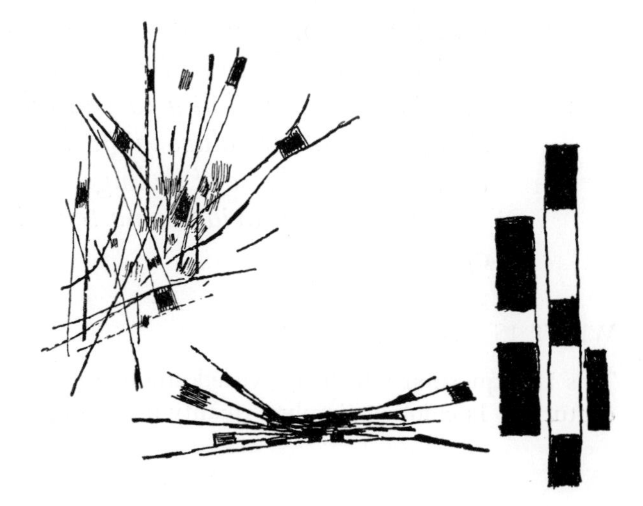

INTRODUCTION

The way in which we manage our emotions has a direct effect upon the health of our personality and our body. If a person strives to eliminate all feeling and emotion from his life, aiming to be rational and intellectual at all times, his relationships with other people will likely be superficial, and he may be jeopardizing his physical health. On the other hand, if a person is unable to control the expression of his emotions and explodes from time to time into tantrums of rage or flights of terror, he will pay for it in various ways. There is a middle ground that is most compatible with optimum health and with the satisfactory conduct of life, and later in this chapter, we will discuss the healthier ways of handling emotion. We can anticipate our discussion, however, by stating that healthy personality calls for the ability to experience and express the full range of human emotion and *the ability to control expression at times when other values might be endangered by unrestrained release of feelings.*

Now, let us provide some technical discussion of emotion.

WHAT IS AN EMOTION?

This is a question which has vexed students of human nature for centuries.[1] Is emotion simply a quality of feeling or tension? Is it a pattern of distinct neurophysiological responses which a physiologist might detect and record with his specialized instruments? Is it a pattern of facial expression, bodily posture, muscular tonus, and tone of voice which a layman can observe with his unaided senses? Actually emotion is *all* these things occurring simultaneously in some given situation. But we are not interested in all aspects of emotion in this volume. What follows is a highly selective discussion of emotion along lines relevant to personality hygiene. Let us begin with the concept of *emotional tension,* or *affect,* as it is often called.

EMOTIONAL TENSION (AFFECT). Most of the time, a person experiences a quality of inner feeling which he might describe as "calm," "ordinary," and "collected." Let us call this quality his *modal tension-level* and *-quality*. Suppose that the person is walking along, feeling nothing in particular, and a complete stranger comes up to him and pushes him off the sidewalk. The person will experience more than an interruption in his walk. He will experience an alteration in his modal tension-state—a distinct change which he has no difficulty in identifying as anger. Something about the fact of having been shoved has produced a radical change in his modal tension-state. He feels he has been insulted, and he always gets angry when insulted. The tension which he has labeled "anger" is one of many which people are capable of experiencing. Emotional tension is the general term which we shall use to refer to these specific affects, which include fear, anxiety, affection, hostility, depression, excitement, and others.[2]

It should be stated that when a person is conscious of angry tension within himself (through introspection), the outside observer can notice certain facial expressions, gestures, signs of autonomic nervous system activity, such as blushing or blanching, changes in the rate and depth of breathing, and muscular tremor.[3] In addition, if the person were to report further on his inner state he might report, not only the presence of angry affect, but also a lot of thinking along lines of this sort: "Why that dirty so-and-so. He insulted me. I'm going to let him have it square on the jaw."

It becomes apparent that emotional tension is only a small part of a much more complex phenomenon which we shall call the *emotional response.* In addition to affect, the emotional response includes cognitive aspects (what the person thinks, perceives), conative aspects (what he intends to do), and complex responses of the voluntary and involuntary nervous and muscular systems. For purposes of simplicity and clarity, and because our interest in this chapter is primarily on emotional tensions, we shall use the term *emotional response* to refer specifically to the emotional tension component of the total response. The reader must not forget, however, that all of the other phenomena are occurring at the same time as the affects.

EMOTIONAL TENSION AND EMOTIONAL BEHAVIOR. Emotional tension may be welcomed by the person and sought as a goal in itself, or it may be unwanted, so that the person will strive to get rid of the tension once it has arisen. Thus, a person may become bored with the sameness of his tension-state and seek thrills and fights, read a detective novel, or play handball, just because he enjoys the experience of mild fear or hot rage. Or, he may have come to detest certain emotional tensions and even to fear them; when such emotional tensions arise, he strives to be rid of them as quickly as he can. Behavior directed toward the changing or reduction of emotional tensions in the self we shall call *emotional behavior*.

THE ORIGIN OF EMOTIONAL RESPONSES

The question may be raised, "How does it come about that some stimulus will provoke an emotional response in a person?" Anyone can observe that the same stimulus will provoke emotional tension in one person but not in another; that the stimulus may provoke entirely different emotional responses in two different persons, or in the same person at different times. Thus, a stern look and a loud bellow from the professor may evoke fear in the student, anger from the professor's wife, laughter from his colleague, and intellectual curiosity in his psychoanalyst. If the student has passed the course, and is no longer dependent upon his professor, he may respond to the stern look and the bellow on that happy day with indifference or with a triumphant counterblast of hostility—he'll tell the professor exactly how he feels about him.

In view of the fact of wide individual differences in emotional responsiveness to a stimulus, and wide intraindividual variability in response to the same stimulus, we may well ask how we come to acquire our emotional habits. By *emotional habit* we are referring to a stable association between some class of stimuli or objects and some emotional tension, such as anxiety and hostility.

On the basis of present-day knowledge about emotion, it may be said that emotional habits are learned (not inborn), and further, they are learned through the mechanisms of *conditioning, identification,* and *socialization.*

CONDITIONING AND EMOTIONAL RESPONSES. The reader is no doubt familiar with the experimental procedure discovered by Pavlov and named conditioning. In brief, the laboratory procedure of conditioning involves:

1. *Discovering some response, or reflex which can regularly be elicited by some stimulus, called the* unconditioned stimulus. Examples of such reflexes and the unconditioned stimuli which stably will evoke them are: eyeblink, a puff of air; knee jerk, a blow on the patellar tendon; salivation, the presence of food or acid in the mouth. The response itself, when considered together with its relevant unconditioned stimulus, is described as an *unconditioned response.*

2. *Presenting a neutral stimulus along with the unconditioned stimulus for a number of trials.* After a suitable number of pairings of the neutral stimulus with the unconditioned stimulus, the former will come to elicit the response ordinarily evoked by the unconditioned stimulus. When this has occurred, the previously neutral stimulus is given the name *conditioned stimulus,* and the response is now called a *conditioned response.*

As a laboratory procedure, conditioning has been used by scientists to study brain functions[4] and to discover some of the "laws of learning."[5] Animal trainers use conditioning principles in order to train animals to perform all manner of tasks. But aside from being the name for a laboratory procedure, conditioning has come to be given a much more generalized meaning; it refers now to any occasion that a neutral stimulus is presented along with an effective stimulus, such that the former comes to elicit the response regularly evoked by the latter.

It has come to be recognized that the manner in which affective responses to stimuli are acquired is analogous with (if not identical to) the laboratory procedure for establishing a conditioned response. The affect *fear,* for example, appears to be a by-product of experience with painful stimulation. The painful unconditioned stimulus produces activity of the autonomic nervous system. Other stimuli, such as the sight, sound, or smell of the painful stimulus become conditioned stimuli for these autonomic responses. Thus, the person comes to respond with emotional tension to conditioned stimuli that were associated with the pain-producing, unconditioned stimulus.[6] In a sense, the conditioned stimuli become signals that the unconditioned stimulus is close by. This signal-function of a conditioned stimulus is what we call the cognitive component of an emotional response. The technical name for this "cognitive component" is *expectancy.*[7]

A person perceives some stimulus. Past experience has led him to expect or predict that some other stimulus will be forthcoming—one which will affect him in a pleasurable or painful way. He sees his girl friend frown, and he becomes anxious—he expects rejection. He sees her smile, and he feels good—he expects to get a kiss. Emotional responses thus are strongly determined by the *interpretation of the stimulus*—by the expectancy which past experience has built up in the person.

EXPECTANCIES AND EMOTIONAL RESPONSES. An expectancy may technically be defined as a prediction that *B* will follow *A*, where *A* is a conditioned stimulus and *B* an unconditioned stimulus. Expectancies are acquired through observation and generalizing from observations. Since generalization is a very tricky activity, even for the professional logician or scientist, it follows that a layman may often overgeneralize from his observations or generalize without an adequate sample of observations. We have all observed night following day with absolute regularity, and so we have accurate expectancies with regard to this fact. We have all heard thunder following lightning with absolute regularity, and so our expectancies will be quite accurate when they predict that soon after we see lightning, we will hear a thunderclap.[8]

But we may have been bitten by one dog—the bite produces pain. On the basis of that one occurrence, a person may generalize that all dogs will bite him. He sees another dog and expects to be bitten. He becomes afraid. If we know that the dog which he fears has never bitten anyone—in fact the dog has no teeth—we would say his expectancy was inaccurate and his emotional response was inappropriate. But appropriate or inappropriate, a person's emotional responses will be predicated on his expectancies, and his expectancies have been grounded on his own experiences with paired stimuli, conditioned and unconditioned. When he observes the contioned stimulus, he expects the unconditioned stimulus to be near, and he will respond emotionally to the conditioned stimulus. When someone responds with fear or hostility to some object which does not evoke those responses in us, we can assume that our expectancies with respect to the object differ from his. If we interpreted the stimulus as he does, and if we had had similar experiences with stimuli of that sort, then we too might display a similar emotional response.

From all of this we may conclude that conditioning, the pairing of neutral stimuli with stimuli that affect us pleasurably or painfully, goes on unremittingly from birth until death; that we continually acquire, revise, and abandon expectancies; and that our emotional responses are elicited by (conditioned) stimuli which have been interpreted by the person in such a way that they acquire signal or predictive properties.

IDENTIFICATION AND EMOTIONAL RESPONSES. A psychologist or layman can readily observe close similarities in emotional habits within a family or between two close friends, or spouses. Father and his sons all display similar emotional responses to politicians, salesmen, women, animals, and so on. A woman, before she became married, responded emotionally after the fashion of her mother and siblings; after several years of marriage, her parents and siblings notice she no longer feels about things the way she used to—she has "changed." She has come to share some of the emotional habits of her husband, and he in turn has acquired many of hers, so that his former bachelor friends notice striking differences in him. He is no longer amused by the same things, angered or afraid of the same things, as he was when he was "one of the boys."

The mechanism responsible for the acquisition of emotional responses which resemble those of someone close is *identification.* Identification is a learning process by means of which an individual, *A*, reproduces in his own stable behavior-repertoire characteristics of person *B.*[9] It may be a conscious, deliberate attempt to imitate the valued traits of another person, or it may be an unconsciously purposeful emulation. It is not known whether emotional habits are acquired through direct identification or whether the similarity in emotional habits between two persons derives from identification with each other's values, expectancies, and attitudes. Nevertheless, it can be asserted that either directly or indirectly persons acquire certain of their emotional habits by means of identification.

SOCIALIZATION AND EMOTIONAL RESPONSES. A sociologist or anthropologist observes that most members of a given social class or of a society share many emotional habits. These emotional responses differ, however, from the modal emotional responses of people in other classes or societies.

It is likely that part of the total socialization process—the efforts of parents, teachers, and others concerned with the molding and shaping of modal personality for a society—is devoted to insuring that the growing and developing children will acquire the appropriate emotional habits. It is desired that most members of a group perceive and interpret aspects of the world in a uniform way and react with similar emotional responses to those objects. This uniformity is probably achieved through formal education—the child knows that pain and fear are associated with danger, and so his elders and instructors teach him to interpret many things as dangerous. It may also be achieved through training-experiences within the family which have the effect of conditioning most members of the society in a uniform way to certain classes of stimuli.[10]

Probably most of the prejudices, fears, likes, and so on, of a given society derive, not from direct and individualized conditioning experiences, but rather as a consequence of socialization experiences and identification with the emotional experience of significant persons in the family or peergroup—who in turn resemble other members of society at large.

EVALUATING EMOTIONAL RESPONSES

When once we have learned to observe, record, and describe our own emotional responses to life situations, it becomes possible to evaluate these responses. But the question arises, "What criteria shall we use for evaluating our emotional responses?" Obviously, there are many criteria possible: intensity of response, duration, similarity of responses to those made by other people, and so on. The choice of criteria depends largely on the specific purpose for which evaluation is to be made. The criteria which appear to be of greatest value in a discussion of healthy emotionality are *appropriateness* and *consciousness*.

Appropriate affects are deemed to be a crucial indicator of over-all personality health. When our affects are inappropriate to the situation, as in the case of phobias, irrational hostilities and affections, and irrational guilts, our capacity to achieve need-satisfactions in acceptable ways is gravely impaired. We may regard the capacity to respond with appropriate affects as a positive personality-hygiene value.

In an earlier chapter (Chapter 2), it was pointed out that only when motives are conscious can a person select his behavior in such a way as to implement them. Emotional tensions are motives which influence behavior selection; when our tensions are conscious, we are better able to select and control our behavior. When affects are unconscious, the probability is increased that we will act in ways which we did not consciously intend. It follows that the capacity to recognize one's own emotional tensions accurately is a positive personality-hygiene value.

APPROPRIATE AND INAPPROPRIATE AFFECTS

If a person became afraid in the presence of a robber holding a loaded gun, we would agree that the situation objectively is dangerous, and we should call his fear rational. The term *appropriate affects*[11] will be reserved for those emotional responses which are associated with accurate expectancies and efficient reality-contact. Such affects are valued by the personality hygienist as indices of personality health. But most of us carry with us emotional habits which do not make sense to another observer or to ourselves. Thus, we may become angry with no apparent adequate provocation; we may like someone when he has done nothing to warrant this like; we may fear dogs and insects when we know from scientific evidence there is absolutely no danger. The term *inappropriate affects* will be used to refer to this class of emotional responses, responses which seem irrational and do not appear to have adequate provocation. We can find no adequate explanation for them. Inappropriate affects are generally interpreted as symptoms of unhealthy personality in general or as signs of unhealthy emotionality in particular. Let us inquire further into their nature. The problem to be solved here is not that of explaining the manner in which such affects have arisen; there is no reason to doubt they were acquired after the fashion of all emotional responses. The main puzzle seems to lie in how they came to be inexplicable. Most affects make sense to us; we fear dogs because we have been bitten. The affects which do not make sense may interfere radically with our life, causing us to restrict behavior considerably or to behave in ways that are not appropriate.

The mechanisms which probably explain inappropriate affects are the following:

1. Repression. Through repression, the individual has "forgotten" the events which resulted in his acquiring an emotional response to some class of objects. The only record that such conditioning did take place is the emotional response itself. Thus we may become angry at all redheaded persons and not know why. It could be that long ago we had been unfairly and cruelly treated by someone with red hair. The memory for the original traumatic experience has long been repressed, but the affect still remains. Possibly if we were able to recall and release our feelings with respect to the original trauma, our automatic hostility toward redhaired persons might disappear.[12]

2. Redintegration.[13] The original conditioning experience involved the association of many conditioned stimuli with the unconditioned stimulus. All of the conditioned stimuli save one may have lost their power to evoke the emotional response. This one remaining stimulus may have no necessary causal connection with the unconditioned stimulus; at the time of conditioning, the neutral stimulus just happened to be present with all the others. The person retains his emotional response to this stimulus and does not know why. This tendency to react to some small part of a very complex whole situation as if it actually were the whole situation is called re-dintegration.

3. *Symbolization.* Language is comprised of symbols that have *shared* meanings. However, a person may construct his own *idiosyncratic* symbols of events and objects past and present. Many of the stimuli for inappropriate, irrational affects may actually be remote symbols of the original unconditioned stimulus; the verbal connections between the unconditioned stimulus and its symbol may have been repressed. Freud explained phobias—irrational fears—in these terms. In one case,[14] a small child dreaded walking in the streets of Vienna because there were horses all about. He dreaded horses, although he had had no traumatic experiences with any particular horses. Analysis of the child's early history revealed that he had much repressed hostility toward his father, with the dread of retaliation by the father for these hostile wishes. The horses had come to symbolize his father, and he was able to keep his feelings toward his father repressed by "displacing" these feelings to horses. The apparent connecting link which made this phobia-development possible lay in the fact that the favorite game which the child and his father played together was "horsey."

4. *Overgeneralization.* Many inappropriate affects derive from the logical fallacy of *overgeneralization.* A person might have been affected pleasantly or unpleasantly by some object or person. Following this experience, he may generalize very broadly, so that he comes to expect similar treatment for good or ill from all objects or persons who even vaguely resemble the original. It is apparent that simply subjecting the expectancy to reality-testing will usually be sufficient to enable the person to discriminate between those objects which will affect him and those which, though apparently similar, say, in appearance, actually differ in basic and fundamental ways from those which will produce the desired or dreaded impact. The common dread of snakes and beetles; the tendency to like or dislike people on first sight; these emotional responses probably derive from overgeneralization.[15] Often, when a person acts on the basis of these overgeneralizations, he gets into some kind of difficulty; as when an employer who trusted a given man hires another man just on the basis of "liking his looks" (the new man resembles the

trusted employee). The new man, however, may actually be a crook. Looks and actual behavior have no correlation with each other, although we have all been conditioned to expect certain kinds of behavior from people on the basis of their facial characteristics[16] and body build. We look at a thin-lipped woman and describe her as highly moral expecting puritanistic behavior from her. We look at a fat man[17] and expect jollity from him. We are often wrong in such expectancies, as experience will attest.

ACHIEVING APPROPRIATE AFFECTS

The capacity to feel, to respond emotionally in life situations, is a personality-health value for many reasons. Emotional tensions add a rich dimension to our experience, making life fuller and more meaningful. Try to imagine how drab life would be without affect of any sort! In addition, emotional responses serve very useful signal and motivating functions for a person, warning him of what to expect and motivating him to do something either to avert the expected event or to hasten its arrival, as in the case of cues which portend pain or pleasure.

But the signal function of affects is of value only when the affects are appropriate. Irrational affects actually interfere with the attainment of gratifications. We will give a general rule for the attainment of appropriate affects and then illustrate this rule with discussions of anxiety, hostility, and guilt.

The rule may be stated as follows: *In order to attain appropriate affects, it is necessary (a) to admit that one has the feeling in question and (b) to subject the cognitive aspects of the emotional response (the expectancies) to reality-testing.* If this is done, the person will fear only those things which realistically are dangerous; he will worry and feel anxiety only when events actually forecast impending danger to values; he will become hostile only when he has actually been insulted, threatened, or thwarted.

ACHIEVING APPROPRIATE ANXIETY. Irrational anxiety is known to play a very crucial role in the development of symptoms of unhealthy personality. Appropriate anxiety, on the other hand, serves a useful biological function to the person, warning him of actual danger to his assorted values.[18] Let us describe the general principles for the attainment of appropriate anxiety:

1. *The person must first experience his anxiety and recognize it as such.* Recognizing anxiety is not so simple as would appear at first glance. Anxiety is very often effectively repressed by a person, so that he is hardly aware he has it. Or it may be warded off by all manner of effective avoidance measures,[19] so that he seldom experiences it. Yet, if the person were directly confronted by the anxiety-provoking situation, he might become overwhelmed with anxiety. The recognition and direct experiencing of anxiety is difficult to achieve in such instances; in fact, it may be necessary for a person to seek help before he can recognize his own anxiety. An expert personality diagnostician or therapist may be able to discern the indirect symptoms of unconscious anxiety and help the patient re-experience his anxiety.

2. *The person must subject his worries, or expectancies, to reality-testing.* Anxiety usually has a cognitive component, namely, *worrying.* Worry is really another term for expectancy, in this case, expectancy pertaining to painful events. Worry may be only momentary, or it may be unremitting and ceaseless. In order to insure that the worry is warranted, it is important for the anxious person to make a realistic appraisal of the probability that the dreaded events will come to pass. Such an appraisal will, in many instances, disclose that the worry is groundless and that the anxiety is thus irrational.[20] In such cases, the irrational anxiety may disappear. In cases where worry continues despite knowledge that the worry is groundless, it can be assumed that the content of worry is symbolic, that the person has anxieties which are still unconscious.

In illustration of these steps, let us assume that a person becomes anxious each time he confronts a crowd for purposes of making a speech. He worries in advance that he will make a fool of himself or that he is a fool already and will reveal this when he speaks. Once in the situation, he expects the people will judge him harshly or ridicule him.

There are many ways in which he can test the validity of his expectancies. First, he can look into the origins of his worries. He may find that on one occasion he made a speech, and people laughed at him. From that one occasion, he generalized to all future occasions. "They laughed at me once, they'll laugh at me in the future." Often, such a logical analysis will dissipate the anxiety and eliminate the worry.

The person may discover through such analysis that he is assuming all people are identical in cruelty with the few who laughed him off the platform the first time he spoke. Observation may disclose there are clear differences between the group he is about to address and the group who laughed at him. Observing the difference may effectively banish anxiety.

It may not be desirable for the person to lose his anxiety entirely, for anxiety can be a useful motive, insuring that a person will work hard or take sensible precautions against danger. But there seems to be little danger that any person will ever succeed in completely eliminating anxiety from his life, unless he remains "doped" with tranquilizing drugs all day every day. If he can rid himself of his irrational anxieties, that will be a worth-while achievement beyond which he need not strive.

Oddly enough, a person may have potential anxiety about facing a group without awareness of the fact. He has never had occasion to confront one and hence cannot recall ever being anxious. He may have all of the false expectancies about groups, but he will never have occasion to test these because he has never experienced the anxiety which would be provoked in the group situation. Only an expert observer might be able to infer from observations of his compulsive avoidance of group situations that he has unconscious anxiety connected with groups. Obviously, the person with unconscious anxiety must experience it before he can go through the procedures that will be effective in rendering anxiety rational. Much of the effort of the personality therapist treating neurotic patients is aimed at helping a patient to recognize and experience his anxieties, when they have been warded off by means of repression and other defensive activities.

Parenthetically, it may be noted that excessive duration and frequency of anxiety-reactions are undesirable and unhealthy. Reality-testing will serve to reduce the frequency with which a person is threatened. Another factor which also serves to reduce anxiety is the increase of one's skill-repertoire. The more one is autonomous and skilled, the less there is to worry about in life. Autonomy and reality-contact thus appear to be among the factors which will reduce the frequency and duration of anxiety-reactions.

Unfortunately, not all persons are able to follow the steps which produce rational anxiety. Instead of striving to recognize and experience their anxiety, they avoid situations thought to be anxiety-provoking; they may drink alcohol so that they don't feel their anxiety; they may swallow tranquilizing pills. Such persons are most likely to move in the direction of unhealthy personality or remain in their present unhealthy state.

Existential Anxiety. Existential philospophers and psychologists have drawn a valuable distinction between neurotic anxiety and existential anxiety. This distinction parallels the one we have drawn between inappropriate and appropriate anxiety, but further discussion is called for to enrich our understanding of the positive role anxiety plays in healthy human existence.

We experience "existential anxiety" when our existence as a human being is threatened by any danger. The ultimate anxiety is dread of death, of nothingness, of the termination of our lives. There is ample reason to suspect that a person only begins to live his life actively, choosing his values carefully, after he has faced death. Such an experience forcibly acquaints him with the fact that his life is impermanent, that he only has the one life to live, and that he had better not waste time with things which are of little importance to him.

We can never eliminate anxiety, which is rooted in human existence, for it is an outgrowth of the inescapable facts that our lives have limited duration and the future is always uncertain. Indeed, it is essential that such anxiety be experienced rather than repressed. Healthy personalities meet existential anxiety head-on; they endure it and struggle to follow their projects and goals in spite of it, showing thereby the "courage to be." Less healthy individuals are more inclined, upon the experience of such existential anxiety, to curtail their lives and their inner experience, seeming to value freedom from anxiety more than a fully lived life.[21]

ACHIEVING APPROPRIATE HOSTILITY. Our society largely condemns hostility as a bad thing.[22] Most of us feel guilty and become anxious whenever we are hostile. We are afraid that if people know we feel hostile toward them, they will reject us. From an early age, we are encouraged to eliminate hostility from our emotional life, with severe punishments whenever we fail to control hostility as we should.

The upshot of training of this sort is that many of us are provoked to hostility by many situations and persons and repress the feelings. Then, neither the offending person nor we ourselves are aware of the hostility. It becomes unconscious hostility, and it "leaks out" in all kinds of ways. The person with unconscious hostility may be very sarcastic toward others; he may bump into people, forget promises and intentions, undermine others' self-confidence—all without any conscious intent to hurt them. From time to time, the hostility may break through into near-homicidal outbursts, and a usually gentle (repressed) person may commit a bloody hatchet murder or otherwise run amok. When do we become hostile? There are only a few general sorts of instigators:

1. Interference with goal-directed activity.[23] We get angry when someone stands in our path or prevents us from reaching our goal.

2. Withholding desired need-objects. When we need money, or affection, or sexual gratification, and someone withholds these things from us, we become hostile. In fact, whenever we are dependent on other persons for different kinds of gratification, it is likely we will experience much hostility toward them from time to time, when they don't immediately gratify us or when they let us down. The reader may be aware of the intensity with which he has sometimes felt hostility toward his parents, spouse, boss, or others on whom he is dependent for many things.

Because of fear or guilt, we may repress (rather than merely suppress) the hostility which has been provoked by the persons on whom we are dependent. When this occurs, the dependent individual will be incapable of perceiving and judging his father, leader, or other dependency-object in a realistic manner, since he cannot criticize him realistically—as it would have the significance of hostility. And so he is likely to *idealize* the object of his dependency, perceiving him as perfect, without flaws—the possessor of magical powers and unlimited strength. All of the hostility which belongs to the object of dependency is likely to be turned inward, in the form of guilt feelings or feelings of inferiority; or the hostility may be "displaced"—directed toward other persons.[24]

In one study, the present author[25] showed that intense moral indignation—hostility toward violators of the social mores—was correlated with an inability to express hostile criticism toward the parents. Those persons who displayed the most intense hostility toward bohemians, graft, sex perversion, and so on, were persons who were least able to acknowledge criticism of their parents' traits.

3. *Violation of ideals.* We all have acquired standards of neatness, morality, decency, kindness, and when a person acts in opposition to these concepts of how things ought to be, we become hostile. Of course, the more rigid these standards are, the more often will the person become hostile.

When is hostility inappropriate? It is inappropriate when it appears to be too intense, in a competent judge's opinion, in comparison with the provocation; in other words, when there does not appear to be adequate provocation for the hostility. A person may explode with hostility when his meal is ten seconds late, or a mother may become enormously irritated when her child gets some mud on his shoes. It must be admitted there are no precise norms to enable us to judge accurately whether or not a hostile reaction is warranted, but certainly crude norms exist in our society, since many of us express surprise when someone gets hostile over something which appears to be trivial.[26]

It may be said that the personality hygienist would not regard a person as healthy who was absolutely without hostility. Appropriate hostility serves a useful purpose in everyday life. It helps get things done which need to be done, as with moral indignation over slums and cruelty to children. Further, expression of hostility in relations with close friends, or family, lets other people know and understand how their behavior affects you. If they know what offends you, they can either change their behavior or leave you.

The personality hygienist would regard it as desirable to eliminate inappropriate hostility, however, since it complicates life considerably. As with anxiety, there are two major steps which must be taken in order to achieve appropriate hostility:

1. The person must experience and recognize his hostility. As with anxiety, recognizing hostility is not always so easy, since we have such strong taboos against experiencing hostile affect. Many of us are unconsciously hostile toward parents, spouse, friends, boss, children, siblings, for reasons indicated above. These persons provoke hostility because of their behavior, but we may not dare to express this hostility toward them openly; indeed, because of strong personal taboos against hating one's family and others, we may have repressed the hostility so effectively we simply are not aware of it. Many a patient undergoing personality therapy is shocked when the therapist examines his behavior and tentatively suggests the patient has a good deal of hostility provoked by and directed toward mother, father, siblings, or wife.

2. The person must subject his hostile reactions to reality-testing. Subjecting hostile reactions to reality-testing really involves an attempt to determine why the person experiences hostility in response to the provocations which occur. If it becomes apparent the hostile reaction is inappropriate, then steps may be taken to eliminate the tendency to react in hostile fashion. If, on the other hand, the hostile reaction seems warranted and appropriate to the instigation, the person can perhaps come to express his hostility in appropriate fashion.

To illustrate, let us imagine that a person becomes hostile, irritated, or annoyed each time his wife straightens his tie, which she does daily. Possibly, he is not aware, fully, of his own irritation, or at least of the stimulus for it. Self-examination may disclose the precise instigator of his hostile reactions in his wife's behavior. When he is fully able to state in words "It makes me angry to have my wife straighten my tie," he may then say: "But that's really silly, to get so intensely furious about something so trivial. I wonder why I react that way?" Further self-scrutiny may disclose that such attentive behavior reminds him of some of the more overprotective and overcontrolling behavior of his mother, which he disliked intensely when he was younger. Simply making this discovery may be enough to eliminate the hostile reaction—it just no longer occurs when his wife fusses with his tie.

Naturally, not all hostile reactions will be so easy to banish through such analysis, but almost any person can eliminate some by such procedures. But even this procedure is impossible unless the person is able to feel and recognize his own hostilities and identify the stimulus for them.

Excessive and unduly prolonged hostility, whether conscious or unconscious, appropriate or inappropriate, is an indicator of unhealthy personality. When a person is chronically in a condition of hostility, his relationships with people will be seriously impaired, his ability to do productive work handicapped, and his physical health itself may suffer. Excessive hostility can be reduced by rational attempts to determine the causes and by undertaking steps to eliminate these causes. If a person becomes hostile because of chronic provocation in a dependency-relationship in which he is embroiled, he might take steps to achieve greater autonomy. If he is encountering too many interferences with his goal-directed activities, he might try to achieve greater skill so as to be better able to avoid or overcome these barriers. If his hostility derives from excessively rigid standards, it might be possible for him to alter his expectations and demands for perfection in himself and other people.

ACHIEVING APPROPRIATE GUILT. Many of us experience intense guilt over apparently trivial breaches of conscience or of other standards for conduct. Thus, some individuals, if they are simply a minute late for an appointment, or if their room is untidy, or if they tell a little white lie, become overcome with an onslaught of guilt. Very often, the guilt may have been repressed and manifests itself in indirect ways without being fully experienced as such.

Guilt itself is a desirable human emotion in the sense that it enables us to recognize when we have done wrong, when we have violated our own consciences and the mores of society; there is no personality-hygiene value in eliminating the capacity to feel guilt. But inappropriate guilt may completely destroy a person's effectiveness and joy in living, so that it should be eliminated or reduced when possible.[27]

It is true there are no precise criteria available for judging whether or not a given guilt-reaction is appropriate, but as with hostility and anxiety, crude norms seem to be available in our society. If the guilt-reaction seems disproportionate to the instigation or persists even after atonement or restitution, then the individual can at least tentatively assume that his guilt-response is inappropriate.

How can inappropriate guilt be replaced by mainly appropriate guilt-reactions?

1. The person must first experience his guilt and recognize it as such. Again, it is common that guilt, like hostility and anxiety, may be repressed and manifest itself only in disguised ways, e.g., chronic self-depreciation, inferiority feelings, avoidance of close relationships with people, vague depression, and so on. The person must reverse the process of alienation from his real self and acknowledge his guilt when it occurs. Such acknowledgment makes it possible to evaluate the guilt-reaction and attempt to alter it.

2. The person must subject his guilt-reactions to reality-testing. Upon recognizing that he feels guilty about something, the person can seek to determine precisely what it was that provoked him to guilt. If it appears that he has violated some deeply affirmed ethical precepts, then he can acknowledge his guilt and seek to make amends or otherwise deal with it. If, on the other hand, the guilt-reaction is made to something quite trivial, the person might be able to recognize he is judging his behavior today from standards appropriate to his childhood years, which are no longer appropriate. Very often such recognition alone is sufficient to eliminate the guilt.

In illustration: A person may feel vaguely guilty each time he kisses a girl, so that he doesn't enjoy the kiss. His fiancée may notice he kisses only occasionally and then in a very perfunctory manner. If she would like more affectionate display, she may ask him why he avoids kissing and why, when he kisses her, he seems uncomfortable. The man may only then recognize he has had guilt-feelings about kissing. If he puts it in words, "Kissing makes me feel guilty," both he and his girl can begin to evaluate the reaction and try to understand its origin. To kiss one's fiancée is not taboo in our society, and so it might be agreed that his guilt over kissing her is not warranted. Then, the man may come to realize that early in childhood he was taught (deliberately or accidentally) by his mother to regard kissing as immoral. In his later years, he no longer believed kissing was immoral, but the early teaching persisted because it was unrecognized.

SOME OTHER EMOTIONS

Thus far, we have discussed anxiety, hostility, and guilt in a rather systematic framework. Our aim was to introduce the student to the problem of evaluating emotion from the standpoint of personality health. In the sections which follow, we shall briefly discuss some other emotions, no less important to healthy personality than the three discussed above, but the discussion will proceed in less systematic fashion.

WEEPING AND HEALTHY PERSONALITY. In our society at least, weeping is acceptable only in women and young children. Grown men are generally regarded as weak, passive, or sissified if they cry when sad, hurt, or helpless. Perhaps the only exceptions are instances where a man has lost someone close to him through death. Then, tears are grudgingly accepted in a man, or at least regarded as understandable.

The personality hygienist regards the *ability* to cry—in men as well as in women—as a desirable characteristic. It is deemed desirable when it does not preclude more active ways of coping with problems and when it is effective in releasing feelings of despair, joy, anger, or a sense of loss. Such emotional catharsis, or release of feelings, seems to have value in freeing the person to resume his life once more on an active basis. Therapists of personality generally find that when their patients are finally able to weep during therapy sessions, the course of therapy proceeds more satisfactorily. This is especially true of male patients who find weeping a drastic threat to their self-esteem and to their identities as men. Therapy calls for the fullest disclosure of experience on the part of the patient, and if he will not permit himself to cry when he feels like weeping, it betokens a lack of trust in his therapist.

The inhibition of weeping which characterizes the average male in our society seems to be but part of a more generalized suppression of many other kinds of feelings, viz., tenderness, sentimentality. Such suppression, if carried to extremes, can have unhealthy consequences for the body and can also render men's relationships with women, children, or other men rather empty and lifeless.

SENSE OF HUMOR AND HEALTHY PERSONALITY. The capacity to see humor in situations and to respond with laughter is regarded by some experts as an indicant of wellness. Indeed, it may be true that loss of the ability to laugh at oneself and at comic situations is one of the early symptoms of more serious personality disorders. When a person can laugh even in potentially grim situations, it implies some degree of freedom from the press of fate and circumstances. Prisoners in the Nazi concentration camps during World War II could even find something to laugh at, though they lived but a hairsbreadth from torture and death.

One psychologist regarded laughter as one of the purest examples of behavior that is characteristically human. That is, laughter is a response to situations which can be made only by persons who have transcended their animal heritage as well as the conformity-producing pressures of society. Laughter is a sort of defiance of necessity, a kind of proclamation of one's independence or of one's ability to transcend the limits of otherwise mundane or grim circumstances.

Of course, there are rough norms extant in society by means of which one can judge the appropriateness or inappropriateness of laughter. Indeed, schizophrenics will often laugh in situations where a more intact person might weep or become angry. But a good sense of humor, the ability to find something ludicrous in situations, is not only a social asset; it is an indication that a person is able to do more than just struggle to exist.

Frivolity As a Defense. Some persons will crack jokes or make light of things which probably should be taken seriously. I have known various people who were afraid to admit their righteous and justified anger, or who were afraid to be taken seriously, and so they cloaked matters of genuine concern in laughter. When people do this chronically, they permit situations to be perpetuated which could be changed for the better if they dropped the humorous façade.

Jokes. There are contexts where a clever and even off-color story can add zest to a gathering, but it takes a certain *savoir-faire* to be able to distiguish between those times when a joke will contribute enjoyable laughter to a situation and when it will bring agonizing embarrassment to the listeners.

Healthier personalities are able to find humor in situations, they are able to laugh at themselves as well as at others who might strut or huff and puff in phony pretense, but they will not be addicted to jokes which inflict harm or which express malice toward various groups. It should not be forgotten, however, that there are some situations, as in dictatorships, where overt hostility against the leaders of a regime might bring death or imprisonment to the rebels. Under conditions of this sort, satire, jokes, and cartoons which cleverly and wittily deride the leading regime may be the only available outlet for feelings. Furthermore, such humor may serve a valuable function in sustaining the morale of the downtrodden people.[28]

ZEST AND HEALTHY PERSONALITY. There is a variety of emotion which has hardly been noticed or studied by psychologists, and hence a suitable technical name for this class of affect has not yet gained common currency. We are referring to the feelings which accompany absorbed, interested activity. Thus, a person who is actively engaged in writing, taking an automobile apart, conversing with someone, or playing tennis will experience and manifest a type of feeling that might be called *zest.* One psychologist[29] called it "activity-affect"; he saw it as a factor which sustained effective coping behavior. This terminology is somewhat esoteric, however, and we shall propose that *zest* is a word which encompasses the same meaning.

The capacity to experience zest as one addresses himself to the diverse problems and challenges of living is highly desirable from the standpoint of personality health. Zest seems to arise when a person encounters situations which are going to "stretch" his resources and muscles, but which he feels confident that he can master. Lack of zest seems to indicate that a person is bored or overburdened with life.

Ordinarily, one can observe zest most frequently in the behavior of younger children, who are often described as exuberant or enthusiastic. Sadly enough, our culture often takes a suspicious attitude toward adults who display zest in their work, regarding it as juvenile or immature. It is as if a sober, joyless mien alone is appropriate to grown men and women wrestling with the serious business of living. Yet, observation of productive artists, scientists, and businessmen will frequently disclose a "boyish," ageless quality of zest, delight, and enthusiasm which seems to facilitate their work and make their lives more enjoyable. Moreover, such productive people seldom seem old because of the zest which they express.

THE FEELING OF FREEDOM. In an important theoretical paper (briefly mentioned in Chapter 2), Frank Barron[30] proposed that freedom be defined, not only as the repertoire of adaptive responses available to a person in a given situation, but also as a feeling. The implication of this view of freedom—seeing it as a feeling in the sense that anger, sex, or guilt are feelings—is that one can study how persons cope with it. Thus, the feeling of freedom can be repressed, projected, and have reaction-formations constructed against it (see Chapter 7 for elaboration of these defense mechanisms), and it can be responsibly acknowledged.

A question that may be raised is, "In what situations, with what other persons, does a given individual *feel* free?" The opposite of the feeling of freedom is the feeling of compulsion, or the feeling of being driven. It may be proposed that maximization of the feeling of freedom is a desirable quality for healthy personality. However, little direct study has yet been made of the conditions upon which the feeling of freedom is dependent. Tentatively, we may propose that persons feel most free when they perceive their environment as safe, when they perceive other people as accepting, trustworthy, and loving, and when they perceive themselves as competent and fundamentally good. This latter point is made because it seems likely that the man who regards himself as good does not have to watch his own behavior carefully in order to make certain that no evil or dangerous behavior will emerge. Instead, he can permit himself to be spontaneous. Spontaneity in expression and behavior is one of the forms in which the feeling of freedom manifests itself.

BOREDOM, DEPRESSION, AND HEALTHY PERSONALITY. When a person is behaving in ways that yield gratification of his various basic needs, his subjective state is likely to be one of happiness, pleasure, excitement, or zest. If, on the other hand, he carries out a daily regime that is not selected for its relevance to his needs, he is likely to suffer the highly unpleasant emotional state called *boredom*. Boredom arises when persons are doing work that has little variety or interest to it. It arises as a consequence of relationships with other persons who have little spontaneity in their behavior and who do not relate to us in ways that meet our needs for affection, understanding, or intellectual stimulation. More generally, persons are likely to experience boredom, perhaps chronically, when they are not actively choosing what they will do with their lives, but are instead permitting their lives to be lived for them by social pressures to conform with rigid roles, concepts of respectability, and the like.[31] Boredom is inevitable in human life, but there are healthy and unhealthy methods of coping with it. The unhealthy patterns include (a) permitting it to continue for indefinite periods of time without making an effort to understand its causes in one's life and (b) impulsively seeking excitement or diversion without striving to understand the causes. For example, some people may drive automobiles at breakneck speeds simply to interrupt monotony. Others may take a flight from their ennui by attending many movies, drinking too much liquor, watching television for long hours, or reading "escape literature." Any of these escapes is harmless as a temporary palliative. They endanger one's personality health when they are the sole reaction adopted by a person to cope with his boredom. The healthier approach to boredom is to use such times as an occasion for careful scrutiny of one's life and one's needs, seeking to ascertain what one truly wants and the ways in which one's existence is failing to provide legitimate, health-yielding satisfaction. If a person is unable to diagnose his own needs, he is serving the interests of healthy personality if he will discuss his life situation and his own personality with any other person whom he can trust. If he has no friend, family member, or relative with whom such an openly disclosing relationship is possible, he might then seek personal counseling from a psychologist or psychiatrist.

Depression, like boredom, is inescapable in life. Depression arises when there has been a loss of an important relationship with another person, because of separation, death, or rejection.[32] Another common cause of depression is a repeated sequence of failures in various missions or projects. Other persons become depressed when they have lost something which has hitherto served as the most important condition for self-esteem; e.g., one individual may become depressed if he gets a grade on an examination which reduces his over-all grade average from an A to a C; another may be depressed if he is not invited to a particular party. And of course persons who have been disfigured in an accident or have lost a limb or their sight will almost inevitably undergo a period of depression.

In principle, there are healthy and unhealthy modes of coping with depression, as with other emotions. The less healthy pattern entails efforts to anesthetize oneself against it, as with alcohol or meaningless busywork. The healthier patterns include making efforts to understand the causes of the depression and making a direct attack on these causes wherever possible. It should be pointed out, however, that it frequently takes a lot of time to understand one's depression and to rearrange one's life so that it may be ameliorated; consequently, the ability to endure the depression with some stoicism may be called for.

BEHAVIOR UNDER EMOTIONAL TENSION

Thus far, we have been primarily concerned with the emotional responses themselves. Let us now examine the behavior to which emotional tension gives rise. It may be said that emotional tensions function in the same fashion as need-tensions or wishes—they give rise to instrumental behavior which has for its aim either (a) the production in the self of certain desired emotional tensions or (b) the changing and riddance of unwanted emotional tensions. In the second instance, the reasons for wanting riddance of the felt tensions may be that the tensions interfere with efficient work or rational thinking, or they may threaten a person's relationships with others upon whom he is dependent for various reasons. He may not want his spouse, parents, or boss to know he has hostile feelings toward them lest he be rejected or punished. Or, the feelings in question may not be wanted because they conflict with and threaten a person's self-structure (see Chapter 6); his self-concept does not include the notion that he is a person with such feelings; or the feelings in question may be opposed to the individual's self-ideal and conscience.

In the first instance (actively seeking to induce certain emotional tensions in the self), the reason may be a desire to escape from the boredom of rationality and everyday work; or it may be that these sought-after feelings were pleasantly experienced in the past, and the individual wants to re-experience them for the sheer joy of feeling them again. Thus, an airplane ride may have induced feelings of omnipotence because it was a thrilling but safe danger; or someone may have said or done very nice things to you, and you want to bathe yourself again in the wonderful feelings induced by the praise, the caresses, or the nurturing.

EMOTIONAL TENSION-SEEKING BEHAVIOR

A person may actively seek out danger for the thrills it gives him, or simply to prove his lack of cowardice. Psychoanalysts give the name *counterphobic character*[33] to individuals who may be ridden with fears which their pride will not allow them to acknowledge. They appear to be engaged in a never-ending demonstration of their own daring and courage; they might be called chronic and compulsive heroes. Such a compulsive pattern of behavior must be judged unhealthy on a number of grounds. The counterphobic tendency in a person may bring him into situations beyond his capacity to handle, thus endangering his life or health. Common sense would have deterred another person, but not the counterphobe. In addition, the counterphobe, by refusing to acknowledge his own basic timorousness, is becoming further alienated from his real self, and he is doing nothing toward the end of understanding his fears and seeking to reality-test them.

Another common variety of tension-seeking behavior is to be found in the sex addict. He (or she) strives for the frequent experience of sexual tension and orgasm. There is nothing unhealthy per se in the quest of sexual gratification. A compulsive quest for sexuality, however, may be undertaken as an escape from boredom, inferiority feelings, or other causes. It is judged unhealthy because the quest for sexuality results in ignoring other important values, such as healthy interpersonal relationships, productivity in work, and the constructive management of the problems which were responsible for compulsive sexuality in the first place. In Chapter 12, we will discuss healthy sexuality in more detail.

EMOTIONAL TENSION-REDUCING BEHAVIOR

Given the fact of emotional tension produced by some stimulus, what does the person do with these tensions? In principle, there is a limited number of alternatives, and each has implications for personality health. The alternative reactions of a person to emotional arousal are: (a) immediate uncontrolled expression and release, (b) suppression of emotional behavior, and (c) repression of emotional tension.

IMMEDIATE EXPRESSION OF EMOTIONAL TENSIONS. This is the characteristic pattern among young children when they have been provoked to emotional tension. They express it immediately, with little if any motor control. They laugh, cry, strike out, jump up and down, throw tantrums—in short, they appear to be almost out of control. It is as if their cerebral cortex had been dethroned from rational control over behavior and their entire organism were being directed by "explosions" of subcortical brain structures, viz., the hypothalamus.

On the positive side, immediate expression of emotional tensions in this uncontrolled manner is effective in getting rid of the tensions. They are given expression, and once out, the person is able to proceed on a more controlled and less tense basis. On the negative side, immediate expression is undesirable especially in an adult because:

1. *Society condemns uncontrolled expression of emotion in an adult on a purely normative and moral basis.* Thus, the adult who throws tantrums or who cannot control his emotions is viewed as an immature person, who cannot be trusted with important responsibilities.

2. *In the process of uncontrolled emotional expressiveness, the person is "out of touch" with external reality.* A person who is out of

touch with external reality does not perceive the world with accuracy—indeed, he is not interested in the external world during his tantrum. Further, he does not protect other important values at the time he is in the throes of an "affective storm." He may break things which he values; he may say or do things which cost him his job, his marriage, his reputation.

SUPPRESSION OF EMOTIONAL BEHAVIOR. Emotional control is made possible through the gradually acquired ability of a person to pick and choose responses to a situation (emotion-provoking or otherwise) that are compatible with the largest number of important values. This picking and choosing in turn is predicated on the ability to postpone immediate responsiveness, to delay responding in order to allow time to reason, plan, or think. A young child cannot do this because he has not yet learned how and because his nervous system has not yet matured to the point where it is physically possible for him to tolerate tension and inhibit motor expression.

When once the nervous system has matured to the point where delay and purposeful planning are possible, then suppression of emotional behavior becomes possible. There are no precise norms available for the age at which control becomes possible and for the quantity of tension which a person can be expected to tolerate without exploding into expressive behavior; however, it can be expected that the ability increases from infancy up to maturity and then probably declines with approaching senescence.

Let us now examine some of the implications of emotion-suppression for personality and physical health.

Physical Consequences of Emotion-Suppression. When a person is provoked to emotional tension, widespread changes occur throughout his body in consequence of heightened autonomic nervous-system activity. If expression is possible and available to the person, in the form of muscular activity, weeping, laughing, sexual behavior, then the physiological processes will shortly be restored to normal.

If no release is possible, if the person suppresses emotion for a long period of time, then the physical events which constitute part of the emotional response will be prolonged. If the prolongation is marked, it is possible that the functions and even the structure of inner organs may be permanently impaired. The field of psychosomatic medicine is devoted to just such a study, the study of the effects of emotionality on the health of the physical organism.[34]

Psychological Consequences of Emotion-Suppression. Suppressed emotional excitement is a factor which interferes with rational activity in many ways. Reich coined the term "emotional plague"[35] to describe the far-reaching impairments of logical reasoning and accurate perception which are produced by prolonged suppression of sexual and emotional tension. It is as if all the energy of a suppressing person is being utilized in holding back affect, with a resultant diminution in the amount of energy available for commerce with reality.

In addition to the effects on rational thinking, emotion-suppression appears to interfere with efficiency of skilled behavior. One cannot play the piano, repair machinery, or knit with efficient speed and dispatch when one is full of unexpressed fear, hostility, grief, or laughter.

Finally, it may happen that the cumulative effects of suppression may eventuate in such a strength of tension that control becomes impossible; the person then explodes with expressiveness of a much more violent nature than would have been the case had he reacted much earlier. Many persons have committed acts of destructiveness when they could no longer fully suppress conscious hostility.

Let us draw a distinction between healthy and unhealthy emotion-suppression. In anticipation, we may say that there are occasions when suppression is compatible with personality health and other occasions when it is not. The following discussion may help us to judge whether or not suppression of emotion is healthy.

Healthy Emotion-Suppression. Let us first assert that for an adult, at least, the capacity to suppress emotional expression and to delay immediate responsiveness is a capacity which is not only valued by moralists, it is also valued by personality hygienists. But the personality hygienist may differ from the moralist in that *he affirms the value of the capacity to express emotional tensions just as much as the capacity to suppress them.* The healthy personality displays neither immediate expression nor chronic suppression of emotion exclusively. Rather, he displays a capacity to choose between the alternatives of suppression and expression. When it will not jeopardize important values, he will express his feelings freely, in an almost unrestrained fashion: He may laugh with gusto, cry without restraint, or express anger with vigor. If other values would be endangered by such emotionality, he is capable of suppressing his feelings and carrying on with whatever behavior was in process at the time of emotional arousal. He displays what psychoanalysts call ego-strength and what other psychologists call stress-tolerance. In the long run, however, this regime of *selective suppression and release* insures that the person's body and his ability to perform will not suffer the effects of prolonged emotion-suppression; and he will not needlessly endanger his job, his reputation, his self-respect, and other important values by heedless emotional explosions. In short, he can suppress when he chooses, and he can let go when he chooses—and it is he who does the choosing.

Unhealthy Emotion-Suppression. Emotion-suppression becomes unhealthy when it is prolonged for any reason. The person who chronically suppresses his emotions generally does so because of fear of the consequences which might follow emotional expression. It often happens that a person's very fear of emotional expression is itself an irrational fear, based on overgeneralization from certain unpleasant occurrences in the past. Perhaps he was severely punished, or lost his job, in consequence of an emotional outburst. From this one event, he may have generalized to the effect that "all emotional expression is dangerous, or bad." The upshot may be that he comes to suppress his feelings—though he is fully aware of them—without discrimination.

The longer-range consequence of chronic suppression *may* be psychosomatic illnesses (provided other necessary and sufficient causes are present), such as elevated blood pressure, mucous colitis, asthma, peptic ulcers; or they may include chronic fatigue (it consumes energy to suppress hostility and other strong feelings), muscular aches and pains, migrainelike headaches; or it may result in impaired work- and study-efficiency, inability to concentrate, impaired reality-contact, and impaired relationships with people. In connection with the latter, most of us value in our friends and loved ones at least some ability to express feelings. The chronic suppresser is often derogated as a "stick," or "stone-face," or an "iceberg"—someone who is "less than human."

REPRESSION OF EMOTIONAL TENSIONS. A person is said to repress his emotions (a) when he takes active steps to avoid experiencing certain affects and (b) when confronted by a stimulus adequate to induce an emotional response, he denies (and believes his own denial) he is experiencing any emotion in particular (see Chapter 7). Repression in the first instance is achieved by regulating one's life so that one will never encounter the objects known to induce certain feelings and also by refusing to think about, or remember, objects or events which might induce unwanted feelings. Repression in the second instance appears to be achieved by means of some form of self-deception or denial—as if the person says to himself, and believes, "I am not angry (afraid, sexy, amused)." Or, in order to rid his awareness of the unwanted emotional tensions, he may think about things and perform tasks that induce feelings incompatible with the emotional tension which is not wanted. Thus, a small child, confronted by a fear-inspiring dog, might say, "Nice puppy"—puppies evoke tender feelings, not fear in the child. Or the nervous and timid speaker at a banquet, who is afraid he will be ridiculed, may address the audience as "My friends." If he believes that they are his friends, his fear will evaporate.

Repression is generally undertaken automatically and unconsciously by a person (although it is possible consciously and deliberately to attempt it), because (a) the emotional tensions serve to trigger off strong anxiety over the anticipated consequences of expressing them and (b) the emotional tensions conflict strongly with the person's conscience and self-ideal—if he admitted he had these feelings, he might have to change his concept of himself, with accompanying losses in self-esteem.

In most, if not all instances, a personality hygienist condemns repression of emotional tensions as unhealthy. The main reason for this condemnation lies in the fact that in spite of repression, the feelings exist—or at least the capacity to experience these feelings remains present and unchanged. When feelings have been provoked but are not recognized by the person, they produce effects both physical and psychological in nature. In Chapter 2, we discussed some of the ways in which unconscious feelings (and needs) manifest themselves in thinking and behavior. In addition to the psychological consequences, repressed affects produce the same effects on the body as do consciously suppressed feelings, only the person is not aware that he has these feelings.

When feelings have been repressed, more or less successfully, it is not only the person himself who is unaware of their presence. Other persons as well will not know how the person really feels. Thus, a husband may irritate his wife for years by certain of his habits. She, however, may have repressed her annoyance and hostility. Then, at some future date, she leaves him or becomes overwhelmed with uncontrollable rage at some trivial annoyance. Naturally, the husband is surprised and shocked. If she had openly vented her feelings long ago, he might have altered his behavior easily and without any complaint.

One of the most important tasks in personality therapy, and in the treatment of so-called psychosomatic illnesses, is that of aiding the patient to recognize his own feelings—to "unrepress" them, to experience and express them fully. This uncovering process generally is met with strong resistance on the part of the patient, however, since the experience of these feelings is quite threatening to security and to self-esteem.

FACTORS WHICH PROMOTE CHRONIC SUPPRESSION AND REPRESSION OF EMOTIONAL TENSIONS

In view of the fact that chronic suppression and repression of affect produce such unhealthy consequences, we shall inquire into some of the factors which are responsible for the adoption of these unhealthy patterns.

DEPENDENCY UPON OTHERS. When a person must depend upon the affection and support of others for the solution of his problems and the satisfaction of his needs, he is thrust into a situation which can promote both suppression and repression. So long as he is in the dependent role and needs the other person's good will, he must do nothing or express nothing which will incur the displeasure of the other person. Thus, a child, an employee, or an inadequate person may have to withhold honest expression of feelings and express (or pretend to feel) only those affects which will improve his status in the eyes of the dominant one. Most of us have had the fantasy at one time or another of telling someone with whom we have been closely associated in a dependent role just how we really feel toward them. Some people, on achieving autonomy, wealth, or courage, come right out and express their long-withheld feelings. Sometimes, the dissolution of a dependency relationship will remove only the motives for suppression, so that the person vents feelings he has long been aware of. Sometimes, however, with the break-up of the dependency relationship, long-standing repressions will be undone, and the person will himself be shocked and surprised at the intensity and nature of feelings which well up for expression.

EXCESSIVELY STRICT CONSCIENCE AND SELF-IDEAL. A person may chronically suppress or repress certain emotions, not only for external reasons, such as avoiding rejection or criticism, but also to conform with demands of conscience. A person may have acquired values which make his self-esteem contingent upon the exclusion of certain feelings and emotions, not only from behavior but even from consciousness. He can accept himself only as kind, pure, generous, strong, and so on, and so he must repress all those feelings which would produce guilt or a threat to his self-concept if they were recognized.

ACHIEVING HEALTHY EMOTIONAL BEHAVIOR

The behavior undertaken by a person when he is aroused to emotional tension is healthy (a) when it is effective in reducing or changing the present tension-level and -quality to one which is more desired and (b) when the emotional behavior does not jeopardize health, self-esteem, or any other things which are valued by the person.

We pointed out above that selective suppression and release of emotional tensions form the desired pattern from the personality-hygiene standpoint. This pattern calls for the capacity to control one's behavior under relatively high degrees of tension. It presumes ego-strength[36] in the person, such that he can refrain from explosive, uncontrolled outbursts if he chooses to, but at the same time, he can also let loose his feelings when he wants to.

What factors promote ego-strength, since this appears to be the most important capacity in the attainment of healthy emotional behavior? One such factor is *autonomy*, the possession of a high degree of skill and competence in many areas, so that the person is not obliged to be overly dependent on others (which we saw to be a factor promoting chronic suppression and repression). *Security* is another factor, whether it is the by-product of diverse skill or an assured source of income. Insecure persons are very prone to anxiety, and they may dread expressing their feelings because they believe that if they do so, they may lose status, their job, or friendships. *Reality-contact* can also promote healthy emotional behavior; the person can determine realistically what values are at stake in an emotional situation and what dangers are associated with suppression and expression of feelings.

Autonomy, security, and reality-contact appear to make it possible for a person to choose how he will react under emotion, rather than reacting in a stereotyped manner with "explosions," with repression, or suppression.

SUMMARY

Healthy personality is manifested by the freedom to experience feeling and also by the capacity to control their expression. A healthy personality will experience anxiety, fear, anger, guilt, tenderness, tears, affection, zest, laughter, boredom, and depression whenever life situations induce such feelings. Since he will have efficient contact with reality, the probability is high that his emotional responses to situations will be appropriate; and since he has the capacity to suppress behavior when it is called for, he will reveal his feelings appropriately and withhold expression when the situation calls for it. His method of controlling emotion can be called selective suppression and release.

Less healthy patterns include chronic suppression of emotional behavior and repression of emotional experience. In the first instance, chronic suppression can contribute to the development of psychosomatic illnesses, and it can interfere with the efficiency of ongoing behavior. Repression of feeling impoverishes life, it makes one's relationships with other people impersonal and shallow, and there is always the danger that repressions will be overthrown and uncontrollable emotional outbursts will ensue.

Factors that contribute to the attainment of selective suppression and release, as a pattern of healthy emotional control, are reality-contact, autonomy, and security. Undue dependency upon others and an overly strict conscience are factors which contribute to excessive suppression and repression of emotion.

NOTES AND REFERENCES

Excellent supplementary reading will be provided by those references marked with an asterisk (*).

*1. While most of the concepts in this chapter are defined in the text, the reader will get a richer understanding if he reviews basic materials. See, for example, Ruch, F. L., *Psychology and Life* (4th ed.; New York: Scott, 1953), ch. 6.

2. There is as yet much controversy and much ignorance about the neurophysiological basis of affects. Probably the "feel" of emotion is produced both by sensory awareness of the visceral changes which occur and by an "upward discharge" of the hypothalamus to the cerebral cortex. See Arnold, M., *Emotion and Personality* (New York: Columbia U. P., 1960), *II*, ch. 1, 3. Also, Gellhorn, E., *Physiological Foundations of Neurology and Psychiatry* (Minneapolis: U. of Minn., 1953), ch. 14. These authors attempt to answer the question of what kinds of neural activity mediate the physiological and psychological phenomena which constitute emotional tension. There is growing evidence to verify the assumption that different affects—viz., fear, anger, depression, and pleasure—are mediated by different patterns of neurophysiological functioning. *Cf.* Arnold, Magda B., "The Physiological Differentiation of Emotional States," *Psychol. Rev., 52,* 35–48 (1945). Ax, A., "The Physiological Differentiation Between Fear and Anger in Humans," *Psychosom. Med., 15,* 433–442 (1953). Stevenson, I., and Matthews, R. A., "Fact and Theory in Psychosomatic Medicine," *J. Nerv. Ment. Dis., 118,* 289–306 (1953). Stevenson, I., "Physical Symptoms During Pleasurable Emotional States," *Psychosom. Med., 12,* 98–102 (1950).

3. Many of the signs of autonomic activity can be detected only with the use of a sensitive instrument called a polygraph, which registers minute changes in the electrical activity of the skin, muscles, and in the brain, some of which are indices of autonomic functioning. "Lie detection" involves the use of a polygraph to register emotion-provoked changes which occur when a person has lied to a questioner. With a poker face, he can mask his inner feeling of guilt or panic, but if these affects exist, the polygraph will often register physiological signs of their expression.

*4. *Cf.* Pavlov, I. P., *Lectures on Conditioned Reflexes* (New York: International Publ., 1928). Also Gellhorn, E., *op. cit.,* ch. 15.

*5. Hull, C. L., *Principles of Behavior* (New York: Appleton, 1943). Skinner, B. F., *The Behavior of Organisms: An Experimental Analysis* (New York: Appleton, 1938).

*6. *Cf.* Watson, J. B. and Rayner, R., "Conditioned Emotional Reactions," *J. Exp. Psychol., 3,* 1–14 (1920). Also Jones, M. C., "A Laboratory Study of Fear: The Case of Peter," *Ped. Sem., 31,* 308–316 (1924); Liddell, H. S., "Conditioning and Emotions," *Scient. Amer.,* 1954, for discussions and illustrations of the conditioning of emotional responses. See also Mowrer, O. H., *Learning Theory and Personality Dynamics* (New York: Ronald, 1950), chs. 1–5, for experimental and theoretical analyses of fear and anxiety.

*7. See Mowrer, O. H., *op. cit.,* ch. 2. In chs. 9 and 10, Mowrer expounds his two-factor theory of learning, which is relevant to the problem of how emotional responses are acquired.

8. Rotter, J. B., *Social Learning and Clinical Psychology* (New York: Prentice-Hall, 1954), pp. 165–183, for a technical discussion of expectancy.

9. See Mowrer, O. H., *op. cit.,* ch. 21, for an analysis of identification in terms of learning theory. The present author borrows heavily from Mowrer's

discussion of identification. A paper by a psychoanalyst which is closely similar in approach to Mowrer's is Hendrick, *I.*, "Early Development of the Ego: Identification in Infancy," *Psychoanalyt. Quart.*, *20*, 44–61 (1951). For a report of a brilliant experimental analysis of identification and imitation, see Bandura, A., "Social Learning Through Imitation," in Jones, M. R. (ed.), *Nebraska Symposium on Motivation* (Lincoln, Nebr.: Univ. of Nebr., 1962).

10. Mowrer, O. H., *op. cit.*, ch. 16.

11. This term is adapted from Mowrer, O. H., *op. cit.*

12. The psychoanalytic method of undertaking personality therapy seeks, among other things, to help a patient discover the origins of many of his irrational affects, to abreact these, and thus to be bothered no more by them.

13. This concept was used to explain some of the phenomena in war neuroses by Hollingworth, H. L., *The Psychology of Functional Neuroses* (New York: Appleton, 1920).

*14. Freud, S., "Analysis of a Phobia in a Five-Year-Old Boy," in Freud, S., *Collected papers*, III (London: Hogarth, 1953).

*15. The importance of making discriminations is well brought out in Dollard, J. and Miller, N. E., *Personality and Psychotherapy: An Analysis in Terms of Learning, Thinking, and Culture* (New York: McGraw, 1950), ch. 19.

16. *Cf.* Secord, P. F., Dukes, W. F., and Bevan, W., "Personalities in Faces: I. An Experiment in Social Perceiving," *Genet. Psychol. Monogr.*, *49*, 231–279 (1954).

17. For centuries, a correlation between body build and personality traits has been postulated. The layman commonly believes in such a relationship. A sophisticated study of the relations between physique and certain personality traits (temperament) is Sheldon, W. H. and Stevens, S. S., *The Varieties of Temperament* (New York: Harper, 1942).

*18. *Cf.* Freud, S., *The Problem of Anxiety* (New York: Norton, 1936). Freud outlines systematically the role that anxiety plays in the genesis of neurotic symptoms. See May, R., *The Meaning of Anxiety* (New York: Ronald, 1950); and Tillich, P., *The Courage To Be* (New Haven, Conn.: Yale, 1952), for excellent analyses of the constructive as well as destructive role that anxiety plays in human life. See also Mowrer, O. H., *op. cit.*, chs. 18–20.

19. It seems likely that rigid character traits—"character-armor"—are acquired during the process of personality growth as means of avoiding anxiety. See Reich, W., *Character Analysis*, Part II (New York: Orgone Institute Press, 1949).

20. *Cf.* Dollard, J. and Miller, N. E., *op. cit.*

21. *Cf.* Tillich, P., *op. cit.*

22. Whiting and Child showed that American parents treat aggression in their growing children with much more severity than do parents from many other societies. See Whiting, J. W. M. and Child, I. L., *Child-Training and Personality* (New Haven, Conn.: Yale, 1953), pp. 98–102.

23. See Dollard, J., Miller, N. E., Doob, L. W., Mowrer, O. H., and Sears, R. R., *Frustration and Aggression* (New Haven, Conn.: Yale, 1939).

24. The so-called "authoritarian personality," a person who is highly dependent upon authority figures for direction, support, and protection, is notoriously hostile toward the authority figure, but at an unconscious level. He is said to manifest ambivalent attitudes toward authority. See Adorno, T. W., Frenkel-Brunswik, Else, Levinson, D. J., and Sanford, R. N., *The Authoritarian Personality* (New York: Harper, 1950). These investigators observed not only signs of unconscious hostility toward authority figures but also evidence for over-idealizing authority figures and displacement of hostility toward minority group members.

25. See Jourard, S. M., "Moral Indignation: A Correlate of Denied Dislike of Parents' Traits," *J. Consult. Psychol., 18,* 59–60 (1954).

26. See Cason, H., "Common Annoyances: A Psychological Study of Every-Day Aversions and Irritations," *Psychol. Monogr., 40,* No. 2 (Whole No. 132) (1930).

*27. Maslow refers to inappropriate guilt-reactions as "silly guilt," and regards them as evidence of the need to grow up. See Maslow, A. H., *Toward a Psychology of Being* (Princeton, N.J., Van Nostrand, 1961); see also Mowrer, O. H., *The Crisis in Psychiatry and Religion* (Princeton, N.J.: Van Nostrand, 1960), ch. 8, for an effective statement of the role of guilt in mental illness.

*28. See Frankl, V. E., *From Death Camp to Existentialism* (Boston: Beacon, 1959), pp. 42–43, for a brief comment about humor in the concentration camps. The view of laughter as an indicant of man's transcendant capacities may be found in Shaw, F. J., "Laughter, Paradigm of Growth," *J. Individ. Psychol., 16,* 151–157 (1960). A more extensive psychoanalytic discussion of humor and wit may be found in Freud, S., *Wit and Its Relation to the Unconscious;* in Brill, A. A. (ed.), *The Basic Writings of Sigmund Freud* (New York: Modern Library, 1938). See also Maslow's comments in Maslow, A. H., *Motivation and Personality* (New York: Harper, 1954), pp. 222–223; and Allport, G. W., *Pattern and Growth in Personality* (New York: Holt, 1961), pp. 292–294.

29. Schachtel, E. G., *Metamorphosis* (New York: Basic Books, 1959), chs. 2 and 3.

30. Barron, F., "Freedom As Feeling," *J. Humanistic Psychol., 1,* 91–100 (1961).

31. See Fenichel, O., *The Collected Papers of Otto Fenichel* (First series; New York: Norton, 1953), pp. 292–302, for a discussion of boredom.

32. There is a growing body of evidence to show that the depression following the disruption of an important relationship, such as marriage or friendship, sets the stage for the onset of various *physical* diseases, such as cancer, tuberculosis, and so on. See, for example, Schmale, A. H., "Relation of Separation and Depression to Disease." *Psychosom. Med., 20,* 259–276 (1958); LeShan, L., "A

Basic Psychological Orientation Apparently Associated with Malignant Disease," *Psychiat. Quart.*, 1961.

33. *Cf.* Fenichel, O., *The Psychoanalytic Theory of Neurosis* (New York: Norton, 1945), pp. 480–485.

34. A good introduction to the field of psychosomatic medicine is Alexander, F., *Psychosomatic Medicine* (New York: Norton, 1950). The most complete review of the bodily changes associated with emotion is Flanders-Dunbar, Helen, *Emotions and Bodily Changes* (4th ed.; New York: Columbia U. P., 1954).

35. Reich, W., *op. cit.*, ch. 12. See Lazarus, R., Deese, J., and Osler, Sonia F., "The Effects of Psychological Stress upon Performance," *Psychol. Bull.*, *49*, 293–317 (1952). This paper reviews experimental studies of the impact on cognitive and performance activities of experimentally produced emotional tensions.

36. The term *ego-strength* originated with the psychoanalysts, but it is gaining increasing usage among psychologists who do both clinical work and personality research. *Cf.* Jourard, S. M., "Ego-Strength and the Recall of Tasks," *J. Abn. Soc. Psychol.*, *49*, 51–58 (1954). Also Barron, F., "An Ego-Strength Scale Which Predicts Response to Psychotherapy," *J. Consult. Psychol.*, *17*, 327–333 (1953). These studies, and others, illustrate the manner in which the construct ego-strength is employed in research work. In clinical work, the psychologist and the therapist are often called upon to make estimates of the strength of the patient's ego. Various indices are commonly employed: viz., estimates of reality-contact, ability to tolerate delay and frustration, and so on.

CHAPTER 5
THE BODY AND HEALTHY PERSONALITY

INTRODUCTION

Study of the body has been relatively neglected by psychologists, and this is a serious oversight. It is serious because of the crucial role the body plays in personality structure and functioning. The body is the meeting ground of psychology and physiology. An individual behaves with his body, and his behavior produces consequences for his body. A person perceives his body and formulates a body-image, or body-concept. He evaluates his body as he knows it and expresses satisfaction, dissatisfaction, or disinterest in his body. Other people react to the appearance of his body, and these reactions strongly influence the person's feelings and attitudes toward his over-all personality. The health of the body is a crucial value, both for its own sake and also because no other values can be achieved unless the body is intact, healthy, and fully functioning. Accidents and injuries which befall the body will impose a strong influence on the personality, calling often for radical changes in the person's modes of gaining satisfactions and even for changes in the satisfactions which will be pursued. Thus, a person who has had both legs amputated is no longer able to pursue an athletic career, and, initially, he will have much difficulty in seeing himself as a whole person able to live his life effectively.

In addition to all these interrelations between the body and personality, the body may serve as a sounding board for all of an individual's life problems. The body becomes sick when the person is unhappy, chronically conflicted, or chronically deprived of psychological satisfactions. The old precept, mens sana in corpore sano *holds intrinsic validity. A healthy mind (personality) is likely to accompany a healthy body, and a healthy body may well be a crucial determiner of personality health.*

SOME TECHNICAL TERMS. The *actual body* refers to the body as it might objectively be described and evaluated by an outside observer. The *body-concept* comprises all of a person's perceptions, beliefs, and expectancies with respect to his body's structure, functions, and appearance. *Body-image* will sometimes be used as a synonym for body-concept. The *public body-concept* refers to the perceptions and beliefs which a person *wants others* to have concerning his body. The *body-ideal* includes all the values and ideals a person has acquired with respect to his body's appearance and functions, his concept of how his body ought to be, or how he wants it to be. The *ideal body* is the culturally valued form, appearance, and mode of functioning of the body.

These terms are introduced so as to enable us to observe variability in the ways in which people relate to their body and to permit us to make evaluations of these relationships from a personality-hygiene point of view.

THE BODY AND PERSONALITY

THE BODY AND THE EGO

The ego is a hypothetical structure within the total personality to which is ascribed, among other functions, the role of co-ordinating and controlling the movements of the body (instrumental behavior) so that various valued ends will be achieved. Psychoanalysts speak, in this connection, of a *body-ego.*[1] One of the first signs that the ego has developed is the infant's capacity voluntarily to control the movements of his body. That is, before the outer environment can be mastered, the person has got to achieve mastery of his body. Before such mastery has been achieved, body movements are diffuse, global, undifferentiated, and not subject to voluntary control. Once such mastery has been achieved, the infant or child is able to *suppress* global, undifferentiated responses to stimulation and respond in a discrete, controlled, instrumental manner. The ability to co-ordinate eyes, hands, and mouth is probably among the first signs that the ego is developing. Psychoanalysts refer to each separate achievement of voluntary control over the musculature and the perceptual apparatus as an *ego-nucleus.*

As physical maturation proceeds, the child gradually acquires increasing mastery over his body and is able to make it perform according to his will. By the time adulthood has been reached, the person, if suitably trained, may be able to achieve such levels of bodily control as are found among athletes and dancers. The contemporary modern dancer, the flamenco dancer, the exponent of Hindu, Balinese, or rock-and-roll dancing, all display a body-ego which has been developed to a relatively high degree.

The loss of control of body functions and body performances is usually experienced as a very threatening catastrophe by most persons. Not to be the master of one's body—its movements, needs, and functions—is a loss of the most basic level of control. An adult who loses voluntary control over his appetite, or over his bowel and bladder sphincters, will feel deep shame and will lose confidence in himself.

THE BODY AND THE SELF

The self-structure of the average individual includes beliefs and ideals pertaining to the body as well as beliefs and ideals with respect to behavior (See Chapter 6). The body-concept, or body-image[2] is an integral part of the self-concept. The self-ideal includes values and ideals which pertain to the appearance and functions of the body; it encompasses the person's body-ideal. The public selves which a person constructs include not only beliefs which the individual wants others to affirm with respect to his personality, they also include beliefs the person wants others to hold concerning the appearance and functions of his body. In order to construct and maintain his *public body-concept,* the individual will clothe himself in preferred ways, use assorted padding, camouflage, corsetry, cosmetics, and other means for looking his best, the way he wants other people to see him. Further he may hide all signs of actual illness, if he wants people to believe him healthy.

THE BODY AND SECURITY. When a person is secure, he is relatively free from anxiety. Insecurity manifests itself as worry and anxiety about expected pains and catastrophes. Since the body is such a highly valued object, it may become the object of anxiety or else the source of anxiety about other expected threats. The appearance of the body is the means to many highly valued ends in our society. From this it follows that if a person's appearance is not attractive, his access to these ends may be limited, and he may suffer anxiety about the prospects of gaining these ends. Some of the ends toward which appearance is instrumental, especially among young people, is acceptance by one's peers and attractiveness to the opposite sex. The unattractive person generally has a more difficult time winning friends, and in being popular with the opposite sex, than the person with a pleasing appearance. One reflection of the importance of beauty in our culture is the annual beauty contests which take place. Women compete with each other for the title of the most beautiful woman of the year, and rich prizes go to the winner.

That one's appearance may be the source of anxiety has been demonstrated in a number of empirical studies. Secord and Jourard[3] showed that *body cathexis* (the degree of acceptance of one's body) was correlated with measures of anxious body-preoccupation and of security. In other words, the more a person accepted his body, or liked it, the more secure and free from anxiety he felt. Persons with a high measured degree of anxiety tended to be dissatisfied with their bodies.

Anxious overconcern with the body is called *hypochondriasis*. The hypochondriac is an individual who is continually preoccupied with his health, who complains about all manner of vague or specific aches and pains, and who may make the rounds of doctors' offices, dose himself regularly with laxatives, vitamin pills, sedatives, and other medicines. It is generally found that hypochondriacal anxiety with respect to physical health is a substitute for, or a displacement of, anxiety that derives from other sources: repressed hostility, sexuality, or achievement problems. The hypochondriac evidently finds it less threatening to think about and worry about his health than to think about these other problems. Health preoccupation takes his mind off more basic problems, as it were.

A person may become excessively concerned and anxious about his or her appearance. This is most likely to occur among persons who use their appearance as their most relied-on means of gaining acceptance from others, of enhancing their social status, or as the means of attracting attention to the self. The name *narcissistic overconcern* seems appropriate to describe this pattern. Such a person will fuss over appearance beyond the point of diminishing returns and will become panic-stricken whenever a wrinkle, gray hair, or change in weight appears.

Hypochondriasis and narcissistic overconcern both may be viewed as *unhealthy* responses to the appearance and functions of the body. They are unhealthy for a variety of reasons. They fail to solve the problems which are basically responsible for the anxiety in the first place. Furthermore, while the person concentrates so much attention on himself and his body, he neglects many other values which are of importance to a healthy personality, for instance, productive work and healthy relationships with other people.

Concern for one's health and appearance are both compatible with personality health, but healthy concern does not place other legitimate concerns in jeopardy. If the healthy personality becomes physically ill, he will take any steps necessary to restore or improve his health, but then he will turn his attention to other matters. Furthermore, he will live in accordance with a habitual health regime—adequate diet, rest, and so on, which maintains his health without requiring too much conscious attention and worry.

With respect to appearance, the healthy personality will take whatever steps are necessary to look his best, and then he will take his appearance for granted. He does not rely totally on his appearance as a means to valued ends. He can make friends, gain professional success, and attract a spouse, not by appearance alone, but by genuine achievement and by means of his usual modes of behaving toward others.

THE BODY AND SELF-ESTEEM. A high degree of self-esteem means that a person accepts and approves his over-all personality. There is a considerable amount of systematic and clinical evidence to show that one's *appearance* is an important determiner of self-esteem, both among men and women.

A number of studies have shown that "self-cathexis"[4] (a technical term roughly synonymous with self-esteem) is correlated with body cathexis. In other words, persons who accept their bodies are more likely to manifest high self-esteem than persons who dislike their bodies.

One reason for this correlation lies in the fact that the self-ideal includes a set of ideals pertaining to the appearance of the body, the so-called *body-ideal.* Each person has a more or less clear-cut concept of how he wants to look. If his body actually conforms, in dimensions and appearance, with his concept of an ideal body, he will then like his body. If, on the other hand, his body deviates from his body-ideal, he will tend to reject and dislike his body.

In one study of college women,[5] it was found that the ideal body proportions (which all girls in the sample shared) were five feet five inches for height, about 120 pounds for weight, and 35 inches, 24 inches, and 35 inches for bust, waist, and hips respectively. The girls liked their dimensions if they coincided with these ideals and disliked them increasingly as they deviated from these ideals. The actual measurements of the girls were slightly larger than these ideals, on the average—except for bust size, where the average size was slightly smaller.

A comparable study of college males[6] showed that acceptance of the body was related to *large size.* While the women all wanted to be slightly smaller in dimensions than they actually were, the men mostly aimed at larger size; they wanted to be taller, with broader shoulders and chests.

It is evident that the body-ideals of the subjects in these studies are closely related to the cultural concept of an *ideal body.*

THE BODY-IDEAL AND THE IDEAL BODY. Each society has its idiosyncratic concepts and standards of personal beauty.[7] The Bushman native on the Kalihari desert, for example, places a value on having enormous hips and buttocks, while in America the desired hip-measurements are much slimmer. The American woman wants to have large (but firm) breasts, a small waist, and narrow hips, and she wants to be relatively tall. In other societies, the standards of feminine beauty differ from this stereotype. In days gone by, the American glamor girl was considerably heftier than our present beauties. Old pictures of burlesque queens look to the modern eye like advertisements for a reducing salon.

The cultural concept of an ideal body has consequences for personality hygiene, since the cultural ideal determines the personal body-ideal and since congruence of the actual body with the body-ideal helps to determine over-all self-esteem. If a man or woman in our society is not able to conform with the ideal-body concepts of his society, he is very likely to face problems growing out of diminished self-esteem. If the ideal-body concepts in the society are highly restrictive and difficult for many people to conform with, the implication is that many people will suffer self-esteem losses.

The widespread dread that many people have for aging may be an outgrowth both of the rigid concept of an ideal body and the role of the body's appearance in gaining valued ends and in determining self-esteem. While a rational degree of concern for appearance is compatible with personality health, too much concern may indicate that the individual's self-esteem is founded on *too narrow a base.* Under optimum conditions, an individual will predicate his self-esteem on a variety of grounds, e.g., achievement, social status, ethical behavior. Attractive appearance is thus only one of many determiners of self-esteem. The healthy personality can face and accept the inevitable changes in appearance that are associated with aging without losses in self-esteem or in the sense of security. He (or she) does not feel that when youthful beauty is gone, so goes personal worth. He believes, in the words of a homely twelve-year-old girl at a summer camp, "After all, beauty is only skin. Be a beautiful *person*, and don't worry so much about how you look!"

SOME PROBLEMS RELATED TO THE CULTURAL CONCEPT OF THE IDEAL BODY

Because the cultural concept of the ideal body is so rigid, and yet so widely adopted by people as their personal body-ideal, a number of anxiety-loaded problems have become a part of our society's preoccupations.

OBESITY. Probably the number one appearance problem in contemporary America is obesity. This is also, of course, a health problem, since overweight people are much more susceptible to certain fatal diseases than thinner people. But the cosmetic aspects of obesity are just as acutely felt and worried about as the physical health aspects. America is the only country in the world where overweight is a public health problem; where food is abundant, yet a slender body is a cultural value.

Obesity usually is, of course, the result of eating too much. Overweight people seem unable to control their food intake to a level which will enable them to lose weight. When a person wants to stop some behavior pattern but finds that will power is ineffective, it is evidence that unconscious motives of great strength lie behind the behavior in question. The overweight person is overeating for reasons other than sheer hunger. The act of eating is serving more functions than simply replenishing the body's energy supplies and maintaining physical health.

Clinical studies of chronically overweight people have shown that they have unhealthy personalities.[8] They may, for example, be unable to derive satisfactions from their relationships with people or from their work. They may be starved for love but unable to get enough love from parents, friends, or spouse to satisfy them. Consequently, rather than live a life devoid of gratification, they resort to a very primitive and basic type of satisfaction—that provided by an overly full and rich meal.

A chronically overweight person is not unlike a chronic alcoholic, in that he is addicted to a practice which is harming him at the same time that it relieves anxiety and provides him with immediate gratification. Like an alcoholic, the obese person might make daily, renewed vows to taper off, but he never seems to achieve this end. In some cities, groups of obese people organize as do the members of Alcoholics Anonymous; they are all dedicated to the aim of reducing, and they lend each other moral support in adhering to reducing diets. Where intensive personality therapy is not available, and when medical aid for appetite suppression has proven ineffective, such groups are probably the most effective means for achieving a weight loss. However, unless the conditions, medical or psychological, which are responsible for the excessive appetite are removed, the person will be obliged to remain dependent upon his group membership in order to preserve his weight loss once it has been achieved.

SKINNINESS. Just as we deplore fatness in our society, so do we pity the "skinny" person. Chronic underweight due to undernourishment is a fairly simple malady to remedy, if suitable food is available. But many persons are overly thin in spite of available food and even in spite of a sizable caloric intake. There are usually reasons for inability to put on weight, e.g., overactive thyroid glands or a finicky appetite; but these may derive from more basic *psychological* causes. An intensive personality diagnosis might disclose many unhealthy personality traits in the chronically thin person. In such instances, personality therapy which produces changes in the ways the person relates to the world may produce as a side effect a desirable increase in weight. Sometimes simply changing the amount of exercise that the person habitually takes will suffice to stimulate appetite and promote a desirable gain in weight.

BREAST-CULTIVATION. Men in our society are highly breast-conscious, and many men equate sexual attractiveness in a woman with a prominent bosom. Since most women want to be considered attractive to men, they consider a flat bust to be a handicap. The reasons for this cultural emphasis on the breasts are not readily determined. Some anthropologists and psychoanalysts believe it is a derivative of painful weaning experiences undergone by male children in our society. Probably, however, the reasons are more complex.

Nevertheless, most women want to have prominent breasts, and if they have not been naturally endowed with them, they may strive to cultivate them by assorted exercises such as are advertised by health clubs, or they will wear brassière padding of one kind or another.

There is nothing intrinsically unhealthy in a woman who wears "falsies" in order to appear beautiful. Personality health is assessed in terms of a number of different criteria, including what the person does to, with, or for her body. So long as males deem breasts to be an index of attractiveness, then women, to the extent that they want admiring male attention, are justified in doing all that is practicable to gain that end.

NOSES. We even have rigid cultural ideals pertaining to noses. The ideal nose is not the majestic protuberance of a Cyrano de Bergerac, nor is it the proud, delicately curved sweep of an aquiline "beak." Instead, it must, at least in the woman, be a short, medium-width, uptilted "snub," so that an onlooker can see the nostrils. Many women feel their facial beauty is marred because their nose differs from this stereotype, and so they undergo plastic surgery in order to achieve the valued snub. Whether or not "nose-bobbing" is a healthy thing to do depends on its consequences for the total personality. Some persons may undergo a healthy personality change following the operation, while others may go through life after such an operation feeling they are a fake.

FACIAL WRINKLES. The appearance of wrinkles in the facial skin and on the neck is an inevitable part of aging. Yet many women, especially, become panic-stricken at the first appearance of a wrinkle. This panic derives from a dread of being old and from an overemphasis of the importance of appearance as a basis for security and self-esteem.

The problem of aging is not a simple one, and an entire medical specialty—geriatrics—has been devoted to a many-faceted study of the problems faced by the aging person. We can do no more in the present context than mention this field *en passant.*

The person who panics at wrinkles, and goes to any length to regain, at age forty, the complexion of a sixteen-year-old, is an unhealthy person. Such an individual might well seek to find more stable sources of self-esteem than facial appearance.

GENITALIA. People have all kinds of problems in connection with their sexual organs. Some men feel they are inferior if they have what seem to be small genital organs. There are cases on record where an entire neurotic personality structure began in consequence of the belief that the sex organs were smaller than those of other men. There is no necessary connection between male adequacy in sexual performance and genital size. There is no necessary connection between "manliness" and the size of genitalia.

In many ways, people in our society are very prudish, almost ashamed, about having bodies with reproductive and eliminative functions. Many persons become panic-stricken at the prospect of being seen nude, and may actually avoid a medical examination if it requires that the genitalia be exposed.

Some women, at least at an unconscious level, may envy not only the apparently privileged social positions of men, but they may also display what the psychoanalysts called "penis-envy"—they resent not having been born males, and they may reject their own feminine role in consequence.

Because of cultural taboos pertaining to sexuality, many persons acquire very unreal concepts both of their own genitalia and that of the opposite sex. These unreal concepts may involve notions that the female organs are dangerous and castrating or that penises are destructive weapons. Some women may acquire attitudes of disgust, resentment and shame over their menstrual functions and needlessly isolate themselves through the duration of their period—as is done in some primitive societies.

MUSCLE-CULTIVATION. In response to the cultural ideal of a muscular male, many sedentarily occupied men will undergo strenuous weight-lifting and body-building courses so as to become visibly muscular. There is nothing inherently healthy or unhealthy in such efforts. They are healthy if they result in an improvement of appearance, vigor, and health without loss of other values. They are unhealthy if they are expressions of unnecessary compensation or overcompensation for other kinds of deficiencies and inferiorities.

A HEALTHY BODY-IDEAL

A person's body-ideal can be assessed with respect to its healthy or unhealthy implications. An unhealthy body-ideal is one that is rigid and unchanging and which includes dimensions and characteristics that are impossible for the individual to conform with. Thus, we observe an unhealthy body-ideal in a woman who, at age forty, feels she is ugly and unattractive because she no longer looks the way she did when she was nineteen. If she devotes extreme attention to her appearance and neglects other values, we should be obliged to adjudge her body-ideal as unhealthy. Similarly, a young man with a slender physique who rejected his body appearance because he was not heavily muscled and proportioned like a football hero might be said to have an unhealthy body-ideal.

A healthy body-ideal is one which is not too discrepant from the cultural concept of an ideal body but *which is revised by the person himself, so as to make allowances for his own, idiosyncratic dimensions and features.* With increasing age, a healthy personality will modify his body-ideal, so that he can continue to regard himself as reasonably attractive at each stage in life. He does not aspire after an impossible (for him) degree of beauty. Rather, at each stage in life, he strives to look his best and then lets the matter drop so as to attend to other important concerns.

THE BODY-CONCEPT

A person's body-concept includes all of his perceptions, beliefs, and knowledge concerning his body: its appearance, functions, limits, and inner structure. As with any other concept—one's concept of self, of other people, of animals—the body-concept may be accurate or inaccurate, complete or incomplete. An accurate body-concept is a personality-hygiene value.

An accurate body-concept implies that an individual perceives, interprets, and formulates beliefs about all aspects of his body with accuracy. When the body-concept is accurate, it provides the individual with a rational foundation for taking adequate care of his body's needs, its health, and its appearance.

Accuracy of the body-concept is achieved by all of the means employed to arrive at reality-tested knowledge in general: through observation, through continual verification of conclusions, and through contact with reliable authorities and sources of knowledge. But many persons have been taught erroneous beliefs about diet, needs, health requirements, and the like. Further, a person may become so alienated from his body (as part of the more general process of self-alienation) that he loses the capacity to "listen" to his body.

Thus, some people may fail to recognize that inadequate diet, excessive amounts of exercise, insufficient rest, and excessive self-indulgence are gradually weakening their bodies. Because of an inaccurate body-concept, such people fail to learn how to take suitable care of their bodies. To the extent that a person has knowledge of the effects of various things on his health, then to that extent his body's welfare is his own responsibility. Just as one can relate to a child in ways that have implications for his health, so can one relate to one's body in ways that have health implications. In order to promote and maintain the child's health, the parents are obliged to formulate accurate concepts with respect to bodies in general and their child's body in particular. In order to promote and maintain one's own health, one must have an accurate body-concept. It may be said that rational body-care becomes possible only when an accurate body-concept has been achieved.

Let us illustrate what we mean by an inaccurate body-concept. In societies where medical knowledge is not available, there may be only imperfect concepts of the causes of health and of illness.[9] Consequently, one may observe that entire sectors of a population suffer from some chronic ailment which they all accept as "natural," as part of the scheme of living, for instance, rickets or TB. It is only from the standpoint of the contemporary scientific concept of the body that it becomes possible to make judgments about how healthy (or sick) an entire society might be.

An inaccurate body-concept and an inaccurate concept of bodies in general are displayed in many ways. Thus, many middle-class people in our society may grow up in ignorance of the process of reproduction; a nineteen-year-old student of the author's once indicated she had no accurate knowledge of menstrual functions and their role in female anatomy and physiology. This ignorance probably derives indirectly from social taboos on discussion of sexual matters.

An aging person with false pride may fail to acquire an accurate concept of the decrease in his powers of muscular strength and endurance. Because he misjudges his strength and endurance, he may endanger his heart through overindulgence in exercise. But just as a person may overestimate his body's capacity, so may he underestimate it. In times of war and other major stress, increasing knowledge is gained of the human's incredible capacity to endure extreme physical conditions.

The attainment of an accurate body-concept is aided by parents who dispense reliable knowledge to their children, by formal education which includes education for physical health, and by rational efforts on the part of the person to acquire reliable knowledge about his own body.

THE BODY AND HEALTH

PERSONALITY, THE BODY, AND HEALTH

Personality refers to the stable and characteristic ways in which an individual behaves in life situations. Behavior produces consequences, not only to the external environment, but also to the body itself. One can evaluate personality with respect to its *physical*-health consequences; thus, it is meaningful to speak of a physical-health-promoting personality and a physical-disease-producing personality.

It goes without saying that personality and body interact; when a person is already sick or handicapped, his behavior will be affected in many ways. For some persons, illness first manifests itself as some slight deterioration in their usual levels of performance or as irritability and depression. However, in the sections which follow, we shall focus more directly on the means by which one's body suffers or flourishes as a consequence of one's customary behavior patterns.

A PHYSICAL-HEALTH-PROMOTING PERSONALITY. A meaningful question to ask is, "What regimen, what ways of behaving in the world will promote health?" The most obvious answer to this question relates to such matters as diet, rest, and sensible exercise. People who have been adequately educated in matters of general hygiene will have learned to eat a diet that maintains health, energy, and weight; they will care for their teeth; they will obtain enough sleep to restore their energy; and they will exercise enough to keep their weight within sensible bounds and their muscle tonus good.

A more subtle factor in the production and maintenance of physical health is morale, or "spirit." Increasing evidence is pointing to the fact that if a person finds his life challenging, purposeful, satisfying, and meaningful, his body works better, maintains its health better, and resists infectious illness better. Such a life, characterized by meaningful work, enjoyable play, and love and friendship thus seems to function as a kind of inexpensive health insurance.

AN ILLNESS-YIELDING PERSONALITY. It is well known that the majority of illnesses, both mental and physical, recur frequently in a relatively small proportion of society. It is as if a small sector of the total population has an especial talent for becoming sick. Defective heredity or a weak constitution goes only part way in explaining this high incidence of recurrent illness in a small proportion of the population—though heredity does play a definite role in proneness to illness. We must look as well into the way of life lived by these people with a flair for becoming sick.

Studies of the frequently ill show many factors in common. Among other things, it is found that they may simply not take sensible care of themselves; that is, they do not eat, sleep, or exercise sensibly. Another, less obvious factor in frequent illness is *stress*. Many people encounter much more stress in everyday life than is objectively necessary. They find everyday interpersonal relationships lacking in satisfactions, and, indeed, positively stressing. One reason for such increments of stress over and above that which can be expected to accompany life has to do with the necessity to play restrictive roles in life (see Chapter 9, pages 280–283). If a person must present himself to others as something which he is not—if he is obliged to seem friendly when he is unfriendly, or if he is obliged to hide his real feelings and wants from others—then every moment spent in the presence of others is a moment of imminent danger. It is as if he is traveling incognito, with his true identity hidden; he feels that if he is truly "found out" by others, terrible harm will then befall him. Consequently, he trusts no one and keeps his guard up. Other people by their very existence then function as stressors, adding thus to the stress of daily life. Such a mode of existence promotes muscle tension, precludes relaxation, and can be readily seen to foster the onset of physical complaints.

Another factor in frequent illness is an overdeveloped sense of duty. Persons who feel obliged by their consciences to keep working at unsatisfactory jobs or to keep involved in relationships that are frustrating and unsatisfactory are actually creating the conditions for their own illness. Periods of being sick are thus periods of respite from a dispiriting way of life.[10] But it is immediately apparent that, if they could modify their way of life, even slightly, to ensure more satisfaction, they would become ill less often. Thus, a brief vacation from work or family is usually less expensive than a stay at a hospital of equal length—and the vacation may forestall the illness.

Chronic fatigue is often an outcome of boring work or unsatisfying relationships with others that are difficult to escape. The fatigue is real enough, because the person is consuming much energy forcing himself to stay in situations that are not congenial. When a person's fatigue can be traced to an enforced but unsatisfactory existence, the best treatment would be some change in work or in ways of relating to others, rather than pills or medicines.

Certain cultural groups and social classes, with their accompanying modal personalities, are more prone to various illnesses than others.[11] The American male has a higher incidence of peptic ulcers than, say, the Chinese male. Diabetes is more frequent, or typical, in some American subcultures than in others. The sociologist is able actually to construct a "sociology" of illness, showing correlations between modal personality for a given class or group and proneness to the development of various illnesses. Thus, the man who is acculturated to the values, practices, and style of life of the advertising profession will probably become afflicted with stomach ulcers. If he attains executive status in some corporation, he increases his chances of developing heart disease.

Various socially defined patterns of indulgence, such as smoking, or overeating, may have the consequence of shortening life or of promoting physical disease. A compulsive smoker, who smokes so heavily as compensation for various unconscious need-frustrations, may prove to be a person who is actually cutting years from his life. A compulsive overeater almost definitely is increasing his likelihood of heart trouble in later years.

Thus, we see that personality has health implications and health consequences. If a person values physical health, it is obvious that his personality—his usual modes of behaving within his life situation—must be of such a kind as will be compatible with physical health.

HANDICAP AND HEALTHY PERSONALITY

It is naturally a very desirable thing for a person to possess an intact body which functions well, is energetic, and which will last a long time. But it may happen that a limb is amputated or otherwise crippled. A sense modality may be lost, e.g., loss of sight, hearing. Or some chronic illness may be contracted, an illness which drastically limits the scope of an individual's potential activities.

If we ignore such psychological factors as pride, values, and goals in the handicapped person and view him strictly as a kind of machine, certain facts become immediately apparent. Although his over-all capacity to come to terms with his environment has been reduced by his handicap, it has not been eliminated completely. Most of the basic functions which an organism is supposed to perform can still be performed, though it may be necessary that these functions be carried out either in different ways or with reduced over-all competence. Thus, a blind person can still be sensitive to all the properties of his physical environment save those which were mediated by vision. The single amputee can still locomote in his environment, though he may have to hop on one leg or limp with a prosthesis. The double amputee could, if necessary, drag his body along by means of movements with his arms and hands. Conceivably, a person with legs and arms amputated might be able to roll his torso in ways which would move him across a room.

Now, let us view a handicapped individual as a whole person again. As a modal member of society, he will undoubtedly share the values of his society. His goals will be similar to those of most members of his society. Like the nonhandicapped person, he will want affection, recognition for achievement, some degree of autonomy or self-sufficiency, and so on. But unlike other members of society, his ability to achieve these ends may be reduced somewhat by his handicaps. In fact, the word *handicap* is meaningless except when used in connection with assorted valued ends. Thus, loss of hearing will only be a handicap in those pursuits where hearing is the sole means to a given end. Loss of sight is a handicap in those activities which are most efficiently directed by the visual sense.

Let us explore some of the possible reactions to handicap and then try to specify which of these reactions are in accord with the principles of personality hygiene and which are unhealthy.

HEALTHY REACTIONS TO HANDICAP. When a person suffers some affliction which results in a handicap, there may be, quite naturally, some rather devastating emotional reactions. These include a sense of hopelessness, anxiety about the future, and losses in self-esteem.

Once the fact of handicap has been accepted by the individual, however, the healthy thing to do is to make an assessment of (a) the residual capacities of the body and (b) the goals and values of the person. When this assessment has been accomplished, it becomes purely a mechanical problem, readily solved (at least in principle), of bringing these two sets of factors into satisfying relationship with one another. If the person's values and goals must remain fixed, then the individual must experiment with his body until he can find ways of accomplishing those ends with new means. Thus, a professional dancer, following the amputation of a leg, may wish to continue his profession. He will be obliged to acquire an artificial leg and practice until he can attain some measure of proficiency that will approximate his previous level.

It is probably easier for a person to leave his goals and values intact and strive to find new ways of achieving them with his now-altered body than it is for the person to change his values and goals. It is common for the handicapped person to feel hopeless and sorry for himself; but with resolve, courage, and encouragement, he can be guided back to the problem of finding new ways of pursuing his former goals. The task which is far more difficult to accomplish is to change the handicapped person's value-system, in order to bring his goals within the realm of possible achievement. Thus, an artist, who derives his livelihood and important personal satisfactions from painting, will be obliged to change some of his goals if he is blinded. He has to learn new goals in some way, in order to obtain satisfactions in living. This is no small task. It can probably be best accomplished through a close relationship with individuals who derive their major satisfactions from activities which will be *possible* for the handicapped person to perform. By means of identification with the value-system of these persons, the handicapped one will come to share those values and thus find new satisfactions.

The blinded artist might establish a very close relationship with a person—blind or seeing—who derives much satisfaction out of teaching or some form of handicraft that a blind man could accomplish. In time, provided the right conditions are met for identification to occur, the blind artist will come to value teaching just as his friend or therapist does and will derive satisfaction from those activities.

It is by means of identification that we acquire our most important values, and it is through identification that we change our values from time to time throughout life. By implication, then, since identification appears to be one of the means by which values are acquired, it follows that people who treat with handicapped persons must learn as much as they can about *the means of promoting new identifications.* If the process of identification could be perfectly controlled, much of the task in rehabilitating handicapped persons would be rendered lighter.

UNHEALTHY REACTIONS TO HANDICAP. In general, a reaction to handicap must be adjudged unhealthy when it interferes with the person's capacity to find meaningful satisfactions in ways that are personally and socially acceptable.

When once blindness, crippling, or debilitating disease have afflicted a person, it is natural that his life will be thrown into some sort of chaos. Plans for the future will have been disrupted. It becomes a physical impossibility for the person to exploit former sources of satisfaction. If his security and self-esteem have been dependent upon certain kinds of activity which are now precluded, then his life will seem empty and futile indeed, following the handicap. Thus, an athlete who earns his living and who derives his self-esteem from athletic prowess will be overwhelmed with depression when a heart ailment necessitates giving up this form of activity. A woman whose self-esteem is predicated primarily on her physical beauty will see little point in living following accidental burning which mars her face with unsightly scars.

The reactions of depression, self-pity, or hopelessness about the future are natural, even inevitable, when handicap occurs. What we are interested in here is the person's reactions to these emotional responses. The healthy reactions already have been described. The most common unhealthy reaction is *resignation.*

Resignation to handicap refers to the response of giving up, of digging in for a life which is devoid of satisfactions. The resigner assumes that there can be found no meaningful gratifications in life, that posthandicap life will consist in helplessness, frustration, emptiness—in short, that it will be an endurance test to be passively submitted to until death comes.

When resignation occurs, and lasts for more than some period of time, say six months to a year, it becomes necessary to assume that the resigner is deriving some kind of masochistic enjoyment out of his affliction and the limitations it imposes on him. In addition, the affliction may give the resigner the "right" to make all manner of unreasonable claims on other people, in accordance with the slogan, "Since the world has handed me such a dirty deal, I am entitled to a lot of support and consideration from other people." Horney[12] has documented this mechanism thoroughly in her discussion of neurotic claims.

Perhaps the best means of rooting a resigner out of his masochistic orgy is to "blast" him out—with scolding, anger, even contempt. Naturally, this blasting should be viewed as a last resort, when other means, such as inspiration, encouragement, and the like have failed. The best person to accomplish this blasting is a person who has himself accomplished a healthy reaction to a similar, or worse, handicap. Such a person is better equipped through personal experience with intimate knowledge of all the advantages accruing to resignation and all the devious defenses and resistances that can be developed against healthy mastery.

Another unhealthy reaction to handicap which may be observed is the attempt to *deny the existence of the handicap.* A "denier" insists that he can do everything which he could do prior to the onset of the handicap and proceeds to attempt this. Objective appraisal may reveal that it just is not so, yet the denier persists in his attempts to live just as he did before the affliction. This adjustment must be called unhealthy because it violates the precept concerning accurate knowledge concerning the self and also because it will probably be impossible for the person to carry out his life as he did earlier. If he can, it will be at the expense of other values which are quite important to happiness and health.

PHYSICAL GROWTH PROBLEMS AND HEALTHY PERSONALITY

As a person grows from infancy, through childhood to adulthood and then to senescence, a number of personality problems arise in consequence of the changes in the body and its performance-potentials. The young child has to learn the limits to the things his body will enable him to do, no less than the aged man or woman has to come to terms with restricted physical powers.

Most of the problems a person has with his body can be traced to *problems in interpersonal relationships* (see Chapter 10).

The young infant, for example, may express through bodily malfunctioning the fact that his relationship with his mother is one that is failing to gratify psychological needs—needs for affection, understanding, and love.

The child's ability or inability to gain voluntary control over bowel and bladder sphincters may reflect inadequacies in the mother-child interaction. Feeding, sleeping, and eliminative disturbances, the stock in trade of the pediatrician, all may derive from the psychological climate in which the child is reared.

By the time a person has attained puberty, a whole host of new problems arise. There is the problem of physical awkwardness, stemming from rapid and uneven growth, at a time of life when muscular agility is highly valued by one's peers. Adolescent acne poses appearance problems at a time when the young person is becoming acutely aware of the importance of being attractive to the opposite sex. Pubescent young women have the problem of coming to terms with their newly developed capacity to menstruate. Many young girls are ill-prepared for this event and experience their first menstruation as a frightening shock. Further, the presence of strong sexual urges, attendant upon maturation of the sexual apparatus, poses problems of morality to most adolescents in our culture.

Aging has its own problems, growing out of the gradual waning of physical vigor and youthful beauty, both highly prized in our society. Perhaps we could say that vigor and beauty are *overly* prized in our society, so that the older person finds it difficult to accept his decreased powers and changed appearance and to find a useful and satisfying role and status in society.

All of these problems attendant upon physical growth and change are made easier to resolve in a healthy way only if a person has a healthy self-structure. The self-structure has got to be sufficiently flexible and elastic, not only to accommodate changes in behavior and personality structure, but also to accommodate changes in the body itself.

HEALTHY ACCEPTANCE OF THE BODY

Another way of stating the optimum personality-hygiene values with respect to the body is as follows: The healthy personality will do all that he can to make his body attractive in appearance and healthy in its functions. Beyond that point, he more or less accepts his body as *one accepts nature.* Up to a point, one can control and master nature; beyond that point, one comes to terms with it. So with the body. To the extent that one can control one's body, it is healthy to strive to make it a thing of health and beauty. Beyond that point, one can best relax and enjoy it. And in truth, if one's attitudes are right, one's body can indeed be a very rich source of pleasure and satisfaction for the self.[13]

TOUCHING AND BEING TOUCHED. Besides the pleasures and satisfactions that come from fulfilling one's bodily appetites, the enjoyment and acceptance of one's appearance, and the "feel" of a healthy body in motion, there is pleasure even in sheer bodily contact. Our society, influenced as it has been by puritanical traditions, tends to make the touching of bodies a thing of shame. Perhaps this is because of the possibilities of sexual arousal associated with touching others and being touched by another. Yet, to be caressed, stroked, touched, or massaged can be a very relaxing and delightful experience. Everyone has had the experience of having his scalp rubbed and massaged by his barber or hairdresser. This experience at being touched is done in the name of the health of the hair and scalp, it is quite impersonal, and so the customer can relax and enjoy the feel of another's hands touching a part of his body. By the same token, patients in hospitals can relax and enjoy a back rub that is given by a nurse without guilt or embarrassment, because the back rub is given in the name of health, to relax muscles. For nurse or patient to admit that there might be sheer delight in the giving or receipt of the back rub might provoke embarrassment, and so the pleasurable aspects of the back rub are seldom discussed, either by nurses among themselves or between nurse and patient. Chiropractors, whose theory of the causes of health and disease is not accepted by medical scientists, doubtless aid many of their patients, not only because of the latter's *faith* in the power of chiropractic ideology, but also because there is much body contact involved in chiropractic healing. The chiropractor massages, manipulates, and otherwise touches his patents' back, and this doubtless has relaxing benefits for the patient.[14]

SUMMARY

A person's body, as he perceives it and evaluates it, plays an important role in determining his security and his sense of self-esteem. Like and dislike for one's own body are determined by one's subjective ideals related to bodily appearance and functioning. The cultural concept of the ideal body is a factor which contributes to various problems in accepting one's body as it presently is. Ideally, a person will construct his own ideals for bodily appearance so that his idiosyncrasies will be acceptable to him.

An accurate concept of one's bodily structure and function has value for the health of personality and for bodily health, because accurate knowledge can serve as a guide to sensible care of one's body. Physical health is fostered by a sensible regimen of diet, exercise and rest, as well as by work and relationships with people which yield satisfactions and which permit self-expression. Physical illness is fostered by neglect of bodily needs and by ways of life characterized by unsatisfying or meaningless work and leisure and inauthentic relationships with people.

Handicapping injuries typically lead to depression and helplessness. Healthy reactions to handicap include assessing the remaining capacities of the body and modifying personal goals and values to bring them within the range of possible attainment.

Changes in the appearance and function of the body associated with growth from infancy to old age pose problems for most people. These problems are best met and grappled with in the con-

text of relationships with other people who are understanding and supporting.

Healthy acceptance of the body implies doing one's best to foster optimum functioning and attractive appearance and then enjoying one's body as a part of life—using it with care and enjoying its capacity to yield pleasure as well as to do work.

NOTES AND REFERENCES

Excellent supplementary reading will be provided by those references marked with an asterisk (*).

1. *Cf.* Hoffer, W., "The Development of the Body Ego," *Psychoanalyt. Stud. Child,* V (New York: International Universities Press, 1950), pp. 18–23.

2. This term was employed by Schilder in his now classic monograph. See Schilder, P. F., *The Image and Appearance of the Human Body* (London: Kegan Paul, 1935).

3. Secord, P. F. and Jourard, S. M., "The Appraisal of Body-Cathexis: Body-Cathexis and the Self," *J. Consult. Psychol., 17,* 343–347 (1953). These findings were confirmed and extended in a study by Johnson, who demonstrated that attitudes of acceptance toward the body were related to the number of somatic complaints. See Johnson, L. C., "Body-Cathexis as a Factor in Somatic Complaints," *J. Consult. Psychol., 20,* 145–149 (1956). A related series of studies has been reported by Fisher on the implications of the unconscious "body-image" (which he approaches by means of the Rorschach test) for psychosomatic illness and for other traits of personality. *Cf.* Fisher, S. and Cleveland, S. E., "The Role of Body Image in Psychosomatic Symptom-Choice," *Psychol. Monogr., 69,* No. 17 (Whole No. 402) (1955). Also, by the same authors, "Body-Image Boundaries and Style of Life," *J. Abn. Soc. Psychol., 52,* 373–379 (1956); *Body-Image and Personality* (New York: Van Nostrand, 1958).

4. *Cf.* Secord, P. F. and Jourard, S. M., *op. cit.* Also Jourard, S. M. and Remy, R. M., "Perceived Parental Attitudes, the Self, and Security," *J. Consult. Psychol., 19,* 364–366 (1955).

5. Jourard, S. M. and Secord, P. F., "Body-Cathexis and the Ideal Female Figure," *J. Abn. Soc. Psychol., 50,* 243–246 (1955).

6. Jourard, S. M. and Secord, P. F., "Body-Size and Body-Cathexis," *J. Consult. Psychol., 18,* 184 (1954).

*7. See Mead, M., *Male and Female* (New York: Morrow, 1949), pp. 138–142, for a discussion of this point.

*8. See, for example, Bruch, H., "Psychological Aspects of Obesity," *Psychiatry, 10,* 373–381 (1947); and *The Importance of Overweight* (New York: Norton, 1957).

*9. See Whiting, J. W. M. and Child, I. L., *Child Training and Personality* (New Haven, Conn.: Yale, 1953), pp. 119–128, for a discussion of different concepts of illness in various cultures.

10. Any textbook which is devoted to the field of psychosomatic illness will give elaborations and documentation of this point. See, for example, Alexander, F. and French, T. M., *Studies in Psychosomatic Medicine* (New York: Ronald, 1948). See also Jourard, S. M., "Healthy Personality and Self-Disclosure," *Mental Hygiene, 43,* 499–507 (1959); "The Role of Spirit and Inspiritation in Human Wellness," *J. Existential Psychiat.,* 1963 (in press); "Some Lethal Aspects of the Male Role," *J. Existential Psychiat., 2,* 333–344 (1962); "Roles That Sicken and Relationships That Heal," *Canadian Nurse, 57,* 628–634 (1961). These papers cite supportive evidence.

11. *Cf.* Ruesch, J., "Social Technique, Social Status, and Social Change in Illness," in Kluckhohn, C. and Murray, H. A. (eds.), *Personality in Nature, Society, and Culture* (New York: Knopf, 1953).

12. Horney, K., *Neurosis and Human Growth* (New York: Norton, 1950), ch. 2.

13. *Cf.* Maslow, A. H., *Motivation and Personality* (New York: Harper, 1954), pp. 206–207.

14. One psychoanalyst has briefly discussed the role of physical massage in promoting relaxation in patients undergoing psychotherapy. See Braatøy, T., *Fundamentals of Psychoanalytic Technique* (New York: Wiley, 1956), pp. 155–197.

CHAPTER *6*
THE SELF-STRUCTURE IN HEALTHY PERSONALITY

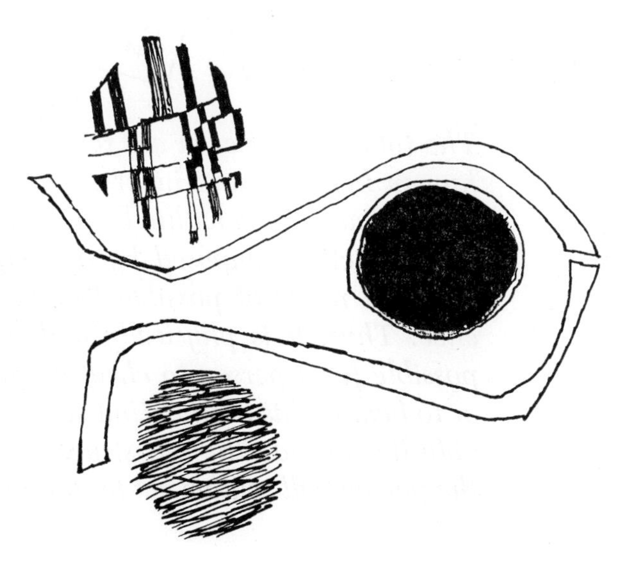

INTRODUCTION

An individual's self-structure is an important determiner of his behavior. Consequently, psychologists have devoted increasing attention to this aspect of personality.[1] *The self-structure imposes certain limits on a person's overt behavior and his inner experience. In general, a person will strive to behave in ways consistent with his self-structure,*[2] *and he will delimit his thoughts, feelings, and wishes to its boundaries. Let us illustrate these points with two diagrams of an arc:*

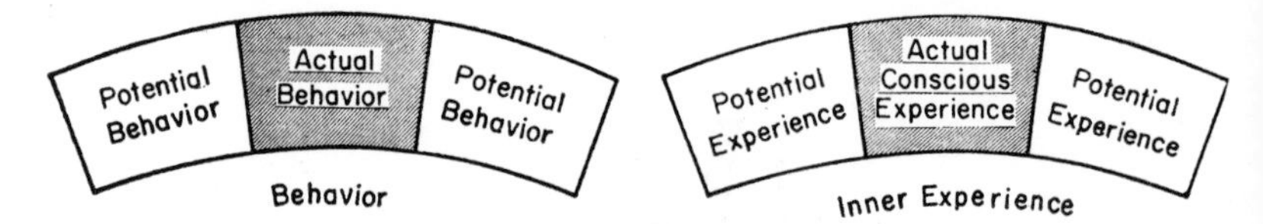

The total area of each arc represents all possible human behavior and inner experience. The narrower shaded area within the total arcs represents the restrictions *imposed by the self-structure on the total range of possible behavior and experience. Thus, it is physically and psychologically possible for a person to cheat on an examination or to beat up his brother, but such behavior probably lies outside the self-structure limits, and so the person will seldom act in those ways. Further,*

it is possible for an individual to feel rage toward his mother or to wish for his father's death, but we seldom experience such feelings and wishes at a conscious level; they usually lie outside the bounds of our self-structure.

What is this self-structure which limits the freedom and spontaneity of our action and experience? Is it possible to observe someone's self-structure and describe it? Is it possible to evaluate the self-structure as healthy and unhealthy? How do we acquire our self-structure? Does the self-structure change? What is a healthy self-structure like? Before we proceed to answer these questions, let us first provide ourselves with some technical definitions.

THE SELF-STRUCTURE AND ASPECTS OF PERSONALITY

In order to obtain a clearer understandinig of what is meant by the self-structure, we shall define some related terms: personality and ego.

THE EGO AND THE PERSONALITY

Personality refers to the totality of an individual's behavior patterns in life situations. A description of personality is a description of how the person typically behaves in specific situations. No description of personality is complete without a description of the situations in which the typical behavior occurs.

Ego is a term long employed by the philosophers to describe the "knower" and the "doer." Psychoanalysts assign a more technical meaning to the term; they regard the ego as one of the three main components of "psychical personality." For the analysts, the personality includes three major structures, or components: the *id,* the *ego,* and the *superego.* The id is unconscious and is the source of basic urges and impulses. The ego is mostly conscious and is the part of personality in contact with external reality; it is responsible for perceiving inner and outer reality, for regulating behavior, and for controlling impulses.[3] The *superego* is synonymous with conscience; it comprises the taboos and ideals with which behavior and experience must conform. It is mostly conscious but has unconscious features as well.

The ego may be viewed as the agent or source of all instrumental behavior. The ego perceives, reality-tests, selects, and rejects behavior patterns. It is responsible for learning, for the control and suppression of impulses. The ego is the agent of cognitive behavior. *The ego is the creator of the self-structure.*[4]

It should be stated that the ego is a hypothetical construct[5]—it cannot be observed directly. We postulate it as a force or agent on the basis of certain observed effects. This is very similar to the concept of electricity; we cannot know or see electricity, but we know what it does, and so we define electricity in terms of its functions and its effects. Just as we can judge electric current to be strong or weak, in terms of its effects on gauges, fuses, or light bulbs, so we can judge the ego to be strong and weak, in terms of certain behavioral consequences. We may assert that a strong ego is personality-hygiene value.

EGO-STRENGTH. Psychoanalysts and clinical psychologists utilize certain behavioral signs as indices of the strength of the ego. The psychoanalysts have constructed an elaborate theory of personality pathology on the basis of variations in ego-strength. The psychotic is regarded as a person whose ego-strength has been severely impaired; the hallucinations and bizarre behavior patterns are interpreted as signs of "ego-breakdown." The neurotic is a person whose ego-strength has partially been impaired; the symptoms of neurosis—obsessions, phobias, hysterical organ-impairments—are interpreted as attempts on the part of a weakened ego to solve problems and to gratify needs. The healthy personality has optimum ego-strength, which is manifested as the ability to reconcile the conflicting demands of the id, the superego, and external social reality.[6]

In terms much more general than those employed by psychoanalysts, we may say that an individual with a strong ego is able to behave in ways which gratify his needs and yet conform with personal and social standards for acceptable conduct. In brief, *a strong ego is a necessary condition for healthy personality.*

The concept of ego-strength is an important one in clinical psychology and psychiatry. Personality therapists often require some estimate of ego-strength prior to undertaking therapy with a patient, on the premise that certain minimal degrees of ego-strength are necessary before a patient can observe his own conduct and achieve insights. Personality researchers utilize the concept of ego-strength as the basis for making predictions about the outcome of certain experiments conducted with human subjects.

Some of the criteria of ego-strength which are employed are:

1. Certain scores on the Rorschach inkblot test; for example, the percentage of accurately perceived forms. The variable scores may be thought to represent an estimate of the degree of reality-contact achieved by the person, and reality-contact is regarded as a sign of ego-strength.[7]

2. Certain measures of rigidity-flexibility in thinking and in behavior. A strong ego is thought to possess the capacity to vary instrumental behavior when it is found that some one behavior pattern is not effective in achieving a goal. Weak egos persist in making a response pattern, even when it is ineffective; in short, weak egos display *rigidity* in thinking and in instrumental behavior.[8]

3. Certain measures of stress- and frustration-tolerance. A strong ego displays the capacity to carry out goal-directed activity in spite of stress, strong needs, and emotions without any disorganization of instrumental behavior. The weak ego is less able to tolerate frustration and stress. Under stress, the weak ego displays disruption in ongoing instrumental action and shows instead emotional behavior of some kind.[9]

4. Minimal evidence for the use by the person of various mechanisms for the defense of the self-structure; namely, repression, rationalization, projection, reaction-formation, and so on. The strong ego is able to face inner reality—his real self—without distortion, selection, or denial of what is perceived there. The weak ego will admit to himself and others only such thoughts, feelings, and wishes as are compatible with the social mores or which are flattering to his self-esteem.

In summary, it may be said that any and all of the behavioral measures utilized by psychologists as indices of "good adjustment" may be reinterpreted as ego-strength indices, since the capacity to "adjust" to one's milieu in need-satisfying ways betokens ego-strength. Most of these adjustment signs, or ego-strength signs,[10] have been discovered by comparing the responses to various test stimuli of people with personality illnesses—neuroses and psychoses—with the responses of normal and relatively healthy individuals, and the responses of those who improve with therapy and those who do not. The premise for such comparisons is the theoretical assumption that if a person has developed a personality illness, it is prima-facie evidence of a weak ego; if he responds favorably to treatment, his ego is stronger than the ego of patients who do not respond. The behavioral and personality tests which discriminate between "normal" and "sick" people are then regarded as different expressions or manifestations of ego-strength.

It is possible that one day the variable ego-strength may be found to correlate with certain modes of function of the cerebral cortex in its interrelationships with lower, subcortical brain structures.[11] Probably a strong ego reflects a situation wherein the cerebral cortex maintains and retains dominance over more primitive structures in the brain, viz., the hypothalamus (which mediates more explosive emotional behavior).

THE REAL SELF, THE EGO, AND THE PERSONALITY

Personality can be observed directly and described in the language of traits, that is, "In such and such a situation, he is most likely to act in such and such a way." The ego cannot be directly observed by an outsider; its "structure"[12] and strength must be inferred from behavioral indices. The *real self* is another hypothetical construct which is gaining increasing usage, especially in the writings of Horney[13] and Fromm.[14] These "neo-psychoanalysts" regard the real self as the basic *inner reality:* the actual feelings, wishes, thoughts, memories, and fantasies of the person as these arise spontaneously. Personality hygienists are in almost universal agreement that the ability to *know* one's real self, to *express* one's real self, and to *act* in accordance with one's real self are optimum goals for childrearing and personality therapy. If we employ the concept of the real self in our thinking about personality and behavior, we should make such observations as the following: "He acts at a real-self level in some situations but not in others"; "He is only pretending to like his girl friend. Actually, he hates her." "I never know what he *really* thinks, feels, and wants."

The term *real self* refers to a process, not to a fixed entity. When one introspects and tries to observe the flow of inner experience as it *spontaneously* occurs, one is in somewhat the same position as a person watching a stream of water that constantly changes color, that has many things floating on is surface, and that has many things only partly visible because submerged: How can one describe what one sees? The term *experiencing* has been proposed to refer to the process or flow of self, and this word may help the reader at least know where to look for data pertaining to his self. In the last analysis, one's real self can never be fully known simply because it *is* a process, not a thing, and hence is continuously changing at faster or slower rates. However, our likes, dislikes, attitudes, feelings, and beliefs do tend to become habitual and recurrent, so that it is at least partly possible to observe and describe these recurrent aspects of our own experiencing.

The ego may be regarded as the perceiver of the real-self process. As with external reality, the ego may perceive the real self accurately or in autistic fashion. If the ego is strong, the individual's perceptions and beliefs about his real self will be accurate.

In order that we shall become the masters of these concepts, let us employ them in some sentences: "His personality reflects a weak ego; he is unable to gain satisfactions through socially and personally acceptable behavior. His behavior tends not to reflect his real self. He does not act in accordance with his real wishes and feelings. His perceptions and beliefs concerning his real self are inaccurate; he has an inaccurate self-concept." The reader may see, from the manner in which the technical terms have been employed, something of their different meanings.

THE REAL SELF, THE EGO, AND THE SELF-STRUCTURE

The real self refers to the real nature of a person's feelings, wishes, and thoughts. The ego is the perceiver of this inner reality. What, then, is the *self-structure?*

The self-structure is constructed by the ego. The ego constructs the self-structure just as it constructs a set of beliefs, conclusions, and ideals pertaining to anything else that can be observed, e.g., horses or women. A Kentucky "colonel" observes horses act, grow, perform. On the basis of his direct observation, supplemented by hearsay, tradition, and authority, he constructs a repertoire of beliefs, expectations, and ideal standards pertaining to horses. Perhaps we could call this body of information his "horse-structure." We could describe his horse-structure after we had interviewed him concerning what he knows, believes, expects, and feels about horses. We could evaluate his horse-structure in the light of scientific knowledge; we could determine how well his various beliefs about horses meet logical standards of consistency; we could compare his ideals and standards with those of other people, and so on. We could even track down the origins of many of his beliefs and feelings by studying his life history in some detail.

If we knew enough about our colonel's horse-structure, we could probably predict many of his overt behavior patterns with respect to horses, and we could also predict many of his feelings, wishes, and decisions as these pertain to horses.

As with the horse-structure, so with the self-structure. The self-structure is a construction of the ego. *It refers to the beliefs, perceptions, ideals, expectations, and demands which a person has come to formulate with respect to his own behavior and experience.*[15]

We are not born with a self-structure, any more than we are born with a horse-structure; it is acquired and constructed by the ego. We can determine the nature of an individual's self-structure, and describe it, if we observe and interview the individual exhaustively enough. We can evaluate his self-structure with respect to the accuracy of the beliefs which it comprises and the feasibility of the component ideals and expectations. If we know a person's self-structure, we should be able to predict and understand his behavior and experience. Indeed, it has been found empirically that when people know each other, they know each other's self-structure in considerable detail. Married couples, for example, know well how their spouses feel about themselves, what they expect of themselves, and what they believe to be true about themselves.[16]

Personality hygienists place a positive value on the construction, by the ego, of a self-structure which is *closely congruent with the real self*. What this means, fundamentally, is that a person should perceive his own inner experience with accuracy, without selection and distortion; he should formulate accurate beliefs about his own modal inner experience; his ideals and values should be experienced as his own and not those of someone else; his expectations of himself should lie within the realm of possible achievement.[17] That is, his expectations of himself are formulated with due attention to his real abilities and potentials for conforming with these expectations.

When an individual's self-structure is markedly discrepant with his real self, he is said to display *self-alienation,* or alienation from his real self.

ALIENATION FROM THE SELF

Horney[18] has listed a number of indications, or symptoms, of self-alienation. These include:

1. *The general capacity for conscious experience is impaired.* The person is living "as if in a fog. Nothing is clear, neither one's own thoughts and feelings, nor other people, nor the implications of a situation."

2. *There may be a decrease in awareness or concern for the body, for its needs and feelings, or for material possessions such as a house, car, or clothing.*

3. *There is a loss of the feeling of being an active determining force in one's own life.*

The factors which Horney sees as responsible for the process of self-alienation include:

1. *The development of compulsive solutions to neurotic conflicts, such as striving for affection, detachment from others, or chronic hostility to others.*

2. *Active moves away from the real self, such as the drive for glory, and strivings to live up to an impossible self-ideal.*

3. *Active moves against the real self, as in self-hate or self-destruction.*

The net consequence of alienation from the self, Horney says, is that the person's "*relation to himself has become impersonal*" (her italics). More specifically, in the self-alienated person, *pride governs feelings*—the individual does not react with spontaneous feeling responses. Instead, he feels what he should feel. Further, the self-alienated person does not feel in possession of his own energies; his powers are not his own. Another consequence of self-alienation which Horney describes is an impairment in the ability to *assume responsibility for the self.* The self-alienated person *is lacking in plain, simple honesty about himself and his life.* The lack in honesty manifests itself, she states, as (a) an inability to recognize oneself as one really is, without minimizing or exaggerating, (b) an inability or unwillingness to accept the consequences of one's actions and decisions, and (c) an inability or unwillingness to realize it is up to oneself to do something about one's difficulties. The person who is self-alienated insists that others, fate, or time will solve these difficulties for him.

Let us generalize from Horney's important contribution to an understanding of self-alienation and restate some of her observations in terms we have defined for this chapter.

Self-alienation means, basically, that the ego is not directing behavior according to the person's real needs, wishes, and feelings; that is, his real self. Instead, the ego is serving some "master" other than the real self. But if the real self is not the source of direction to the individual's behavior, what is the direction-source for the self-alienated person? Let us distinguish among the following sources of behavior-direction, namely, *pride-direction, conscience-direction, au-*

thority-direction, other-direction, impulse-direction, and, finally, *real-self-direction.*

PRIDE- AND CONSCIENCE-DIRECTION. Riesman's concept of the "inner-directed character"[19] is an excellent illustration of the person whose behavior expresses the dictates of conscience and self-ideal rather than the real self. When choices for action arise, such a person experiences a conflict between what he really wants to do and what he believes he *ought* to do. In this connection, Horney has written of the "tyranny of the should."[20] Implicitly, such a person believes his real self is an unreliable guide to conduct, and so he represses, suppresses, or ignores his real self. Instead of following his real self, he habitually follows some inflexible moral code or some stringent ideals which he believes he must conform with. The net consequence of ignoring the real self in favor of the conscience and self-ideal is that the person may behave in a moral and exemplary fashion, but his real needs are ignored, and he will be perpetually thwarted.

AUTHORITY-DIRECTION. The "authoritarian-character" is a person who seeks or allows the dictates of some authority figure to serve as the source of direction to his conduct.[21] He strives to discern what behavior the authority figure expects of him, and he hastens to comply. If there is any conflict between his own wishes and the demands of authority, he habitually suppresses his own and compulsively complies with the authority's wishes. Indeed, he experiences his real self as evil or weak—not worth considering. Fromm[22] interprets the manner in which authoritarian-characters perceive authority as a by-product of real-self repression, followed by a projection to the authority figure of all of one's own repressed "powers." Hence, the authoritarian-character perceives himself as weak and the leader as all-powerful and possessing unusual strength and wisdom—the "charismatic" leader.

OTHER-DIRECTION. Riesman's concept, the "other-directed" character,[23] describes an individual who allows the wishes and expectations of his social peers to direct his actions. The other-directed character becomes sensitized to other's wishes and actively seeks to comply with them. The result may be popularity and acceptance, but it is purchased at the cost of knowledge of the real self and at the cost of thwarting many basic needs.

IMPULSE-DIRECTION. Impulses and emotions are a part of the real self, just as are will and ideals. The ego has the function of reconciling the often conflicting demands of impulses, ideals, the will, and the demands and expectations of other people. An impulse-directed person is one who habitually ignores all demands upon his behavior save those imposed by his impulses and feelings. He ignores his conscience, the rights of other people—even his own long-range welfare and growth. All is subordinated to the immediate gratification of his needs and impulses and the immediate expression of his feelings. Psychoanalysts refer to such individuals as "instinct-ridden" characters; they idealize and rationalize their drives and emotions because they cannot voluntarily control them.

REAL-SELF-DIRECTION. In the instances mentioned above, the person's ego has been directed and guided by sources other than the real self. The real-self-directed person is the healthy personality. His ego is sensitive and perceptive of his real self. The person affirms the value and worth of his real self. He trusts his real self as the best guide for his own conduct.[24] Consequently, his behavior is a true expression of his real self. He knows his real needs, his own values and ideals, and strives to satisfy the needs in accordance with his own values. In contrast with the other types of characters, the real-self-directed person is *autonomous*.[25] His ego selects the promptings of his real self, rather than other sources of direction, as the guide to conduct.

Real-Self-Being: The Honest Disclosure of Self. We have asserted directly and indirectly that to be one's real self is essential to healthy personality. A good question to raise in this connection is, "How does one go about *being* one's real self?" One indication of degree of real-self being is found in the nature of a person's *self-disclosure*.[26] Humans have the capacity to fake, to dissemble, to seem to be what they are not, and they also have the capacity to reveal their true feelings and thoughts and true information about themselves. True disclosure of self in "dialogue"[27] with one's fellow man seems to be the most direct indicator of real-self being. When a person lets others know what he genuinely thinks and feels, and when he answers their questions about him truthfully and without reserve, he is said to be engaged in real-self-being. Obviously, such openness, or transparency, exposes a person to real danger, because to be that open with others means to be without defenses. The interests of healthy personality are served if a person is able to disclose himself fully, honestly, and spontaneously to others when there is no great danger likely to follow such disclosure. People are much more likely to be overly cautious than they are to be excessively open, with the result that they are relatively safe but lonely and misunderstood by others.

It may seem paradoxical, but one comes best to know one's real self, and to be able to introspect honestly, as a consequence of unselected, spontaneous disclosure of self to another person. The individual who has a trusted friend or relative to whom he can express his thoughts, feelings, and opinions honestly is in a better position to learn his real self than the one who has never undergone this experience, because as he reveals himself to another, he is also revealing himself *to himself*. The act of stating one's experience to another, making oneself known to him, permits one to "get outside oneself" and see oneself. This process of self-discovery through making oneself known to another is facilitated if the other person *reflects back* what he has heard you say. His reflection or restatement, like a mirror, then permits you to compare your words with your experience as you feel it directly and immediately.

COMPONENTS OF THE SELF-STRUCTURE

Thus far, we have distinguished among the personality, the ego, the real self, and the self-structure. Let us investigate the self-structure in further detail. The self-structure may be broadly defined as a by-product of the cognitive activity of the ego; it is constructed by the ego, in the last analysis. It comprises three broad components, the *self-concept,* the *self-ideal,* and various *public selves.* More broadly, the self-structure is everything that a person can say about his own experiencing.

An individual's self-structure is seldom in the forefront of his thoughts, but it is possible for him to verbalize its contents. An observer can often determine the nature of an individual's self-structure through inference and through direct questioning. Personality investigators have devised rather ingenious methods for making the self-structure explicit for research purposes. The basic procedure has been to develop a list of statements concerned with behavior and inner experience: "I never lose my temper"; "I have a good sense of humor"; "I have many fantasies about success," and so on. The person then responds to this list in various ways, depending upon what aspect of the self-structure is under study. Thus, if the self-concept is being studied, the subject is asked to indicate which of the statements are accurately descriptive of him and which are not. If the statements are printed on cards, the subject sorts them into piles, where one pile represents statements that are very true for him, other piles include statements which are less true, and still others contain statements which are definitely not descriptive of the person.

If the self-ideal is being investigated, then the individual again sorts the statements into piles, but this time he selects those statements which would describe him if he were *the way he wanted to be.* If the public selves are to be explored, the person sorts the cards so they will describe the way he behaves in the presence of others: the way *he wants others to think of him.*

This procedure has been described in the literature as "Q-methodology," and a number of important researches have been made possible by its invention.[28]

In the last analysis, the self-structure of an individual can be formulated by an observer through asking him to describe himself as he believes he is, as he would like to be, and as he wants others to think of him. The research procedures are little more than a refinement and extension of this basic procedure.

THE SELF-CONCEPT

The self-concept comprises all the beliefs the individual holds concerning what kind of person he *is;* i.e., conclusions concerning his *modal* or typical reaction patterns to typical life situations. Although a person seldom formulates all of these beliefs, yet a sample of them can readily be obtained simply by asking a person to describe himself. Generally, he will proceed to enumerate a series of trait-names: "I am lazy, happy-go-lucky, even-tempered; I have a good sense of humor; I don't rattle easily; I am polite." It can be seen that these words and phrases refer to consistent modes of behavior. They are in a sense statistical formulations. When a person says "I am even-tempered," he is asserting that he has observed his own experiencing and behavior in a broad variety of situations and over an extended period of time; during that period of observation, the person believes that very few occasions could be found when he became angry or excited.

Yet it should not be concluded that the beliefs which comprise the self-concept are all grounded in the individual's direct observations of his own conduct. Many of the beliefs that the individual holds concerning his personality have been acquired from other people—"significant others," as Sullivan described them[29]—from parents, friends, spouse, siblings, and so on. These other people have observed the behavior of the individual and have formulated beliefs concerning his personality, beliefs which they convey to him. He, in turn, adopts or affirms these beliefs. As they believe he is, he comes to believe he is. Many of the beliefs which a person has acquired from other people are not simply statistical conclusions, free from value-judgments; rather, many of them derive from a comparison of the individual's behavior with various moral standards. Thus, parents may say to a child, "You are bad." "You are lazy." The child has no reason to doubt the veracity of his parents, so he comes to agree with them. He believes he is lazy and bad.

Since the self-concept is actually a system of beliefs, we can apply the principles of logical and scientific criticism to those beliefs. We can ask, for example, "On what evidence does the person believe he is energetic? Bright? Even-tempered? Is this belief warranted? Or is it a generalization based on insufficient data or on a biased sample of observations?" In other words, we can determine whether or not the beliefs correspond with the individual's modal behavior.

We can inquire further as to the logical compatibility or coherence of the beliefs with one another, much as we would examine any system of beliefs with respect to its logical coherence. Are some beliefs contradictory with one another? Does a person believe that he is both kind and unkind? Honest and dishonest? Lazy and energetic? Easygoing and tense?

Examination of the beliefs which an individual holds concerning his modal behavior will often disclose many that are patently inaccurate and contradictory. Further, there may be a wide range of behavior and experience which the individual himself does not observe or misinterprets—just as a scientist who is defending some pet theory will ignore or misinterpret "negative instances." This is done so as to avoid drawing undesirable conclusions about his personality and to defend his present self-concept.

WHAT CONSTITUTES A SIGNIFICANT OTHER? Sullivan, the late prominent American psychiatrist, accorded considerable attention to the role played by "significant others" in the acquisition of the self-structure, or "self-dynamism," as he called it. He stated[30] that the self (-structure) was made up of "reflected appraisals," appraisals of the individual which were made by "parents and significant others." The implication of his comments is clear: As the parents and significant others defined and evaluated the person, so would he come to define and evaluate himself.[31]

Another way of looking at this problem is as follows: The self-concept comprises the beliefs which an individual holds with respect to his behavior, as well as a number of moral conclusions, based on a comparison of the behavior with some moral standards. Now, a person can arrive at beliefs and moral judgments through his own independent observations and comparisons, but he can also arrive at them simply through *listening to the conclusions which another person makes and believing the other person.* Thus, I can examine my past behavior and assert: "I hardly ever stole anything in the past. Therefore, I can say that I am honest and trustworthy. Honesty and trustworthiness are very valuable traits in our society, and since I have them, I can also say that I am a good person." Suppose my mother then said: "Look here. You are overlooking a lot of things. Remember all the times that you stole and told lies? I believe you are dishonest, untrustworthy, and bad." Whom shall I believe? My mother or myself?

Let us define another person as a significant other *when his beliefs and feelings about us make an important difference to us and when he has a status which implies his opinions and judgments must be considered as authoritative.* By these criteria, it is clear that one's parents are highly significant others when one is very young—on both counts. Their opinions and beliefs about us will strongly influence the way they treat us, and further, when we are very young our parents appear omniscient. If they say we are bad, they punish us, and we believe we are bad. What child can pit his opinion against that of his parents? Why should the child doubt his parents' conclusions?

All of us are surrounded by significant others, and we are continually modifying our self-concepts so they will accord nicely with the opinions and judgments of these significant others. When one's superior says, "You've done a nice piece of work, you're a good craftsman," one can hardly escape believing that one is a good craftsman and glowing with pride. If one's friend says the same words, it doesn't feel the same, and it leaves one with a certain measure of uncertainty concerning one's skill, for the friend is not really qualified to judge.

An individual may believe that he is insane. His friends may reassure him, but they are not significant others when it comes to making judgments about sanity. The individual will not be reassured until be hears a qualified psychiatrist or psychologist pronounce the words "you are sane."

THE SELF-IDEAL

The self-ideal refers to a set of beliefs which an individual holds concerning how he *should* behave.[32] These specifications of ideal behavior usually derive from the more abstract moral and ethical precepts which are current within the society at a given time. The beliefs of the self-ideal can be stated as "self-expectations," or "self-demands." The individual expects it of himself that he will behave with honesty, punctuality, morality. If he fails to live up to these self-expectations, he will experience self-hatred, or guilt. (See Chapter 8.)

The self-ideal has its beginnings in early childhood in the form of demands and expectations which parents and other significant persons held of the child. As the child conformed with these demands and expectations, he was rewarded and received approval. When he failed to conform with parental demands, he was punished and rejected. Usually, the child conformed with the parental demands for very concrete reasons—to maximize very concrete rewards and to minimize very concrete punishments and reprimands. Later, the demands or ideals came to be formulated as moral absolutes, as abstract statements of what is right and good and what is wrong and bad. The child gradually adopts these demands (which others have made of him) as *his own demands on himself*. When the parents asserted to their children that they should be prompt, clean, neat, obedient, high achievers in school, and so on, they generally assumed the children had the ability or the potential ability to conform with those expectations. But often, the demands and expectations were set beyond the real ability of the child to conform with them. The child, however, again has no reason to doubt his parents. If they say he can and should conform with their wishes, he believes them. When he cannot, he questions his goodness, obedience, or persistence, not his parents' demands. One sees no reason to doubt that if a mother said to her child, "You should grow wings and fly," the child would try and try, and when he observed that no wings were sprouting, he would feel guilty and unworthy of his mother's love. He would hate himself, because he *should* be able to grow wings; Mother said so.

We can examine the beliefs that comprise the self-ideal from a number of viewpoints. We can inquire: "How possible is it for this particular person to conform with this particular ideal?" "How compatible are these ideals one with another?" "To what extent do the ideals or expectations conform with the mores of society at large?" "To what extent are the ideals compatible with gaining physical satisfactions?" "To what extent does fulfillment of the ideals bring satisfaction?"

When once a self-ideal has been formulated (it is continuously in process of formulation and reformulation), it provides a standard in terms of which the individual appraises his own conduct (and personality). Just as a person intermittently observes his own conduct, so does he evaluate it in terms of his moral or ideal precepts. There is no self-observation which is not also a self-evaluation—a comparison between what is done and what should be done. It is only under special conditions of sophistication that an individual can attempt to observe and describe his conduct without evaluating it in moral terms.

In view of the continual self-evaluation which goes on during a person's life, it should be apparent that when the self-ideal is violated by the person's conduct—when he does not behave as he believes he should—he will hate himself or believe he is a failure, a sinner, or just plain "no good." If he behaves as he should, he will experience self-esteem and believe that he is a worth-while, likable, acceptable person. The self-ideal is such an important factor in personality health that we shall devote a chapter (Chapter 6) to fuller discussion.

THE PUBLIC SELF

Other persons who have observed an individual formulate beliefs about his personality. They not only observe his behavior, however; they also evaluate it in terms of their own value-system. The small child soon learns that when his parents believe he is one kind of person, they punish and reprimand him; when they hold different beliefs, they reward and approve of him. Consequently, he acquires a vested interest in promulgating certain *preferred beliefs about his personality* in the minds of other people.

At this point, we must draw a distinction between the valid beliefs that other people hold concerning an individual, which constitute his "real personality," and the carefully monitored set of beliefs which the individual *strives* to *induce* other people to formulate. It is the latter which constitute the *public selves* of the individual. Students of the history of psychology will observe a close parallel between the "social self" described by William James[33] and the present writer's concept of the public self. James stated "*a man has as many social selves as there are individuals who recognize him* and carry an image of him in their mind" (italics his).

The layman's term for the public self is "wanted reputation." Everyone strives to construct a reputation with respect to his modal behavior; i.e., he carefully restricts his behavior before other persons so they cannot help but formulate the kinds of beliefs which he wants them to possess. Almost everyone in our society draws a distinction between his "public" life and his "private" life. Ordinarily, only those persons whom an individual loves or trusts absolutely are allowed to observe the full range of his behavior-repertoire. Outsiders are permitted to observe only the "expurgated" edition of his behavior. One author spoke, in this connection, of "on-stage" behavior, as opposed to backstage or off-stage behavior.[34]

The most important reason for constructing public selves of various sorts is *expedience.* It is only when others believe certain things to be true of you that they will like you, marry you, give you jobs, refrain from imprisoning you, appoint you to public office, buy things at your store, or consult you professionally. If, for any reason, other people believe undesirable things to be true of your modal behavior, they will ostracize you, jail you, and so on.

A person may construct highly diversified public selves, depending upon his needs and values. The young man seeking a spouse strives to behave in ways that the girl will be likely to value and approve. He does not allow her to see the rest of his behavior, which may be tremendously discrepant with the censored version of him which she does see.

The construction of public selves bears a resemblance to sculpture. A sculptor manipulates clay, then steps back to see whether the statue he is creating resembles the image he has in mind. If it doesn't, he continues to work at it, until by successive approximations, he has brought into reality something which hitherto existed only as a preferred idea or image.

By the same token, a person may hold an image of his own being and personality that he wants to construct in the mind of another person. Instead of clay, he employs his own carefully selected behavior and conversation. From time to time, his audience will offer feedback, indicating how he has been seen. If the way he is being seen does not yet coincide with the preferred image, the individual engages in more behavior and talking, until he is assured by the other's responses that he is now seen as he wishes to be seen.

A person's public selves are usually incomplete versions of his total self, since he seldom allows other people to observe or know about *all* of his behavior. This implies that the individual knows more about himself than any one other person. It is only in principle that another person could know more about me than I know myself. If he could accompany me at all times, and if I related everything I thought and felt aloud to him at all times, then he might know me better than I know myself, for he is less likely to make biased observations than I am.

Very often, a person may slip during the process of constructing, or living up to, a given public self. He may want his audience to believe one thing about him, say, that he is blameless and morally scrupulous; yet, he may forget himself and curse or lose his temper, and thus destroy the image he was constructing. Such experiences produce embarrassment, to say the least. The reading public has an insatiable curiosity for details which conflict with the public selves of newsworthy people.[35]

A person is generally very sensitive to the impression his behavior produces in his audience. When it appears that the other person is formulating nonpreferred beliefs about him, he will become disturbed and say, "You have the wrong impression of me. I am not like that," and he will strive, with words and action, to convey a set of beliefs he wants the other person to adopt.

With respect to the preferred impressions which comprise an individual's public selves, we can ask: "Do these desired impressions correspond with his self-concept? Do they correspond with his usual private behavior? Do they correspond with his self-ideal? Are his public selves compatible with one another? Are his public selves accurate versions of his total behavior-repertoire?"

We have related in some detail the definitions of the parts of the self-structure. Let us now ask: "What difference does it make what a person believes himself to be, or what he believes he ought to be, or what he wants other people to believe about him? Will variations in these assorted beliefs make a difference in the way in which the person behaves?" We shall answer these questions with a "yes."

THE SELF-STRUCTURE AND BEHAVIOR

A person tends to show marked consistency in his behavior. A neat individual is usually neat in almost everything he does. An honest person is usually consistently honest. A poor speller generally shows consistency in making errors.[36] A thorough person generally does everything in a thorough fashion. What factors are responsible for this observed consistency in behavior? One answer may be found in the realm of learning theory. Consistent behavior is *habitual* behavior. As a general rule, habits persist so long as they are "reinforced"; i.e., so long as they continue to be instrumental toward the attainment of satisfaction or toward the avoidance and reduction of pain.

Another reason for consistency in behavior, not necessarily incompatible with that derived from reinforcement theory, is to be found in the theory of the self-structure. It may be asserted that *people behave with consistency in order to maintain or to justify their present beliefs about their personality.* In other words, an individual believes he is such and such a kind of person, that he "has" certain traits. He continues to behave in ways that will enable him to continue believing that he has those traits.

Why should the person *want* to continue believing he has those traits? What difference could it possibly make whether he believes or doubts that certain trait-names describe his behavior accurately?

There are three separate but related answers to this question. A person must believe certain things about himself (a) in order to maintain self-esteem, or to avoid guilt and shame, (b) in order to maintain his sense of identity, and (c) in order to continue to believe he is acceptable to other people.

SELF-CONCEPT, BEHAVIOR, AND SELF-ESTEEM

Self-esteem, a variety of self-appraisal highly valued by personality hygienists as well as by the person himself, is highly dependent upon behavior which conforms with the self-ideal. So long as a person *acts* in self-approved ways, he can justifiably believe he is a worth-while person, at least in his own eyes. Thus, we can assert that a person behaves in certain ways, not only to secure satisfaction of assorted wants, but also to verify or justify certain beliefs about his personality. He must justify these beliefs in order to maintain self-esteem.

Let us imagine that a person values the ability to speak with elegance. His self-esteem may be highly dependent upon his own ability to speak with elegance. So long as he speaks in this fashion, he holds his personality in esteem. When he speaks crudely, he despises himself. This individual literally must believe, if he is to maintain self-esteem, that he is an effective and elegant speaker. As a consequence he will strive continually to speak in this fashion. It is only as he speaks that way that he can (a) believe he is such a speaker and (b) hold his personality in esteem.

It may readily be seen, then, that a person actually *strives* to behave with consistency. He strives to behave in those ways which will continually verify or justify the beliefs he holds with respect to his personality. Only so long as these beliefs can be affirmed will he be able to maintain self-esteem.

THE SELF-CONCEPT, BEHAVIOR, AND THE SENSE OF IDENTITY

The sense of identity may be defined as the subjective experience of "being one's real self." Psychologists have not as yet paid much attention to this variable. Erikson,[37] a psychoanalyst, has used the term "ego identity" to refer to the identity-sense, and he mentions at least four meanings for his term: "At one time, ego identity will appear to refer to a conscious *sense of individual identity;* at another time to an unconscious striving for a continuity of personal character; at a third, as a criterion for the silent doings of *ego synthesis;* and, finally, as a maintenance of an inner *solidarity* with a group's ideals and identity" (italics his).

For us, the sense of identity is a conscious, subjective experience of "being oneself" which derives from self-observation and judgment. The person observes his actions as he goes along through life and compares them, consciously or unconsciously, *with a standard provided by his memory of how he has been throughout the recent and immediate past.* It is as if each action of a person yielded a proprioceptive and kinesthetic "feedback" that is judged as being "like me" or "not like me." The "me" which is referred to is the individual's self-concept.

When a person acts in accordance with his self-concept, his sense of identity is reinforced. When he acts in ways discrepant to his self-concept, he feels what we shall call *a loss of the sense of identity.*[38] It is probably verbalized by the person: "I am not myself." When a person is acting in ways counter to his self-concept, he experiences anxiety, apprehension about the probable reactions of other people to his behavior. So long as he is "himself," he can predict fairly well how others will react. When he is in process of changing his identity, he will likely experience "identity-crises" marked by intense anxiety.

Behavior which conforms with the self-concept may thus be viewed as behavior which preserves the sense of identity; like anxiety and guilt, the sense of identity is a factor which promotes consistency in behavior and resists change in behavior.

Another way of defining the sense of identity is to describe it as a person's *beliefs* concerning the ways in which *other people* think about him. This is not the same as the public self or personality. Public selves are preferred or valued beliefs which a person *wants* other people to have about him; personality formulations are beliefs which other people actually have with respect to the individual's behavior, independent of his wishes, knowledge, or preferences. The sense of identity, on the other hand, refers to the individual's conviction—accurate or inaccurate—of his "stimulus value," of how other people think about him. He may like or dislike, be proud or ashamed, of his identity. Yet it seems valid to assert that even a shameful identity is preferable to a person than no identity—being nobody.

Therefore, a person who believes he is bad, or unskilled, or sloppy, will tend to behave with consistency, thus continually reinforcing those beliefs, *because they constitute his identity.* It is as if being John Smith means being bad, lazy, and sloppy—but better to be John Smith than to be nobody. If he were to behave in other ways, John would feel strange, "not himself"; in order to get rid of the feeling of strangeness, he snaps back to the old ways of behaving.

Many overweight people have constructed a public self, a self-concept, and a sense of identity which are all predicated on overeating, being happy and jolly and clownlike. Such persons do not feel they are "themselves" when they are eating small meals, and they fear that should they change their body shape, they will not be known and recognized by their friends and associates. They fear the prospect of creating a new identity for themselves. Hence, they may find it very difficult to reduce.

THE SELF-CONCEPT AND THE BELIEF THAT ONE IS ACCEPTABLE TO OTHERS

We have stated that a person must believe certain things about his personality in order to maintain self-esteem and his sense of identity. In addition, he must believe certain things about himself in order to justify the belief that he is *acceptable to others.*

Early in childhood, the individual learned that only when he acted in certain ways was he acceptable to his parents. As he consistently acted in those acceptable ways, he would come to believe he *was* the kind of person who acted that way. A child's sense of safety, or security, is strongly dependent upon the belief that his parents like him.[39] We may generalize further and assert that any individual's sense of security is dependent upon the belief that other people like him.

Because only a certain range of behavior is acceptable to others, a person will strive to behave in acceptable ways and hide unacceptable behavior from the public gaze or eliminate it. So long as he does behave in acceptable ways, he can believe (a) that he is the kind of person others will like and (b) that other people actually do like him. If he behaves in ways which challenge his self-concept, the person is likely to experience guilt, a feeling of not being himself, and also a sense of anxiety or insecurity—the conviction that other people will not like him.[40]

THE PUBLIC SELVES, SELF-IDEAL, AND BEHAVIOR

The public selves which a person has established, or is trying to establish, constitute an important determiner of behavior, especially in behavior which comes under the observation or scrutiny of other people. In contemporary society, where privacy and secrecy are difficult to find, this naturally includes most of a person's behavior-repertoire.

A person will strive to behave before others in ways that will construct or preserve a set of beliefs about him he wants them to have. Riesman has[41] described vividly the changes in the contemporary American social structure which compel a person to become concerned with the opinions of others about him. His other-directed character is a superb description of a type of man, or personality-structure, which is becoming increasingly common.

In the presence of others, an individual may often behave in the ways which *they* expect him to behave, irrespective of his real feelings or wants. Since many of the satisfactions in contemporary living can be achieved only through the good will of other people (lone wolves are no longer fashionable), the person must present at least the appearance of being an "acceptable" individual.

The public selves constructed by a person will generally correspond closely with his self-ideal. He may know with certainty that he doesn't really want to act in certain ways; he doesn't really have the opinions which he expresses; he doesn't really have the feelings which he pretends to have. Yet he must behave as if he had those feelings, opinions, and desires because he believes that he *should* (as specified by his self-ideal) and because if he fails to act in those ways, other people will formulate undesirable beliefs about him. These beliefs will jeopardize his status, his marriage, his job, and many other things which he values highly. Accordingly, the person will strive to control the impression others form of him by selecting his behavior for its desirable effect on others. Such "public-self-being," or contrived self-presentation, is much like the performance of an actor before an audience.

Thus far, we have defined the components of the self-structure and attempted to show how the self-structure influences behavior. Let us now pose the question, "What is an unhealthy self-structure?" Later, we shall describe healthy-self structure in more detail.

VARIETIES OF UNHEALTHY SELVES

INACCURATE AND INCOMPLETE SELF-CONCEPTS. This is perhaps the most common variety of unhealthy self. A person may entertain only a limited repertoire of beliefs about his personality, refusing to acknowledge entire realms of behavior as part of him.[42] He might, for example, refuse to acknowledge the proposition that he is an aggressive person, even though he behaves often in an aggressive manner. Instead, he may believe he is basically a gentle, kindly person. When he loses his temper, he will assert that "I was not myself at the time" or else forget about it.

We are all familiar with the person who defends some cherished theory by ignoring all evidence which would refute his theory. The self-concept is very closely analogous with a cherished theory. Thus, from a strictly logical point of view, the person's beliefs about what kind of a person he is may be grossly incomplete.

In addition to incompleteness, a person's beliefs about how he behaves may be logically contradictory with each other. He may, for example, believe he is both aggressive and kind, competitive and co-operative, highly moral and also a "jolly good fellow"—"one of the boys."

Finally, a person's beliefs may be drastically inaccurate. His beliefs about how he behaves—i.e., how his behavior should be classified—may do violence to the science of taxonomy. Thus, many people may label his behavior with his children as cruel and brutal, while he calls it "good parenthood." Or, many people might call his behavior in business sheer piracy or dishonesty, while he chooses to call it "business acumen."

One of the important aims of psychotherapy can be stated as the attempt to help a person formulate beliefs about how he behaves (i.e., what kind of person he is) which are accurate, complete, and logically compatible.

UNDULY HIGH SELF-IDEALS. The self-concept refers to the way that a person believes he acts. The self-ideal refers to his concepts of how he *should* act. The penalty for failure to behave as one "should" is *guilt*—a hatred of the behavior in question and, more than that, hatred of the total personality and of the real self.[43] When a person has acquired values or ideals which are well out of the range of human capacity to implement, he has the groundwork prepared for chronic guilt. More than that, he has the groundwork prepared for inaccurate beliefs about the self. When it is so painful to doubt certain beliefs about one's personality, one may be driven, by the need to maintain self-esteem, to formulate inaccurate and incomplete beliefs. Thus, a "tyrannical" self-ideal often leads to inaccurate self-concepts and promotes chronic guilt, or loss of self-esteem.

INACCURATE AND INCOMPLETE PUBLIC SELF. Like the inaccurate self-concepts, inaccurate and incomplete public selves are very common forms of the unhealthy self. People seldom allow other people indiscriminately to observe all of their behavior or allow others to know what they think and feel about things. They monitor their public behavior carefully in order to promote censored beliefs concerning the kind of people they are.

As a consequence of this felt necessity to promulgate highly selected concepts of their personality to others, people often develop highly contradictory concepts among different groups of people. Thus, a college student might promote the view in his home town that he is highly obedient to his parents, a conformer, and so on. At college, in his fraternity, he encourages the view that he is a "devil with the ladies," a man who can hold his liquor, and a bit of a nonconformer. With one girl friend, he behaves in ways which will promote a concept of him as the kind of person she might like to marry; with another, he presents a different conception.

None of these public conceptions of his personality correspond with the individual's real personality, with his self-concept, or with his self-ideal. As a consequence, the individual with such conflicting public conceptions of his personality will often believe he is a hypocrite (since a common value is that of consistency), hate himself for it, and live in continual dread of being unmasked.[44]

MOVEMENT OF THE SELF-STRUCTURE

A healthy self-structure probably does not exist; it is rather an ideal formulated by the personality hygienist. People differ in the extent to which they presently have a healthy or unhealthy self.

We can study an individual, however, and come to conclusions concerning whether or not this self-structure is "moving" toward a healthier, or less healthy, self-structure or whether it is remaining static and unchanging. Naturally, the personality hygienist is concerned with promoting movement toward a healthy self-structure.[45]

How do we go about deciding in what direction a person is moving, with respect to common vicissitudes of the self-structure?

As observers, we have to take into account the following factors: (a) the person's actual behavior and subjective experience (his real self), (b) the nature of his self-concept, self-ideal, and public selves, and (c) the degree of congruence of each of these factors with every other factor. Let us illustrate how judgments might be made concerning movement toward and movement away from a healthy self-structure.

Peter believes the following things about his personality: that he *is* a highly moral person, and according to his standards, this implies that his behavior, thoughts, feelings, and fantasies all conform with social norms; also he believes he *should* be moral. Finally, he wants other people to believe that he is moral.

Let us now imagine that careful observation of Peter's behavior discloses that much of the time, Peter has fantasies and wishes which are in violent opposition both to his self-ideal and to social mores; for example, he wants to abandon his wife and establish a romance with another woman. Further, when he is certain that nobody who knows him is around, he cheats on his wife, drinks lavishly, and is not averse to petty theft.

When Peter examines *all* of his behavior and labels it accurately, we should expect him to experience guilt and fear of rejection and criticism. These emotional tensions are painful, or unpleasant, and serve as a drive to some kind of activity which will eliminate or avoid them. What kind of activity is most valued by the personality hygienist as movement toward a healthier self-structure? What kind of activity is, on the contrary, condemned as movement away from a healthy self-structure? Actually, we are restating a question dealt with in other sections (Chapter 8: healthy and unhealthy reactions to guilt; Chapter 4: healthy and unhealthy reactions to fear and anxiety). In the present context, the focus of our discussion is somewhat different, however, and so the question warrants restating.

ACTIVITY TOWARD A HEALTHIER SELF-STRUCTURE

When a person experiences guilt or fear of rejection, punishment, and ostracism, it is usually because his behavior is not consistent with his self-concept. It will be recalled that the person *must* hold certain beliefs about his personality, on pain of guilt, loss of a sense of identity, and loss of status and the approving reactions of others. In principle, the healthy reactions to guilt and anxiety, prompted by inconsistent behavior, are:

1. *Restrict behavior and experience so that they conform with the self-concept.* Restricting behavior and experience is not entirely desirable, since it implies a static self-structure, and the personality hygienist values change (growth) of the self.
2. *Change the beliefs which comprise the self-concept so that they encompass* all *behavior and experience.*
3. *Change the self-ideal, leaving the self-concept intact.* (When this can be effected, the individual's behavior does not change, but his negative evaluation of it will. He will no longer experience guilt for the behavior that formerly was culpable.)
4. *Change his various public selves so that he strives to convey to other people, by his behavior, a set of beliefs more congruent with his actual behavior and his self-concept; he strives to get other people to know him as he really is.*

Any activity which produces these consequences may be regarded as movement toward a healthier self-structure, as this was defined in an earlier section.

Throughout the course of a person's life, many of these activities take place spontaneously. People actually do change their self-concepts, self-ideals, and public selves from time to time. Changes of this sort may be experienced sometimes as emotionally charged crises, or they may occur so gradually as to be unnoticed. Many personality therapists have observed people in the process of amending their beliefs about the kind of person they really are. Generally, these alterations in the self-concept are forced upon the patient as he observes the full extent to which his actual behavior, thoughts, and feelings diverge from the presently held self-concept. Probably in the natural course of events, the self-concepts change gradually, almost without the awareness of the person involved. He just realizes at one time or another that he no longer believes something about himself which he always had before, and it doesn't particularly bother him. This is most likely to occur as a consequence of identifications with persons in groups that have different values. College students living away from home are often unaware they have changed their behavior patterns, their concepts of self, and their self-ideals. It is only when they return home that their parents and former associates "hardly know them." This often produces discomfort, conflict, and embarrassment.

In a later chapter, we will inquire in more detail into the conditions under which movement toward a healthy self-structure can be promoted, even controlled. This is actually the problem of psychotherapy, or personality therapy, as the present author prefers to call it. We can anticipate this chapter, however, by stating that movement toward a healthy self is most likely to be promoted within the framework of relationships with other people. More of this later. We are merely asserting here that it is difficult if not impossible for a person to move toward self-health without the assistance of others.

Let us illustrate at this point, with concrete examples, the above-mentioned healthy moves.

The author understook personality therapy with a middle-aged man who complained of the following symptoms: marked sensitivity to light and an absolute panic when in the company of other people (including the therapist).

Over a period of several months, it was discovered that, among other things, he believed (but without being absolutely certain of it) that he was intellectually superior to other people. Further, he valued intelligence, culture, and poise very highly and demanded of himself that he manifest all these traits. As he talked about his daily round of activities, his past, his feelings and fantasies, it soon became apparent to the therapist (and to him) that his belief in his own intellectual superiority to all others was a shaky one at best. He lived in constant dread lest others outsmart him, which would prove his self-concept was without foundation. Under the impetus of panic, he could not display his really considerable background of reading and general culture. He would instead block, stammer, giggle, get embarrassed, be unable to answer questions coherently, and so on. These panic-produced reactions made him hate and despise himself. He "moved away from people," as Horney puts it, and spent much solitary time in his room. In addition, he believed that his eyes betrayed his inner feelings, so he wore very dark glasses when among other people. Naturally, this made him very sensitive to light whenever he removed them. As years passed, light became a source of agony, and so he was obliged to live almost as a blind person, in darkened rooms. So much for the "presenting symptoms."

At one point he stated: "I am a hypocrite; I am stupid; I hate myself so much I don't see how you or anyone else could possibly be concerned about me. I don't deserve to live."

In the course of time, however, he came to modify his self-concept in important ways, bringing it much more into line with his actual behavior and feelings. His self-ideal underwent marked changes, mainly with respect to the stringency of his ideals. Finally, when among others, he behaved much more in accord with his feelings, constructing thereby more accurate public selves. It could be said about him that he manifested all of the active moves toward a healthy self-structure.

Here are some quotations from his remarks which illustrate these moves: "I know that I am not the smartest person in the world, but I really am smarter than many people I come into contact with. Not long ago, I'd have died rather than put that into words. Wasn't that stupid?" "I used to think that it was the most important thing in the world to be perfect, never to make a mistake in grammar, never to state an unfounded opinion. It's funny, but now I curse quite a bit, I sometimes speak like a hillbilly instead of a cultured person, and do you know, it doesn't bother me?" "You know, I'm getting brassy. I don't seem to give a damn what other people think of me. I just speak my piece, let them know what I think, and if it satisfies me, then that's all that counts. I don't mean that I'm a wild man; don't get me wrong. I just mean that when I'm with other people, I don't feel so phony, like I'm trying to get them to think about me in a special way. I'm finding out who my real friends are."

Lest the reader get the wrong impression, these statements were made after long months of agonizing, emotion-charged sessions during which the patient talked about his thoughts, feelings, wishes, past events, fantasies, with many attempts to hide and cover up important experiences.

A HEALTHY SELF-STRUCTURE

Probably the best single indicator of a healthy self-structure is to be found in an individual's threat-threshold. The more easily threatened the individual, the less healthy is his self-structure. It will be recalled that threat to the self-structure is experienced subjectively in the form of guilt, as loss of self-esteem, anxiety, or dread of being "found out," and as dread of finding out things about oneself.[46] The more accurate the individual's self-concept, and the more congruent one with the other are his self-ideal, self-concept, public selves, and real self, then the less readily can a person be threatened. We are all familiar with the person who, when his motives are questioned, becomes upset and defensive. He is striving to hide the motives in question from the viewer and also from himself. He wants to be opaque before others. The individual with a healthy self-structure can face and admit all of his motives and feelings and all of his past and present actions. Moreover, he is not afraid to be "transparent," to be known by others as he authentically is.

In more formal terms, a healthy self-structure[47] is comprised of the following components:

1. A self-concept which, at any given time, is based on the individual's real self. He has no vested interest in believing anything about his own motives or actions which is untrue. He can acknowledge to himself and to others (if need be) all of his feelings, wishes, fantasies, needs, and experiences.

2. A self-ideal which is feasible, comprising values which are roughly congruent with social mores and which the person has had an active role in formulating and affirming.

3. Public selves which are accurate, compatible with one another, and expressive of the real self.

It is fair to state that no person ever has an absolutely healthy self-structure; rather, a healthy self-structure is a goal or value, and it is never maintained for long. The real self is in continuous process of change, as is the actual behavior of the individual. If he is to maintain a healthy self-structure, the person must continually reformulate his self-structure so that it keeps in touch with the realities of his inner self and his overt behavior. Each time the self-structure becomes discrepant from the real self and the individual becomes aware of the discrepancy, he will again experience threat. *Whether or not his self-structure moves in the direction of health will depend upon how he has handled the threat—whether in a growth-promoting way, as a challenge to be met, or in a defensive manner.*

Thus, it is not only the threat-threshold which depicts the health of the self-structure; the manner in which the individual deals with threats to his self-structure must also be considered.

A NOTE ON THREAT

Threats to the self-structure arise from inner and outer sources. Inner threat refers to all of those thoughts, feelings, wishes, fantasies, and memories which are likely to be discrepant with the present self-structure. Thus, a person may strive to avoid thinking certain things because to do so would cause him to doubt certain aspects of his self-concept.

Outer threat comprises the reactions of other people to the self. If another person holds a concept of you which is different from your self-concept, you may experience threat. If he assigns a different interpretation of your motives than the one which you want him to hold, you will experience threat. Threat is a very powerful motive. It can lead to behavior pathology, and it can lead to further personality growth in the direction of health.

SELF-CONSCIOUSNESS IN A HEALTHY SELF-STRUCTURE

Young children are spontaneous and lacking in self-consciousness. At some point during the process of being socialized, they learn that some of their spontaneous behavior is unacceptable to their parents and other adults because they are punished for some actions and not for others. In order to avoid future punishment, the child learns to control or suppress his spontaneous behavior and verbalization in order to *select* those acts and expressions which will be acceptable. The necessity to avoid punishment and to obtain desired consequences to his action appears to be a factor in the development of self-consciousness.

The capacity to be self-conscious is probably unique to man, because of the relative size of his cerebral cortex. Doubtless, the ability to observe the flow of one's experiencing in order to select whatever aspects are to be revealed in behavior has some adaptive and adjustive value. However, chronic self-consciousness can be an agonizing, cramping experience, one which reduces the enjoyment of living; in extreme instances, self-consciousness can so handicap a person he becomes unable to act at all, until he has first checked and rechecked his proposed action or communication. When self-consciousness is carried to this extreme, the individual may become well-nigh paralyzed by doubt and indecision, as in a pattern of neurosis called "doubting compulsion."

But chronically unreflective, spontaneous behavior can likewise yield undesirable and unhealthy consequences. The individual who is unable to delay his responses in order to pick out those most compatible with goals and values may run into much difficulty in his relations with others or even with the law. Psychiatrists refer to persons who seem incapable of introspection, delay of response, and the planned selection of appropriate behavior as individuals who "act out." The condition of acting out is observed in so-called psychopathic personalities and some hysterics.

In the healthy personality, there is no longer an irreconcilable conflict between spontaneous acting out and self-consciousness. Instead, the healthier personality has been able to reconcile the contradiction, and can be spontaneous and unself-consciousness when it is safe and appropriate to do so. When spontaneous behavior seems likely to yield difficulties or when it does in fact bring some form of pain or failure, the healthy personality has the capacity to suppress his spontaneity, and with full self-consciousness he can examine himself in order to select more effective modes of behavior. Once he has done this, he can permit himself to become unselfconsciously absorbed in his work, hobbies, other people, and any other interests.

Clearly, to be able to attain this transcendence of the opposition between self-consciousness and unpremeditated spontaneity calls for a considerable degree of *trust* in the ultimate goodness and competence of one's real self.[48] Probably, the moments in everyday existence when a person is most involved in, most fascinated and absorbed with, a task, a conversation, a book, or music, are moments when he is most unself-conscious and most fully integrated. These moments of "loss of self" are moments when there is optimum congruence among real self, self-concept, and public selves. Probably, the absence of self-consciousness, except on occasions when it is called for, is one of the best indices of a healthy self-structure.

EGO-STRENGTH, AND GROWTH VERSUS DEFENSE OF THE SELF-STRUCTURE

We have stated that the self-structure should be maximally congruent with the real self if it is to be adjudged healthy. But the real self is a continually changing thing. One's needs, wishes, feelings, values, goals, and behavior all change with age and experience. This continual change in the real self—its "unfolding" and "becoming"[49] —poses a problem for the individual. There is always the danger his real self will outgrow his self-structure in much the same way that a person outgrows his clothes. One knows his shoes or clothes no longer fit when they feel tight and produce discomfort. One knows that his self-structure no longer "fits" the real self when threat occurs unduly often.

When a person experiences threat to his self-structure (which is a common, even daily, occurrence), he has a limited number of alternative paths to action. Which path he will take hinges greatly on the strength of his ego.

If the ego is strong, the person will acknowledge the threat and explore the factors responsible for it. On the basis of this reality-testing activity, he may suppress the threatening activity or repress the unwanted feelings or impulses (but through conscious choice). Or, the person may accept and act upon the threatening feelings and strive to modify his self-concept and self-ideal so they again fit his real self. A strong ego thus facilitates growth of a healthy self-structure.

But if the ego is weak, the individual may not be able to tolerate the threat to his self-structure. Instead of striving to determine what is threatening him and why, he may, quite automatically and involuntarily, resort to actions designed to *defend and protect his present self-structure*. There is a wide variety of "mechanisms" for the defense and maintenance of the self-structure which a weak ego will adopt. In the next chapter, we shall discuss these.

SUMMARY

A person's self-structure influences his experiencing and his behavior. The self-structure is a set of beliefs, attitudes, and ideals constructed by a person in reference to his behavior and experience. If the individual has a strong ego, his self-structure will be fairly congruent with his real self. The real self is defined as the process or flow of spontaneous inner experience. When the self-structure is not congruent with the real self, the individual is said to be self-alienated, showing symptoms of being driven by pride, conscience, external authority, the wishes of others, or by his impulses. The healthy personality is not self-alienated, but rather displays responsible real-self-direction of his conduct. Real-self-being is manifested by authentic self-disclosure to others.

The self-structure comprises the self-concept—the individual's beliefs about his own personality; the self-ideal—his views concerning how he ought to be; and various public selves—his preferred modes for presenting himself to others. The person's self-concept and the self-ideal are partly shaped by the beliefs and expectations held by significant others with respect to the person.

Self-esteem, the sense of identity, and a sense of secure acceptance by others are fostered by behavior that conforms with the self-concept. Persons will strive to confine their behavior to limits set by the various components of their self-structure.

Unhealthy self-structures are characterized by inaccurate self-concepts, unduly high self-ideals, inaccurate public selves, and conflict among the components of self-structure. A healthier self-structure is fostered whenever the individual behaves in ways more consonant with his real self. A healthy self-structure is one in which the components are congruent with one another and with the real self. Chronic self-consciousness is an indicant of an unhealthy self-structure, as is a chronic sense of threat.

NOTES AND REFERENCES

Excellent supplementary reading will be provided by those references marked with an asterisk (*).

*1. The study of the self by psychologists and sociologists has a history that is longer than that of experimental psychology. William James wrote most lucidly on the subject and anticipated much of the contemporary empirical research findings with respect to the self. See James, W., *Principles of Psychology* (New York: Holt, 1890); or his *Psychology: Briefer Course* (New York: Holt, 1892), ch. 12. The social psychologist, Mead, has contributed richly to present-day interest and formulations with respect to the self. See Mead, G. H., *Mind, Self and Society* (Chicago: U. of Chicago, 1934). A highly articulate formulation of the theory of the self is given in Rogers, C. R., *Client-Centered Therapy* (New York: Houghton, 1951). Sullivan, Fromm, and Horney have been most explicit about the self among the psychiatric group of writers.

*2. Prescott Leckey was highly influential in directing the attention of contemporary psychologists to the phenomenon of *consistency* in behavior as a function of the self. See Lecky, P., *Self-Consistency: A Theory of Personality* (New York: Island Press, 1945).

*3. See Freud, S., *An Outline of Psychoanalysis* (New York: Norton, 1949), for Freud's last systematic presentation of his conception of personality structure. For a systematic account of ego-psychology, see Hartmann, H., "Comments on the Psychoanalytic Theory of the Ego," *Psychoanalyt. Stud. Child*, 1950, V, International Universities Press, New York. An excellent survey of ego functions is given in Redl, F. and Wineman, D., *Children Who Hate* (Glencoe, Ill.: Free Press, 1951), pp. 61–196.

4. This distinction between the ego and the self parallels that made by Symonds, P., *The Ego and the Self* (New York: Appleton, 1951).

*5. *Cf.* MacCorquodale, K. and Meehl, P. E., "On a Distinction Between Hypothetical Constructs and Intervening Variables," *Psychol. Rev.*, *55*, 95–107 (1948).

6. Fenichel, O., *The Psychoanalytic Theory of Neurosis* (New York: Norton, 1945), ch. 10.

7. It was Beck who suggested employing the "form-level" on the Rorschach as an index of ego-strength. Following his suggestion, a number of experimenters have employed this index, or some adaptation of it, in various experiments and with varying degrees of predictive efficiency. See Williams, M., "An Experimental Study of Intellectual Control Under Stress, and Associated Rorschach Factors," *J. Consult. Psychol.*, *11*, 21–29 (1947); McReynolds, P., "Perception of Rorschach Concepts As Related to Personality Deviations," *J. Abn. Soc. Psychol.*, *46*, 131–141 (1951); Eriksen, C. W., "Psychological Defenses and Ego Strength in the Recall of Completed and Incompleted Tasks," *J. Abn. Soc. Psychol.*, *49*, 45–50 (1954); Jourard, S. M., "Ego Strength and the Recall of Tasks," *J. Abn. Soc. Psychol.*, *49*, 51–58 (1954); Feldman, M. J. *et al.*, "A Preliminary Study to Develop A More Discriminating F-Plus Ratio," *J. Clin. Psychol.*, *10*, 47–51 (1954).

8. *Cf.* Cattell, R. B., *Description and Measurement of Personality* (Yonkers, N.Y.: World Book, 1946).

9. See Personnel Research Branch Technical Research Note 22, *A Bibliography for the Development of Stress-Sensitive Tests* (Washington, D.C.: Psychological Research Associates, 1953).

10. *Cf.* Davidson, H. H., "A Measure of Adjustment Obtained from the Rorschach Protocol," *J. Proj. Tech.*, *14*, 31–38 (1950); Barron, F., "An Ego

Strength Scale Which Predicts Response to Psychotherapy," *J. Consult. Psychol.*, *17*, 327–333 (1953).

11. *Cf.* Gellhorn, E., *Physiological Foundations of Neurology and Psychiatry* (Minneapolis: U. of Minn. Press, 1953), pp. 434–438.

12. The "structure" of the ego may be described as the total repertoire of instrumental behavior patterns which a person has acquired up to any given time in his life.

13. Horney, K., *Neurosis and Human Growth* (New York: Norton, 1950).

14. Fromm, E., *Escape from Freedom* (New York: Rinehart, 1941), pp. 256–276.

15. This definition is similar to that expounded by Rogers. See Rogers, C. R., *op. cit.*, pp. 497–510.

16. Dymond, R. F., "Interpersonal Perception and Marital Happiness," *Can. J. Psychol.*, *8*, 164–171 (1954); Corsini, R. J., "Understanding and Similarity in Marriage," *J. Abn. Soc. Psychol.*, *52*, 327–332 (1956).

17. These phenomena are found to occur among patients who have undergone successful personality therapy. *Cf.* Rogers, C. R. and Dymond, R. (ed.), *Psychotherapy and Personality Change* (Chicago, U. of Chicago, 1954).

18. Horney, K., *op. cit.*, ch. 6. See also "Symposium on Alienation and the Search for Identity," *Amer. J. Psychoanal.*, *21*, 117–279 (1961).

19. Riesman, D., *The Lonely Crowd* (New Haven, Conn.: Yale, 1950).

20. Horney, K., *op. cit.*, ch. 3.

*21. Fromm, E., *op. cit.;* Maslow, A. H., "The Authoritarian Character Structure," *J. Soc. Psychol., S.P.S.S.I. Bulletin*, *18*, 401–411 (1943); Adorno, T. W., Frenkel-Brunswik, Else, Levinson, D. J., and Sanford, R. N., *The Authoritarian Character* (New York: Harper, 1950). See also Bettelheim, B., *The Informed Heart. Autonomy in a Mass Age* (Glencoe, Ill.: Free Press, 1960). This book is a superb discussion of the problem of resisting the forces which seek to eliminate autonomy.

22. Fromm, E., *op. cit.*, pp. 174–177 (discussion of the "magic helper"). Also Fromm, E., *Man for Himself* (New York: Rinehart, 1947), pp. 145–146.

23. Riesman, D., *op. cit.*

*24. *Cf.* Rogers, C. R., *The Concept of the Fully Functioning Person*, in Rogers, C. R., *On Becoming a Person* (Boston: Houghton, 1961), pp. 183–198.

25. *Cf.* Riesman, D., *op. cit.*

26. A discussion of self-disclosure as an indicator of real-self-being is given in Jourard, S. M., "Healthy Personality and Self-Disclosure," *Ment. Hyg.*, *43*, 499–507 (1959).

27. See Buber, M., *Between Man and Man* (Boston: Beacon, 1955), pp. 1–39, for a discussion of dialogue.

*28. See Mowrer, O. H. (ed.), *Psychotherapy: Theory and Research* (New York: Ronald, 1953), for a detailed discussion of "Q-methodology." This technique was employed in the extensive studies of therapy conducted at Chicago. See Rogers, C. R. and Dymond, R. F. (eds.), *op. cit.* A critical review of this and other research approaches to the self is given in Wylie, Ruth, *The Self-Concept. A Critical Survey of Pertinent Literature* (Lincoln, Nebr.: U. of Nebr. 1961).

29. Sullivan, H. S., *Conceptions of Modern Psychiatry* (Washington, D.C.: William Alanson White Psychiatric Foundation, 1947).

30. Sullivan, H. S., *op. cit.*, pp. 10, 131.

31. Jourard, S. M. and Remy, R. M., "Perceived Parental Attitudes, the Self, and Security," *J. Consult. Psychol.*, *19*, 364–366 (1955).

32. The concept of the ideal self is employed in the studies cited in Rogers, C. R. and Dymond, B. F. (eds.), *op. cit.* Horney also uses the term extensively in Horney, K., *Neurosis and Human Growth* (New York: Norton, 1950).

33. James, W., *Psychology* (New York: Holt, 1892), p. 179.

34. The concepts of "public self" and "social role" are systematically related to each other; each involves the selection by the person of "appropriate" behavior to perform in the presence of other people. See Goffman, E., *The Presentation of Self in Everyday Life* (Garden City, N. Y.: Doubleday Anchor, 1960), for further discussion of this point.

35. Compare the versions of movie stars' private lives as these are portrayed in the popular movie magazines and in the "scandal sheet" magazine *Confidential.*

36. Lecky, P., *op. cit.*

37. Erikson, E. H., "The Problem of Ego Identity," *J. Amer. Psychoanalyt. Assoc.*, *4*, 56–121 (1956). See also Bugental, S. and Zelen, S. L., "Investigations into the Self-Concept, I. The W-A-Y Technique," *J. Pers.*, *18*, 483–498 (1950). More extensive discussions from varying points of view may be found in Bettelheim, B., *op. cit.*, pp. 60, 73, 94, 98–100; Wheelis, A., *The Quest for Identity* (New York: Norton, 1958); Lynd, H., *On Shame and the Search for Identity* (New York: Harcourt Brace, 1958); and Stein, M. R., Vidich, A. J., and White, D. M. (eds.), *Identity and Anxiety; Survival of the Person in Mass Society* (Glencoe, Ill.: Free Press, 1960).

*38. See Sherif, M. and Cantril, H., *The Psychology of Ego-Involvements* (New York: Wiley, 1947), ch. 12, for extensive discussion of the loss of identity.

39. Jourard, S. M. and Remy, R. M., *op. cit.*

40. Horney sees the conviction that others do not like you as an important component of "basic anxiety"—the feeling of powerlessness in a potentially hostile world.

41. Riesman, D., *op. cit.*

42. The psychoanalysts speak of this unacknowledged aspect of the real self as the "unconscious"; Sullivan referred to it as "dissociated" aspects of the self.

43. *Cf.* Horney, K., *op. cit.*

44. Mowrer's theory of anxiety and the development of neurosis is related to this interpretation. See Mowrer, O. H., *op. cit.*, chs. 2, 6. See also Jourard, S. M., "Healthy Personality and Self-Disclosure," *Ment. Hyg.*, *43*, 499–507 (1959), for a discussion of real-self-being *versus* contrived self-presentation.

45. This movement is interpreted as "growth." For examples of some criteria of "growth," or improvement, see Rogers, C. R. and Dymond, R. F. (eds.), *op. cit.;* Conrad, D. C., "An Empirical Study of the Concept of Psychotherapeutic Success," *J. Consult. Psychol., 16,* 92–97 (1952); Barrabee, P., Barrabee, Edna L., and Finesinger, J. E., "A Normative Social Adjustment Scale," *Am. J. Psychiat., 112,* 252–259 (1955).

*46. See Combs, A. W. and Snygg, D., *Individual Behavior* (2nd ed.; New York: Harper, 1959), ch. 9, especially pp. 170–189.

47. Rogers and collaborators found that the subjects who profited from therapy showed essentially the characteristics indicated in the text. See Rogers, C. R. and Dymond, R. F. (eds.), *op. cit.*

*48. This discussion is adapted from ideas presented by Alan Watts, in Watts, A W., *The Way of Zen* (New York: Mentor, 1959).

49. *Cf.* Allport, G., *Becoming. Basic Considerations for a Psychology of Personality* (New Haven, Conn.: Yale. 1955).

CHAPTER 7
DEFENSE VERSUS GROWTH OF SELF

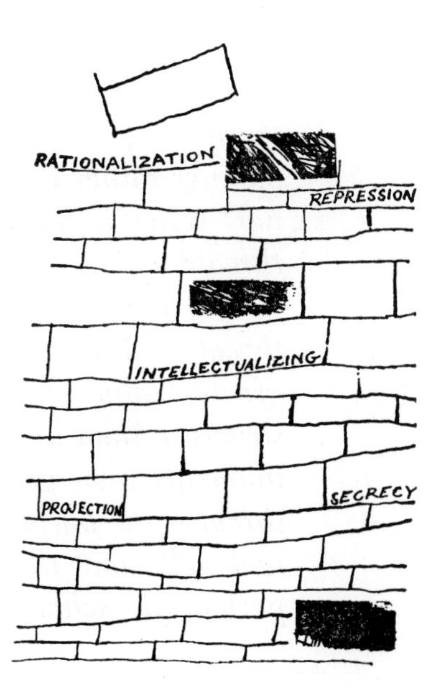

INTRODUCTION

If a person's ego is strong, it is likely his self-structure will "grow" with actual changes in his real self and in his behavior. Each time that threat is experienced, the person with a strong ego will face the threat, analyze it, and respond to it in a way which promotes further growth of his self-structure. His self-concept will keep pace with changes in the real self; and his self-ideal, public selves, and self-concept will continually be in a process of mutual adjustment toward congruence with each other and with the real self.

But no one possesses an ego of optimum strength at all times, and so we all respond to threat at least some of the time in a defensive *manner rather than in a growth-promoting manner. What is meant by a defensive response to threat?*

When a person responds defensively to any threat to his self-structure, he is actually placing a greater value upon maintaining his present self-structure than he is upon being his real self and upon his own growth. For in the last analysis, threat is the by-product of a conflict between the real self and the self-structure. Threat is experienced whenever some impulse, feeling, thought, memory, or perception conflicts with the person's beliefs about himself, with his self-ideal, or with one of his public selves. It is experienced as guilt, loss of the sense of identity, anxiety about the reactions of other people, and so on. And so, in order to preserve self-esteem, the present sense of identity, and the desired reactions of others to the self, the threatened individual may strive to ignore, hide, *or* distort *the inner experiences that produced the threat. Defense of the self-structure against threat is achieved by means of ignoring and distorting the perceptions that have induced threat. When the defenses have been effective, the experience of threat is eliminated from consciousness, but the person has missed an opportunity to grow.*

WHY DEFENSIVE REACTIONS TO THREAT ARE REGARDED AS UNHEALTHY

Personality hygienists regard indiscriminate defense of the self-structure as unhealthy because of the long-range consequences which it produces. Threat is very analogous with pain. When a person experiences pain, it is a signal that something is wrong with his body.[1] If he utilizes pain as a signal, the person will take active steps to remove the causes of the pain, thus prolonging his life. If the person anesthetizes his pain, *the factors which are responsible for the pain remain active;* as soon as the drug or anesthetic wears off, pain is again experienced. Further, since no action has been undertaken against the causes of the pain, the destructive action of these causes may have progressed considerably.

So it is with defensive reactions to threat. The various patterns of defensive behavior function much like anesthetics; they may be effective in neutralizing or reducing the unpleasant emotions of guilt and anxiety, but they do nothing to remove the factors which are producing the threat. Consequently the defensive person becomes addicted to defenses just as a pain-evader might become addicted to aspirin, codeine, serpisil, or alcohol. Neither person has the courage or ego-strength to investigate the causes of the unpleasant feelings and to take the steps necessary to remove the causes.

The person who habitually responds to threat with defense mechanisms eventually becomes alienated from his real self. He consumes energy in defending his self-structure and hence has little left over for constructive work. His relations with people are impaired because he does not have all of his real self accessible to him for interpersonal relationships. Ultimately, he must remain lonely and unknown to others, because he does not dare make himself known to others. In time, the habitual addict to defense mechanisms may display the clinical symptoms of neurosis and psychosis.[2]

WHAT ASPECTS OF THE REAL SELF TYPICALLY PRODUCE THREAT?

In our society, there are strong taboos directed against three classes of impulses, or feelings: viz., *sexuality*, *hostility*, and *dependency longings*.[3] Most individuals who have been socialized in the usual fashion internalize these taboos and embody them in their self-ideals. Thus, persons come to believe they should not experience sexual impulses at any time except during marriage. They come to believe they should not feel hostility and hatred toward anyone except those who violate the social mores. And men especially believe that once they have grown beyond childhood, they should not admit weakness and helplessness and longings to be taken care of.

The self-concept and the public selves of the average adult generally include these taboos. The average person wants, even needs, to believe he does not have socially disapproved sexual strivings, hostile feelings, or dependency longings; and he certainly doesn't want anyone else to believe he experiences these unwanted feelings and impulses.

Yet, the circumstances of life and of growth are such that, at the real-self level, these impulses and feelings all exist in everyone. People do become aroused to sexuality before they are married, and they have sexual longings for persons whom they are not supposed to be interested in as sexual partners: family members, people of the same sex, and so on.[4] People are aroused to hostility by provocations and provokers which society does not recognize as legitimate. We all experience hostility toward our parents, our children, our spouses, or close friends. And no adult is so self-reliant he has not experienced the wish to be a protected child at one time or another.

Another, more subtly threatening aspect of one's real self is the experience of *positive feelings* (that is, liking) toward another person. We do not have taboos directed against liking as we do against some aspects of sexuality, yet many persons are afraid to like another person and to let this liking be known. Instead, we commonly *pretend* to like many persons or things, even though the self-reported liking is not spontaneously experienced. Perhaps the repression of authentic liking reflects a fear that, in so transparently liking someone, we make ourselves more vulnerable to hurt than when our true likes are kept secret.

WHAT ARE DEFENSE MECHANISMS?

Defense mechanisms are automatic, involuntary ways in which a person reacts to threatening perceptions so that his self-structure will remain unchallenged and unchanged.[5] Whenever anything of value is threatened, the person will naturally strive to defend it. But there are realistic and rational ways of defending something of value, and there are unrealistic and irrational shortsighted ways of defending our values. If we value our body, and our body is threatened by disease, the rational means of defense is to study the disease, determine its cure, and administer this cure. The unrealistic and irrational means for defense is to ignore the pain, or anesthetize ourselves against the pain, and pretend there is no threat operative against our life and health.

If we value some theory, we can defend it unrealistically by distorting any evidence which conflicts with it or by ignoring this unwanted evidence. The earlier discussion of *autism* (Chapter 2) illustrates this kind of autistic cognition.

The defense mechanisms are autistic means of defending the self-structure. They make it possible for a person to continue believing he is the kind of person he wants to believe he is when there is much evidence (from the real self) to refute these beliefs.

DEFENSE MECHANISMS ARE INSTANCES OF UNCONSCIOUS INSTRUMENTAL BEHAVIOR. Instrumental behavior may be defined as any behavior undertaken by the individual so as to achieve some valued end. Most instrumental behavior is conscious or potentially subject to voluntary control. Defense mechanisms may be viewed as "preconscious," or unconscious, instrumental behavior. The defensive individual is not aware he is defending himself against threat. As a matter of fact, once a defensive person recognizes he *is* being defensive against some threatening impulse or feeling, he may achieve voluntary control over his defensive behavior.

We say that defense mechanisms are instances of instrumental action because they are potentially subject to voluntary control and because they are directed toward a valued end, namely, the reduction of the unpleasant experience of threat and the preservation of the present self-structure. In the language of learning theory, defense mechanisms illustrate both "avoidance" behavior and "escape" behavior; they help a person to avoid threat and to escape it once it occurs.

HOW DEFENSE MECHANISMS MILITATE AGAINST GROWTH. Growth may be defined as *change in a valued direction.* One of the goals of personality growth is a healthy self-structure, i.e., a state where the real self, the self-concept, the self-ideal, and the public selves are all mutually congruent. Whenever such a state of affairs exists, it can only be temporary—a sort of unstable equilibrium.[6] Any change in the real self is likely to disrupt this equilibrium, and such changes in the real self are always occurring. The self-structure grows when the necessary adjustments are made following real-self changes. But if the person defends his self-structure, then he will strive to ignore or distort the messages of his real self, thus preserving his present self-structure despite its increasing alienation from the real self.

The person who defends his self-structure against change and growth is like the aging matron who keeps wearing the clothing of an 18-year-old beauty queen, in spite of increasing girth. Her girdle may be so tight that she nearly faints daily, but she will not admit her clothing does not fit. So with a defended self-structure; the underlying real self may have become so discrepant from the self-concept, self-ideal, and public selves that the individual is really two distinct persons: the one he *believes* he is and the one he *really* is.

If the real self could be knocked out of commission by defense mechanisms, the individual would not suffer in consequence of his defensive operations. But the real self inevitably finds its way to expression. A real self which has been excluded by defense mechanisms manifests itself through the experience of suffering, boredom, frustration, vague anxiety and guilt, depression, unconscious motivation (see Chapter 2), and the symptoms of alienation from the self (see Chapter 6); in short, the whole repertoire of clinical psychopathology with which psychiatrists are familiar in their daily practice. Clinical symptoms of neurosis and of psychosis may be regarded as a by-product of the conflict between the real self and the attempt to preserve a self-structure markedly discrepant with it.

EXCESSIVE DEFENSIVENESS: A SIGN OF A WEAK EGO

A strong ego enables a person to face reality—inner and outer—without distortion or selection and to come to terms with this reality. When the ego is weak, the person ignores reality or reconstructs it so as to make it conform with his wishes and needs.[7] Before World War II broke out, the French believed the Maginot Line was adequate defense against any invasion. Evidently, they were unable to appreciate that the kind of threat imposed by Germany could not be stopped by stationary blockades. They probably ignored or distorted any evidence which carried the implication that France could easily be invaded. If the French military leaders had appreciated the full extent of danger, it would have been necessary to revise drastically their concepts of defensive warfare, and this would have required extensive reorganization of their entire army.

In the case of the self-structure, a person with a weak ego needs to believe he is the kind of person he *now* thinks he is. When conflicting evidence arises, he will distort or ignore this evidence and thus blithely believe that nothing has changed; he *is* the kind of person he believes he is. If he were to admit the conflicting evidence, it might call for all manner of changes. And so, against evidence, he wishfully believes there is no conflicting evidence.

BEHAVIOR PATTERNS COMMONLY EMPLOYED TO DEFEND THE SELF-CONCEPT

The mechanisms of defense might just as legitimately be called mechanisms for increasing self-alienation or methods of evading growth[8]—for such are their consequences. They are modes of behavior undertaken by a person with a relatively weak ego when threat to the self-structure arises. If they are effective, they reduce anxiety and guilt; but whenever the defenses are themselves weakened, threat is again experienced, for its causes continue to be operative. A defense is like a drug; it must be kept operative if it is to remain effective in removing discomfort. But a defense, like a drug, does not remove the causal conditions which are responsible for the pain and discomfort.

What are the major patterns of defensive behavior, and how may they be recognized? The person himself can seldom recognize his own defensiveness except under special conditions. The observer may be able to infer, from certain signs, the nature of the defense, the consequences of the defense, and the aspects of the real self which are being defended against.

REPRESSION. Repression is the most basic mode of defense.[9] It consists in actively excluding from awareness any thought, feeling, memory, or wish that would threaten the self-structure. The represser will actively resist even thinking about any theme or topic if it seems likely to induce anxiety or guilt. Freud introduced the concept of repression in order to explain some phenomena which he regularly observed in his efforts to treat neurotic patients. He found his patients displayed resistance to the injunction that they speak freely about *everything* which came to mind. He used the term *resistance* to describe any and every deviation from the injunction to speak freely. The term *repression* was invoked to explain the efforts of the person to avoid, not merely speaking about embarrassing or threatening topics, but even *thinking* about these topics.[10]

Repression manifests itself by the *omission* in the person's speech, emotion, and behavior-repertoire of responses which might ordinarily be expected under given circumstances. For example, if a person has been deeply insulted by someone and he displays no overt signs of hostility, the hypothesis can be entertained that he has repressed these feelings.

It should not be assumed that because some thought, feeling, or need has been repressed, it simply fades out of existence altogether. Rather, what appears to occur is that the repressed feelings and tensions continue to operate as *unconscious determiners of behavior* (see Chapter 2), because the causes of these feelings persist. The represser may betray many signs of his repressed feelings to a keen observer—in his dreams, accidents, slips of the tongue, and so on.

An important indicator of repression is a *refusal by the person to examine and consider any other motives for a given action than the one which he will consciously admit.* Thus, a person may spank his children quite severely, he may forget their birthdays, he never spends time with them at enjoyable activity, and he continually scolds them. An observer may gather the impression that such behavior expresses hatred and dislike of the children. He asks the father why he treats his children so. The father says, "Because I love them, and I am trying not to spoil them. I am trying to raise them right." If the observer asks him, "Could it be that you don't like your children?" the father might become quite indignant and refuse to explore the possibility that this might be true. He is repressing his hostility to his children. To admit that he dislikes his children might threaten his self-structure to a profound and catastrophic degree.

Another important indicator of repression is *selective recall of the past.*[11] In relating aspects of the past, much may be omitted from the account. If the observer knows what has been omitted he may confront the person with these details only to have him deny that the events occurred or else admit them reluctantly and with much tension. It is as if he had a vested interest in forgetting these details—so as to preserve his present concept of self. Many experimental research studies[12] have shown how our recall and our forgetting are determined to a high degree by the need to maintain self-esteem and to preserve the present self-concept.

In principle, a person can repress any aspect of his real self, whether it is socially desirable or socially reprehensible. Thus, a person may repress sexual urges, hostility, and so on; but *he may also repress his feeling of liking, his own intellect, and his own strength and resources,* if these real-self aspects imply some threat to his self-structure. There is reason to believe that the authoritarian-character, who exaggerates his own weakness and the strength of his hero or boss, is repressing his own powers and ascribing them (projecting them) to the authority figure in question. Fromm has detailed this point in his discussion of authoritarianism in everyday life and even in religion; he has suggested that the image of an all-powerful god, in contrast with weak, powerless man, rests on man's repression of his own powers and the ascription of these very powers to the deity.[13]

Repression is a very primitive means for the defense of the self-structure—it consists, fundamentally, in a denial that something real actually exists. The represser is denying that some aspect of his real self, past or present, actually exists. To admit that the feeling or wish exists as part of the self would call for a reorganization of the self-structure, and this may be too threatening and beyond the present strength of the individual's ego.

Yet, repression is quite an unstable mechanism, calling as it does for unremitting (but unconscious) effort from the person. Whenever there is any reduction in the energy which is devoted to repression, there is likely to be a *breakthrough of the repressed aspects of the real self.*[14] When this occurs, the person may be incredibly threatened by feelings and impulses he did not know that he possessed. It may happen that the feelings are so intense that the person explodes into uncontrolled activity—for instance, sexual or hostile violence. Probably many of the sex and homicide crimes which one reads about in the papers—"Nobody would have expected him to do that, he was always so nice, so moral"—illustrate the breakthrough of repressed feelings and impulses.

When repressed aspects of the self increase in strength, or when the energy available for repression decreases, these are the occasions when breakthroughs are most likely to occur. Thus, when fatigued, as before falling asleep, or during illness, a person may be overwhelmed with fantasies, feelings, and impulses that are shocking to him and to those who know him.[15]

Although repression is usually an involuntary and unconscious mechanism, recognizable only by its consequences of omissions in the person's behavior-repertoire, it is sometimes a conscious and deliberate activity. Every reader will recall occasions when he has had thoughts, feelings, or fantasies which were fully conscious but quite repugnant and threatening. On those occasions, he may have striven to get rid of the unwanted mental contents, by just putting them out of mind or by trying to change the subject of thinking, in order to think of more pleasant things. Such efforts, if successful, may be called voluntary and conscious repression. They are analogous with a conversation between two persons; when an unpleasant subject comes up, the person who finds it is unpleasant will ask that the subject be changed, or else he may skillfully guide the conversation so the dangerous topics are avoided before they arise. Some persons are quite skilled at sensing when an unpleasant subject is about to be discussed; they subtly direct the talk around and away from the loaded topic.

Thus, whenever some aspect of the real self provokes threat, a person with a weak ego may repress this aspect. The repression is carried out by means of refusing to think about it or by stopping thinking after a start has been made; or by not remembering aspects of the past; or by refusing to examine and accurately label motives for action. The reason for repression is that the self-structure must be protected against threatening, conflicting elements. Repression protects the individual against anxiety, guilt, and the loss of the sense of identity.

One of the aims of personality therapy is to undo the process of repression and to help the patient face, and acknowledge, the previously repressed aspects of his real self. Patients undergoing therapy are often quite shocked by some of the feelings and wishes they find within themselves. If their egos have been strengthened during the process of therapy, however, this increased contact with the real self does not necessarily lead to overt action upon the new impulses nor to renewed efforts at defense. Rather, the person is able to incorporate these newly experienced feelings into a more complete self-concept, and he is able to control his conscious impulses by voluntary suppression rather than automatic, involuntary, and unconscious repression.

RATIONALIZATION. Instrumental behavior is carried out usually in the service of fully conscious aims and goals. These aims are called motives. If a person is asked why he is doing something, or why he has done it, he is seldom at a loss to explain his motives. But a curious observation may be made. It is striking that whenever a person is asked why he did anything, his motives usually appear exemplary, to him and to the observer. A person will seldom admit any intentions of an immoral or antisocial sort. Yet the consequences of many actions are often discrepant with the admitted motive. Thus, a person intends to help his friend and actually interferes drastically with his friend's success. A man loves his wife, yet his behavior toward her may produce grief, pain, and discomfort for her.

For any given action that a person undertakes, it can be roughly assumed its *consequences were desired by the person.* If the aim is denied, or if the consequences appear at variance with the aim, then the observer may assume the *intent has been repressed.* The motive that the person admits may be called a *rationalization.* It is an explanation for an action and its consequences which is compatible with the individual's self-structure. The motive behind rationalization is not to give a factual account of the real intentions; rather, it is to do some justice to the need to explain conduct and yet, at the same time, protect the self-structure.

A more succinct definition of rationalization may be stated as follows: *A rationalization is an explanation of one's own motives and behavior which has been selected from among many possible explanations because it enhances and defends the individual's self-structure.*

A rationalization is not a conscious lie. When a person rationalizes his behavior and motives, he believes that his rationalization is true. The observer only begins to suspect the person is rationalizing when he finds the same behavior could be explained by other motives than the one which is admitted or when the consequences of action are strikingly inconsistent with the admitted aim.

If a person were not rationalizing, but rather was sincerely interested in discovering his own motivation, he would at least consider a number of different possible explanations for his conduct and select one or more which did the greatest justice to his conscious aims and to the actual consequences of his conduct. This quest might be threatening to the self-structure, but it would insure that the person was learning his own motivations. If a person with a weak ego needs to defend his present self-structure, he will rationalize his motives and actions and strongly resist any attempts from others to get him to explore his motives beyond the one motive he admits.

Patients who have undergone successful therapy will find themselves acknowledging a much broader range of motives for action than they did earlier; they are much less threatened by the act of exploring freely their own motivations, and they are better able to incorporate frankly admitted motives into their broadened self-structure.

The reader can assume that any explanation which he gives for his own conduct is at least in part a rationalization; i.e., the explanation is a by-product of an unconscious selection from among many motives, the one which is most compatible with self-esteem and the self-structure. If we assume, as the psychoanalysts do, that there is an unconscious component to *all* of our motivation, then it becomes increasingly clear that rationalization is a continuous activity for all of us; our conscious motives explain only part of our behavior. Our behavior serves unconscious aims as well as conscious ones. These aims are unconscious, or repressed, *because* they conflict with the self-structure.

Let us suppose a young man asks a girl for a date. His friend suggests he is asking for a date with this particular girl because it is known she is a "heavy petter." If the young man does not like to think of himself as a sexy young man, he may be threatened by this explanation. He will indignantly insist he is dating this girl because, and *only* because, he wants to discuss the lecture they both attended. He is probably rationalizing his motives.

Rationalization may be regarded as an attempt by the person to fill in the vacuum which repression leaves. We all have a strong need to make sense of our behavior to ourselves and to others. It is intolerable for us to act without knowing reasons. And so, if we have repressed our genuine, real-self motives, we replace them by constructing explanations which go part way in explaining the conduct but which serve the more important function of defending the self-structure. A crude rule of thumb for inferring rationalization is to ask a person to consider some motives other than the one which he admits. If he becomes intensely indignant at the suggestion, it may be provisionally assumed he is rationalizing his motives.

VERBAL REFORMULATION. There is a very subtle kind of defense mechanism which is closely related to rationalization. It is adopted usually by persons who have been well educated and who have an extensive vocabulary. Psychoanalysts originally called the mechanism in question *isolation,* and some psychiatrists and clinical psychologists refer to it as *intellectualizing.* We shall give it a more general name—*verbal reformulation.*

What verbal reformulation amounts to, in the last analysis, is selecting words to describe one's feelings, motives, perception, and behavior *on the basis of the feelings which they induce in the self.*[16] Thus, the same perception, thought, or motive, if stated one way, might invoke threatening feelings and meanings; if stated another way, with different language, these meanings and feelings are avoided. Let us illustrate with *euphemisms.* A euphemism may be defined as a nice way of talking about something which produces threatening feelings. Thus, some people are made uncomfortable by frank discussions about biological functions; they refer to pregnancy with the term "infanticipating" or with the French word *enceinte.* Menstruation may be referred to as "falling off the roof" or "a visit from Aunt Nellie." Most of us have been trained to avoid obscene words; only nasty, evil people swear. And some of the words to describe excreta are regarded as obscene; children who employ four-letter Anglo-Saxon words in reference to bodily wastes are severely punished. Even to think these words is enough to induce anxiety and threat. And so euphemisms or technical terms may be learned as substitutes.

The mechanism of verbal reformulation—earlier called isolation and intellectualization—was discovered by personality therapists. They found that their patients, in talking about past experiences or present feelings, were avoiding any unwanted emotions by carefully choosing their language on the basis of its "feel." Thus, a patient who might break into tears if he admitted he hated his father might relate to the therapist, "You know, I do have some antipathy against my father." If the therapist reflected back, "You mean you hated the old boy," the patient might become severely upset. A patient from a lower-class background was striving to elevate her socio-economic status. She spoke of her sexual affairs, not in the four-letter language of her partners, but rather in pseudotechnical terms: "Well, I had an intercourse with him, and then I had an intercourse with that other fellow, and an intercourse with still another man, and so on."

Words are very powerful conditioned stimuli; they carry with them emotional meanings as well as cognitive ones. Jung[17] regarded certain words as "complex-indicators"—stimuli for strong but repressed emotional responses. The familiar word-association lists are illustrations of how words are associated with both cognitive and emotional responses.

It is in order to avoid the unwanted emotional tensions which some words produce that verbal reformulation is adopted as a defense. Verbal reformulation, as a defense, takes many different forms in usage. Thus, it may be manifested through chronic *understatement.* The Englishman is stereotyped as a man who might describe some horrible and terribly emotional experience as follows: "It was a bit thick, a bit of a shaky do."

Intellectualizing, the use of technical language to describe events, behavior, and motives, often reflects defensive verbal reformulation. If the person were to use other language to describe the same things, the feelings which might be provoked would be overly threatening. One patient could not even think, much less say, the common vulgar word for *flatus.* The four-letter word, when spoken or even thought, would bring back the memory of a very painful episode which occurred early in childhood involving flatulence in a social situation.[18]

Obscenity[19] itself may be an instance of verbal reformulation for purposes of defense of the self-structure; a person may be able to accept himself only if he is rough and tough and virile, and he believes that swearing is synonymous with masculinity or emancipation from parents. Thus, an educated person who compulsively uses profane words may be employing them to keep dependency feelings and "sissy" feelings in a repressed status.

Verbal reformulation thus takes many forms. In a sense, this defense may be regarded as an adjunct to repression as well as a positive means of defending the self-structure against the real self. As long as the person formulates his inner experience in the particular language which he employs, he is protecting himself against the feelings and memories which other language might invoke. The unwanted feelings and memories remain repressed.

A person with a strong ego and a healthy self-structure is not obliged to limit the vocabulary with which he will think about and describe his inner experience; he can pick words and concepts, not on the basis of the feelings they induce in him and the associations they stir up; rather, he can think and talk in the words which are the most richly descriptive of his experience.

Scientists are probably among the worst offenders in the use of verbal reformulation. In scientific work, it is important to use language which is neutral with respect to emotional meanings; emotion is deemed a barrier to effective experimentation; it distorts perception and steers thinking into autistic channels. But in everyday interpersonal relations, emotions play an important role. The scientist may be actually afraid of his own emotions, and so he depersonalizes his relationships with his wife, children, and friends and may use the language of technical science in his interpersonal relationships outside the laboratory and the classroom.

REACTION-FORMATION. A person may defend himself against unwanted, threatening thoughts, feelings, and wishes, first by repressing them and then by compulsively thinking and striving to feel the opposite. It is as if it were not sufficient for the person to free himself of threat by merely eliminating the unwanted thoughts and feelings from his mind and overt action. He can only convince himself (and others?) he is not that kind of a person if, and only if, he displays the *opposite* kinds of behavior in extreme degree. Reaction-formation reveals itself through the compulsive and exaggerated nature of the behavior and attitudes which the person manifests;[20] yet the repressed aspects of the real self may still leak out. Thus, a compulsively generous person may betray his repressed egocentricity and selfishness by giving gifts which the receiver does not like or cannot use: he gives expensive cigarette lighters to nonsmokers and bottles of expensive Scotch whiskey to teetotalers. The person who is *compulsively* kind to animals betrays underlying sadism by the brutality with which invective is leveled against those who experiment with animals.[21] The devoted, overprotective mother prevents her child from growing by her exaggerated overconcern with his health and safety.[22] The guilty, philandering husband showers his wife with lavish gifts and with surprising and unusual tenderness and solicitude. The man with repressed dependency-strivings displays exaggerated self-reliance, until he gets sick, when he becomes a virtual baby.

A person with a strong ego can acknowledge a wide range of his real motives and feelings, and his behavior is much more guided by reality-contact than by the need to defend his self-structure. The person who employs reaction-formation displays a rigidity and an exaggeration in his everyday behavior which leads the observer to exclaim, with Shakespeare, "The lady [or man] doth protest too much, methinks." Whenever one observes exaggerated behavior of the sorts described above, one can suspect that it exemplifies reaction-formation; one can look for evidence of repressed aspects of the real self in other aspects of the person's behavior-repertoire: in dreams, accidents, and so on.

Aside from manifest attitudes and behavior, reaction-formation may be revealed in the actual content of the person's thoughts. It was pointed out that repression may take the form of stopping thinking or refusing to think about threatening topics and themes. A represser may "tamp down" the repressed material by compulsively occupying his thoughts with content that is opposite in moral significance; he thinks the opposite, as it were. Thus, a person with repressed sexual strivings may frantically preoccupy himself with thoughts of a religious nature, often to an obsessional degree. He cannot rid his mind of the religious thoughts, and so his work-efficiency may be impaired. The overprotective mother who is repressing much hostility toward her child may become obsessed by thoughts that the child's health and life are in danger. A solicitous wife, who is repressing hostility to her traveling husband, may say on his return: "I couldn't sleep or eat while you were gone. I kept thinking your car turned over and that you had been seriously injured or killed."

PROJECTION. The ability to perceive the world accurately is an achievement that is relatively difficult to attain. The probability is high that persons will perceive the world autistically unless they have taken active steps to reality-test their perceptions. Autistic perception is animistic and "physiognomic." The young child, the regressed psychotic, and to some extent, primitive people, all manifest primitive perception.[23] Primitive perception is characterized by the tendency for the individual to assume that animals, trees, water, nature, and so on, are personalized; that they have motives, feelings, and wishes just as the perceiver himself has motives, feelings, and wishes. The defense mechanism of projection is a special case of primitive perception. *Projection is the name given to the tendency to assume that another person has motives, feelings, wishes, values, or, more generally, traits which the individual himself has.*

If a person assumes that someone else is similar to himself, the term *assimilative projection* is used to describe such an assumption. If the person assumes that someone else has motives or feelings which are denied, disowned, or repressed in the self, the term *disowning projection* is employed.[24] Both varieties of projection manifest themselves in the perceptions and beliefs one formulates concerning another person.

Projection as such is not a defense mechanism; rather, it might be called *mis*perception of another person. Or, it may be regarded as a sort of logical fallacy—the act of formulating beliefs about another person's motives and feelings without adequate evidence. Thus, I may notice that some man resembles me in age, sex, educational level, and so I assume he is responding to some situation in a manner identical with my own response. Both of us look at a pretty girl. I notice I am pleasantly affected by the girl, and I assume that the other person is similarly affected. Further questioning of the other person may prove my assumption is wrong, but my assumption itself illustrates *assimilative* projection.

But suppose I have repressed any interest in pretty girls; to admit any such interest might threaten my self-structure. I may assume the other fellow is very interested in the pretty girl, but I would myself vehemently deny any such interest. I could be just as wrong. But if I assumed the other fellow had erotic wishes that I denied in myself, I would be displaying *disowning projection.* This unwarranted assumption about the other person's motives would be a defense mechanism. I would be protecting my self-concept by repressing certain feelings in myself and assuming without warrant that other people, not I, are motivated by such unacceptable drives.

The evidence which prompts the observer to suspect disowning projection is to be found in the beliefs which a person holds concerning his own motivation and that of others. One suspects disowning projection if (a) the motives imputed to others are derogatory and immoral, (b) such motives are vigorously denied in the self, (c) there is not much evidence to support the belief that the other person has the motives imputed to him, and (d) the person himself gives evidence of these imputed motives, but at an unconscious level.

As was suggested earlier, a person can disown and project not only unsavory aspects of his real self, he can also repress and project his own positive potentialities. Where this occurs, the person perceives himself as imperfect, weak, and base, while the object of his projection is perceived as perfect, strong, and ideal. Authoritarian-characters appear to do this. Many a romantic lover, too, has seen himself as worthless and evil and has projected his own moral potential to his object, perceiving her as the embodiment of all that is clean, wonderful, and morally perfect. He may become disillusioned when reality sets in.

Both varieties of projection are manifested in persons with weak egos; assimilative and disowning projection are actually instances of impaired contact with social reality. Disowning projection is the only kind of projection which can properly be called a defense mechanism. Bigoted persons appear to predicate many of their beliefs about the shortcomings of minority group members on disowning projection. They perceive themselves and their fellow group members as free from all kinds of moral shortcomings and ascribe these shortcomings to the members of the minority group. The bigot would strongly resist any suggestion that the same undesirable traits existed in himself, although at an unconscious level.[25]

Projection is often a very subtle mechanism, difficult to detect because it may happen that the motives imputed (through projection) to the other person are almost accurate. One can only become reasonably sure that a person is projecting if one knows the other person actually does not have the traits imputed to him or if one knows that the suspected projector has not yet had an opportunity to know the personality and motives of the person whom he is describing.

DEFENSIVE DISCRIMINATION. Perception is strongly dependent upon classification and discrimination. We classify things into categories and assign different labels to them on the basis of perceptible differences.[26]

One important aspect of normality is the ability to form categories similar to those formed by the majority of group members and the ability to make discriminations, i.e., to notice differences among objects and situations, in socially shared ways. A person may defend his self-structure by *not* noticing differences which are apparent to others, and he may likewise defend his self-structure by *making discriminations* which no one else would make. It is the latter which we call defensive discrimination. To illustrate: A situation may be one which calls for honest behavior. The individual takes pride in his honesty. But if he stands to gain richly from dishonest behavior, he might pick out some aspect of the situation which enables him to say, and believe, "*This situation is different.* Conventional morality does not prevail here." The disinterested observer fails to see the difference. But the defensive discriminator will strongly resist any attempts that are made to show him that the situation in which he is cheating is really no different from a situation where morality prevails. Thus, some persons may be scrupulously honest in their dealings with individual persons, but they cheat the government or large corporations without blushing. "It's different," they might say.

A person might relieve himself of fear and anxiety if he can single out some aspect of a fear-provoking and dangerous situation which differentiates it (for him) from other, similar situations. Yet, the detached observer may notice the situation objectively is dangerous. So long as he can believe in the difference, however, the defensive individual can remain relatively free from fear and anxiety.

In extreme forms, this tendency to make discriminations which are not shared by others is a symptom of serious personality illness: schizophrenia. The schizophrenic not only classifies his experience in deviant ways, he also makes deviant discriminations.[27] Perfectly safe food may be perceived as poisonous because of some barely noticeable difference in color or temperature between the food-serving today and the same food which was served yesterday. The healthy personality can tell the difference between a difference which *makes* a difference and one which does not.

DEFENSIVE CLASSIFICATION. A person may classify completely different things into the same category, not because they belong together, but so as to defend his self-structure. Things are classified into categories on the basis of fundamental or essential properties: viz., function, structure, color, and so on. One of the signs of psychiatric normality is the ability to form concepts or to classify objects in ways that are shared by the majority of persons.[28] A loss in this ability is deemed to be a sign of schizophrenia or of brain damage. Among persons with only moderately impaired ego-strength, classification of objects, persons, or situations may be made in the service of defense rather than on the basis of real (i.e., socially agreed-upon) similarities. Thus, a person may classify persons into categories on the basis of superficial and unnecessary similarities because he *needs* all the members of the group to be similar to each other. He needs them to be similar so as to defend his present ways of behaving toward those persons. If he recognized individual differences among all the members of the particular class which he has constructed, it might call for self-threatening readjustments of his present interpersonal behavior-repertoire. Thus, a person may say, "All women are alike," when it is apparent that there are important individual differences among women. But so long as he believes they are alike, he does not have to alter his present ways of behaving toward women. Or, he may believe that all Negroes are alike, and so on.

Not all faulty classification can be regarded as defensive in function. Autistic classification may simply reflect impaired ego-strength. We can regard faulty classification as defensive only when there is evidence to show that the person actually is protecting and enhancing his self-structure by his deviant modes of classifying.

In another context (Chapter 9) we speak of *attribution* as a means by which inaccurate other-concepts are formed. Attribution refers to the assumption that because a present person has one trait in common with someone in the past, then the present person has many or all of the traits which were known in the person from the past. Attribution is an instance of defensive classification. So long as one believes that the present person is similar to the past person, one does not have to learn new ways of relating to him. In personality therapy, the phenomenon of "transference" illustrates attribution and defensive classification. The therapist may be classified into the category "just like mother" or "just like father." Much therapeutic gain follows when the patient is able to know that the therapist is really different from his mother and father, in spite of superficial similarities.

PERCEPTUAL DEFENSE. Repression is really an instance of refusing to see or hear aspects of inner reality: the real self. But one can defend one's self-structure by refusing to see or hear aspects of outer reality if such perception would result in threat to the self-structure. The psychoanalyst coined the term *denial* to describe this tendency to ignore aspects of outer reality which induced anxiety, fear, or losses in self-esteem. Experimental psychologists use the term *perceptual defense* to describe the same phenomena. Sullican spoke of "selective inattention" in this connection. In Chapter 2, the concept of perceptual defense was discussed and documented in greater detail. In the present section, we shall only restate some of this material.

Humans seem to have a very strong tendency to ignore or reconstruct reality when reality is pain-producing. It is such a stubborn tendency that Freud spoke of it as one of the "principles" of mental functioning—the *pleasure principle* in contrast with the *reality principle.*[29] It is as if when there are two possible meanings which might be assigned to some perception, one pleasant but untrue and the other true but painful, we must actually *fight* the pleasure principle in order to arrive at accurate cognition. Thus, we do not hear derogatory remarks uttered by someone about us even though our hearing is quite adequate to notice whispered praise. We do not see the blemishes in our loved ones if our self-esteem rests on the premise that we have made a wise choice of a perfect mate. In extreme forms, among persons with very weak egos, we may actually see something quite clearly but then deny we saw it and believe the denial. For some persons the death of a loved one is so catastrophic, calling as it does for much reorganization of behavior and the self-structure, that they will not believe the person is dead.

PERCEPTUAL SENSITIZATION. If a person is habitually quite anxious, he may become quite sensitized to all stimuli which have the significance of danger. He might be able to detect their imminence and onset at very low degrees of intensity. It is as if eternal vigilance is the price he must pay, not to protect just his self-structure, but even his life.[30] Thus a person may actually perceive hostility in others long before a nonanxious individual might. He is sensitized to it, as it were. It is probably true that we have become extremely sensitized to the feelings of other people toward us, insofar as we are becoming other-directed characters (as Riesman suggests).

While sensitization may well serve a defensive function, it may actually lead us to misinterpret the motives and feelings of other people. We may misinterpret others' motives because we interpret too quickly, before enough evidence is available. Oversensitization and vigilance are similar to the behavior of the "bomb-happy" discharged soldier who reacts to each car-backfiring as if it were an 88mm shell.

ISOLATION. Much of the meaning which psychoanalysts imputed to the term isolation has been incorporated into the concept of verbal reformulation. We shall employ the word *isolation* to describe any activity which a person undertakes so as to divest a perception, thought, or act of its threatening emotional implications.[31] Thus a person may commit some crime or some immoral act. If he allowed himself to think about these things freely, he might be led inevitably to guilt and condemnation of himself. However, he might be able to avoid these threatening feelings if he isolates his acts from the rest of his life. He may admit he has done these things, but he refuses to allow himself to make moral judgments. Isolation most often takes the form of refusing to evaluate one's own actions. One admits they were performed, but one does not evaluate them as other acts might be evaluated. So long as this evaluative thinking is repressed, the threatening action is encapsulated, as it were. It has no connection with the total self.

"Sunday Christians" may be viewed as individuals who employ the mechanism of isolation. All week, they may violate most of the moral precepts they supposedly affirm, but they experience no guilt because this behavior is isolated from evaluative judgments. A term which has often been employed as nearly synonymous with isolation is "living in logic-tight compartments." As we have used the term, isolation is actually a case of repressing value-judgments so as to avoid guilt.

COMPENSATION. For most of us, success in any undertaking is an important determiner of self-esteem. But our coping efforts do not always meet with success. When we fail at some endeavor, some threat to the self-structure is the consequence. In order to rid ourselves of the unpleasant feelings of inferiority that failure might produce, we often pursue some substitute goal. The response to feelings of failure by pursuing substitute, second-best goals is termed *compensation*. Considered by itself, compensation is neither healthy nor unhealthy. We can judge compensation from a health point of view only in terms of its long-range consequences. If a person perpetually failed, and satisfied himself with second-best all his life, we would regard his compensatory activity as unhealthy, for he might always carry unconscious inferiority feelings. It would be healthier if he could lower his level of aspiration or modify his self-ideal. But the ability to compensate is actually a healthy one, because no one meets with success all the time, in every venture.

Overcompensation is the name given to a special kind of compensatory activity. If a person has failed in reaching some goal because of some personal inadequacy, he may devote so much effort toward altering his inadequate traits that they actually become overdeveloped. For example, a person may have failed to win a certain girl because of his "97-pound-weakling" physique. Instead of compensating for this failure by pursuing some other girl, he might enroll in a physical culture course, devoting all of his time and money to the quest for a Herculean, muscle-bound physique. This might be called overcompensation.

Actually, overcompensation is a special case of reaction-formation—it could be renamed "denial by overdoing."

Persons with strong egos will adopt compensation, not necessarily as a defense of their self-structure, but rather as a means of insuring for themselves at least some gratifications after their efforts at some goal have failed. The person with a weaker ego is profoundly threatened by his failures; we can speak of compensation as a defense mechanism only when there is enough evidence to show that the person is pursuing some other goal, not to make up for missed pleasures, but rather to restore self-esteem which has been threatened by failure at some instrumental activity.

PSYCHIC CONTACTLESSNESS. This term, which was coined by Wilhelm Reich,[32] refers to an inability, or a refusal, to communicate with or get emotionally involved with another person. If one has been deeply hurt in relationships with people, one might protect oneself against further hurt and losses in self-esteem by walling the self off from people. One is *among* people without being really *with* them. Avoidance of close contact and emotional involvement with others serves many defensive functions, not the least of which is the fact that others will never come to know you. Since others are never given the opportunity to observe his real self, the contactless person can entertain all manner of grandiose fantasies about himself, and these are never known or criticized by others. Horney's concept of "moving away from people" is closely similar in meaning to the concept of contactlessness.

DEPERSONALIZING OTHERS. If an individual does not allow himself to think of others as human beings with feelings, hopes, and so on, he can protect himself in many ways. He may be afraid to become personally involved, and so he stubbornly refuses to pay any attention to the other person as a feeling, sensitive human being. Instead, other people are just the embodiment of their social role; they are workers, or wives, or doctors, not men and women or *human persons*. The act of depersonalizing others may thus protect the person against guilt feelings he might experience if he knew he was hurting others. Or, if he suffers from an inability to love, he might protect himself against such a disquieting insight through depersonalizing others. Physicians, nurses, and dentists often depersonalize their patients or clients, adopting a "bedside manner," or a "chairside manner," when dealing with them. The adoption of such contrived patterns of interaction permits them to treat their patients without being disturbed by the latters' suffering. Further, it permits them to hide their true feelings of like or dislike behind a professional mask.[33]

FIXATION AND REGRESSION

There are two defensive maneuvers, fixation and regression, that cannot be understood properly without a preliminary discussion of the concepts of growth and of age-grading. Personality *growth* refers to changes in the various aspects of personality, so that the individual conforms with his successive *age-roles*.[34] Each society has its concepts of expected behavior for each age level, and socialization practices are designed to promote the acquisition of behavior patterns which are deemed appropriate to each age level. For each aspect of personality, a growth-sequence which is typical for a given society can be observed and described. Thus, the food and the eating habits of the infant differ from those of the child, the adult, and the senile person. The sexual fantasies, objects, and practices differ from age level to age level. In our society, psychologists have made attempts to specify in explicit fashion the behavior patterns which are believed to be modal or typical for the various age levels. Intelligence tests,[35] and growth norms such as those established by Gesell,[36] are examples of formal, scientific age-grading in our society. The psychoanalytic theory of stages in psychosexual development is another example of descriptive norms for personality development.[37] Maslow's theory of a hierarchy of needs is, in a sense, a normative developmental theory.[38] Murphy's doctrine of stages in the development of perception—global, differentiated, and integrated perception—is a developmental theory.[39] Werner's distinctions between primitive and developed mental activities are illustrative of crude growth norms.[40] Fromm's distinction between authoritarian and humanistic conscience may be viewed as a rough developmental distinction.[41] The reader is urged to acquaint himself with the details of these various theories of developmental stages as they apply to various aspects of personality, for they serve as the basis for judgments which have high importance in our society—judgments about maturity, rates of growth, retardation, fixation, and regression.

At any given chronological age, it is possible to describe the various aspects of a personality and make judgments about how mature, developed, or appropriate to that age are each of these aspects. Thus, we might study John's personality in detail, and on the basis of our observations and comparisons with age norms, arrive at conclusions of this sort: "In terms of breadth of knowledge, John is quite *advanced* for his age. His skill-repertoire is greater than that which is typical of other sixteen-year-olds. His emotional responses, however, are similar to those usually found in five-year-olds; his emotionality is *fixated*. Also, we find that his needs appear to be fixated; he strives after goals similar to those pursued by much younger children. Whenever John meets with frustration, we find there is a generalized *regression* of all aspects of personality; his perceptions become autistic, his emotions appear infantile, his fantasies become juvenile, his instrumental behavior becomes diffuse and disorganized, and so on."

From this discussion, it should now be apparent that the concepts of growth, fixation, regression, precocity, retardation, deterioration, and so on, all are meaningless except with reference to explicit age or growth norms.

Growth of personality—learning ways of solving problems and satisfying needs which correspond with the ideals and expectations for each age level—is highly valued by personality hygienists. In fact, some theorists hold that all varieties of personality illness derive from either growth-resistance (fixation) or from growth-regression. The psychoanalytic theory of neurosis, for example, explains neurotic symptomatology as a case of fixation or regression in growth.

Obsessive-compulsive neurosis is thought to derive from stress applied to a person who has been *fixated* at the phallic stage of development. In consequence of the stress, the fixated individual regresses to the anal level of psychosexual development. The obsessive and compulsive symptoms are interpreted as infantile attempts to master conflicts and solve problems which are appropriate, or normal, in a five-year-old but neurotic when they arise in an adult.[42]

Now that we have discussed norms for growth, we shall focus more directly on fixation and regression as modes of defense.

FIXATION AS DEFENSE. The self-structure is a very powerful determiner of *fixation* of behavior. When new problems arise for solution, then new patterns of behavior are required from the person. But new situations—the "unknown"—generally provoke *anxiety* in a person. Further, the new behavior patterns might conflict strongly with the present self-structure. If the individual acts in the new ways that the situation demands, he might become threatened. Therefore, he may *resist the new learning*, and his old behavior patterns will become more strongly reinforced—fixated.[43]

We can visualize the total personality of an individual as being comprised of traits which differ in the degree to which they are fixated. Some traits are quite flexible and easily modified, while others are stubbornly resistant to change. It is the latter which are fixated. The fact of fixation helps us to understand why we can often find, even in a very mature and healthy personality, some traits which appear paradoxically juvenile, childish, or undeveloped. They have been fixated as a defense against the threat to the self-structure which abandonment of the trait and learning new traits would produce.

Thus, we may know a person who strikes us as being very mature and relatively healthy in most aspects of personality. But he persists in relating to women in a manner similar to the way in which he related to his mother when he was very young. This particular interpersonal trait has been fixated; for him, other ways of relating to women may be greatly threatening. Even though this fixated trait might produce all kinds of problems for the man in his dealings with women, yet he is able to keep his present self-structure intact only as long as the trait remains unchanged.

REGRESSION AS DEFENSE. Regression means, basically, growth "in reverse." When a person regresses, it may be a highly *selective* regression, where only one trait changes from its present form to one which was typical of the person at a younger age; or, it may be a more *global* regression, where all aspects of the personality become more "primitive."

Clinical and experimental studies have warranted the generalization that regression is a reaction to stress, frustration, and deprivation.[44] If ego-strength is relatively low, the person cannot preserve his present level of performance under stressing conditions, and so he might come to manifest more primitive and childish reactions. Regression may be a *transient* reaction to stress, or it may be a relatively permanent, almost *irreversible* reaction. Transient regression is very common—it happens to all of us. We may burst into tears when we have been thwarted, but later we learn to master the obstacles to gratification of our needs in a more adult manner. We may deliberately regress from our adult, formal roles and become apparently childish in our behavior just for purposes of fun and enjoyment. It is possible that the ability to regress is an important determiner of many forms of creative work.

Permanent regression is more properly indicative of a defensive process. If a person has been finding it difficult to gain satisfactions in conforming to an adult role, he may regress to some level of functioning which yields him greater satisfactions. This regression serves the function of defending the self-structure or at least the sense of identity of the individual, and it may further defend the value of gratification-richness. If the person, through regressing, is able to force others in his social situation to take care of his needs, his regression may become permanent. If the regression is extreme, as in severe psychoses, the person is able to obtain only fantasy-gratifications; but in less severe regressions, very real satisfactions may be obtained.

It should be pointed out that regression itself may be a strong threat to the present self-structure. In order to reduce the threat which regression might produce, the individual may have to formulate elaborate rationalizations in order to justify the regression. The real reason for regressing may be a fear of inadequacy in present situations. The rationalization for regressing might be: "I deserve to be taken care of because I am sick."

DEFENSE OF THE PUBLIC SELF

The repertoire of public selves constructed by an individual is very important to him for practical reasons. It is only so long as the other person holds the desired set of beliefs about him that the individual can feel reassured his needs will be satisfied and his valued ends secured. Consequently, it is not enough for him simply to construct the public selves by appropriate behavior and verbal definition of his personality to others. Once he has constructed a public self, he is obliged to defend and maintain it. How is this done?

The most general means of defending and maintaining the public self is by means of *selective suppression of* behavior and emotional expression which is inconsistent with the public self.

Sometimes, in order to defend a public self, the individual is obliged to lie. A mother may have heard reports about her son's behavior which conflict with her concept of him. She confronts him with the report, and he denies it flatly. He does not want her to believe that he behaves in such a way.

Secrecy is more common than lying as a means of defending public selves. We can do almost anything without fear (though not necessarily without guilt) if only no one observes or discovers what we have done. The secret activities may be incredibly disparate with the public selves of the individual. Men at conventions sometimes display behavior markedly different from their usual home-town behavior and are quite disconcerted if their family and neighbors hear reports of their conduct.[45]

A really intelligent person can construct various public selves with ingenuity and finesse—sometimes fantastically diverse and contradictory selves. The more diverse they are, however, the greater the difficulty in maintaining them; very often persons who hold contrasting concepts of the individual may meet him simultaneously, and he is at a loss to know how to behave.

DEFENSE OF THE SELF-IDEAL

The self-ideal is comprised of values. The individual may formulate these values in various ways: as abstract propositions of right and wrong or as very specific prescriptions and formulas which specify how he should behave in various situations. When once a self-ideal has been constructed, or "built into" a person, it becomes a fairly fixed structure, strongly resistant to change. In fact, when confronted with social pressure to change his values, a person may diligently resist all such external pressures. We might ask here, "Why will a person resist efforts to alter his values, i.e., his self-ideal? Consider, for example, an individual with a very pathological level of aspiration. He sets incredibly high standards of performance in situations involving competitive achievement, never attains those levels, and as a consequence believes that he is worthless, a complete failure. If only his self-ideal could be altered, his behavior and his self-concept could remain unchanged, and he would experience self-esteem, perhaps for the first time in his life. Yet, when he is urged to relax his standards, he will refuse or else say, "I wish I could, but I can't."

One of the reasons why a person finds it difficult to examine, criticize, and alter his values is because they came from sources he dares not question—his parents, teachers, God, the Bible, and so on. His values have been acquired in the context of an authoritarian relationship, and he dreads all manner of horrible consequences should he question or defy the "commands."[46] Values and ideals acquired in this way are quite analogous with orders from a superior officer in the army. The private is "not to reason why," he must obey. If he has been rigorously trained in authoritarian fashion, he is likely to get anxious at the bare thought or mention of disobedience, criticism, or personal alteration of the orders. Many people deal with their self-ideal in the same fashion. For them to question their values is unthinkable. They just obey. They are afraid (for reasons unknown to them) to examine their values in the light of critical reason, and they will not brook anyone else's questioning their values. In short, they will avoid thinking about, that is, they will repress, all criticism of the self-ideal and its component values and "shoulds." Freud said, "As the child was once compelled to obey its parents, so the ego submits to the categorical imperative pronounced by its superego."[47]

This fear of obscure consequences, if one should examine, criticize, and change one's values, presents a powerful conserving force in the self-structure. Although the self-concept is very resistant to change, observation discloses that the conscience is even more resistant to change. A person may anesthetize his conscience with alcohol, he may lull it with self-deceptive arguments and rationalizations, he may even repress it by refusing to think of his values and refusing to compare his behavior with his ideals; but he will rarely change it and then only under highly specialized circumstances.[48]

DEFENSE VERSUS GROWTH OF THE SELF-STRUCTURE

The many ways to defend the self-structure all have the consequence of keeping the self-structure constant. If the self-structure is fixed and resistant to change, the likelihood is great that the behavior patterns of the person will become increasingly fixated, or crystallized. His responses to life situations will become increasingly predictable, sometimes to an almost caricatured degree; people can set their watches by the individual in question.

Such fixity in behavior and in the self-structure is perfectly fine—or would be, if the environment in which the person lived was absolutely unchanging. Then like the dinosaurs during their epoch on earth, he would be remarkably well adjusted to his surroundings. Like the dinosaurs, he would live as long as physical health allowed and would find a maximum number of satisfactions in living. But when the dinosaurs' environment changed, the beasts died off. Their physical structure was such that they could not alter their highly fixed repertoire of responses so as to survive. Humans living in modern cultures are unlikely to die because of rigidity in their behavior; but they are likely to experience a good deal of misery if they are unable to change. Modern personality hygienists and therapists assert that it is only as a person continues to meet new situations, and modifies his behavior and his self-structure, that he will grow. This is another way of asserting that the personality hygienist values change of behavior and self-structure of a special kind. He does not value the kinds of changes which a psychiatrist would call regressive, or psychotic. He does, however, value changes which move the person in the direction of greater productivity, of mastery over the environment (see Chapter 1 for the heuristic portraits of healthy personality), and which produce increasing congruence among the self-concept, behavior, self-ideal, and public selves.

The defense mechanisms actually interfere with personality growth, as this has been defined. They preserve, even "freeze", the individual's self-structure. When it has become unduly frozen, it becomes also brittle, and can crack. The individuals whom psychiatrists call neurotic, or psychotic, or who have "nervous breakdowns," are generally individuals who have a frozen self-structure which cracks under the pressure of too much conflicting evidence—evidence which conflicts with the self-concept, evidence which results in catastrophic losses of self-esteem, and evidence which results in the person's living in dread of public shaming and ridicule.

RECOGNIZING DEFENSIVE BEHAVIOR

The preceding list of defense mechanisms does not include all that have been recognized and described by students of behavior; it may be regarded as a list of those which are relatively common. In principle, any behavior pattern whatsoever may serve defensive functions as well as other aims. It is desirable, at this point, to suggest the means by which an observer can recognize defensiveness when he sees it.

In general, defense mechanisms are behavior patterns which are motivated by anxiety and guilt. When they are operating, the person does not directly experience these unpleasant affects. But defensive behavior differs from positive, goal-oriented instrumental behavior in a fundamental respect. Where positive, goal-directed behavior is quite flexible within certain limits, defensive behavior is not. Any interference with defensive behavior is apt to induce anger, anxiety, guilt, depression, or other unwanted affects in the defensive individual. Defense mechanisms are like emergency measures;[49] they are the crutch upon which the individual's security hinges, that is, the security of a person with diminished ego-strength. And when anyone's security and self-esteem are threatened, he will become upset. And so, the best means for ascertaining whether or not some behavior is defensive is to observe what happens when this behavior is interfered with. If it gives rise to anxiety, hostility, depression, or guilt, then one is justified in at least suspecting that some aspect of the real self is being hidden by the behavior in question.

EGO-STRENGTH AND GROWTH OF THE SELF-STRUCTURE

The self-structure is not synonymous with personality; rather, the self-structure is only a part of the total personality. If an individual's ego is strong, his self-structure at any given time is likely to be quite congruent with his real self. But again it should be stated that the congruence of the self-structure with the real self, at any point in time, is only temporary. The real self is continually changing; new needs arise, new feelings, memories, and so on, crowd into conscious awareness; and usually (but not always) these new experiences induce threat, for they do actually threaten the present self-structure.

If the person has a strong ego, and if he values self-honesty, he will respond to the threat, not by defensive behavior, but rather by reformulating his self-structure. It may thus be seen that ego-strength is a very important determiner of a healthy self-structure and, more generally, of a healthy personality. When we learn better ways of measuring ego-strength, it may some day become possible to discover more adequate means for promoting it. The net consequence will be that more persons will achieve a healthy self-structure and healthier personality.

SUMMARY

A person with a strong ego is able to keep his self-structure in congruence with his real self, following threat, by making modifications and adjustments within his self-structure. If a person's ego is weak, however, he is likely to respond to threats to the self-structure in a defensive manner. Defense mechanisms are deemed to be unhealthy responses to threat because they do not come to grips with the cause or source of threat.

Some common sources of threat to the self-structure are sexuality, hostility, *and* dependency longings.

Defense mechanisms *are automatic, involuntary ways of reacting to threatening perceptions, feelings, impulses, and so on, with the aim of preserving the present self-structure intact. The defense mechanisms enable a person to continue believing that he is the kind of person he believes he is, when there is much evidence (from the real self) to refute this belief. They may be regarded as examples of unconscious instrumental behavior, motivated by anxiety and guilt and directed toward the valued end of preserving the present self-structure.*

Defense mechanisms interfere with healthy growth *of the self-structure, and they produce the consequence of self-alienation. They are symptomatic of a weak ego. Many mechanisms for defending the self-concept have been identified:*

repression, rationalization, verbal reformulation, reaction-formation, projection, defensive discrimination, defensive classification, perceptual defense, perceptual sensitization, isolation, compensation, overcompensation, psychic contactlessness, depersonalizing others, fixation, and regression. Most of these maneuvers entail the ignoring or the distortion of some aspect of the real experiencing of the person.

Individuals defend their public selves by lying or by suppressing any behavior or experience which might give rise to unwanted perceptions of them in the minds of others.

Defensive behavior generally manifests itself as rigid and compulsive patterns of conduct. Whenever defensive behavior meets interference, or when it is challenged, the individual will manifest anxiety, guilt, hostility, or other evidence of threat.

NOTES AND REFERENCES

Excellent supplementary reading will be provided by those references marked with an asterisk (*).

1. *Cf.* Szasz, T. S., "The Ego, the Body and Pain," *J. Amer. Psychoanalyt. Assoc.*, 3, 177–200 (1955). See also, Szasz, T. S., *Pain and Pleasure* (New York: Basic Books, 1957).

2. See Freud, S., *Inhibitions, Symptoms, and Anxiety* (London: Hogarth, 1948), for the psychoanalytical view of the relationships among defenses and symptoms.

*3. Whiting and Child show that socialization practices in our society with respect to these three classes of motives are very strict in comparison with other societies. See Whiting, J. W. M. and Child, I. L., *Child Training and Personality* (New Haven, Conn.: Yale, 1953).

4. *Cf.* Kinsey, A. C., Pomeroy, W. B., and Martin, C. E., *Sexual Behavior in the Human Male* (Philadelphia: Saunders, 1948).

5. See Menninger for a systematic account of the ways in which a person preserves his identity and integrity under stress. Menninger, K., "Regulatory Devices of the Ego Under Major Stress," *Int. J. Psychoanal., 35,* 1–9 (1954). Also, by the same author, "Psychological Aspects of the Organism Under Stress. Part I. The Homeostatic Regulatory Functions of the Ego," *J. Amer. Psychoanalyt. Assoc., 2,* 67–106 (1954). "Part II. Regulatory Devices of the Ego Under Stress," *J. Amer. Psychoanalyt. Assoc., 2,* 280–310 (1954).

6. The concept of *homeostasis,* originally used in reference to physiological functions, has been extended to describe and explain psychological stability. See Stagner, R., "Homeostasis As a Unifying Concept in Personality Theory," *Psychol. Rev., 58,* 5–17 (1951).

7. See Werner, H., *The Comparative Psychology of Mental Development* (Chicago: Follett, 1948), for illustrations of "primitive" cognition—indices of ego-weakness. See also Fenichel, O., *The Psychoanalytic Theory of Neurosis* (New York: Norton, 1945), ch. 4, for a discussion of the "archaic ego." See Nunberg, H., "Ego Strength and Ego Weakness," in *Practise and Theory of Psychoanalysis* (New York: Nerv. and Ment. Dis. Monogr., 1948), *74,* 185–198.

8. See Angyal, A., "Evasion of Growth," *Amer. J. Psychiat., 110,* 358–361 (1953) for one psychiatrist's formulations concerning the means by which people strive to evade personality growth. Whitaker and Malone have organized their book on psychotherapy around the concept of growth. See Whitaker, C. A., and Malone, T. P., *The Roots of Psychotherapy* (New York: Blakiston, 1953).

9. See Freud, Anna, *The Ego and the Mechanisms of Defense* (London: Hogarth, 1937), for a formal psychoanalytic presentation of the mechanism of repression. Also, see Fenichel, O., *op. cit.,* pp. 148–151.

*10. See the analysis of repression from the standpoint of contemporary learning theory in Dollard, J. and Miller, N. E., *Personality and Psychotherapy,* (New York: McGraw, 1950), ch. 12.

*11. Shaffer and Shoben provide the reader with a treatment of experimental studies that have been done on repression. See Shaffer, L. F. and Shoben, E. J., *The Psychology of Adjustment* (Rev. ed.; New York: Houghton, 1956), ch. 8.

12. See Rosenzweig, S., "An Experimental Study of 'Repression' with Special Reference to Need-Persistive and Ego-Defensive Reactions to Frustration," *J. Exp. Psychol., 32,* 64–74 (1943). Alper, Thelma G., "Memory for Completed and Incompleted Tasks as a Function of Personality: An Analysis of Group Data," *J. Abn. Soc. Psychol., 41,* 403–420 (1946). Eriksen, C. W., "Psychological Defenses and Ego Strength in the Recall of Completed and Incompleted Tasks," *J. Abn. Soc. Psychol., 49,* 51–58 (1954). For a different, promising experimental attack on the problem of repression, see Eriksen, C. W. and Kuethe, J. S., "Avoidance Conditioning of Verbal Behavior Without Awareness: A Paradigm of Repression," *J. Abn. Soc. Psychol., 53,* 203–209 (1956).

*13. *Cf.* Fromm, E., *Psychoanalysis and Religion* (New Haven, Conn.: Yale, 1950).

14. Freud spoke of the "return of the repressed" as one of the determiners of neurotic symptoms.

15. Bettelheim discusses the difficulty which emotionally disturbed children have in establishing ego control upon awakening from sleep. *Cf.* Bettelheim, B., *Love Is Not Enough* (Glencoe, Ill.: Free Press, 1950), ch. 4

16. It is well known both by clinical and experimental psychologists that words and symbols are powerful conditioned stimuli for emotional responses.

17. Jung, C. G., *Studies in Word Association* (New York: Moffat, Yard, 1919). See Eriksen and Kuethe, *op. cit.*, for a recent demonstration of how feelings may experimentally be associated with stimulus words.

18. See Feldman, M. J., "The Use of Obscene Words in the Therapeutic Relationship," *Amer. J. Psychoanal.*, *15*, 45–48 (1955).

19. Feldman, M. J., *op. cit.* See also Ferenczi, S., *Sex in Psychoanalysis* (New York, Brunner, 1950).

20. Reich and other psychoanalysts view many rigid traits of character—"character-armor"—as a by-product of reaction-formation. See Reich, W., *Character Analysis* (New York, Orgone Institute Press, 1949).

21. *Cf.* A letter received by Jules Masserman from a woman antivivisectionist, quoted in Coleman, J. C., *Abnormal Psychology and Modern Life* (New York, Scott, 1950), p. 89.

22. See the case histories in Levy, D. M., *Maternal Overprotection* (New York, Columbia U. P., 1943).

23. *Cf.* Werner, H., *op. cit.*

*24. This distinction has been adapted from Cameron, N. and Magaret, Ann, *Behavior Pathology* (New York, Houghton, 1951), pp. 381–387.

25. Students of prejudice assume that projection plays at least some part in the development of bigoted beliefs about minority group members. See Allport, G., *The Nature of Prejudice* (Cambridge, Mass.: Addison-Wesley, 1954).

*26. *Cf.* Dollard, J. and Miller, N. E., *Personality and Psychotherapy* (New York, McGraw, 1950), chs. 17, 18, 19.

27. See, for example, Rapaport, D. (ed.), *Organization and Pathology of Thought* (New York, Columbia U. P., 1951), for various approaches to the analysis of schizophrenic, or primitive, thinking. See also Werner, H., *op. cit.*

28. See Feldman, M. J. and Drasgow, J., "A Visual-Verbal Test for Schizophrenia," *Psychiat. Quart. Suppl.*, Part I, 1–10 (1951), for a description of a test which measures the ability to make socially agreed-upon classifications.

29. Freud, S., "Formulations Regarding the Two Principles in Mental Functioning," ch. 1 in Freud, S., *Collected Papers*, IV (London: Hogarth, 1953).

30. See ch. 2. See also Cameron, N. and Magaret, Ann, *op. cit.*, pp. 70–74.

31. *Cf.* Fenichel, O., *op. cit.*, pp. 155–159.

32. Reich, W., *op. cit.*, pp. 316–328. See also, for some examples, Albert Camus' novel *The Stranger* and Colin Wilson's essay *The Outsider.*

33. See Jourard, S. M., "The Bedside Manner," *Amer. J. Nursing, 60,* 63–66 (1960).
34. See Parsons, T., *Essays in Sociological Theory* (Glencoe, Ill.: Free Press, 1954), ch. 5, for a discussion of age-grading in the United States.
35. Terman, L. M. and Merrill, Maud A., *Measuring Intelligence* (New York, Houghton, 1937).
36. Gesell, A. and Ilg, F. L., *Infant and Child in the Culture of To-day* (New York: Harper, 1942); see also the subsequent volumes which provide norms for various aspects of behavior up to adolescence.
*37. A good secondary source which describes the psychoanalytic theory of psychosexual development is Brown, J. F., *Psychodynamics of Abnormal Behavior* (New York: McGraw, 1940), ch. 10.
*38. Maslow, A. H., *Motivation and Personality* (New York: Harper, 1954), ch. 5.
*39. Murphy, G., *Personality: A Biosocial Approach to Origins and Structure* (New York: Harper, 1947), ch. 14.
40. Werner, H., *op. cit.*
41. Fromm, E., *Man for Himself* (New York: Rinehart, 1947).
42. *Cf.* Fenichel, O., *op. cit.*, ch. 14.
*43. See Cameron, N. and Magaret, Ann, *op. cit.*, ch. 5, for an excellent and well-documented discussion of fixation.
*44. See Cameron, N. and Magaret, Ann, *op. cit.*, ch. 8, for a thorough discussion of regression. Bettelheim has noted the degree to which prisoners in Nazi concentration camps during World War II regressed to more primitive levels of functioning. See Bettelheim, B., *The Informed Heart* (Glencoe, Ill.: Free Press, 1960), pp. 131–134.
*45. See Goffman, E., *The Presentation of Self in Everyday Life* (Garden City, N.Y.: Doubleday Anchor, 1959), ch. 4.
46. *Cf.* Fromm, E., *op. cit.*
47. Freud, S., *The Ego and the Id* (London: Hogarth, 1927), p. 69.
*48. See Mowrer, O. H., *Learning Theory and Personality Dynamics* (New York: Ronald, 1950), ch. 22, for a discussion of "conscience-killing." Mowrer has written extensively about the interrelations of guilt and anxiety.
49. *Cf.* Menninger, K., *op. cit.*

CHAPTER 8
CONSCIENCE AND GUILT IN HEALTHY PERSONALITY

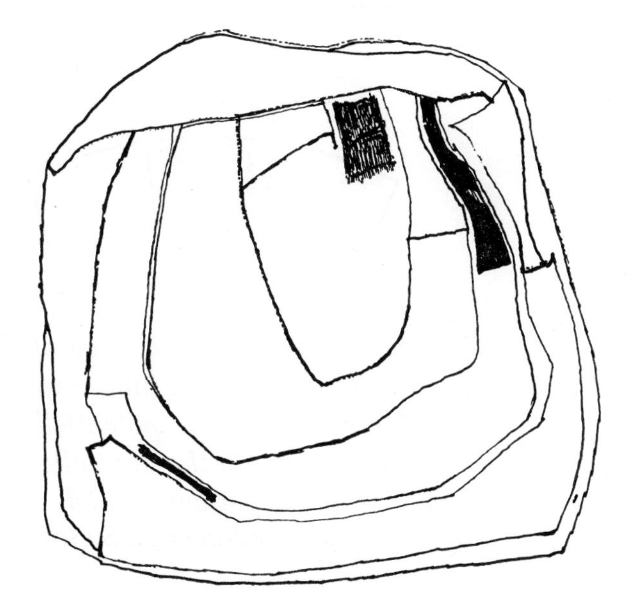

INTRODUCTION

Each society has its set of rules that the members must obey if they are to continue to live in that group as accepted members. The various means for producing conformity with social mores are called techniques of social control.[1] *Social control of behavior ranges from overt force to such subtle techniques as omitting an offensive person's name from the list of people invited to a party. We can depict the impact of limits and social control over an individual's behavior by recourse to the image of an arc:*

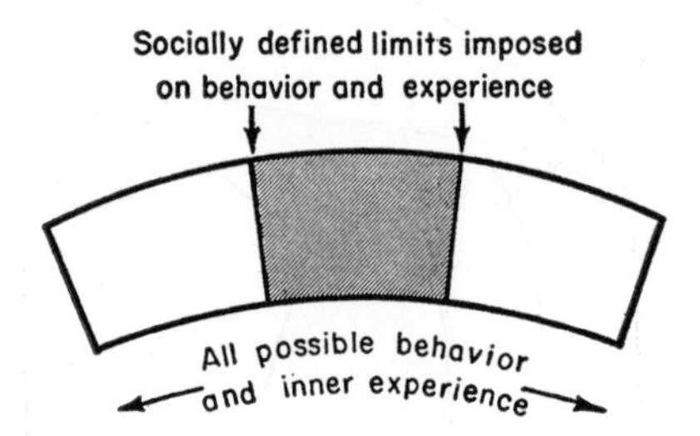

In the diagram, the total area of the arc encompasses all behavior and inner experience of which the human being is potentially capable. The shaded area within the arc indicates the range of behavior and experience which a society will recognize, value, and accept. So long as a person re-

stricts his behavior within those limits, he will avoid punishment from the law and from his peers, and he can retain the respect and esteem of others.

The actual behavior encompassed by the social mores is the expression of that society's value-system.[2] *The value-system refers to the more or less explicit statement of the valued goals that are pursued by the group members and the kinds of behavior prescribed as means to those goals. Some common goals in our society are a sizable income, a high-prestige profession, a wife or husband who will be deemed desirable and attractive by our peers, and so on. A person who achieves these goals in the* right *ways will enjoy a high degree of status. The person who achieves these goals the* wrong *way*[3] *will be judged harshly and will not be accepted in the groups in which he desires membership.*

External sanctions are not the only means by which society controls the behavior of individual persons. Each member of a society is subjected to a fairly rigorous training process—socialization—which indoctrinates him with the values characteristic of his society.[4] *Each socialized person acquires a* personal value-system *which resembles the social value-system. By the time he becomes an adult, he conforms with social limits on behavior because he fears external punishments for deviant behavior and also because* he wants to conform with his conscience. *If the person violates the group code (and his own conscience), he will experience anxiety, the dread of being caught and punished; and he will also experience* guilt, *an acute moral condemnation of himself. Guilt may be more severe than any punishment that society could mete out to an offender. Persons who could easily escape punishment for a crime have been known to give themselves up and actually beg for external punishment, just so they could be relieved of agonizing guilt feelings.*

Guilt and the conscience, when seen from a sociologist's point of view, serve the very important function of augmenting social control over behavior and insuring conformity with the social value-system. The necessity for the external control of behavior is reduced when all the members of a society have a conscience and are capable of experiencing guilt. People with consciences control their own behavior and strive to remain within limits which will keep them free of guilt.[5]

From a psychological standpoint, the conscience is one component of individual personality structure and a highly important determiner of personality health and personality illness. It is meaningful to ask, "Does this person have a healthy conscience, or is his conscience unhealthy?" The problem, of course, is to determine the characteristics which earmark a healthy conscience and those which describe an unhealthy conscience.

The conscience is a determiner of guilt and of self-esteem, both powerful motives and deter-

miners of behavior, especially interpersonal behavior. A self-respecting individual behaves quite differently with other people than a guilt-ridden person. The self-respecter "has nothing to hide" from others; the guilty person is very defensive, withdrawn, and prone to avoid close and confiding relationships with others.

ROLE OF CONSCIENCE IN MENTAL ILLNESS

An unhealthy conscience is known to play a crucial role in the determination of neurosis and psychosis. Freud and his followers believed that neurosis was partly determined by an overly severe but unconscious conscience (he called it the *superego*). The neurotic is obliged to refrain from certain kinds of behavior, such as sexuality; more than that, he must refrain even from thinking about or wishing to act in the forbidden ways if he is to be guilt-free. The therapeutic aim in such cases is to help the patient to reformulate his conscience along more conscious, rational, lenient, and adult lines. If that aim can be accomplished, the patient will have no further need to repress his inner experience, because it would no longer induce guilt.

Mowrer differs with the orthodox psychoanalytic theory concerning the role of conscience in the development of neurosis. He differs also in his concept of therapeutic aims with respect to the conscience.[6] According to Mowrer, a neurotic is not a person with an overly strict conscience, who must repress his sexuality in order to remain guilt-free. Instead, he sees the neurotic as a person who persists beyond childhood in the pursuit of irresponsible pleasures, including sexuality, and *who represses his guilt and his conscience.* Neurotic symptoms arise as defenses against guilt, not merely as defenses against infantile sexuality, as the Freudians might maintain. Consequently, Mowrer claims, the aim in therapy is not to render the conscience more lenient, but to make it *conscious,* so that a person will feel guilt more acutely and seek in future to obey his conscience rather than ignore or repress it.

Clinical experience suggests that neither Freud nor Mowrer is wholly correct or wholly incorrect. Rather, it can be found that some neurotic patients do indeed have a conscience that is too strict; in order to remain guilt-free, they must refrain from *all* pleasurable activities, including those which society condones.[7] Other patients may be found with the make-up which Mowrer has regarded as nuclear to all neurosis—they repress conscience so they can break social taboos without conscious guilt.

If we paraphrase Freud's therapeutic aim to read "change the conscience in lenient directions" and Mowrer's to read "strengthen the conscience, and help the person to conform with his conscience," we are thrust into an acute impasse: We find that contradictory roles are assigned to the conscience in neurosis, and contradictory therapeutic aims are proposed. This impasse can be resolved if we recognize that consciences *are not all alike* among all members of a given society. Some consciences are stricter than the society requires, some are more lenient, some are quite deviant from the social value-system, and many are highly conflicted. Further, consciences differ at various age levels; a child's conscience differs from that of an adult—although adults can be found with the conscience of a child. In other words, the conscience is a highly variable thing. We could state that if a person has a *healthy* conscience, then *healthy personality will be fostered if he conforms with his conscience.* But if a person's conscience is *unhealthy,* then conformity with it will only perpetuate or promote unhealthy personality. The healthy thing for a person to do, if his conscience is unhealthy, *is to change it.*

THE DEFINITION OF CONSCIENCE

Conscience is made up of ideals and taboos for a person's behavior. Each socialized person internalizes the *social* value-system and acquires a *personal* value-system. The personal value-system is more comprehensive in its scope than conscience, since it defines the person's goals, his standards for judging other people, and his standards for judging himself. Conscience refers only to the values and ideals which pertain to the self. Values and ideals pertaining to other people may be similar to those pertaining to the self, but they cannot be called part of the conscience. Rather, they are part of the more comprehensive concept of the personal value-system.

In the literature on personality theory, many terms have been employed to describe what we call conscience. The psychoanalysts use the term *superego* in this context, but superego has a somewhat different technical meaning from conscience. The superego is a hypothetical substructure within personality structure as a whole, with conscience being one of its *functions*. The literal meaning of conscience is roughly "simultaneous knowledge, or awareness"; that is, conscience means observing and judging one's own behavior and experience during the actual process of behaving and experiencing. The superego is regarded as a derivative of another psychological structure, the *ego*. The ego constructs the superego and also the *ego-ideal*. The ego-ideal sets the goals and ideals which the ego will strive to attain.[8]

Other personality theorists[9] have employed the term *self-ideal*, or *ideal self* (in contrast to the real self, perceived self, or self-concept) to embody the facts which we are summing up with the term conscience.

In order to avoid confusion in terminology we shall use the word conscience throughout this chapter to refer to the values, ideals, rules, taboos, goals, and so on, which an individual holds with respect to his own behavior and inner experience.

HOW THE CONSCIENCE IS ACQUIRED

The conscience is gradually acquired during the process of growing up by means of *identification*.[10] Identification is the name given to the process of adopting traits of some *valued model*. It is through identification that intrafamilial resemblance in behavior, gesture, values, attitudes, and morals are acquired. It is through identification with the parents' value-system that the growing child acquires his personal value-system and his conscience.

The growing child begins life without a preformed conscience. Rather, he comes into the world only with the *capacity* to form one. He acts in accordance with his momentary needs and feelings, but his parents are usually watching him closely, making value-judgments about his behavior. If the child acts in ways which violate the parents' concepts of what is right, they will generally punish him for behaving in that way. If the child fails to conform with their expectations about achievement, they may punish him, sometimes making him feel rejected and unloved. The parents appear huge, powerful, admirable, and wonderful from the child's standpoint; he wants to become like them. In order to avoid punishment, to retain the parents' love, and to acquire their wonderful attributes, the child strives to become like his parents in very many ways. He identifies with their demands and expectations of *him;* these gradually become the child's expectations of himself. In short, he comes to forbid in himself what his parents forbade. He comes to demand of himself what his parents demanded. He comes to expect of himself what his parents expected. In this manner the conscience is acquired.

SOME CHARACTERISTICS OF THE CONSCIENCE

THE CONSCIENCE IS NOT ALWAYS CONSCIOUS. The conscience is gradually acquired beginning in early childhood, and so the individual cannot verbalize all of its component taboos and ideals. All he knows is that when he acts in certain ways he feels guilty and when he acts in other ways he feels all right. It may happen, indeed, that a person *thinks* certain modes of behavior are perfectly all right and virtuous, but if he behaves in those ways, he experiences guilt. He doesn't know why he feels his guilt, but he feels it none the less. Since he does not know why he feels guilt, the implication is clear that certain aspects of his conscience are *unconscious.* As we pointed out earlier in this chapter, the individual may have repressed his conscience.

If a person always acts in accordance with his conscience, he never feels guilt anyway; in fact, he may be said to be unaware that he *has* a conscience. His conscience manifests itself only indirectly, through his automatic choice of behavior patterns which accord with his conscience.

THE CONSCIENCE IS AGE-GRADED. Just as society expects varying kinds of behavior from a person at various age levels, so does the person make age-graded demands upon himself. The child does not expect the same performances from himself that he will when he reaches adult status. The child does not feel guilty about the same things an adult would feel guilty about. If total personality development proceeds smoothly, the conscience will change in the appropriate way at each growth stage. However, conscience-*fixations,* conscience-*regressions,* and *precocity of conscience* occur commonly, and they are important causes of unhealthy personality.

THE CONSCIENCE IS OFTEN VERY STRICT.[11] The conscience is a set of demands which a person makes upon himself. If he fails to conform with these demands, he may experience guilt, depression, or inferiority feelings of incredible intensity. Some people would never dream of judging their worst enemy as harshly as they judge themselves when they fail to live up to some self-expectation. The problem becomes quite complicated when the self-demands are unconscious, that is, unstated in words. For in such instances, the person experiences only the guilt and is unaware of the self-demands with which he has failed to comply. The causes of this severe self-punishment have been investigated by psychoanalysts; they have suggested that severe self-criticism reflects severe punishments and stringent demands the parents imposed upon the child when he was younger. In identifying with his parents, the child came to evaluate himself, to make similar demands, and to impose taboos upon himself similar to those imposed on him by his parents. Violation of these taboos results in a "punishment" of the self similar in intensity to the punishments the parents imposed.

THE CONSCIENCE OFTEN HAS ELEMENTS IN CONFLICT. The conscience is acquired through identification with the values and ideals which others held with respect to the self. These origins may result in *conflicting* values and ideals. The parents may disagree on what they demand of their child, and so he acquires conflicting self-expectations. As the child becomes involved with other significant adults, such as teachers, ministers, relatives, maids, and so on, he internalizes some of their demands on him, and these may conflict sharply with his present conscience. As he becomes involved in various peer groups, he may adopt many of their values, which can be at variance with his present value-system. His conscience will thus comprise demands upon the self which are logically contradictory with one another. In conforming with one set of values, the person is violating another set. The result may be chronic guilt, or chronic moral indecision.

THE CONSCIENCE IS USUALLY AUTHORITARIAN. The "authoritarian character" is a person who believes authority figures are omnipotent and must be obeyed and submitted to without question or criticism. Indeed, to disobey or to question authority is synonymous with sin for the authoritarian character; he becomes overwhelmed with guilt at even the thought of disobeying or challenging vested authority. A person may experience his own conscience in the same manner that he experiences external authority—it is to be obeyed blindly, without question, hesitation, or criticism. Its commands have the feeling of certainty and unquestionable rightness. Fromm has named a conscience with such characteristics an *authoritarian conscience.*[12] He regards an authoritarian conscience as an undesirable thing from the standpoint of healthy personality. An authoritarian conscience will most likely be acquired by a person reared by authoritarian parents—they brooked no disobedience and no questioning of their authority. Most persons have aspects of conscience they acquired out of the authoritarian relationship with their parents or other significant persons. A high degree of rigidity or resistance to change in the typical conscience reflects its authoritarian nature.

THE CONSCIENCE CAN BE REPRESSED AND PROJECTED. To repress is to refuse to think about something or to refrain from engaging in some mental operation, such as thinking, remembering, daydreaming, or *evaluating*. Conscience functions by means of the comparison of one's own behavior, feelings, or motives with relevant taboos and "shoulds." A person may have learned to refrain from making value-judgments about aspects of his own behavior so as to avoid the painful experience of guilt.[13] *This avoidance of making value-judg-*

ments concerning one's own behavior is what we mean when we speak of the repression of conscience. Laymen speak, in this connection of a "hardened heart." The most vivid proof that one has repressed aspects of his own conscience is provided by experiences of the following sort: Suppose you have done something without thinking too much about its moral implications, such as stealing office supplies for home use. You feel no guilt. But then, another person discovers it and reminds you this is theft. You become threatened and overwhelmed with guilt. What the other person has done is to reactivate your tendency to evaluate yourself. On doing so, you feel guilt. Probably one of the more important functions of a revivalistic minister is that of reminding his congregation they have values and they should compare their deeds with these values. He is striving to undo the process of conscience-repression so the church members will again feel guilt whenever they violate their consciences.

A person can project his conscience as well as repress it.[14] Concretely, this involves repression of the process of self-evaluation and *ascribing evaluations of the self to others.* Thus, a person might engage in some act but deny it is wrong for him to do this. However, he may impute condemnation of himself to some other person and feel without warrant that the other person is criticizing and condemning him. In extreme cases of personality illness, for example paranoid schizophrenia, the patient projects all of his self-criticism to others and believes that everyone is criticizing him and persecuting him.

THE CONSCIENCE CAN BE DECEIVED. A person skilled in argument and debate can persuade a gullible individual that black is white and that wrong is right. Such a person can direct his rhetoric at himself, or rather at his conscience. Most of us have at one time or another faced some moral conflict, where strong temptation confronted us. We took the easy path, the one which procured some forbidden pleasure for us and stifled our self-condemnation by means of subtle self-debate. Much of our *rationalization* serves the function of duping or deceiving our conscience (i.e., ourselves as a whole person) into believing that we really have done no wrong.[15]

The above list of characteristics of the conscience could be extended at some length, but it should suffice to acquaint the reader with this aspect of his own personality. Now that we have some idea about the range of variability of conscience in society, let us proceed to evaluate conscience from a personality-hygiene point of view.

THE EVALUATION OF CONSCIENCE

What are some of the more common indications and patterns of unhealthy conscience? What are the characteristics of a healthy conscience? These are questions we shall attempt to answer in the following sections.

SOME INDICATIONS OF AN UNHEALTHY CONSCIENCE

If a person has an unhealthy conscience, his growth toward personality health will be fostered by efforts to change it in the directions indicated in a later section (pp. 247–251). Let us now list some signs of an unhealthy conscience.

UNREMITTING GUILT. If a person experiences guilt chronically and yet his behavior does not appear to an observer to warrant such guilt, it is likely that the person has an unhealthy conscience. This chronic guilt may be fully conscious, or it may be unconscious, disguised even from the person who is victimized by it. Unconscious guilt assumes many forms.[16] It may manifest itself through repetitive accidents; through repeated failures in important ventures, failures which easily could have been avoided if the simplest precautions had been taken; through habitual self-depreciation in the presence of others; through habitual, uncalled-for justifications and explanations of one's past and present actions, and so on. All of these signs of unconscious guilt, as well as conscious guilt, indicate that the conscience which is responsible is unhealthy in at least some respects; if may be unconscious, too rigid, too strict, or not suitable to the person's present age level.

ABSENCE OF GUILT IN SPITE OF OBVIOUS MORAL VIOLATIONS. If a person violates many ethical precepts and yet seems free from conscious guilt, it may be assumed that his conscience is strikingly deviant from the modal conscience. Or, he may have repressed both conscience and guilt. Psychiatrists use the term "psychopathic personality" to describe individuals who violate mores without guilt.

GUILT OVER APPARENTLY TRIVIAL LAPSES. If a person suffers an onslaught of guilt over something trivial, such as coming late to an appointment or failing to return a borrowed book on the exact date that was promised, it betokens unhealthy conscience. His conscience is unhealthy because it is too strict, too exacting, or childish. Such a disproportionate reaction may indicate the person has repressed guilt that was induced by a very grave violation of conscience and then *displaced* his guilt-response to the less serious crime. Edmund Bergler, a psychoanalyst, illustrated this mechanism with an analogy: "I couldn't be guilty of that murder, because I was robbing a bank on the other side of town at just the time the killing occurred."

SOME PATTERNS OF UNHEALTHY CONSCIENCE

We will describe *excessively strict consciences, excessively permissive consciences, deviant consciences,* and *consciences in conflict.*

EXCESSIVELY STRICT CONSCIENCE. This pattern of unhealthy conscience limits guilt-free behavior more drastically than law and custom. The unfortunate bearer of such a conscience allows himself fewer need-satisfactions than other members of his social group; he expects more of himself, more difficult achievements, and a sterner morality than his group peers. In America, it might be quite acceptable, and certainly not immoral, for a middle-class girl to smoke, take an occasional drink, neck, go to dances. Her friend, with an excessively strict conscience, might want to do these things but find herself so ridden with guilt they are rendered unenjoyable for her. Many people have been subjected to socialization influences from parents, ministers, and other moral models, so that they must not only avoid certain kinds of activities (which are defined as wrong, or sinful), but they must even avoid thinking about such activities. Thus, many persons may have been taught that sexy or hostile fantasies and thoughts are equivalent in sinful significance to sexual and hostile activities. In order to remain guilt-free, they must not only restrict their activities but also their thoughts. It is probably this type of excessively restrictive conscience which Freud saw as a factor responsible for the development of neurosis and which he sought to modify in his patients.

In terms of our arc-image, we would depict the excessively strict conscience as follows:

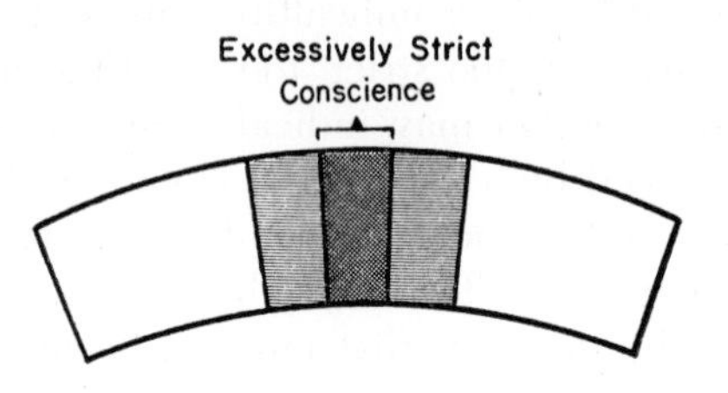

The horizontally shaded area in the diagram represents all of the behavior patterns which are theoretically available to members of a given group but which are taboo for the person with an excessively strict conscience; he must confine his behavior to the narrower, cross-hatched area.

EXCESSIVELY PERMISSIVE CONSCIENCE. An excessively permissive conscience is one which allows a person to engage, guilt-free, in a range of behavior broader than that which is usual or allowed by the laws and customs of the group. The person shares most of the moral values of his group, but his behavioral boundaries are broader than those of the group. It should be stated that the word *excessive* is always in reference to the social group in question. Obviously, what is regarded as "loose living" in one group may be regarded as strictly moral in another. In terms of the arc-image, the overly permissive conscience would be depicted as follows:

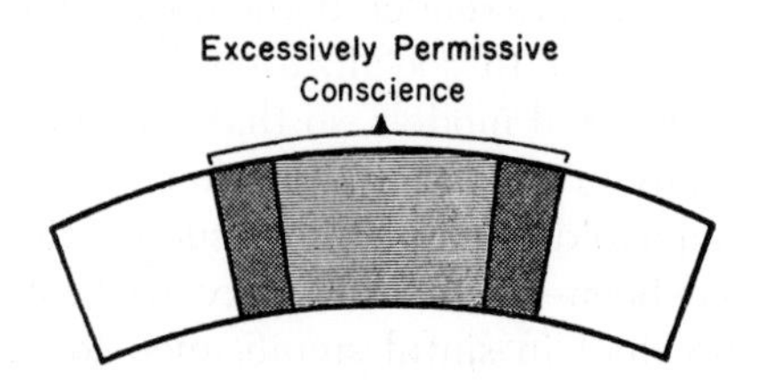

The persons in our society most likely to have an excessively permissive conscience (as seen from the viewpoint of the average person) are the "beatniks." Such individuals conform in some respects with conventional moral standards, but they may refuse to delimit their behavior in some selected area, such as sexuality. The beatnik inveighs against "middle-class morality," all the while conforming with it in most respects, excepting sexual morality. If he is successful in his reformulation of modal morality, he may be quite capable of indulging himself in promiscuous sexuality without guilt.

Many parents, eager to apply "newer concepts of child-rearing," may inculcate an excessively permissive conscience in their children. They refuse to set and enforce limits on the behavior of their children (so as to avoid thwarting them) and inculcate a conscience (or lack of one?) which enables the children to transgress the limits of conventional morality in a guilt-free manner.

DEVIANT CONSCIENCE. A deviant conscience is one which comprises values markedly different from the values prevalent in the person's present social group. His standards for conduct may overlap in important respects with those of other people, but they will differ strikingly in other areas of activity. The goals which he considers important are not the goals emphasized by his group. His concepts of right and wrong diverge in many ways from those of the group. In actuality, the person with a deviant conscience may be evaluated in comparison with his "home group" as having a strict or permissive conscience, but with reference to the new group, he has a deviant conscience. The persons in our society who have deviant consciences are primarily first-generation immigrants. The immigrant who has not as yet been acculturated to American ways still behaves in accordance with the values of the culture from which he has come. Thus, many of the American practices seem scandalous to him, and he would be overwhelmed with guilt if he emulated them. Similarly, many of his guilt-free activities may be viewed as sinful or even criminal to the American.

Another version of deviant conscience is to be found in certain groups in American society, especially groups of teen-agers. They may evolve a set of values which differ markedly in many important respects from the values represented by their parents or by society at large. Thus, the teen-ager may have an extremely exacting and strict conscience, based on identification with the values of his gang or group. In order to maintain his self-esteem, he may feel compelled to perform all kinds of actions repugnant to the person with a modal conscience. He may lie, cheat, steal, rape, and so on. These actions may serve not only to preserve his status within the group but also to maintain his self-esteem.

CONSCIENCES IN CONFLICT. A conscience in conflict is a very common version of unhealthy conscience. It is composed of values, ideals, and taboos which contradict one another. Thus, conformity with one component value requires violation of another, with consequent guilt. The conflicted conscience is developed out of identification with persons who have contrasting demands, expectations, and prohibitions with respect to the individual's behavior. A common source of conflicted conscience is parents who have different standards for judging the behavior of their children. The mother may value gentleness, submissiveness, obedience, and "womanly things," while the father affirms self-assertion, aggressiveness, muscular strength. Prior to the establishment of a conscience, the child may experience considerable confusion and conflict as he strives to obtain the approval and affection of his parents. In pleasing his father, he displeases his mother, and vice versa. When once he has identified with the values of each parent, the interpersonal conflicts are changed into *intra*personal conflicts. He acts one way, in order to maintain self-esteem, only to experience guilt for the violation of contrasting values.

An additional source of conflicted conscience is to be found in the fact that very often the parental values with which a person has identified differ markedly from the values of teachers, peers, or the values of other groups with which the person is involved. He may identify with many value-systems, incorporating them into his conscience, and increasing the frequency of value-conflicts.

Some people attempt to resolve the value-conflicts by compartmentalizing their lives: They follow one set of values at work, another set in the home, another set when they are among their peers, and so on. A more desirable way from the personality-hygiene viewpoint is the attempt to reconcile one's values with one another so they constitute a harmonious and hierarchically arranged system.

Now, let us discuss healthy conscience.

CHARACTERISTICS OF A HEALTHY CONSCIENCE

A person with a healthy conscience will follow personality-hygiene precepts if he strives to conform with it. Such conformity will have a number of consequences. It will enable the person to obtain enough basic need-gratifications to make life worth living, but in a guilt-free manner. The person will enjoy relatively high self-esteem. His behavior may be quite highly approved by other members of his social group—at least to the extent that his conscience is congruent with the group's value-system. A healthy conscience will be compatible wth continual personality growth; indeed, it may be a strong motivating force toward personality growth. In view of all these important and valuable consequences of a healthy conscience, it is important to define its characteristics as clearly as our knowledge will allow. This clear definition might then facilitate the personality-hygiene goal of promoting healthy conscience-development in more people. Let us turn, then, to a listing of some of the more salient attributes of a healthy conscience.

ACCESSIBILITY TO CONSCIOUSNESS. A healthy conscience is a *conscious* conscience. The person is able, when he wants, to formulate its component taboos, ideals, and ethical precepts in words. That is, he can state his moral-ethical convictions to himself. This accessibility to consciousness is very important for such problems as *moral conflicts*. If a person is faced with a decision which he must make, he can make his decision along moral lines much more readily when his conscience is clearly stated. A conscious conscience provides the person with explicit standards in terms of which he can evaluate his own behavior in a rational manner.

When we say that a healthy conscience is conscious, we do not mean the person is always thinking about his moral standards. Most of the time, the healthy conscience will be unconscious; the person will conform with his conscience automatically. But when he does feel guilt, he will be able to determine what aspects of his conscience he has violated; and when he has to resolve some conflict, he will be able to make all of the relevant moral aspects explicit, so that his decision will be made after due consideration of the moral issues at stake.

SELF-AFFIRMED. A healthy conscience is not experienced as an "alien power" within the total personality structure, a power compulsively obeyed out of dread. Rather, it is composed of a set of ideals and taboos, each of which has been examined by the person and *affirmed* by him so that it becomes a true part of his real self. A self-affirmed conscience is one with which the person conforms *because he wants to,* not because he is afraid of disobeying. Another way of saying this is to assert that the person feels he *owns* his conscience; it is *his.* He has had a voice in determining the rules by which he will live. He is like the citizen in a democracy who does not mind conforming with rules he has helped formulate.

FLEXIBILITY. A healthy conscience is based upon general values and ideals which remain fixed throughout life. But the specific behavior which these values call for is not rigidly defined. The person can change many of his self-demands when it becomes apparent they are no longer relevant to his present life-circumstances. Let us illustrate what we mean by flexibility of conscience: Early in life, a person may have been trained to believe that smoking is a sin. Since he wants to be considered a good person, the individual refrains from smoking. Actually, smoking may be considered to be morally wrong only within his family. Later in life, the person discovers there is no necessary connection between goodness and refraining from smoking. Consequently, he may revise this aspect of his conscience and start to smoke with enjoyment, free from guilt. He has not changed his affirmation of the over-all value of being a good person; he has merely dropped one specific taboo which he earlier thought must be observed if one were to be good. Smoking has ceased to be a moral issue for him. Of course, he may still refrain from smoking, but not on moral grounds; rather, to save money or protect his health.

The flexibility we are talking about as a property of a healthy conscience depends on freedom to examine one's specific taboos and self-expectations to evaluate these in terms of more general values, and to abandon, change or reaffirm the specific aspects of conscience on the basis of such examination. This flexibility is most likely to be found in consciences which are *not authoritarian* in nature. Such flexibility insures that a person will be observing only those taboos which he wants to observe, and it insures that the individual's conscience will be up-to-date. That is, he will not be observing taboos or pursuing ideals in adult years that are appropriate only to a child.

MATURITY. The healthy conscience is comprised of ideals and taboos which are appropriate to the individual's present stage of over-all maturity. Healthy conscience is not fixated nor regressed to less mature levels. A person with a healthy conscience does not demand things of himself which would be more suited to a person of more advanced years or a person with more skill, knowledge, or ability.

REALISTIC. The specific taboos and ideals which comprise a healthy conscience are formulated with due consideration for the person's actual ability to conform with these self-demands. The person does not impose taboos upon himself which no human being could be expected to conform with: viz., absolute perfection, absolute blamelessness, absolute freedom from hostility, absolute freedom from thinking about socially tabooed activities. Rather, the healthy conscience may affirm the person's right to absolute freedom to think and fantasy anything imaginable without guilt; it is only the overt behavior which would be self-condemned and productive of guilt.

HIERARCHICAL STRUCTURE. The values which make up a healthy conscience are organized into a hierarchy of relative importance. This arrangement enables the person to make moral decisions, when conflicts arise, on a rational basis. He will be able to see what values are at stake and make decisions which implement his most important values. Probably the value which would lie at the pinnacle of the hierarchy would be the person's concern for his own integrity and growth as a whole, with all other values assigned lesser importance. Fromm has implied this in his discussion of a *humanistic* conscience in contrast to an authoritarian conscience.[17] The humanistic conscience includes a positive affirmation of the importance of full development of the latent capacities of the self. Maslow[18] also regards full development of one's potential self as a value more important than other goals.

SOME DEGREE OF CONGRUENCE WITH THE SOCIAL VALUE-SYSTEM. The person with a healthy conscience is living among other people, and so he will be obliged to share at least some of their values, ideals, and taboos. This is not to say that his conscience must be absolutely congruent with the social mores. It may happen that the person finds his values more ethical than the prevailing mores, and so he will follow his own conscience rather than the moral expectations of his peers and contemporaries. It may be necessary for the person with a healthy conscience to be able to *resist* the efforts of others to make him conform with their moral precepts. He may even be obliged to leave some group, or locale, because of moral-ethical differences and seek a group more congenial to his outlook or else live on in active opposition to the group.

To state this point another way, the person with a healthy conscience may choose to conform to some degree with the mores of his group, but he will preserve a certain degree of inner freedom from the group's demands. His self-affirmed conscience is his guide to conduct, and not the expectations of others.

HUMANE. When we say that a healthy conscience is humane, we mean that the person does not treat himself cruelly and sadistically when he violates his own ethical precepts. He will feel guilt, to be sure, but it is not likely to be harsh or brutal. Rather, he will experience his moral lapses as mistakes which can be rectified by him through any suitable restitutive and expiatory measures. And he does not condemn himself outright and wholly for his lapses; in spite of his "sins," he can continue to love and esteem himself as a person, with the same compassion for his own frailties that he would show to some child who made moral mistakes. We do not kill a child who steals and lies, so it is difficult to see how it could be healthy for a person to kill himself—literally or symbolically—for some deviation from his own conscience.

A person with a healthy conscience, as defined above, will have the capacity to experience guilt, but he will not likely suffer from chronic guilt. It is not implied that a healthy conscience will be highly lenient, permitting any antisocial behavior. Indeed, it may be very difficult to accord with the precepts of a healthy conscience. Fromm has stated that the voice of a humanistic conscience may be only dimly heard, because it is readily masked by the authoritarian elements of conscience. As Fromm puts it, "[conscience] is the voice of our true 'selves' which summons us back to ourselves, to live productively, to develop fully and harmoniously—that is, to become what we potentially are." He points out further that guilt arising from a violation of a healthy conscience may be very difficult to identify; we might feel guilt arising from our *authoritarian* conscience when we ignore its demands in order to pursue the requirements of a *healthy* conscience.[19]

MODES OF RELATING TO THE CONSCIENCE

It should not be forgotten that the conscience is a part of a person's self-structure. Consequently, when we speak of "modes of relating to the conscience," we are really speaking of different ways in which a person relates to his real self. In principle, a person can relate to his conscience, or his real self, *in almost all of the ways that he might relate to another person.* Thus, one can listen to oneself, ignore oneself, obey and disobey oneself, love and hate oneself, rebel against oneself, kill oneself, aggress against oneself, worship, deceive, drug, reason with the self, and so on. Since the conscience is one aspect of the self, a person can relate to his own conscience in all of these ways. Let us describe the healthy ways of relating to the conscience and then comment upon some of the more obviously unhealthy ways of relating to the conscience.

A HEALTHY RELATIONSHIP WITH THE CONSCIENCE. Since the conscience is really the self observing, evaluating, and "talking" to the self, it is healthy for the person to pay attention and to listen. Presumably, the conscience is that part of the real self which is actively concerned with the growth and the "goodness" of the whole person and so should be attended to. The voice of the conscience is heard, however dimly, whenever some action is being considered which will have consequences for the over-all growth and moral worth of the whole person. The individual will then experience a conflict between his immediate wishes for need-gratification and pleasure and his desire to grow, to become a better person, or to remain a good person. If the person is relating in healthy fashion with his conscience, he will listen at these times to what it has to say to him. This message will neither be ignored nor compulsively and unthinkingly obeyed. Rather, the person will "hear himself out" and strive to make a realistic appraisal of all the issues that are involved in the proposed behavior. If he discovers that no important values are being violated, he will so inform himself (his conscience) and proceed with his actions. If, on the other hand, he discerns that he will violate important values by acting in this way, he may decide to conform with his conscience. Let us call this mode of relating to the conscience *reasoned consideration.*[20] It is obviously comparable with the reasoned consideration an adult will give to the opinions, objections, and requests that other people might express to him when he is planning some sort of activity which affects their welfare. He has to decide upon that line of action which will reconcile all of the conflicting values that may be at stake.

UNHEALTHY RELATIONSHIPS WITH THE CONSCIENCE. A person can interact with his conscience, as with another person, in ways that undermine health. Let us examine some of these ways:

1. Compulsive conformity with the conscience. This is an unhealthy pattern which is most likely to be observed in a person with an authoritarian conscience. Such a person very likely experiences himself as "split," or divided in fundamental ways; he has a "bad" self, which is impulsive, childish, selfish, and immoral, and a stern, powerful "good" self—his conscience—which orders him to suppress his bad self and to be good. Habitually, the person acts in accordance with the literal dictates of his conscience, upon pain of intense guilt for failures to conform. This pattern parallels very closely the relationship that a "good boy" might establish with very stern and autocratic parents or that an obedient and well-trained soldier establishes with his superior officers.

2. Compulsive rebellion against the conscience. A person who has acquired a strict and authoritarian conscience may set out deliberately and systematically to rebel against it. His manifest guide to conduct might then be, "Would my conscience (meaning my parents, authorities, and so on) become shocked by such behavior?" If the answer is affirmative, he will then act in the shocking ways, even enjoying the dismay of others and the possible punishment which he receives for acting in those ways. The compulsive rebel is not aware that in compulsively violating the social mores and his parents' wishes, he is actually violating a repressed aspect of his real self; namely, his conscience.

3. *Anesthetizing the conscience.* Fiction is full of examples of people who have taken to drink and in so doing have violated their consciences high, wide, and handsome. Just as one might induce someone else to do all kinds of things when drunk that he would never do when sober, so can one "dissolve" one's conscience in alcohol. Alcohol appears to function as a "conscience solvent" by impairing the accuracy and precision with which the person makes (moral) judgments, and also by anesthetizing the person against the painful experience of guilt which he would ordinarily experience following moral lapses.

4. *Conscience-killing.* If a person is being followed, threatened, and persecuted by some accusing individual, he may resort to the extreme expedient of killing the accuser so as forever to still his voice. By the same token, all attempts on the part of a person to suspend, repress, or eliminate the act of self-judgment and self-criticism might be contrued symbolically as conscience-killing.[21] In extreme instances, a guilt-ridden person might kill himself because that is the only way that he can kill his conscience.

5. "*Sending the conscience on vacation.*" An employer who has an annoying, self-righteous partner or employee can sometimes gain temporary respite against the other's reproaches by sending him away for some period of time. In many ways, people may put their own consciences on vacation and place a definite moratorium on moral self-criticism. For example, a highly righteous man may go on a wild spree when he is out of town at a professional convention. There is a sort of tacit agreement between him and his fellow conventioneers that no one shall judge conduct during the convention time by home-town moral standards. However, if some neighbor from the home town who is not part of the convention should see the man in the midst of his revels, the latter might become guilty as well as embarrassed.

All the preceding ways of relating to the conscience may be regarded as unhealthy. In the long run, these unhealthy patterns have the consequence of promoting increased alienation from the self and of mobilizing increasing amounts of guilt. Now, let us examine the "voices" of conscience themselves: guilt and self-esteem.

GUILT AND SELF-ESTEEM

When a person behaves in opposition to his conscience he experiences guilt, just as he received punishment from his parents when they caught him behaving contrary to their expectations. When he behaves in conformity with his conscience, he experiences a heightening of the feeling of self-esteem, just as he received signs of love and lavish praise from his parents when they observed him doing something meritorious during childhood days. Guilt and self-esteem may be regarded as the internalized version of the punishments and rewards which earlier in life were accorded the child by his parents and other significant persons.

Guilt and self-esteem are both *emotional responses* to one's own inner experience and overt behavior. The emotional responses to *other people's* behavior which are analogous with guilt and self-esteem are moral indignation[22] and admiration,[23] respectively. Thus, when we see someone else treating an animal cruelly, we may become infuriated with that person, just as we would feel guilty for ill-treating the animal ourselves. If we see someone doing something which we wish we had the moral fortitude to do ourselves, we admire them for the exemplary deed.

As emotional responses, both guilt and self-esteem include cognitive, affective, expressive, and instrumental components. We can evaluate these responses with respect to their rationality, their congruence with social norms, with the person's age-roles, and so on. Further, we can evaluate the emotional behavior which guilt and self-esteem motivate the person to perform. Guilt-motivated behavior may be adjudged healthy or unhealthy, depending upon the consequences which follow from this behavior. Self-esteem-motivated behavior likewise can be assessed with respect to its consequences. Let us examine, discuss, and evaluate guilt and self-esteem.

SELF-ESTEEM

Self-esteem is the name given to the complex cognitive-affective response which accompanies behavior in accordance with the conscience.[24] Most of the time, we are not aware of the experience of self-esteem. It peeps, or leaps, over the threshold of awareness when we have accomplished some fairly difficult task that reflects favorably upon our moral worth in our own eyes and in the eyes of those who share our values. We most often become cognizant of self-esteem when we have lost it through some morally unacceptable activity or through some failure in achieving our self-appointed goals.

The cognitive aspects of self-esteem include verbal judgments of the following sort: "I am a good and worthwhile person"; "I respect myself as a person because of the way that I act"; and so on. The affective aspect of self-esteem is something analogous to the feelings which accompany the expectation of pleasant things. When a person has high self-esteem, he probably anticipates affection, praise, or admiration from others, and this expectancy feels good per se.

Self-esteem is rational when it derives from an accurate comparison of actual behavior and achievement with the relevant ideals of the conscience. It is irrational when the person esteems himself for traits which he actually does not possess and achievements he has not actually performed. The extreme case of irrational self-esteem is found in the patient who displays a manic psychotic reaction and in paranoid patients who believe they are someone great and wonderful.

Rational self-esteem is a personality-hygiene value, both in its own right and because of its influence upon the individual's interpersonal relationships. A person with self-esteem is much more likely to be able to establish healthy personal relationships with others (Chapter 10) than one who is chronically guilty or plagued by inferiority feelings.

Self-esteem is very highly dependent upon the continued receipt of affection, approval, and admiration from other persons, even in the individual with a healthy conscience. If one is perpetually criticized by others, one is likely in the long run to suffer a loss of self-esteem, even if one knows the criticism is not warranted. But a healthy personality is much more independent of external praise and approval than an unhealthy individual. The healthy personality may be said to display relatively *autonomous self-esteem*—he experiences it when he accords with *his* values, and he loses it when he violates *his* taboos. A person with a less solidly established conscience is likely to be what Riesman called an other-directed character, one whose self-evaluations and self-esteem are almost totally dependent upon a continued supply of favorable evaluations from others. The person who displays *self-esteem dependency* is much more at the mercy of people about him than the person with autonomous self-esteem; he may be subject to depressions and acute attacks of inferiority feelings every time there is some decrease in the flow of "narcissistic supplies"—praise and love from others—upon which his self-esteem rests.[25]

A fairly stable level of self-esteem is most likely to occur in persons with a healthy conscience who have received abundant supplies of love and appreciation during the process of growing up and who have been able to achieve a fairly adequate number of socially valued successes throughout their life. Self-esteem is of course highly dependent upon success, that is, achieving at one's level of aspiration. The more one has achieved, the more solidly established will one's self-esteem be. Finally, under optimum conditions, self-esteem will be predicated on a *broad base* of achievements and traits, and not dependent on some one, temporary and insecure basis, such as income or appearance.

GUILT

Guilt involves both cognitive judgments (I am no good; I am worthless) and strong affective components. No feeling is so agonizing to a well-socialized person as acute guilt, except, perhaps, an acute anxiety attack. Since guilt is such a powerful feeling, it incites the person to do something quickly in order to get rid of its pain. As we noted in an earlier chapter (Chapter 4), we can distinguish between appropriate and inappropriate guilt, and we can recognize healthy and unhealthy guilt-motivated behavior.

HEALTHY REACTIONS TO GUILT. In principle, a healthy reaction to guilt is one which (a) gets rid of the guilt feelings and restores self-esteem and (b) either preserves personality health or moves the person closer to the goal of a healthy personality.

There are some fundamental rules which, if followed, will insure that a person is handling his guilt in a healthy fashion. These rules may be listed as follows:

1. *When guilt is experienced, acknowledge it.* Suggesting the acknowledgment of guilt is no more than saying that a person should pay attention to all of his inner experience, whether it be pleasant or unpleasant.

2. *Following the recognition of guilt feelings in the self, the person should strive to determine why he feels guilt.* Determining why a person feels guilty involves a careful appraisal of whatever behavior, thoughts, wishes, or fantasies occurred just prior to the guilt-reaction. More important, it involves the necessity of making the rules and taboos of the conscience explicit, stating them in words in somewhat this fashion: "Since I feel guilty after doing that, I must hold the conviction, consciously or unconsciously, that such activity is wrong."

3. *Once the relevant taboo has been put into words, the person can then* examine the taboo itself, *in order to ascertain how he acquired it, how appropriate it is for a person in his present situation and with his present degree of development.*

4. *If critical assessment indicates the taboo is one which he believes should be observed, then the person can* reaffirm *it consciously, do whatever is necessary to make amends or to undo the "wrong" he has committed, and strive thenceforth to* conform with his conscience *in that respect.*

5. *If, on the other hand, the person discovers that the taboo responsible for his guilt is childish, or no longer relevant to his present situation, this very discovery may eliminate the guilt.* The person can say to himself, and believe it, "Why, I no longer believe it is wrong to do that." He has, in effect, actually *changed his conscience.*

From that time onward, he can perform, guilt-free, whatever actions he earlier had avoided because they induced guilt in him.

These steps toward the healthy management of guilt have been described earlier as *conformity with the conscience* and *changing the conscience.* That is, a person who has faced his guilt and acknowledged it has two healthy alternatives at his disposal for the riddance of his guilt: subsequent avoidance of the guilt-inducing behavior and conformity with his conscience (which has been made *conscious*), or changing his conscience and thus feeling free to do what earlier made him guilty.

Although we have spoken about changing the conscience, it must not be assumed this is an easy task to accomplish. There are many obstacles which make it a very difficult problem indeed. Yet it is not so difficult as to be impossible. We do know that conscience changes by itself many times during the process of growing up, usually in a way that is unconscious and automatic. As the person makes new identifications with new significant people, he often adopts many aspects of *their* consciences which come to replace the relevant taboos and rules of his own. As the person becomes involved in various groups which follow moral codes different from his own, he may come to adopt these new codes. These changes in conscience, however, are not deliberate and willed by the person. They just happen. It is the deliberate changes in conscience which probably are most difficult to achieve. Yet, if the person can make his conscience *conscious,* he will have gone a long way toward altering his taboos in the light of common sense and mature judgment. Probably one of the most effective means for changing an infantile conscience into one which is more conducive to adult living and adult satisfactions is intensive personality therapy. In therapy, the patient exposes his real self to the therapist, and in the process of self-exposure, he may verbalize many of his presently unconscious taboos for the first time. Further, he may get a clearer idea how he acquired these immature rules for conduct. Simply seeing all this *may* help the person change his conscience.[26]

What of conformity with the conscience? When is it healthy to conform with the conscience, and when it is healthy to attempt to change the conscience? The obvious answer is as follows: If the conscience is healthy, then the guilty person should strive to conform with it. If the conscience is unhealthy, then the person should strive to change it.

UNHEALTHY REACTIONS TO GUILT. Guilt is like pain or any other kind of suffering; it motivates the person powerfully to do something to get rid of the unwanted feelings. With physical pain, a person has three alternatives. He can simply endure the pain, doing nothing to ease it. He can take drugs to relieve himself of pain, the while doing nothing to remove the causes which are responsible for the pain. Or, he can treat the pain rationally—seek out its causes and do whatever is necessary, even go through greater pain in order to alter or remove these causes.

So it is with guilt. The person experiences guilt for a reason; he has acted in some way that violates his conscience. Upon experiencing guilt, the person can endure it, sedate himself so as not to feel it too keenly, or deal with it rationally. The rational means for dealing with guilt were discussed in an earlier section. Here, we shall examine some of the unhealthy reactions to guilt. They are called unhealthy because they do not get at the causes of the guilt and because they promote or perpetuate unhealthy personality.

Repression. A person may behave in ways which violate his conscience and then repress the consequent feelings of guilt. Repression is the name given to the process of excluding from awareness any painful or undesirable thoughts, feelings, or impulses. When a person represses his guilt feelings, we may assume that they continue to exist and function as all unconscious motives do. That is, we may expect the unconscious guilt to influence the person's behavior in subtle and unforeseen ways; we may expect a "return of the repressed" from time to time, when either the repression is weakened or the guilt feelings are increased in intensity. When this occurs, we would expect the person to experience an overwhelming onslaught of self-hate, worthlessness, depression, unlovability, feeling like a fake, or phony, and other like reactions. Another indicator of unconscious guilt might be the frequent recurrence of accidents that hurt the person's body, his property, or his career.

As long as the repression is effective in removing the guilt from awareness, the person can continue to act in ways that violate his moral precepts without any conscious loss in self-esteem. But he is actually compounding guilt. In the intervals when the repression is less efficient, he may review his long history of morally reprehensible conduct and feel so full of self-hate and so unworthy of being accepted by others that he may commit suicide. The author has known cases where a person has repressed guilt for a long interval. When the guilt "returned," the person was so full of loathing for himself that he became dramatically converted to a religious viewpoint, believing the religious affirmation would help him behave morally and regain self-esteem as well as the esteem of others. He has also known persons who reviewed their "sinful" pasts, evidently felt they were unsalvageable, and so committed suicide.

Projection. When a person is guilty, he despises himself. It is possible for a person to attribute his own psychological processes to another person, e.g., his feelings, thoughts, values, and so on, without recognizing that he has done so. But when this projection has occurred, he believes it is the other person who has these feelings and attitudes. A person with repressed guilt will of course deny he *experiences* guilt, but he may believe very strongly that other people condemn and despise him (disowning projection). This belief will be acted upon—he lives in a world of people whom he assumes despise him—yet careful study may disclose that other people have nothing but esteem for him, since they have not seen his sins and crimes.

Displacement. A person may successfully have repressed guilt for some major crime or sin against his own values, but then, for some minor omission or deed, he is overwhelmed with a guilt-onslaught which is disproportionate to the crime. Here we are probably observing the displacement of guilt. Thus, a man may have been cheating on his income tax for years, but he does not experience any conscious guilt for so doing. He may then forget to pay the paperboy and be overwhelmed with guilt.

Rationalization. Rationalization refers to the selection of explanations for action which will preserve self-esteem. In one's dealings with conscience, motives or reasons for actions are all-important. One can perform an apparently immoral action, but if one's motive is pure, no guilt is felt, no matter what the results of the action. If the motive itself violates the conscience, then, no matter if the action be saintly, the person will feel guilty. Consequently, of all the motives or explanations a person could find for a given action, he has a vested interest in choosing and believing only those motives which are consistent with his conscience. Take, for example, the act of killing another man. In our society, this action violates our moral code. If a person killed another individual intentionally, because he didn't like him, he would feel guilty. If he killed a person to protect his household, he would feel less guilty. If he killed a man who was trying to kill him, perhaps he would feel proud.

Redl and Wineman[27] described some ingenious rationalizations which a group of aggressive and delinquent children used in order to justify, without guilt, a wide variety of immoral actions. These included:

1. *Repression of intent.* An inability to recall the original motive for performing the crime, though there was full recall of the details of the crime itself.

2. *"He did it first."* Though the action was wrong, the fact that another person had done such a thing evidently served as a precedent, and this precedent made the action "legal."

3. *"Everybody else does such things anyway."* If everybody does such things, then they can't be wrong, and so I need not feel any guilt for doing them.

4. *"We were all in on it."* Since it was a group activity, the responsibility, and hence the guilt, either belongs to the leader or else to no one person.

5. *"But somebody else did that same thing to me before."* Because I once was the victim of such an act before, I am entitled to do the same thing to some present innocent party without having to feel guilt for it.

6. *"He had it coming to him."* The wronged person was such a sinner himself that he deserved to be sinned against; ergo, I need not feel guilty.

7. *"I had to do it, or I would have lost face."* Justifying one's actions on the assumption that status in a group with deviant values is more important than conformity with society's morals.

8. *"I didn't use the proceeds anyway."* An appeal to the "Robin Hood" mechanism. If I used the proceeds of illegally gotten money, and so on, for charitable or highly moral purposes, there need be no guilt.

9. *"But I made up with him afterwards."* If I befriend the victim of my immoral activity, I have thus undone the crime and need feel no guilt.

10. *"He is a no-good so-and-so himself."* Similar to number 6.

11. *"They are all against me, nobody likes me, they are always picking on me."* Since the person is living as if he is in an enemy camp, then all activity is justifiable.

12. *"I couldn't have gotten it any other way."* Self-exculpation on the premise that what was gained immorally was somehow the person's inviolable right; he is entitled to get it by any means.

Though these rationalizations were collected from a group of preadolescents, the reader might find them to be prototypes of many adult rationalizations.

One of the criteria which psychotherapists use in determining whether or not a patient has profited from the treatment is his willingness to consider seriously, and to compare with evidence, a wide range of *possible* motives for some action, rather than violently affirming some one self-enhancing motive and vigorously denying all others. The healthy personality will be less prone to such instant selectivity in the choice of possible explanations for his conduct and will be able to entertain even guilt-provoking motives as possible explanations for his action.

WHY THESE REACTIONS ARE UNHEALTHY. When a person has repressed, projected, displaced, or rationalized his guilts away, he has not really gotten rid of his guilt. All of the factors which are responsible for his guilt in the first place are still present; his conscience still includes the taboos he has been violating, and he is continuing to behave contrary to these taboos. Consequently, it can be assumed he is continually adding to his fund of guilt, in spite of the temporary effectiveness of his defenses against feeling it. The more guilt he accumulates, the more drastic must his defenses become in order to keep it from conscious awareness. The eventual consequences to these unhealthy reactions to guilt will be increased alienation from the self, increased ease of being threatened, and reduction in the capacity for free, honest communication with others—all unhealthy consequences. Finally, it should be stated again that these guilt-evasion tactics are seldom effective for very long. When the person is confronted by the full intensity of his previously repressed guilt, he may become neurotic, psychotic, or perhaps commit suicide.

PROMOTING HEALTHY CONSCIENCE

Parents, teachers, spouses, and friends can all assume they will have at least some influence on the conscience-development of the children, students, spouse, and friends with whom they interact. How can people in these roles promote the development of a healthy conscience in the individuals whose growth and well-being they influence?

One obvious thing they can do is avoid making unreasonable and excessive demands on the other person. If the relationship is one in which identification is likely to be fostered, then the demands made upon the other person are likely to become internalized as self-demands; that is, they are incorporated as part of the individual's conscience. Thus, if the demands and expectations made of a person have been reasonable and humane, the ground is prepared for the development of a healthy and humane conscience.

Another factor which can promote the development of a healthy conscience in a growing person is the presence of a healthy conscience in the significant others with whom he deals. When we identify with another person, we may identify with *his self-expectations* as well as with his expectations of us. If his demands upon himself are reasonable, then it is likely that we will make reasonable demands upon ourselves, following his example. A significant other who tortures himself with excessive demands and undue strictness with himself may promote the development of an excessively strict conscience in his child or student—even though he has never openly called for such achievement or moral strictness from him.

Yet another factor which can help promote the development of a healthy conscience in one's child, or friend, is to act at the real-self level when in the presence of the child, student, or friend. When this is done, the person who is doing the identifying will be able to acquire an accurate concept of his identification-model, complete with foibles and frailties. Parents often strive to hide many of their weaknesses and faults from their children, thus portraying themselves as perfect, flawless beings. The child may base his conscience upon this unrealistic model, thus paving the way for chronic guilt and inferiority feelings; that is, he strives to become "just like Daddy" and feels worthless when he finds he has many faults which Daddy seemed not to have. It might come as a shock to the son to discover that his father probably had these faults too but hid them from his son's gaze.[28]

We can help another person achieve a healthy conscience in still another, more direct way by commenting upon and evaluating his conscience from a realistic and health-oriented point of view. If we do not share our friend's ideals and taboos, we can let this be known to him and let him know why we disagree with his moral precepts. Just the experience of hearing another person comment upon his conscience may make him conscious enough of its contents to begin to assess it critically by himself.

PERSONAL VALUE-SYSTEMS AND HEALTHY PERSONALITY

Our personal value-system derives from the social value-system. If the social value-system is fraught with many conflicting values, taboos, and ideals, it can only be expected that the personal value-systems and the consciences of individual members of society will likewise be conflicted. A number of observers[29] of the contemporary American scene have called attention to sharp conflicts in values at the cultural level. We all value competitive success, but we also value co-operation. We value obedience to parents, but we also value independence. We value economic self-sufficiency, but we also value government support of industry and public relief. These conflicts at the cultural level are all reflected in the personality structure of individual members of the society. A culture which has conflicting and rapidly changing values is one which makes it difficult for its members to achieve a personal value-system which will serve as a guide to a life that has direction, meaning, and challenge.

A phenomenon which occurs in people's lives from time to time is the collapse of values, with accompanying collapse of conscience. This refers to the loss of the sense of values or the discovery that the aims which one had pursued with such cost in time, effort, and resources turned out to be meaningless and lacking in satisfaction or importance once they have been attained. Thus, some people may have defined wealth as their most important value and devoted their lives to becoming wealthy, only to find that once they had money, their life seemed to have lost its zest and purpose. Under these conditions, they may abolish their consciences and behave in amoral ways. They have no new values which might guide them, for example, in the worth-while expenditure of their wealth, and they see no reason for "being good."

Religion provides direction and a source of conscience for many persons. The more profoundly religious individuals see themselves as engaged in an endless dialogue with God.[30] They experience themselves as continuously challenged, in this dialogue, to fulfill their potentials, to discover and employ their talents, to love their fellow man, and to live as ethically as they can. A religious orientation of this humanistic sort, which does not foster an overly strict conscience or unnecessary repression, is a factor in healthy personality. Religious behavior which follows an authoritarian pattern, requiring the individual to repress his intellect and much of his emotion, by contrast, can be a factor in the development of unhealthy personality.[31]

In healthier personalities, the values in life and the ideals of conscience are hierarchically arranged, in an order from the least important to the most important, and such a personal value-system provides the individual with a guide, not only to ethical conduct, but also to the good life, one that remains zestful, satisfying, and challenging.[32]

SUMMARY

Conscience is a constraining influence upon a person's behavior and experiencing. In some forms, conscience can undermine the health of personality, whereas in healthier patterns, it can foster the fullest development of the individual and permit guilt-free gratification of needs.

Conscience is sometimes unconscious; it is age-graded; it is sometimes strict, conflicted, and authoritarian; it may be projected as well as repressed; and it can be deceived.

Unhealthy conscience is manifested by unremitting guilt, by the absence of guilt in the face of moral violations, and by guilt over apparently trivial lapses. Some patterns of unhealthy conscience include those which are excessively strict, those which are unduly permissive, deviant consciences, and those with elements in conflict. Healthy consciences are accessible to awareness, self-affirmed, flexible, mature, realistic, and with component values arranged in a hierarchy of degrees of importance. In addition, healthy consciences are more or less congruent with the social mores and are humane.

Given a healthy conscience, the desirable response to it is reasoned consideration—neither blind obedience nor compulsive rebellion. Unhealthy relationships with one's conscience include compulsive conformity and compulsive rebellion; efforts to "knock the conscience out of commission" by drinking to excess, by suicide, or by declaring holidays for conscience.

Self-esteem is the emotional state accompanying conformity with conscience, while guilt is the penalty for violation of conscience. Guilt should be acknowledged and responded to either by atonement or by efforts to change the conscience if its commands prove to be unduly strict or inappropriate.

Collapse of values and of conscience arises when a person finds the values he has hitherto pursued have become meaningless. Such collapse can be forestalled by affirmation of a positive philosophy of life, one which sets goals that continually challenge the person, no matter what he has accomplished.

NOTES AND REFERENCES

Excellent supplementary reading will be provided by those references marked with an asterisk (*).

*1. See LaPiere, R., *Social Control* (New York: McGraw, 1954), for a systematic account of social control. See also Parsons, T., *The Social System* (Glencoe, Ill.: Free Press, 1951), pp. 297–321.

2. See Parsons, T., *op. cit.*, for a sociological account of value-orientations.

*3. This phenomenon is one aspect of what sociologists call *anomie*. See Merton, R. K., *Social Theory and Social Structure* (Glencoe, Ill.: Free Press, 1949).

*4. See Parsons, T. and Bales, R. F., *Family, Socialization and Interaction Process* (Glencoe, Ill.: Free Press, 1955), ch. 2.

5. Riesman calls the person whose behavior is primarily controlled by his conscience an *inner-directed character*. See Riesman, D., *The Lonely Crowd* (New Haven, Conn.: Yale, 1950).

*6. See Mowrer, O. H. (ed.), *Psychotherapy: Theory and Research* (New York: Ronald, 1953), especially chs. 3, 6, for the most systematic account of

Mowrer's theory of the origins of neurosis and of the aims of therapy. Also, by the same author, "Learning Theory and the Neurotic Paradox," *Amer. J. Orthopsychiat., 18,* 571–610 (1948); "Symposium, 1952. The Therapeutic Process. III. Learning Theory and the Neurotic Fallacy," *Amer. J. Orthopsychiat., 22,* 679–689 (1952); "Some Philosophic Problems in Mental Disorder and Its Treatment," *Harvard Educ. Rev., 23,* 117–127 (1953); and *The Crisis in Psychotherapy and Religion* (Princeton, N.J.: Van Nostrand, 1961), chs. 2, 13. A more sophisticated view of conflicting theories of neurosis is given in Waelder, R., "The Principle of Multiple Function," *Psychoanalyt. Quart., 5,* 45–62 (1936), especially pp. 54–55.

7. A patient undergoing personality therapy once remarked to the present writer, "I've been brought up to believe if I enjoy doing something, then it *must* be a sin, so I mustn't do it."

8. *Cf.* Freud, S., *The Ego and the Id* (London: Hogarth, 1927). Also Fenichel, O., *The Psychoanalytic Theory of Neurosis* (New York: Norton, 1945), ch. 6.

9. Rogers, C. R., *Client-Centered Therapy* (New York: Houghton, 1951), p. 140. Also Rogers, C. R. and Dymond, Rosalind F. (eds.), *Psychotherapy and Personality Change* (Chicago: U. of Chicago, 1954).

10. For a psychoanalytic formulation of identification and the superego, see Fenichel, O., *op. cit.,* ch. 6; for a more general learning theory analysis of identification, see Mowrer, O. H., *Learning Theory and Personality Dynamics* (New York: Ronald, 1950). See also Hendrick, I., "Early Development of the Ego: Identification in Infancy," *Psychoanalyt. Quart., 20,* 44–61 (1950). See also Bandura, A. and Huston, A. C., "Identification as a Process of Incidental Learning," *J. Abnorm. Soc. Psychol., 63,* 311–318 (1961).

*11. See Flugel, J. C., *Man, Morals, and Society* (New York: International Universities Press, 1945), chs. 4, 9, 11, 12, for an analysis from a psychoanalytic viewpoint as to why the superego (conscience) is often so strict.

12. Fromm, E., *Man for Himself* (New York: Rinehart, 1947), pp. 143–175.

13. *Cf.* Mowrer, O. H., *op. cit.*

14. Fenichel, O., *op. cit.,* pp. 109–110.

*15. *Cf.* Redl, F. and Wineman, D., *Children Who Hate* (Glencoe, Ill.: Free Press, 1951), chs. 4, 5.

16. Horney describes strict conscience as the "tyranny of the should." See Horney, K., *Neurosis and Human Growth* (New York: Norton, 1950), ch. 3. See ch. 5 for discussions of guilt, self-hate, and self-contempt.

17. Fromm, E., *op. cit.*

18. Maslow, A. H., *Motivation and Personality* (New York: Harper, 1954), ch. 12.

*19. Fromm, E., *op. cit.,* pp. 159 ff. Also Buber, M., "Guilt and Guilt Feelings," *Psychiatry, 20,* 114–129 (1957).

20. Such reasoned consideration seems to be easier to give to others than to the self; we are often harsher in our demands on ourselves than on others.

21. See Mowrer, O. H., *op. cit.*, for an elaboration of the concept of "conscience-killing."

22. See Riesman, D., *op. cit.*, for a discussion of moral indignation. Also Jourard, S. M., "Moral Indignation: A Correlate of Denied Dislike of Parents' Traits," *J. Consult. Psychol.*, *18*, 59–60 (1954).

23. See Jourard, S. M., "Identification, Parent-Cathexis, and Self-Esteem," *J. Consult. Psychol.*, *21*, 375–380 (1958). In this paper, positive cathexis for parents (admiration) is demonstrated to be a correlate of the extent to which the parents' personality traits and behavior accord with the child's ideals for parents' personality.

24. Jourard, S. M., *op. cit.* See also Maslow, A. H., *op. cit.*

25. Fenichel, O., *op. cit.*, ch. 17.

26. Rosenthal demonstrated that among patients who showed improvement under therapy, there was a change in moral values in the direction of those held by their therapists. See Rosenthal, D., "Changes in Some Moral Values Following Psychotherapy," *J. Consult. Psychol.*, *19*, 431–436 (1955). Rogers *et al.* found changes in the "self-ideal" of patients who had undergone therapy—changes in the direction of the real self. See Rogers, C. R. and Dymond, R. F., *op. cit.*

27. Redl, F. and Wineman, D., *op. cit.*, pp. 145–156.

28. Interestingly enough, research has shown that people tend to disclose less about themselves to their fathers than to their mothers or their peers. Furthermore, fathers seem to disclose less about themselves to their sons and daughters than mothers do. See Jourard, S. M. and Lasakow, P., "Some Factors in Self-Disclosure," *J. Abnorm. Soc. Psychol.*, *56*, 91–98 (1958).

29. *Cf.* Horney, K., *The Neurotic Personality of Our Time* (New York: Norton, 1937).

*30. See Buber, M., *Between Man and Man* (Boston: Beacon, 1955), pp. 1–39, for amplification of the concept of dialogue.

*31. See Fromm, E., *Psychoanalysis and Religion* (New Haven, Conn.: Yale, 1950) (paperback edition, 1959), for the contrast between authoritarian religion and humanistic religion.

*32. Maslow, A. H., *Toward a Psychology of Being* (Princeton, N.J.: Van Nostrand, 1962), pp. 76–79; chs. 11, 12.

CHAPTER 9
INTERPERSONAL BEHAVIOR AND HEALTHY PERSONALITY

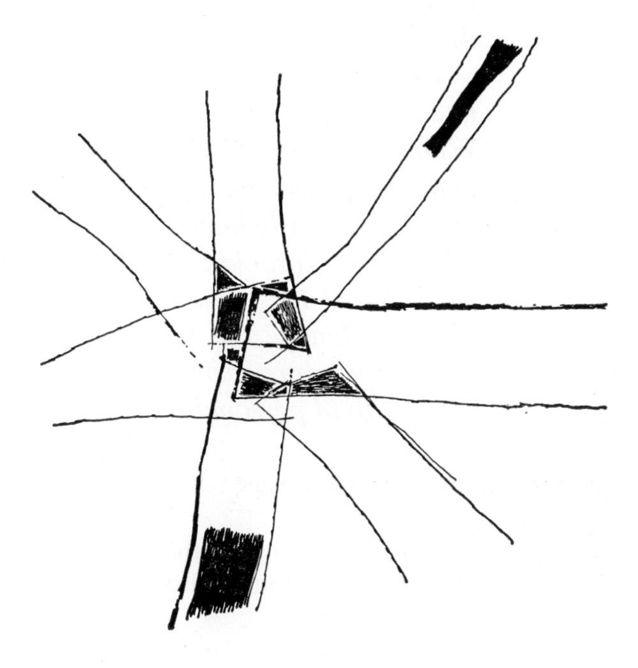

INTRODUCTION

Many of our basic needs can be satisfied only through relationships with other persons. Other people are frequently the source of frustration or irritation, but we can hardly remain fully human without some form of communicative contact with our fellow man.[1] *This is not to say that moments of separation from others are dangerous to one's well-being; indeed, there is some evidence that the healthiest personalities need and actively seek periods of solitude in order to contemplate and to discover their authentic feelings and beliefs.*[2]

Why do we need other people? What do we need them for, and what do we need from them? What are some of the more common bases for man's dependency upon his fellows? And how must a person behave toward others so that they will, in turn, provide him with whatever he needs from them? First, we will examine some aspects of dependency, and then we shall turn to a discussion of interpersonal behavior in its relation to the health of personality.

DEPENDENCY IN INFANTS

A newborn human infant is among the most helpless of living organisms. The repertoire of instrumental action which the human infant can perform is limited to a few automatic reflexes: swallowing, eliminating, crying, and gross motor movements. For sheer survival, the infant needs other people—parents or parent-surrogates—to behave in ways which will bring all manner of need-objects to him. The mother must provide food and arrange the environment so that the child will stay alive, relatively free from pain, and able to grow. As the child develops physically, so that he becomes more capable of learning, he needs other people as identification-models so he can become increasingly socialized. He needs to hear people talk, for example, so he can learn to talk. He needs, in his early days, a lot of mothering[3]—caressing, holding, and social stimulation; there is evidence that without such close mothering, his physical development will be impaired, and his social development will be deviant. The child needs other people to reward and punish him so he can learn to behave in socially acceptable ways. He needs to be in contact with peers, other children his age, so he can learn to compete, co-operate, play games, and so on. Contact with other people is thus seen as crucial for many aspects of a child's healthy development: physical survival and health; the learning of many skills important in the solution of problems and the gratification of assorted needs; and the learning of attitudes, values, morals, and social roles, essential in defining the child's membership in varied groups.

DEPENDENCY IN ADULTS

The adult, by virtue of a vastly increased skill-repertoire, is much more self-reliant than the infant or young child, but he still needs other people for many reasons. Most of the satisfactions which make life worth while in fact can be gratified only in relation to, or with the co-operation of, other people.

TECHNICAL DEPENDENCY. In a society so complex as ours, no man can ever hope in his lifetime to encompass all the skills necessary to solve all his problems and gratify all of his wants. Division of labor and specialization in knowledge and technique are enormously developed in the Western world, so each man is dependent upon many other people for their specialized skill and knowledge.

The question may be asked, "How can an individual get the other person who has the needed skills to utilize them in his behalf?" In our society, this is generally accomplished on a *quid pro quo* basis; the needful individual "buys" the knowledge or skill from its possessor with money or anything else that is deemed of value equivalent to the skill. In some instances, if the skill or knowledge is very scarce, the possessor will set high or unusual prices for the purchase of his skill-commodity.

SELF-ESTEEM DEPENDENCY. The adult may need other people to behave toward him in certain prescribed ways in order to maintain his self-esteem. Thus, if a person has acquired a "self-ideal" which specifies, essentially: "I am not a worth-while self-respecting individual unless other people (in general, or else certain classes of people) admire me, or listen to me seriously, or just plain like me," then it becomes apparent that he needs them to behave in the requisite ways. When they do not, he will be overwhelmed with feelings of inadequacy, worthlessness, or what is commonly called depression.[4] In our society, almost everyone's self-esteem is strongly determined by the presence of approval or accepting-responses from others; but there is also great variability to be found in just how a person needs others to act toward him in order to maintain self-esteem. These individual differences stem from individual differences in life experiences. To illustrate: The author knows several men who feel depressed and inadequate if an attractive woman does not seem to be favorably impressed by their appearance and behavior. A student undergoing personality therapy had a very curious set of conditions which had to be met in order that he might experience self-esteem. It was necessary that his father, *and only his father*, approve of his behavior. When the needed approval-response was obtained from his father, he would be elated, happy, and would hold himself in very high esteem. At the faintest indication of paternal disapproval, the student would be literally overwhelmed by self-hate, depression, and the conviction that he was a worthless individual. In his most severely depressed moments, he would even consider self-destruction. However, no one but his father could affect him in this way.

The reader might well ask himself this question: "How do I need other people [be specific in referring to other people, e.g., mother, father, spouse, boss, friend, and so on] to behave toward me in order that I continue (or begin) to feel self-esteem?" The answers should provide considerable illumination to the motives for much behavior which occurs in the presence of those people. Very often, in order to obtain the needed behavior from the other, the individual has to "buy" it with behavior that conforms with the other's demands and expectations. This means that wherever there is a conflict between one's own wants and the other's demands, the wants must be sacrificed; when they are acceded to, the consequence is that the other withdraws the needed praise or approval, and the person loses self-esteem.

SECURITY DEPENDENCY. Security has been defined in many ways. In this context, security means the belief that everything one values and needs is safe from threat. People need and value many things for many reasons. So long as the need- and value-objects are available and assured, the person is secure. Anything which threatens to remove, or restrict, the availability of the need- and value-objects provokes insecurity, or more precisely, *anxiety*. Anxiety always implies the anticipation of pain or some form of unpleasantness; in this context, the pain or unpleasantness is produced by deprivation of the need-objects. It is, literally, "frustration-anxiety," the apprehension of frustration.

Since other people do provide us with many things we need and value, then to that extent we are dependent on these other people for our security.[5] As long as the other people are willing and able to act in ways that satisfy our wants (wants which we cannot satisfy by ourselves), then we feel secure. Anything which threatens the relationship with the "dependency-object" will provoke anxiety in the dependent person. He cannot satisfy all his wants by his own behavior; he needs the other person. If the other person is not available or is no longer willing to act in need-satisfying ways, then the dependent person faces the frightening prospect of deprivation.

As with self-esteem dependency, the individual whose security is dependent upon the intervention of other people must buy their skill, knowledge, or needed behavior in assorted ways. He must conform with their expectations and demands; he must get them to like him; in more general terms, he must govern his behavior by their wishes so as not to jeopardize his friendly relationships with them.

In our society, there are many satisfactions which are possible to achieve *only if other people in general like you.* This objective state of affairs makes "likability" a trait of fundamental importance to the individual and the experience of being disliked a near catastrophe. (Later in this chapter, we will discuss this in greater detail.) When one is disliked, it may have the consequence of making many valued ends and many satisfactions completely inaccessible. Riesman's "other-directed" character is the logical outgrowth of the social conditions which make each of us dependent upon others for important need-satisfactions. Since other people will "come across" only if they like us, then we come to seek their approval and affection just as we seek money: not for its own sake, but for what it will enable us to acquire. And so in our society, many people dread being disliked just as they dread financial bankruptcy, and for the same reasons.

IDENTITY-DEPENDENCY. A person's sense of personal identity may be defined as a conviction or belief he *is* somebody, that he has characteristics which set him off from other people. In order that the sense of identity be strengthened, it is important that other people recognize, appreciate, value, encourage, and react to these individual idiosyncrasies. When other people react to an individual on a *formal* basis, when they see him as simply one member of a broad class or category of people, they actually deindividualize the person. Such behavior makes him feel much less an individual person and much more the embodiment of his social role. For example, a wife may be perceived and reacted to by her spouse as "the wife": "I'll have to ask the wife." For him, she is a wife, not a person. A recruit in the army soon learns that his personal idiosyncrasies, so lovingly recognized and catered to by his mother, are ignored by his sergeant; for the latter, he is just another GI. And the army chef cooks for "the men"—not for John, Bill, or Arthur.[6]

The sense of identity is an important aspect of personality health; a person could not be called healthy if he lacked a sense of identity or if he suffered a weakened sense of identity. But it is clear the sense of identity is strongly dependent upon the reactions of other people to the self. If others will not recognize and respond to one's idiosyncrasies, the person loses palpably in the sense of identity and feels much less a person. We conclude that people are dependent upon others for the reinforcement of the identity-sense.

DIRECTION-DEPENDENCY. Personality hygienists place a positive valuation on autonomy, one aspect of which is self-direction (or, more literally, real-self-direction). By this is meant the person makes his own decisions; he follows his own will and not the will of others. But it happens that people become, in consequence of certain kinds of life-history experiences, "alienated from their real selves." When this has occurred, the individual loses the sense of being self-directing, and he will experience the need for some source of direction other than his own will. Earlier (Chapter 6) we noted certain patterns which emerge from self-alienation. From among these patterns of behavior-direction, let us discuss *authority-direction* and *peer-group direction.* The authority-directed character, or *authoritarian-character,* is an individual who feels lost unless he is in a position subordinate to some authority figure.[7] The directing agents for his behavior might be his parents, his superior officer in the armed services, or his boss. The peer-group-directed character has substituted the will of his peers for his own; he strives to ascertain what others do in a given situation and allows their example or their wishes to be his guide to conduct. He is the compulsive conformer which Fromm[8] and Riesman[9] have described; more recently, experimental psychologists have begun investigating his traits in more detailed fashion.[10]

LOVE-DEPENDENCY. Love is a basic requirement for personality health and for happiness, and it is obvious we are dependent upon other people for their love. We need the love of (selected) other people. One of the reasons we pursue affection so assiduously is that affection in another person is a signal that loving-behavior will be forthcoming from him. Love-dependency is a form of dependency which is quite compatible with personality health. In our culture, we place such great emphasis on the positive value of independence and autonomy we are likely to overlook the fact that the need for love is a healthy need, and its satisfaction does not necessarily rob a person of his identity or independence. Indeed, a person deprived of love will find difficulty in relating to other people in socially acceptable and personally satisfying ways. Or, he may become quite indiscriminate in his quest for persons to love him.[11]

We have reviewed man's dependence upon his fellows for survival during infancy, for technical assistance, approval, security, reinforcement of his identity, direction, and love. Let us now turn to a discussion of interpersonal behavior—man's ways of behaving toward his fellow man—and explore its implications for his personality health.

INTERPERSONAL BEHAVIOR

The behavior of a person in relation to or in the presence of his fellows has been subjected to intense study over the past decade, and will doubtless remain a subject of keen interest to psychologists for many years to come. The reason for this aroused interest in interpersonal behavior stems from the observation that man's personality characteristics are strongly determined and influenced by his relations with others. Martin Buber, a philosopher whose writings have stimulated many contemporary psychologists and psychiatrists, has made the statement, "The *I* in the primary word *I-Thou* is a different *I* from that of the primary word *I-It*."[12] In another context, Buber asserts that the essential nature of man will reveal itself for study only as man is involved in relations with other men as distinct individuals.[13] Buber's statement about the difference between the "I" of I-Thou and the "I" of I-It means that man, when he interacts with other men as persons, behaves and functions *differently* from man when he deals with things or with other people who are treated as things. An observer who studied man only in relation to an impersonal environment would get an entirely different view of man from one who observed men in their relationships with other people.

INTERPERSONAL COMPETENCE

Man, living in society as he does, is obliged to suppress and delimit his behavior to that range which is compatible with the smooth functioning of the over-all group or society. To the extent that his behavior conforms with rules, laws, customs, and the legitimate expectations of others, the man will remain free from criticism, punishment, and censure. In order that conformity with social expectation be facilitated, people are obliged to learn *roles* —patterns of approved and expected behavior—that are associated with one's sex, one's age level, one's position in the family: viz., father, mother, son; occupational roles; and so on. Healthy personality calls for facility at the learning and enactment of these roles in relationships with other people. But a potential threat to health is implicit to roles. Roles call for *suppression* of all behavior and emotion that is inappropriate to the role-definition. This suppression is necessary so that ordinary social relations will proceed along smooth, frictionless paths. People need to be able to predict the responses of others in their everyday transactions. We depend upon our parents behaving like parents, not like children. We expect a physician to behave like a physician when he is in his clinic, not like a playboy. But we have shown elsewhere (Chapter 4) that prolonged suppression of feelings and behavior tendencies can undermine health and that spontaneity and expressiveness are positive factors in wellness. This suggests that healthy personality calls for the ability to reconcile the often conflicting demands of role-behavior and "real-self" behavior. That is, healthy personalities should be able to confine their interpersonal behavior to the limits prescribed by their roles, when this is appropriate, and they should be able to abandon such formality and be themselves in the fullest spontaneity in their relations with others when the situation permits it. Such openness and spontaneity is appropriate in "personal relations" between people, and we shall devote the next chapter to discussion of factors in healthy personal relations. But if a person can assume a variety of roles in his transactions with others, and if he can abandon formal roles and be himself in his personal relations, he is manifesting a special type of skill which we shall call *interpersonal competence.*[14] Such interpersonal competence is an identifying characteristic of healthy personality. Two aspects of such competence are *role-versatility* and *role-adequacy.* These terms refer to the desirable ability to fulfill a variety of roles (versatility) in socially acceptable ways (adequacy). Let us discuss role-behavior and explore its relation to the health of personality.

ROLE-BEHAVIOR AND HEALTHY PERSONALITY

An individual will enact many roles in his relationships with others. He may be obliged to play the role of husband, father, son, employee, boss, and so on. Each social role a person adopts carries with it certain prescriptions concerning how he must or should behave. Naturally, as a person plays any role, *he is obliged to suppress behavior which is not relevant to the role in question.* If, for example, the role of son requires that the person display only respect, obedience, and submission, then the son must suppress all rebellious, hostile, or self-assertive behavior. A person may avoid certain roles, or strongly resist having the role thrust on him, when the behavior required by that role threatens his self-structure or else interferes with the satisfaction of important needs. Thus, a person may reject the role of husband because such a role will require him to assume responsibility for others, and he may believe he is incapable of holding down a job. Marriage may require him to give up a close relationship with his mother, or with some friends, and since he needs those relationships in order to maintain a sense of identity, security, or self-esteem, he will avoid marriage.

Some roles dovetail nicely with the needs and values of the person, allowing him to find many important satisfactions. Thus a man may seek out the role of the leader, or the follower, because these roles require him to engage in interpersonal behavior which guarantees him safety, satisfactions, and self-esteem.[15]

Although an adult person has some freedom to choose various roles, e.g., occupational roles, some are ascribed to him by society because of sex, age, and the social group into which he has been born. As with all roles, the sex-role, the age-role, and the roles that are assigned because of group membership involve restriction and prescription of certain behavior patterns. The idiosyncratic needs of the person may be satisfied or thwarted by these roles, and so a discussion is warranted of *assigned* roles and personality health.

SEX-ROLES. One's sex is determined at the instant of conception, but masculine and feminine behavior and personality are *culturally* defined and determined. Each person has to learn or be trained in his sex-role. Each society differs in its concept of masculine and feminine behavior, as Mead has convincingly demonstrated.[16] She showed that in three New Guinea tribes, there was considerable difference from tribe to tribe in the typical male and female roles. In one group, the Arapesh, men and women alike were passive, "maternal," co-operative, and nonaggressive. In the Mundugamor, a tribe geographically close to the Arapesh, men and women alike were fierce, cruel, aggressive, and self-assertive. A third tribe, the Tchambuli, showed a different pattern of sex-typing. The men were passive, dependent, individuals who spent their time cultivating the arts, while the women were assertive, and had to cultivate the gardens and make a living.

In America, rigid definition of sex-roles is gradually breaking down. Thus, many middle-class men take an active role in child care, in housekeeping, while their wives do many things which once were deemed to be a male prerogative: They keep the budget, spend the money, and work at occupations that formerly were strictly male. In some European countries, male and female behavior contrasts in certain ways with the American concept of masculinity and femininity. Thus, in Latin countries, a man can comfortably kiss another man, and he can cry openly without shame. But these men might look askance at the American woman who likes to wear trousers. For them, women belong in dresses.

In order to "wear" one's sex-role comfortably, a person has to be trained into it. Yet, some men have been reared in ways that promote the development of traits ordinarily regarded as effeminate; they may also have acquired, in process of growing up, the cultural concepts of the male role. Therefore, they find it a strain to "be a man." In acting in manly ways, they are going against their (acquired) "nature." But if they were to act in the ways which were most natural for them, they might experience a considerable threat to their sense of identity as a man and expose themselves to much ridicule. The same considerations apply to women. The individual who has acquired a rigid concept of male and female roles may experience a high degree of inner discomfort and conflict. If he acts just as he feels, he may undergo a threat to his self-concept. If he acts in accordance with his sex-role, he may suffer from considerable frustration of strong needs for self-expression. Some individuals are so insecure about their sexual identity that they must "overprotest." Instead of being content to be manly, they must be "supermanly." They exaggerate their manly traits as if to convince themselves and others that they are indeed men. If anyone questions the masculinity of such a person, he may become dangerously aggressive. His life involves a continual quest for reassurances of his own masculinity. A woman who questions her own femininity may adopt the same adjustive procedures.

A common occurrence is that of role-conflict. Sociologists have pointed out that this is becoming increasingly common, especially among women, as our social system undergoes changes. The woman is obliged to be a housekeeper, a glamor girl, and a stimulating companion to her husband. It may be difficult for her to do justice to all of these roles, so that she comes to doubt her identity as a woman.[17]

Some women, as the psychoanalysts have pointed out, are very resentful of the woman's role in society and envious of the apparent freedom and more privileged position of the male in our society. This pattern has been metaphorically described among the analysts as "penis-envy." Mead has shown that just as women may envy the male, so some men may envy certain female prerogatives, such as their role in the bearing of children. In this connection she speaks of "womb-envy."[18]

Since sex-roles are relatively fixed by society, each person, man and woman, must find ways of fitting himself to his sex-role, of coming to terms with it. Some men and women find their sex-role too constraining, and they adopt many of the patterns of the opposite sex, both sexually and behaviorally.

The healthy personality is able to redefine his own personal sex-role in ways that dovetail better with his needs. Consequently, he has greater freedom to express and act out his real self and is much less easily threatened. Thus, a healthy man can do many things that might be deemed effeminate by other men, and yet he will not experience any threat to his masculinity. He may wash dishes, change babies, perform jobs such as hairdressing or ballet, yet still feel manly. A rigid concept of one's sex-role can promote the development of unhealthy personality.

AGE-ROLES. Each society expects a progression of behavior in its members, a progression that will keep pace with the person's chronological age. If a person is keeping pace with his age-roles, he is said to be mature. If he is behind other people his age, he is said to be immature, or *fixated*. If he reverts to behavior characteristic of a younger age, he is said to display *regression*, and if he shows a premature development of traits expected from older persons, he is said to display *precocity*. As with sex-roles, age-roles may conflict sharply with the person's needs. He may not be ready to progress to the next age-role when the time for it comes. Or, he may enforce conformity with his age-role on himself, at considerable cost in satisfactions.

By the time an individual has become an adult, as this is defined in his culture, he acquires a vested interest in regarding himself as mature. Yet, need-gratifications may be possible only if he behaves in immature ways.

The healthy personality feels sufficiently secure about his identity as a mature adult that he can regress when he wants to or when he feels like it without any marked threats to self-esteem or to his sense of identity. A person who is insecure about his maturity may strive to convince himself and others that he is mature and avoid any regressive behavior like the plague. Thus, some men may not allow themselves to be taken care of even when they are gravely sick because it would imply that they had regressed. Some women may refuse tenderness and solicitude from a man because of the implication that they are not independent adults. Some adults cannot play because frolicsomeness feels childish to them and threatens their self-esteem.

ROLE-VERSATILITY AND -ADEQUACY IN THE HEALTHY PERSONALITY

An individual who is unable to assume a variety of roles in his daily life, and enact them in socially acceptable ways, is foredoomed to social censure. On the other hand, the individual who delimits his behavior too stringently to the roles he plays—never appearing "off stage," as it were, never letting his hair down—is likely to be prone to recurrent illness.

Thus, a student who has attained some measure of role-versatility and -adequacy might, in the course of a day, be a student to his teacher, a roommate to his friend, a "date" to a casual female acquaintance, a son to his parents, and a brother to his siblings. These roles call for a broad repertoire of behavior, and it is clear that any inner factors, such as an unhealthy self-structure (see Chapter 6), might impede the smooth performance of these roles. However, given a healthy self-structure, the required behavior could be enacted without inner stress. When the social situation permits it, as in personal relations, the student could relax and simply be himself. For example, a student might spend an hour with his professor and portray himself as interested, deferent, and absorbed in the topics of conversation. In fact, the student may authentically *be* interested, deferent, and absorbed, but consciously or unconsciously, he is delimiting his behavior to the range that is appropriate for teacher-student relationships. When he goes back to his dormitory and starts "horsing around" with his fellow students, he will doubtless be more at ease, more expressive of his feelings, and he may even speak disparagingly about eccentricities of the teacher he has just left. If he lacks role-versatility, he might display the same modes of behavior with his fellow students that he did with the professor. Such *might* betoken admirable consistency, but more likely it would exemplify a type of unhealthy rigidity.[19]

Let us turn now to further discussion of interpersonal behavior, looking at it from the standpoint of its effectiveness or ineffectiveness in fulfilling the purposes of various transactions. The point at issue here is whether the individual is able to achieve his purposes in his relationships with others without jeopardy to other values such as his health, his comfort, his morality, and so on. The concept of interpersonal competence must be expanded to include, not only role-adequacy and -versatility, but also the dimension of *effectiveness* in relating to others. We will confine our discussion primarily to factors in ineffective interpersonal behavior, but the reader can readily transpose terms in the discussion that follows and arrive at a statement of some factors in effective interpersonal behavior.

FACTORS IN INEFFECTIVE INTERPERSONAL BEHAVIOR

Literature abounds with examples of persons who do not know how to behave with others. The wallflower, the obnoxious character, the sycophant—these are well-known illustrations. Why does a person act in ways which alienate people from him, and why does a person not act in ways which will bring him affection, admiration, and love? Naturally, there are many possible explanations, but we shall content ourselves with only a few of the more obvious factors which promote ineffective interpersonal behavior.

DEVIANT SOCIALIZATION. If a person has been reared in atypical ways, or in another culture, his idea of acceptable interpersonal behavior is likely to be unrealistic for our society. For example, a man reared in some foreign country may assume that an American girl will be flattered if he flirts with her in a frank manner. His face may be abruptly slapped before he learns that his advances have been interpreted differently than he intended.

DEFECTIVE EMPATHY. Empathy may be defined as the attainment of an accurate imaginative picture of the *present* subjective state of another person.[20] One has empathy with another person when one correctly infers that he is, right now, friendly, or afraid, or puzzled and lets him know this in some way. Usually, one formulates one's empathic guesses on the basis of facial cues, or from the person's ongoing overt behavior, as well as from past experience with the individual in quetion. One is better able to achieve empathy with one's long-time friend than with a stranger. If an individual lacks the ability to imagine the probable inner experience of another, or if he fails to confirm his empathic guesses, he may well behave toward the other in ways that defeat his purposes. Thus, if my aim is to teach a student, and I fail to discern that he is bored and uninterested, my teaching efforts will likely be without their intended effect.

IRRATIONAL ANXIETY. Past experience may have produced a dread of behaving in certain ways so that these modes of acting are suppressed. Yet the suppressed behavior patterns may be the very ones which, if manifested in his present life situation, would bring rich gratifications to the person. Thus, he may have been severely rejected once when he displayed spontaneous affection for another person. The experience was so traumatic for him he suppressed any tendencies to express spontaneous affection for other people. But it happens that openly expressed affection is one of the most efficient means of eliciting affection-responses from another person. The consequence of suppressing affection may be that the suppresser is obliged to suffer an extreme lack of affection. Any other interpersonal behavior which has been suppressed because of irrational anxiety will have the consequence of limiting the person's behavior-repertoire and hence will limit the range of gratifications which he can obtain in relationships with other people.

EXCESSIVELY STRICT CONSCIENCE AND SELF-IDEAL. Strict morality and unrealistic pride may so limit a person's interpersonal behavior that he cannot act in ways which provoke friendliness in others. In order to be free of guilt and to maintain self-esteem, he maintains a strict and rigid adherence to some behavioral code. The consequence may be that people find him cold, aloof, stilted, and uncommunicative. The overly proud and the overly moral person will thus have to face the consequences of a friendless and empty interpersonal existence.

EXCESSIVE PRIVATION. If a person is starved for food, sex, affection, fame, or other gratifications, he may pursue these goals at the expense of his own dignity and integrity, as well as the integrity of others. Under high deprivation, the individual perceives others as means to his ends, or obstacles to the pursuit of his ends. A person under strong need-tension is less able to perceive others' needs and reactions accurately and is likely to "use" others, ignoring the while their individuality and their privilege of being treated as "ends in themselves."

DEFECTIVE KNOWLEDGE OF PEOPLE IN GENERAL. When a person's contacts with other people have been restricted for any reason, e.g., through isolation, lack of travel, lack of exposure to others, he will have had little opportunity to learn the similarities and differences to be found in people. Some socially inept people, for example, become shocked when they learn that others have traits in common with them and even more shocked when they learn that others may differ from them in attitudes, feelings, goals, and so on.

FAKING AND MANIPULATING. One who chronically fakes his feelings, for example, pretending to be friendly when in fact he loathes the other person, is bound in time to be "found out." The confirmed "phony" may, if he persists in masking his authentic feelings and purposes, eventually lose sight of them in himself. That is, in hiding his true feelings from others, he will ultimately hide them from himself and become increasingly "self-alienated."

Many people dream of being able to manipulate other people into doing what they want them to do. The average student is fascinated with accounts of the effects of subtle propaganda in shaping the attitudes of the populace; of the shrewdness of advertisers at molding the buying habits of people; at the skill of the college Romeo who can boast of his conquest with the opposite sex by virtue of a "smooth line." The extreme case of manipulation of others is provided by hypnosis, in which the subject will apparently behave with unquestioned compliance to the wishes and commands of the hypnotist.

When manipulation becomes the most usual mode of interacting with others, it is a serious sign of impaired personality health. It implies, among other things, a profound distrust of the other person, even a contempt for him. Furthermore, the habitual manipulator of others, in his efforts to manipulate, must repress his real self, thereby promoting further self-alienation.[21]

The contriving, manipulative, insincere individual, often without conscious awareness, places popularity and "success" at the peak of his value-hierarchy. He sells his soul (his real self) to achieve it. He strives to determine what kind of behavior the other person likes and then pretends to be the kind of person who habitually behaves in that way. The net consequences are that the other person formulates an inaccurate concept of the individual, and the latter finds it a growing burden to maintain a variety of conflicting and false public selves (see Chapter 6). And finally, he may come to feel he has acquired friends on false pretenses—if people found out what he was really like, they might ostracize him.

The major factor responsible for habitually contrived interpersonal behavior is the belief, conscious or implicit, that to be one's real self is *dangerous,* that exposure of real feelings and motives will result in rejection, punishment, or ridicule. Such a belief stems from experiences of punishment and rejection at the hands of the parents and other significant persons. In order to avoid punishment in the future, the child represses or suppresses his real self in interpersonal situations and learns to become a contriver: an other-directed character. Of course, more serious outcomes are possible, too: neurosis, psychopathic personality, and so on.

One of the aims of a course in healthy personality should be to help students become aware of the extent to which their interpersonal behavior may be contrived, that is, selected to please others or to achieve desired effects but at the cost of repression of the real self. Healthier personalities, certainly, become less afraid to be known as they are; that is, they can be more authentic and "transparent" in their dealings with others.

Scientific students of the learning process, following the lead of Pavlov, Watson, and Skinner, have been able to demonstrate that people's behavior *can* be manipulated in subtle ways, without their awareness. Recently, for example, a psychologist was able to get subjects in an experiment to increase the frequency with which they uttered plural nouns simply by murmuring "Mm-hmm" whenever the subject spontaneously uttered the desired class of words.[22] Many other experimenters have demonstrated that the content of another's conversation can subtly be controlled by properly timed "reinforcing" stimuli, such as saying "That's good," and so on. There seems little doubt that, with a little training or practice, almost anyone could improve the efficiency with which he could thus manipulate or influence the behavior of others without their immediate awareness that they had been so manipulated. All it calls for is study of the other person to discern what things will function as reinforcers to his behavior and then supplying these things (words, rewards, and so on) whenever the desired behavior occurs. However, most people resent being manipulated, and they become properly angry when they discover that they have been treated like puppets or like experimental animals.

A nineteen-year-old male student once consulted with the writer, seeking help at improving his relations with people. He stated that he had studied Dale Carnegie's book, *How to Win Friends and*

Influence People, and found the advice given there extremely helpful to him in "conning" others, especially girls. He was very successful as a campus lover, and had up to six of the most attractive coeds in love with him at the time of seeking help. The help he sought was any suggestions that psychology might offer to him in his campaign to win over the affections of the campus queen, who rejected him, telling him he was a "phony." This rejection upset him very much, and he wondered if there were some new gimmicks he might learn in order to convince her that he was desirable. Parenthetically, he mentioned that, once he won over the affections of a girl, he rapidly became bored by her, stating, "Once you've won a girl, its like a book you've just read; you don't want to have anything more to do with her." The author refused to help the student learn new manipulative methods, but it was possible, through more prolonged personality therapy, to help the young man gain some insight into his motives and background, such that he became a more sincere person and less the unscrupulous user of other people.

ACQUIRING HEALTHIER INTERPERSONAL BEHAVIOR

When a person is ineffective at relating to others, the over-all health of his personality is likely to deteriorate. Moreover, his existence is likely to be somewhat barren, devoid of the satisfactions that can come only from effective relationships with others. What can an ineffective person do to improve his interpersonal competence?

The answer to this question, of course, depends upon understanding the causes of the interpersonal ineptitude. If the lack of competence is the outgrowth of deviant socialization, the socially inept person can take steps to study the customs, mores, roles, and values of the social group in which he presently is living. This may entail reading, taking courses, or, better, the effort to establish contact with an "informant," as is done by anthropologists who are intent upon studying an entire society. Anthropologists learn much about the taboos, ideals, beliefs, and expectations of the societies they study through interviews with informants.

If the lack of facility at interpersonal transactions stems from impaired empathic skill, the person can seek to improve his empathy with others. Empathy with others—the capacity to form an accurate imaginative picture of the present subjective state of the other person in a transaction—improves with insight into oneself. Moreover, it improves with increased exposure to the self-disclosures of the persons with whom one wishes to become empathic. That is, the more a person has been a confidant for others, the more he has heard them reveal about their usual feelings, thoughts, reactions, and so on, the easier it becomes to establish empathy with them. Hence, any experiences in introspection which enhance a person's insight into himself will at the same time improve his empathic abilities. And any experiences at close, communicative contact with others will increase the accuracy of empathic guesses which one makes in dealing with others. Moreover, contact with a variety of people, such as occurs through travel or through work-experiences, will increase one's knowledge of people in general and promote *savoir-faire.*

If the incompetence at relating to others stems from irrational anxiety or an excessively strict conscience, then personality therapy may be the most direct type of help. Troubled individuals frequently come to understand themselves better during the process of therapy with a psychologist or psychiatrist. Through this self-understanding, they can often modify their consciences and be rid of irrational anxieties.

When a person's interpersonal relations are rendered ineffective because of various privations, he can make efforts to identify just what it is he most needs from others, in what ways he is "starved," and seek to gratify these needs more effectively. If he is unable to gratify apparently insatiable needs for affection, or reassurance, or status, then he will serve himself best if he seeks professional therapeutic aid.

Contrived, manipulative interpersonal behavior is perhaps the most difficult of the inept patterns to modify in healthier directions. The mode of interpersonal behavior deemed most compatible with health is authenticity or "real-self" behavior in the presence of others. Real-self interpersonal behavior is not effortful, planned, or deliberately assumed. Rather, it is spontaneous and unpremeditated, and it authentically expresses the subjective state of the person as he is at that moment. Such behavior, in the long run, turns out to be flexible and versatile and usually appropriate to the situation. However, it is usually difficult for the habitual contriver and manipulator to abandon this mode of relationship because he usually fears that if he spontaneously reveals himself, others may dislike or hurt him. Sometimes this will be true, but not always. Furthermore, if a person has long been a contriver, *he may have lost the ability to distinguish between contrived and real-self interpersonal behavior.*

This distinction is impossible until real-self behavior has actually occurred. In such cases, the person requires the assistance of a trained therapist to point out the difference between contrived and real-self behavior. During the process of therapy, the patient discloses his thoughts, feelings, memories, and so on to the therapist. The therapist has been professionally trained to be alert to the distinction between authentic, transparent real-self behavior in the presence of others and the more common, contrived interpersonal behavior which aims at concealing a person's real self. Whenever the patient does express something which impresses the therapist as authentic, he points this out to the patient, so that the latter will gradually learn to tell the difference.[23]

CHARACTER AND INTERPERSONAL BEHAVIOR

Despite the fact that spontaneity in interpersonal behavior is desirable for the health of personality, nobody is perpetually spontaneous. Instead, careful study will show that modes of interacting with others are usually patterned, even though the situation or role may change. The term "character" has been defined in various ways. In the present context, we will follow (but modify) the usage proposed by Fromm[24] and state that character refers to the habitual modes by which a person interacts with others. Fromm classified character into broad categories named, respectively, the "receptive orientation," the "hoarding orientation," the "exploitative orientation," the "marketing orientation," and, finally, the "productive orientation." Patterns of interpersonal behavior differ markedly in these various types of character. The receptive character limits his interpersonal behavior to that range which gets love and support from others; he strives to become lovable so other people will give him what he needs. The hoarding character shows predominately interpersonal behavior which keeps people at a distance so they can get little from him. The exploitative character displays predominately force or cunning in his interpersonal behavior, getting what he needs from others by these means. The marketing character is a person who "experiences himself as a commodity, and his value as 'exchange value.'" His main aim in interpersonal behavior is to cultivate those traits which pay off in economic success. If money is to be earned by having a pleasing personality, then he strives to cultivate a pleasing personality; if money is to be earned when one appears industrious, then he strives to give the impression of industry.

The productive character corresponds in our terminology with the healthy personality. The productive character strives, through his own efforts, to produce what he needs through his own behavior. In interpersonal behavior, he actually produces his own satisfactions by behaving toward others in ways which will satisfy them and thus make them willing to satisfy him.

Other authors have constructed characterologies, which consist in a description of types.[25] Thus, the psychoanalysts speak of the oral character, the anal character, the phallic character, and, finally, the genital character. Rank[26] classified people into types: the normal, the neurotic, and the creative. Riesman[27] grouped people according to the source of direction for their behavior: the "tradition-directed" character, the "inner-directed" character, and the "other-directed" character. Each of these types may be "anomic" (maladjusted or confused), "adjusted" (feeling no inner conflict), or "autonomous" (real-self-directed—the person has personally endorsed tradition, conscience, or others' will, and they are synonymous with his own will).

These characterologies are useful means of classifying different kinds of interpersonal behavior. Want of space precludes our doing more than mentioning them here; the serious student is advised to consult the appropriate sources directly. We will assert, however, that these character types do not exist as pure cases. Like healthy personality, they are hypothetical extremes which are useful as base lines against which to compare living persons, a sort of standard against which comparisons can be made with actual behavior.

Yet, there is a case to be made for constructing these characterologies. It is true that persons develop consistencies in their instrumental behavior in general and their interpersonal behavior in particular. The very fact of predictability in interpersonal behavior attests to this. A character description of the single case has many important uses in interpersonal relationships. Our other-concepts actually are composed of generalizations about the modal behavior of the other person, especially his interpersonal behavior. Thus, we describe John as the "kind of fellow who will tell his boss what he thinks of him," or we describe Mary as "the kind of girl who behaves with gentleness and consideration for other people's feelings."

We may define a healthy character as a person whose total repertoire of interpersonal behavior patterns meets the criteria for healthy interpersonal behavior (see above).

It is obvious, however, that not all the component interpersonal behavior traits of a person will be healthy; the person may, for example, be able to gratify his needs for esteem from others, but he cannot seem to obtain love. He may relate to one person in a healthy way, but to others in his social milieu he may display either ineffective or contrived interpersonal behavior. Further, some of his interpersonal behavior patterns may be quite rigid and resistant to change. Let us discuss these rigid interpersonal habits or, as Reich terms them, *character-armor*.[28]

CHARACTER-ARMOR: RIGID INTERPERSONAL BEHAVIOR PATTERNS. We may regard a person's interpersonal habits, his habitual modes of behaving toward other people, as a kind of record of interpersonal problems which he has encountered in the process of growing up. Each interpersonal pattern was presumably learned as a means of gaining affection and approval from significant others or as a means of avoiding or escaping punishment, criticism, or rejection. Adopting the terminology of learning theory, let us refer to the habits which secured affection and approval as *interpersonal reward habits;* the term *interpersonal avoidance habits* will describe those modes of relating to others which were learned as means of warding off expected punishment and criticism.

From students of the learning process, we learn that reward habits are generally more amenable to extinction and to alteration than avoidance habits; the latter appear to be much more rigid and resistant to attempts at alteration.[29] These generalizations were predicated mainly on studies of learning in rats, but there is little reason to doubt they hold up for human learning. In fact, most of the interpersonal behavior which psychotherapists call "ego-defensive" may be regarded as instances of interpersonal avoidance habits. Reich called the attention of psychoanalysts to a phenomenon which he called *character-resistance;*[30] in psychoanalytic therapy, the patient is obliged to relate to the observing therapist all that passes through his mind. Analysts noted that patients developed various resistances to the enjoinder they must speak all they think and feel. Character-resistance referred to subtle ways of relating to the therapist which served to bypass the free-association rule; further observation led Reich to note the character-resistances were but special cases of the more general concept, character-armor. Character-armor may be regarded as the sum total of an individual's interpersonal avoidance habits.

The reader can detect instances of character-armor in himself if he will strive to discern some consistency or pattern in the way he behaves toward, say his mother. If he is very respectful toward his mother and tries to alter this way of behaving, he may become aware of considerable anxiety; in order to reduce the anxiety, he may find it necessary to revert back to the pattern of respect.

Character-armor—rigid interpersonal habits—is an obstacle to the attainment of healthy personality. Rigid interpersonal habits impel a person to behave toward others in ways which are inappropriate to the feelings, wishes, or traits of the other person; in spite of their inappropriateness, the individual cannot abandon or alter these rigid habits, and so his potential gratifications in interpersonal relationships are reduced. A further outcome of character-armor is obvious: it insures that the individual's real self will not be revealed to others. This means others will not come to know him as he truly is.

A special problem in personality therapy is that of "loosening the character-armor."[31] What this involves is attempts on the part of the therapist to lead the patient, who has sought help because of some neurotic symptom such as an obsession or an hysterical complaint, *to regard his interpersonal habits as symptoms.* Up to this time, the patient may have taken his interpersonal behavior for granted, never bothering to examine it. Once he begins to examine it, he becomes extremely self-conscious, self-analytical, and usually quite anxious. The consequence is that the person no longer relates to others in the smooth, long-rehearsed, automatic ways he previously did. Instead he is obliged to suppress his automatic reaction-patterns and to attempt to replace them by newer, more flexible, appropriate, and self-revealing interpersonal behavior. Although this entire process is accompanied by much anxiety, it is intended that the patient should learn healthy interpersonal habits, ways of behaving predicated on accurate perception of others, which are more spontaneous, flexible, and expressive of his real self.

AFFECTION AND INTERPERSONAL BEHAVIOR

We have pointed out already that affection is one of the need-objects a person can gain through interpersonal behavior. Affection is valued for its own sake, as a determiner of self-esteem and also because it is an important means to many other need-objects. What are the consequences of not getting it? Are there healthy and unhealthy ways of getting it? Let us inquire into some of the answers to these questions.

CONSEQUENCES OF RECEIVING AFFECTION. A considerable amount of attention has been paid by students of child development and of personality to the role of affection in personality development.[32] Personality hygienists are unanimous in asserting that unrestricted affection is as important to optimum personality development as food, shelter, or medical attention. The experience of being liked by significant others makes it possible for the growing person to like himself and to express affection openly to others. Both these responses are important indices of personality health.

To the adult, being liked will certainly contribute to an increase in self-esteem and to a feeling of security—but the identity of the other person must not be overlooked. It feels different to be liked by one significant person, or class of persons, rather than another. It feels different because of the different meanings associated with different people. Nobody wants to be liked by criminals if he is not a criminal himself; in fact, he is likely to become uneasy if it becomes known among polite society that criminals like him. People will wonder what he has done in order to earn the affection of criminals. A young man will feel more pleasant if he is liked by an exquisitely beautiful woman than if he is liked by one who is homely.

The pleasant feelings associated with being liked stem from two major sources: the increase in self-esteem which follows the receipt of affection responses and the anticipation, or expectation, that many important wants and valued ends will be satisfied or obtained in the near future. In our discussion of emotions (Chapter 4), we pointed out that expectancies play an important role in determining the emotional response to some object. Fear and anxiety are associated with the anticipation of pain; the pleasant feelings associated with being liked stem from the prediction that the liking-responses shown by the other person are a signal that your wants will be gratified in the future with the collaboration of that other person.

CONSEQUENCES OF NOT RECEIVING AFFECTION. A life history marked by scarcity of affection-responses is characteristic of most mental illness.[33] As a student examines psychiatric literature or studies case histories in abnormal psychology, he finds with regularity that the patient has seldom felt loved or liked. Criminologists have found that in most instances of criminal behavior, the offender had a childhood and adult life which was poverty-stricken with respect to affection—nobody liked, or likes, him. Ribble, Spitz, Goldfarb,[34] and others have observed that psychiatric afflictions are frequent outcomes when children grow up in an atmosphere devoid of affection.

A bountiful supply of affection-responses is a necessary precondition for the development of healthy personality. Why should this be the case? Why do people need affection in order to grow into adults who are happy and with whom others can live in harmony? Probably because affection-responses serve the function of a "pay-off" for the pains and frustrations associated with socialization. The socialization process largely entails learning to forego immediately gratifying impulsive behavior, and such suppression is intrinsically unpleasant. The child "paid" for these pains with affection-responses becomes willing to forego immediately gratifying impulsive behavior and is able to learn socially acceptable behavior. The reasons why affection acquires "pay-off" value is a problem in learning theory; affection is an example of *secondary reinforcement*.[35]

The adult in our society who doesn't receive enough affection from others (the amount which is sufficient differs between persons) generally *suffers*. He regards himself as unworthy or inferior and feels there "must be something wrong with him." He is generally anxious; he anticipates all manner of dire events at the hands of "hostile" people, which includes everyone who withholds the symbols of affection from him. In our society, not to be liked seems to symbolize "being hated" by others, rather than neutrality on the part of others.

The person who is not liked enough may react in a variety of ways. He may become vengeful and aggressive and "move against people," as Horney puts it. Or, he may "move toward people," striving compulsively to please in order to seduce others into giving him the affection responses which he so desperately needs. Basic anxiety, the feeling of helplessness and loneliness in a potentially hostile world, is perhaps the best term to describe the general consequences of an insufficiency of affection as this is experienced by people in our society.[36]

AFFECTION AND HEALTHY PERSONALITY

We have asserted that affection-responses are needed by a person for many reasons: for the maintenance of self-esteem, for promoting security, and for reassuring him that other people who like him will not withhold many other kinds of need-objects. Much interpersonal behavior that a person engages in, then, has as its aim, consciously or unconsciously, the securing of affection-responses from the other person. We can appraise this interpersonal behavior from the standpoint of efficiency and, more generally, from the standpoint of personality hygiene. Healthy interpersonal behavior is successful in obtaining affection and acceptance from others and at the same time is expressive of the individual's real self.

Unhealthy interpersonal behavior may be inefficient, contrived, antisocial, or in conflict with the individual's real self. We would have to assess as unhealthy, then, the pursuit of affection-responses at the expense of other valued ends, such as self-esteem and growth. The quest "to be liked at all cost" is not worth the cost. Very often, in order to be liked, a person is obliged to suppress and repress many of his own feelings and wants; in short, he is obliged to become alienated from his self.

Behavior aimed at securing affection may be just plain inefficient. It may be inefficient because the seeker is so anxious that he loses control over his behavior and loses the ability to assess what responses will be effective. Many of the obnoxious behavior patterns which a patient manifests with his therapist are almost "tests" of the therapist, as well as characteristics of his relationships with many other people in his present and past social orbit. If the therapist can accept these patterns without seeming to reject the patient or to dislike him, then the patient will begin to like and trust his therapist, feel less anxious, and begin to recognize how he behaves toward the therapist and others. Finally, he may learn to behave in more likeable ways toward the therapist. This ability may then carry over to other persons in his life.

We will assert that it is healthy (a) to want affection, (b) to be able to accept it without anxiety when it is genuinely offered, (c) to be able to behave toward others in ways which will elicit affection, (d) to be able to give affection, and (e) to be able to choose rationally between affection and other values. In connection with (e), affection may not be worth what it costs. However, one cannot tell this to a starving individual. Taste and the ability to make discrimination is a by-product of plenty, not of scarcity. Under extreme deprivation of any sort, canalizations, or preferences in need-objects, become relatively ineffective, and the person will take what he can get. The affection-starved individual shows a similar lack of discrimination in his choice of friends (sources of affection) and in his choice of behavior patterns which he will engage in in order to get affection. It is not uncommon for persons to rob, cheat, kill, degrade themselves, swallow their pride and steal in order to be liked by somebody.

Affection is not the only need-object which can be obtained through interpersonal behavior. In fact, it is convenient and valid to think of another person as a "cafeteria display" of actual and possible need-objects of varied kinds. We already touched on the fact that other people possess skills which we need; all kinds of material need-objects which they will give us only when appropriately paid, either in money or in conformity with other conditions which they impose; affection; self-esteem-enhancing responses. Let us examine in more detail the role an individual's need will play in influencing interpersonal attractions and repulsions.

NEEDS AND INTERPERSONAL RELATIONS IN GENERAL

We can regard another person as an animated collection of need-objects. The other person's appearance, his status, his values, his modal behavior, all can serve as need-objects at one time or another to a given individual. The securing of need-objects possessed by the other person presents a continual challenge to an individual; he must learn the appropriate interpersonal behavior patterns which will be effective in obtaining the needed responses from the other person. In a sense, we can regard many of the personality traits of an individual, his recurrent modes of relating to other people especially, as a record of his past relationships with others. These interpersonal habits represent his solutions to past problems, problems which involved his learning effective ways to getting what he needed from the other person. Thus, a persistent habit of politeness, or of deference, may tell the observer that in order to get what he needed from others, the individual was obliged to behave politely, or deferentially. A strongly aggressive individual may reveal to the observer that in order to get what is needed from others, it was necessary for him to take it by force. It should be possible to infer many of the needs of a person by studying the characteristics of the other people whom he likes, dislikes, and is indifferent to. Further, it should be possible to make valid predictions about whom an individual will like,[37] whom he will choose as a friend or spouse, how long a friendship will last, or a marriage, on the basis of knowledge about what the individual needs in order to maintain security, self-esteem, and so on.

Let us illustrate some of these points. We will discuss the role of certain needs on the choice of friends, fiancées, fellow workers, and so on.

NEEDS AND THE CHOICE OF FRIENDS.[38] A person will choose as a friend that individual whose characteristics will satisfy his varied needs. A very passive and helpless individual will be attracted by competent and highly skilled persons. A man with strong sexual tensions will be attracted toward women who seem willing to serve as potential sexual partners. A person with shaky self-esteem will like those people who seem to hold beliefs about him which correspond with his self-ideal rather than with his self-concept. A social climber will be indifferent to persons of his own social class but will be strongly attracted to someone who comes from a higher socioeconomic class.

One can regard the behavior of one person in front of another as a variety of advertising, or of wares display. In a very short time, each person will size up the other with respect to his suitability as a potential need-satisfier. One looks the other over and sees signs in his behavior which indicate "This fellow will be a good companion on a camping trip; a sympathetic audience when I am in trouble; a good source of jokes; a rich source of money to borrow; he can introduce me to the right people." The other person, in turn, might see the first as "a guy who knows all the answers; a first-rate technician; someone who can show me a lot about getting along with people." If each has what the other person needs for assorted purposes, then a more lasting friendship might develop out of the encounter. If, on the other hand, either sees or thinks he sees signs which point to various frustrations, the relationship will not be cultivated. Thus, one of the individuals might think he sees a certain intolerance for some of his own modal behavior; in order to save himself from future frustrations, he will terminate the relationship or tell the other, "I know you don't like certain kinds of behavior, and I happen to behave in those ways."

Friendships and love affairs generally begin with such a period of mutual exploration, or diagnosis. The initial attraction which brought the two people together may have been the result of such factors as appearance or behavior samples which constitute possible need-objects. For example, in a crowded room, you might overhear a person expressing tastes in music just like your own. A girl might see some boy whose appearance corresponds with her most romantic dreams of a lover. Once two persons meet, however, the process of diagnosis really begins. Each looks the other over, asks questions, sounds out the other's values, biases and attitudes, and tries to make formulations concerning the other's modal behavior. These formulations are often grossly wrong. On the basis of this diagnostic behavior, a decision may be made to spend more or less time with the other individual.

NEEDS AND THE MAINTENANCE OF FRIENDSHIPS. So long as no external factors interfere, a friendship will endure (or a marriage or any other association between two persons) only as long as the behavior of each partner provides more satisfactions than it does deprivations or frustrations. As soon as the needs of either are satiated, or as soon as either partner withholds the need-objects required by the other, then the relationship will no longer have any "cement" to hold it together.

NEEDS AND INTERPERSONAL AVERSIONS. Just as a person can be seen as attractive insofar as his behavior will serve as need-objects to the chooser, so can he be repulsive for the same reasons. If your self-esteem is dependent upon being chosen as a friend only by the "best" people, you will be repelled by the "not best." A person who values manners will be repelled by the uncouth. A prude is repelled by a satyr. Whether or not you will be indifferent or repulsed by another person seems to be a function of the relevance of that person's traits to your needs. If his behavior interferes with or prevents need-satisfaction, you will dislike him.

INTERPERSONAL BEHAVIOR AND HEALTHY PERSONALITY

In this chapter, we have concentrated on interpersonal behavior in a given individual without paying much attention to the characteristics of the other persons with whom he may interact. Moreover, we have made no attempt to describe the characteristics of the *relationships* which people establish with each other. Our focus instead has been upon interpersonal behavior as a kind of skill, as a type of operant or instrumental behavior, which may be effective or ineffective, compatible with health or destructive of health. If an individual is able to assume a variety of roles in his everyday life, fulfill them adequately, and at the same time not place other values in jeopardy, we can assert he displays interpersonal competence. If he cannot do these things—neither fulfill role-requirements nor protect other values, such as health, self-esteem, a sense of identity, and so on—then we would regard him as interpersonally incompetent. Speaking in more general terms, the class of interpersonal behavior which is most compatible with over-all health of personality is real-self behavior, that is, behavior with others that accurately depicts the real self of the behaver in spontaneous response to the other.

A convenient definition for *healthy* interpersonal behavior in the light of the preceding discussion is as follows: Interpersonal behavior is healthy when it expresses the individual's real self, is effective in producing satisfaction, and is congruent with the limits set by conscience and others' expectations (i.e., role-definitions).

SUMMARY

Man is dependent upon his fellows for many vital satisfactions; his survival during infancy is contingent upon the care of others. As an adult, he needs the help and the responsiveness of others in order to cope with life problems and to produce or maintain his sense of security, self-esteem, and identity. Interpersonal behavior is the term used to describe man's behavior with his fellows, behavior he engages in to attain gratification of his needs through the responses of the other. A man displays interpersonal competence when he can enact a variety of roles (role-versatility) in ways acceptable to other (role-adequacy). Roles are ways of behaving that others expect from one because of one's age, sex, occupation, or social status.

Ineffective interpersonal behavior is associated with deviant socialization, defective empathy, irrational anxiety, unduly strict conscience, excessive need-privation, limited knowledge of people in general, and efforts to misrepresent the self.

"Character" is the term commonly employed to refer to patterns of interpersonal behavior. Rigid interpersonal behavior patterns are referred to as "character-armor" because they protect the individual from possible hurt, and they serve to hide the individual's real self from the gaze of others.

Interpersonal behavior may be called healthy when it is effective in yielding satisfaction of various needs, when it expresses the individual's real self, and when it is compatible with conscience and the demands of the social system.

NOTES AND REFERENCES

Excellent supplementary reading will be provided by those references marked with an asterisk (*).

*1. The reader perhaps has known people who live far away from other people or who never interact with others, and he may have noticed that such individuals seem "odd"—different in their values, emotional reactions, and so on, from the average person. Fromm regards interaction with others as a *sine qua non* for being *human. Cf.* Fromm, E., *The Sane Society* (New York: Rinehart, 1955), pp. 30–36. For an account of *desocialization* and its bearing on "behavior pathology," see Cameron, N. and Magaret, Ann, *Behavior Pathology* (New York: Houghton, 1951), ch. 16. For an account of the effects of sensory deprivation, as well as isolation from people, see Fiske, D. W., "Effects of

Monotonous and Restricted Stimulation," in Fiske, D. W. and Maddi, S. R., *Functions of Varied Experience* (Homewood: Dorsey Press, 1961), especially pp. 122–143; also Heron, W., "The Pathology of Boredom," *Sci. Amer., 196,* 52–56 (1957); Byrd, R., *Alone* (New York: Putnam, 1938); and Solomon, P., Leiderman, H., Mendelson, J., and Wexler, D., "Sensory Deprivation. A Review," *Amer. J. Psychiat., 114,* 357–363 (1957).

2. Maslow notes that "self-actualizing people" have periodic strong needs for privacy and solitude. *Cf.* Maslow, A. H., *Motivation and Personality* (New York: Harper, 1954), pp. 212–213.

*3. See Ribble, M., *The Rights of Infants* (New York: Columbia U.P., 1943). This small volume is devoted to a discussion of what the infant needs a mother *for* and what he needs *from* a mother in order optimally to grow. Rene Spitz, a child psychiatrist, has undertaken some interesting research on mother-infant relationships and their consequences. See Spitz, R., "Hospitalism," in *Psychoanalyt. Stud. Child,* I (New York: International Universities Press, 1945).

4. Horney has called attention to the various conditions which must be met in order that a neurotic person will not unleash upon himself a veritable onslaught of self-hate. See her *Neurosis and Human Growth* (New York: Norton, 1950), ch. 5. Fenichel also has indicated how neurotics come to depend, for the maintenance of self-esteem, on "external sources of supply." See Fenichel, O., *The Psychoanalytic Theory of Neurosis* (New York: Norton, 1945), pp. 387 ff.

5. Blatz, W., *Understanding the Young Child* (Toronto: Clarke, Irwin, 1944), ch. 9.

6. The child psychoanalyst Erikson has recently been calling attention to the role of the sense of identity in personality growth. *Cf.* Erikson, E. H., *Childhood and Society* (New York: Norton, 1950). See also, by the same author, "The Problem of Ego Identity," *J. Amer. Psychoanalyt. Assoc., 4,* 56–121 (1956). Jeanne Watson, in an ongoing study, sees interpersonal behavior (sociability) as a means by which identity is defined: Watson, Jeanne, "Sociability as a Medium for Definition of the Self." (Mimeographed manuscript, 1956, Committee on Human Development, University of Chicago.) See also Maslow, A. H., *Toward a Psychology of Being* (Princeton, N.J.: Van Nostrand, 1962), chs. 7, 9.

*7. See Fromm, E., *Escape from Freedom* (New York: Rinehart, 1941), pp. 141–178, for a discussion of authoritarianism. For an empirical study of authoritarian characters, see Adorno, R. W., Frenkel-Brunswik, Else, Levinson, D. J., and Sanford, R. N., *The Authoritarian Personality* (New York: Harper, 1950).

8. Fromm, E., *op. cit.,* pp. 185–206.

*9. Riesman, D., *The Lonely Crowd* (New Haven, Conn.: Yale, 1950)—the discussion of the other-directed character.

10. *Cf.* Crutchfield, R. S., "Conformity and Character," *Amer. Psychologist, 10,* 191–198 (1955).

11. See Horney, K., *op. cit.,* ch. 9.

*12. Buber, M., *I and Thou* (2nd ed.; New York: Scribners, 1958), p. 3.

13. Buber, M., *Between Man and Man* (Boston: Beacon, 1955), pp. 199–205.

14. This term has been borrowed from Foote, N. N. and Cottrell, L. S., *Identity and Interpersonal Competence* (Chicago: U. of Chicago, 1955).

*15. There is an extensive literature on role-theory. The interested student will find an excellent introduction to this area in Lindzey, G. (ed.), *Handbook of Social Psychology,* I, (Cambridge, Mass.: Addison-Wesley, 1954), ch. 6.

*16. See Mead, M., *Male and Female* (New York: Morrow, 1949). This is an excellent discussion of cultural variation in sex-typing by a leading anthropologist.

*17. See Parsons, T., "Age and Sex in the Social Structure of the United States," in *Essays in Sociological Theory* (Glencoe, Ill.: Free Press, 1954). See also Jourard, S. M., "Some Lethal Aspects of the Male Role," *J. Existent. Psychiat., 2,* 333–344 (1962). In this paper, I speculate on the possible relationship between the tendency of men to die sooner than women and the tendency of men to be less "self-disclosing" than women.

18. Mead, M., *op. cit.*

*19. Block, J., "The Assessment of Communication. Role Variations as a Function of Interactional Context," *J. Pers., 21,* 272–286 (1952). One psychiatrist developed an entire theory of psychiatry out of the study of interpersonal relations. See Sullivan, H. S., *The Interpersonal Theory of Psychiatry* (New York: Norton, 1953). An interpersonal system for conducting research into personality is Leary, T. *et al., The Interpersonal Diagnosis of Personality* (New York: Ronald, 1956). See also Heider, F., *The Psychology of Interpersonal Relations* (New York: Wiley, 1958), and Schutz, W., *FIRO. A Three-Dimensional Theory of Interpersonal Behavior* (New York: Rinehart 1958), especially pp. 13–33.

20. See Foote, N. N. and Cottrell, L. S., *op. cit.,* ch. 3; and pp. 71–77 for further discussion of the role of empathy in interpersonal competence. See also Stewart, D., *Preface to Empathy* (New York: Philosophical Library, 1956), chs. 5, 6. Research approaches to empathy and person perception are given in Steiner, I. D., "Interpersonal Behavior and Accurate Social Perception," *Psychol. Rev., 62,* 268–273 (1955); Foa, U., "Empathy or Behavioral Transparency?" *J. Abnorm. Soc. Psychol., 56,* 62–66 (1958). A more general discussion of issues in perception of the other person is given in Heider, F., *op. cit.,* pp. 59–78; and Allport, G. W., *Pattern and Growth in Personality* (New York: Holt, 1961), pp. 497–522 and pp. 533–537.

*21. This point is developed further in Jourard, S. M., "I-Thou Relationship Versus Manipulation in Counseling and Psychotherapy," *J. Individ. Psychol., 15.,* 174–179 (1959). The "psychopathic personality" is often seen as very charming and well liked. This is probably a by-product of the fact that the psychopath is not restricted in interpersonal behavior by his conscience to the same extent as most people. In consequence, he can behave in very contradictory ways with different people in order to "charm them," and yet he will not feel any guilt over the inconsistencies in his behavior. *Cf.* Cleckley, H., *The Mask of Sanity* (St. Louis, Mo.: Mosby, 1941). See also Rogers, C. R. and Skinner, B. F., "Some Issues Concerning the Control of Human Behavior: A Symposium," *Science, 124,* 1057–1066 (1956); and Krasner, L., "Behavior Control and Social Responsibility," *Amer. Psychol., 17,* 199–204 (1962).

22. Greenspoon, J., "The Reinforcing Effect of Two Spoken Sounds on the Frequency of Two Responses," *Amer. J. Psychol., 68,* 409–416 (1955). See Krasner, L., "Studies of the Conditioning of Verbal Behavior," *Psych. Bull.,* 55, 148–170 (1958), for a more extensive review of studies of this sort.

23. *Cf.* Horney, K., *op. cit.,* ch. 14, for a discussion of therapy from the standpoint of "self-realization." Also Jourard, S. M., reference 21.

24. Fromm, E., *op. cit.,* pp. 54–118.

*25. See Notcutt, B., *The Psychology of Personality* (London: Methuen, 1953). His discussion of typology (ch. 4) is unsurpassed, in the present writer's opinion.

26. Rank, O., *Will Therapy, and Truth and Reality* (New York: Knopf, 1945).

27. Riesman, D., *op. cit.*

28. Reich, W., *Character Analysis* (New York, Orgone Institute Press, 1949), pp. 40–76.

29. *Cf.* Keller, F. S. and Schoenfeld, W. N., *Principles of Psychology* (New York: Appleton, 1950), p. 315. These authors state: "Our present knowledge, gleaned mainly from animal study, indicates that *the extinction of an avoidance response is often extremely difficult,* even in well-controlled experimental situations." (My italics.)

30. Reich, W., *op. cit.,* pp. 40–51.

31. Reich, W., *op. cit.,* pp. 67–76.

32. John Bowlby has written extensively on maternal deprivation and affection-lack. See Bowlby, J., "Maternal Care and Mental Health," *Bulletin World Health Organization, 3,* 335–534 (1951). Also, his popular book, *Child Care and the Growth of Love* (London: Penguin, 1953).

33. Bowlby, J., *op. cit.* Check index of both volumes under heading of affection.

34. Ribble, M., *op. cit.* Spitz, R. A., *op. cit.* Goldfarb, W. His studies are summarized in Hoch, P. F. and Zubin, J. (eds.), *Psychopathology in Childhood* (New York: Greene, 1955).

35. The words, gestures, and actions which signify affection and approval are thought to acquire their meaning to the individual through the association of these signals with more "primary" stimuli, such as caresses, food, and so on. See Wolfe, J. B., "Effectiveness of Token-Rewards for Chimpanzees," *Comp. Psychol. Monogr. 12,* 1–72 (1936), for an example of an experiment which demonstrates secondary reinforcement with animals. Probably the same principles, or at least similar ones, will account for the effectiveness of words and gestures as rewards and punishments at the human level. See Skinner, B. F.,

Science and Human Behavior (New York: Macmillan, 1953), for a more recent treatment of reinforcement.

36. This analysis is a paraphrase of Horney's writings. See Horney, K., *Our Inner Conflicts* (New York: Norton, 1945).

37. See Newcomb, T., "The Prediction of Interpersonal Attraction," *Amer. Psychologist, 11,* 575–586 (1956), for a cogent discussion of this point, with some experimental data. Also his book, *The Acquaintance Process* (New York: Holt, 1961).

38. There have been hosts of studies aimed at the discovery of the personality characteristics which are typical of individuals with high sociometric status. See Northway, M. L., Frankel, E. B., and Potashin, R., "Personality and Sociometric Status," *Sociom. Monogr.* No. 11, Beacon House, 1947), for one review of the literature on this subject. The present author reported a study which showed that those children in a summer camp who were the most highly chosen by the other children were the most active and highly skilled participants in the camp program (unpublished manuscript).

CHAPTER *10*

HEALTHY INTERPERSONAL RELATIONSHIPS

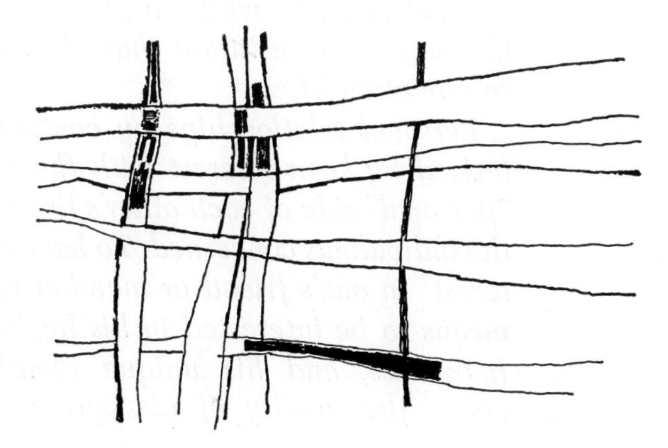

INTRODUCTION

Let us first draw a distinction between interpersonal *relationships and* interrole *relationships. In the latter instance, two people enact certain social roles, e.g., salesman and customer, physician and patient, teacher and student, sergeant and private. The participants in such role-relationships may interact with one another for years and never become acquainted with each other as* persons.[1] *Participants in role-relationships are concerned that each individual do his part—each is concerned primarily with the overt behavior of the other, with his performance, not with his feelings, problems, likes, dislikes, hopes, tastes, and so on. In fact, participants in role-relationships may not even care about the other individual's subjective side. "I don't want to know about his private life; it might interfere with our relationship" expresses the impersonal attitude that characterizes many role-relationships.*

Personal relationships by contrast are characterized by keen interest with the subjective and "personal" side of each other's lives on the part of the individuals concerned. To have a "personal interest" in one's friend or member of one's family means to be interested in his health, well-being, happiness, and his unique identity over and above the quality of his various role-perform-

ances. As more is learned about the conditions of health, the suspicion grows stronger that inability to enter into and sustain such personal relations with others is either symptomatic of personality illness or else contributes to the onset of such illness.

Professional therapists of personality are necessarily interested in the study of relationships between people[2] *(see Chapter* 13*), because it is through the quality of the relationship which they establish with their patients that the latter improve in wellness or else fail to improve. Moreover, as therapists seek to understand their patients better, they find they must obtain information about the nature of the patients' relationships with parents, friends, spouse, and so on. Employing standards that are not yet very explicit, a therapist might say, "This patient has a healthy relationship with his wife, an unhealthy relationship with his parents, and unhealthy relationships with several of his friends." When is a relationship between two persons healthy? What are the characteristics of relationships between persons which are compatible with the health of both, and what are the characteristics of such relationships which undermine the health of personality?*

CHARACTERISTICS OF HEALTHY PERSONAL RELATIONSHIPS[3]

Personal relationships which foster and maintain health have the following characteristics:

1. *The participants know each other as distinct individuals.*
2. *The participants like more traits in one another than they dislike.*
3. *Each participant feels concern for the happiness and growth of the other.*
4. *Each participant seeks to behave in ways which will promote happiness and growth in the other.*
5. *Each participant can communicate effectively with the other and make himself known and understood.*
6. *Each participant imposes reasonable demands on the other.*
7. *Each participant values and respects the autonomy and individuality of the other.*

These criteria may be used to assess the health-yielding quality of personal relationships after they have evolved beyond the period of initial acquaintance, when the partners may still be involved in some interrole relations; that is, the partners may first have behaved formally and impersonally with one another. Let us turn now to the problem of explaining how formal impersonal relationships evolve into personal relations.

Almost all lasting relationships between people begin with initial attraction between them. (Of course, some begin in indifference and others even with mutual hostility.) This initial attraction is a function of each person's needs. When an individual meets another person, he sees that other person as a source of potential satisfactions and frustrations. If the other person has traits or characteristics which can serve as need-objects for the individual, he will be attracted to him; he will like him. When two people meet and are mutually attracted, however, they do not yet know each other. Their other-concepts will comprise accurate as well as autistic beliefs and expectations. The partners must make further observations of one another, continually testing their present impressions before we could assert they "knew" each other.[4] Frequently, getting to know the other person better results in termination of the relationship. To know a person means to form an accurate concept or set of beliefs about him. Let us devote attention to study of such other-concepts—how they are acquired and how *accurate* other-concepts are achieved.

KNOWLEDGE OF THE OTHER

The term self-concept refers to an individual's beliefs about his own personality; the term *other-concept* refers to beliefs one holds concerning someone else's personality. We can evaluate a person's other-concepts in terms of their accuracy and completeness.

Formulating an other-concept is no different from formulating a concept of a particular motor or cow. We observe, generalize, make further observations, and then uphold, reject, or revise the generalizations. But emotions are more likely to influence observation of a person than of a motor. It is very difficult to form an accurate concept of another person. The observer's needs, values, prejudices, hopes, and expectations all exert a powerful influence on the activities of observing the other person and formulating conclusions (beliefs) concerning his nature, or structure. Accurate other-concepts are very difficult to achieve, but they are of utmost importance for healthy personality in general and healthy interpersonal relationships more directly. Only when our other-concepts are accurate can we behave in ways which make the other happy, help him grow and help us in communicating with him. In more general terms, we will state dogmatically a person is healthy *only* to the extent that he has accurate other-concepts. Now let us turn to the process of forming other-concepts and observe some of the factors which make it difficult to acquire accurate ones.

FIRST IMPRESSIONS OF THE OTHER PERSON

A number of controlled experiments[5] have demonstrated that we perceive a person in an organized, meaningful way in our first contact with him. We immediately classify him into some category—for example, male, adult, Protestant, middle class, teacher, American-born, Yankee—rather than postponing judgment or experiencing puzzlement about him. On the basis of such an immediate classification, we then ascribe to that person all of the modal reaction patterns, values, attitudes, motives, beliefs, which we have been led to expect from such persons.[6] The initial other-concept which we formulate of a new acquaintance thus comprises a host of expectations and assumptions. Some of these expectations and assumptions may prove later to be accurate, but for the most part they will be inaccurate. How do we get these other-concepts in such a short time? It behooves us to find answers, because these first impressions, though wrong, often last a long time. The following factors play an important role in determining other-concepts: (a) *projection,* (b) *attribution,* (c) *needs,* and (d) *social pressures to conformity.*

PROJECTION AND OTHER-CONCEPTS. Cameron and Magaret[7] distinguish between *assimilative projection* and *disowning projection.* Assimilative projection refers to the assumption by an individual that the other person is similar to him in personality structure, in motives, values, goals, attitudes, and past experiences. The person ordinarily adopts this assumption when the other individual appears similar in age, social class, appearance, or other obvious and observable characteristics. In the usual course of events, the average person is not aware that his first impression, or his initial other-concept, is the by-product of a very rapid *observation* of the other person, a *comparison* of him with the self, and then a *conclusion* that the other person is indeed similar to the self. Often enough, the traits imputed to the other person through assimilative projection are sufficiently accurate to enable meaningful communication with him and to enable appropriate interpersonal behavior to occur. This accidental accuracy in first impression results from similarities in personality that stem from similarities in socialization. Yet, there is enough variation in people's life experiences, variations which produce differences in personality, to produce errors in first impressions. Hence the very common experience of "being wrong about the other person," of having "sized him up wrongly."

Disowning projection refers to the assumption that the other person is different from the self; but more than being different, there is implied the notion the other person has many traits the observer deems repugnant and objectionable. Disowning projection was described earlier as a mechanism for the defense of the self-concept.[8] The disowning projector represses certain objectionable characteristics in himself and imputes them to the other person. Indeed, the traits which one sees in the other person one would be most reluctant to acknowledge in the self. Disowning projection is thus a means of maintaining an invidious difference between the self and the other person. If one's self-esteem is dependent upon the belief (a) that one is perfect and highly moral and (b) that other people are inferior to the self in these respects, then one will need to believe that other people do have all manner of morally reprehensible motives and traits.

A man may need to believe he is without hostile impulses. He may need, for various reasons, to believe he is morally superior to other men. Therefore, to maintain self-esteem, he will repress hostile strivings in himself, but he will be very quick, even eager, to see signs of hostility in other men. On first meeting someone he will believe the other person is just waiting for an opportunity to engage in hostile, malicious activities—yet the person in question may actually be very warm, friendly, and unselfish.[9]

Disowning projection will play a role in the formulation of other-concepts primarily when the person has a very strict conscience and when his self-esteem is strongly dependent upon his belief that he is different from, or superior to, other people. Many people have very bizarre concepts about the personality of minority group members, foreigners, and so on, which derive in part from disowning projection. They also derive, however, from the popular folklore of the society in which they live.

Psychiatric literature has many examples of unhealthy personalities whose other-concepts seem to be the consequence of disowning projection. Thus, a person who represses sexuality may believe other people are full of sexual desires. If he becomes able to acknowledge his own sexuality, he may then begin to change his other-concepts. Rogers found that patients who completed psychotherapy successfully manifested pronounced changes in their other-concepts; specifically, they showed a decrease in the difference between their self-concepts and other-concepts.[10]

ATTRIBUTION AND OTHER-CONCEPTS. Attribution is defined as *the assumption by a person that some new individual whom he has encountered for the first time has traits identical with those of a significant person from his past.*

The psychotherapists called attention to this phenomenon in various ways. Freud used the term "transference" to refer to the observation that a patient would behave toward the psychoanalyst as if the latter had characteristics of the patient's parents or spouse. Sullivan coined the term "parataxis"[11] to describe the same facts (*para:* strange, or distorted, and *taxis:* pertaining to classification; literally, distorted classification).

When you meet another person, you may see characteristics in him which are apparently similar to traits of your mother, former teacher, the family domestic, or a childhood friend. The characteristic which leads to this assumption of similarity may sometimes be very trivial, for example, hair color, or voice intonations. Yet, once the assumption of similarity is made, it is acted upon. If you liked the person from the past, you will feel warmth and trust for this new person. If the person from the past had very stern moral standards and always condemned you, then you will feel on probation with the new person, even though you do not as yet know him. Many of the most poignant disturbances and misunderstandings in interpersonal relationships stem from attribution (as well as from projection). A young woman, after one or two failures at shy flirting with attractive men, may conclude that men have one trait in common: they *all* dislike her. When she meets a new man, she assumes that he too hates her—if not at first sight, then when he gets to know her. And so she abandons all attempts to develop a relationship which might lead to marriage. Yet, the man may in fact be wildly in love with her at first sight. Her logic, if it could be formulated, runs like this: "Bill and John disliked me. They were men whom I knew ten years ago. Tom, whom I have just now met at a party, is a man. Therefore, like Bill and John, he too dislikes me."

Secord and Jourard demonstrated attribution in a picture-rating study.[12] From previous studies, it had been found that judges agreed markedly in assigning personality traits to a group of young women whose facial photographs were employed in these studies. One group of faces—young women with thin lips and plain features—regularly suggested to the judges that the women were highly moral creatures, "good mothers." Another group of faces—young women with thick lips, narrowed eyes, and so on—regularly suggested to judges that the women were very sexy and had loose morals. In the Secord-Jourard study, the subjects were asked to rate their own mothers on a list of traits; then they were asked to rate the personalities of the women whose faces were shown on a screen. Strong similarities were found between the personality traits assigned to the "high moral" faces and the mother-ratings; while this similarity was much less between mother-rating and the "low-moral" faces. The authors concluded from these data that in the high-moral faces, the subjects saw some physiognomic traits which resembled those of their mothers and hence assumed that the young women had traits just like mother's. If mother was rated as having low morals, then even the high-moral pictures were rated as low-moral.

Thus far, we have mentioned projection and attribution as determiners of initial other-concepts. In addition to these factors, the needs of the observing individual and social pressures of many kinds also can help determine the other-concepts which an individual will formulate.

NEEDS AND OTHER-CONCEPTS. Other-concepts are formulated as conclusions or inferences drawn from observations of the other person. We have shown in an earlier chapter the ways in which perception and cognition are influenced by the needs of the individual. Autistic factors strongly influence the perception of persons and the concepts of their personality derived from such "social perception."[13] A person constitutes a complex and highly ambiguous stimulus; as we have seen, needs and other subjective factors such as interests, values, and emotions are most likely to influence perception when the stimulus is ambiguous.

We can raise this question: What does an individual need to see in another person's behavior? What does he need to believe about the other individual's personality in order to feel safe, to be satisfied, or to maintain self-esteem? When we state the question this way, it helps us to understand why some people see evidence for certain traits in a friend, spouse, child, boss, or enemy which no disinterested person can see. Thus, a fond wife interprets her husband's unscrupulous business activity as evidence of the trait of intelligence. She needs to believe that he is intelligent. Or an inept employee who cannot recognize his ineptitude must believe that his boss is a harsh tyrant. He can see no evidence in his boss's behavior to justify the belief that his boss is a kind and fair man. If he were to conceive of his boss in such terms, it would mean his boss was right—he, the employee, really was a poor worker—and this conclusion might produce an unbearable loss of self-esteem.

The romantic lover, of course, provides us with the classical example of the influence of needs on other-concepts. He needs a sweetheart who is perfect. He meets a woman who has one or two of the signs of perfection. Immediately, as in the Gestalt psychology examples of "closure," he fills in the missing details; he sees her as perfect and believes she is indeed perfect. He may later be sadly disillusioned when reality—evidence—rears its ugly head and compels him to revise his concept of her.

Emotions, such as fear or guilt, can strongly influence the formation of other-concepts. The guilty individual believes that other people hate him. The anxious individual believes other people are just on the point of hurting him, or venting hostility on him.[14]

SOCIAL FACTORS AND OTHER-CONCEPTS. Many of our other-concepts have been derived, not from intimate, firsthand observations of the other person, but rather as a result of being told by someone what the other person is like. Everyone is very free in passing judgments about someone whom they "know" to anybody who is interested in listening. These premeeting sessions have a marked influence on an individual's expectations and on his perceptions of the other person's behavior when once a meeting occurs. When one meets another person for the first time, armed with a predetermined other-concept, it is difficult for this concept of the other person to be altered. Psychologists have turned this fact to advantage in personality research and research into the phenomena of suggestion. By explaining to one group of subjects that the person who is about to address them is a very cold, harsh, mean man, the group will respond differently to his speech and behavior than another group who have been told he is warm, gentle, and kindly. Yet, the man may behave identically before both groups.[15]

Not only do we acquire many other-concepts about specific individuals from other people; we also acquire concepts about entire classes of people from our friends, teachers, parents, or associates. The stereotypes we have acquired about Negroes, Jews, and foreigners strongly influence our perceptions of single members of those categories and strongly influence the other-concepts we formulate about them. The influence of others in determining our other-concepts is so strong that we never say to ourselves when meeting a new person, "I just don't know what kind of a person he is, or what to expect from him." Instead, as the new other person behaves, we see a corroboration of the other-concept which we brought with us into the situation.

A fruitful line of study might be that of manipulating experimentally the influence of other people on the process of other-concept formation. At Berkeley, California,[16] an ingenious apparatus has been devised for the study of social conformity. Subjects are seated in individual stalls, and before them they see several rows of lights. Each row of lights is supposed to be under the control of another person, and each light in the row stands for a certain response to questions, or a certain judgment. Then problems, or questions, are directed at each subject, and he is asked to push a button which will turn on the light that signifies his answer. But before he responds, he has to wait his turn. He must watch the lights on the panel which indicate how the five or ten other people have responded and then give his response. Actually, there are no other people. The experimenter controls these lights and only gives the illusion that a group of people are making responses.

Suppose in this situation the subject was required to observe the behavior of a person and then signify a rating on certain traits with his row of lights. Suppose, for example, he was asked to rate the sense of humor of a person who had just finished cracking a number of very weak jokes. The experimenter could then manipulate the lights on his panel so the person would believe nine other subjects rated the stimulus person as having a very keen and witty sense of humor. How would our subject rate the person? Previous studies in conformity suggest he would rate the person as the "group" rated him. It is difficult to go against the judgments of a group; when one disagrees with the group, one feels uncomfortably eccentric.

Because of the pressure to conform we tend to develop fairly fixed other-concepts concerning all manner of people—other-concepts which fellow members of the group hold and which we acquire from them. Indeed, qualification for membership in some groups consists in affirming some peculiar other-concepts, e.g., the belief that if a person is white, he is superior to all colored people. Or a communist must affirm a certain concept of capitalists before he can gain entry into the Party.

In view of all the factors which operate so as to produce distorted and inaccurate other-concepts, how exactly does one develop accurate other-concepts? This question is very important in personality hygiene, since it is only when an individual has an accurate other-concept that he can establish a healthy interpersonal relationship.

THE FORMATION OF ACCURATE OTHER-CONCEPTS

The formation of accurate other-concepts is a special case of the more general problem: How does a person acquire accurate knowledge about anything? He does so by following the scientific method of inquiry.[17]

Scientific inquiry commences with doubt, or uncertainty. The investigator asks a question about some state of affairs and formulates as many possible answers as he has the imagination or precedent to suggest. Then under conditions as rigorously controlled as possible, he makes detailed observations in order to get facts. On the basis of these facts, he upholds some one of these hypotheses and rejects all others.

In the special problem of getting accurate knowledge of another person, we are concerned with formulating beliefs congruent with the usual behavior of the individual and with his actual personality structure. If we are to acquire accurate other-concepts, we must be glad to get as many hypotheses as we can. But we must believe none of these in advance of actual observation of the person. *It is this crucial step of hypothesis-testing that even a trained scientist overlooks in his perception of people.*

The present author knows a man who is a very rigorous scientist. This person carries out meticulously controlled experiments dealing with isolated bits and pieces of behavior in animals and humans. If I told him that reinforcement in learning was caused by brain cells moving together in order to make new contacts with each other, he would doubt me, demand endless proof, and insist that I show him anatomical slides. But if I told this same man "Say, did you know that Professor *X* (whom he doesn't like) drowned some rats which didn't behave according to his pet hypothesis?" Although, in fact, Professor *X* did not, the man would without doubt reply, "He did? Why that crook! He ought to be tarred and feathered." No demands for proof or even evidence; instead, immediate belief of an untested hypothesis—a cardinal sin for scientists.

Other-concepts probably enjoy the unique advantage of being the last of the theories which an individual will test, much less abandon. A person will abandon the belief that the world is flat. He will abandon the belief that Santa Claus brings his Christmas presents.[18] He will abandon the belief that storks bring babies. But he will not abandon his present beliefs about the other person—his other-concepts. By some curious quirk of vanity, each man believes he is an expert psychologist and that his other-concepts are accurate and irrefutable. *Never has so much been believed about people, by people, on so little evidence.* It should perhaps be stated here that as a general rule, the more thoroughly one comes to know himself, the more capable will he be of knowing others. Patients who have undergone effective personality therapy report that with gains in self-knowledge they have also gained in knowledge of others.

There is one direct means by which one acquires valid knowledge about the other person, and that is through his self-disclosure.[19] This fact is so obvious that it is often overlooked. If the other person *wants to be known,* he will not hesitate to disclose his true opinions, feelings, past experiences, and anything else that is relevant. However, since people, unlike animals, can lie, such transparency of the self is likely to occur only under conditions of trust and assured good will.

In the last analysis, each person has some measure of control over the concept of him which the other people in his life will formulate. In our discussion of the "public self" (see page 167) we pointed out that each individual presents himself to others in the way that he *wants* to be seen. Hence, I can, if I wish, misrepresent myself to others so that their concepts of me will be as false as a counterfeit dollar. By the same token, if I want to be known as I am, I will take pains to reveal myself in authenticity to my personal friends and loved ones.

A SPECIAL CASE—THE ASSUMPTION THAT THE OTHER PERSON CAN BE CHANGED

An important component of an other-concept is accurate knowledge concerning the other person's susceptibility to change. Psychologists know that human nature is not fixed, that modal behavior and personality structure are quite subject to change within very broad biological limits. Psychologists even have acquired some rudimentary knowledge of the conditions under which behavior and personality will change, and they stand in a position where they can influence, or control, the rate and direction of changes in behavior and personality structure. Teachers, psychotherapists, social workers, military training personnel, all of these professional workers seek to control the process of behavioral change in other people.

Individual people often get involved in interpersonal difficulties, however, because their concept of the other person includes an *inaccurate estimate of the changeability of the other person.* They will either overestimate the changeability, underestimate the changeability, or fail to identify the variables which must be manipulated in order to produce change.

THE EFFECTS OF UNDERESTIMATING CHANGEABILITY. A person may believe that other people's behavior is a fixed, unyielding, and immutable fact; nothing will change it. In consequence, he may develop compulsive, or fixed, modes of relating to others—which may have the consequence of perpetuating the undesirable behavior of the other person. For example, a man may believe that human nature is basically evil, that people are "just no damn good"; no matter what is done for them, they will remain untrustworthy, dishonest, selfish, animal-like, lustful, and everything else that is bad. If a person with this belief has children, his child-rearing behavior will necessarily be influenced. It makes a difference to a parent whether he is dealing with a child who will turn into a savage beast unless curbed or whether he is dealing with a malleable piece of "clay" who will become, roughly, what he is trained to become. In the former instance, child rearing will consist primarily in a tense battle of the parent with the forces of evil that are assumed to be inherent in the child; one false step, one weak moment of unwatchfulness, and catastrophe will result.

Probably many marriages have been terminated, or endured with resignation and martyrdom, because one spouse has incorrectly diagnosed the changeability of his partner. The husband may assume his wife cannot be changed, and the wife has tried unsuccessfully to change her man. The couple then "digs in" for a life of dissatisfaction, or else they institute divorce proceedings. Many a spouse, following a bitter divorce, has been dumbfounded to observe that, like magic, the discarded partner has become everything which was desired during the marriage. The husband about whom the wife forever complained "He is such a stodgy, unimaginative, unromantic man" becomes after the divorce a veritable movie star hero—more attentive to his appearance, more considerate of women, more romantic and impractical. This is certainly evidence that he was capable of change, but more than this, it is evidence *he did not want to change for her* and that *she did not know how to behave so he would want to change for her.*

THE EFFECTS OF OVERESTIMATING POTENTIAL FOR CHANGE. While behavior is mutable, yet there are powerful forces which militate against behavioral change. These factors include the need to feel safe, the need to maintain self-esteem, the need to maintain a sense of identity, other people's expectations, and so on. Each time a person alters some accustomed mode of response, he may feel anxious about disapproving responses of others; he may lose self-esteem, if his present value-system opposes the new behavior; he may fear that other people will no longer recognize him. These factors thus operate as a kind of gyroscope, restricting behavior to a certain relatively fixed range. But a man may choose a friend, or a spouse, with a view to transforming this person, like Pygmalion, into something new and different. The person "as is" is not acceptable. A sort of silent wager is laid down that the chooser will in time be able to change the other person. Thus, a woman may displace her zeal as a sculptress from clay to people. She chooses a bum, dead beat, or criminal as husband, not because he is attractive the way he is, but because she believes she can change him into a new man. In theory, it is possible to arrange conditions so that a man will change his modal reaction patterns, but few laymen are so skilled they can manipulate conditions in precisely the ways which will promote behavioral and personality change. For that matter, trained psychotherapists, criminologists, and other professional personality-changers have a difficult time doing their job, since knowledge about personality change is as yet incomplete and incompletely tested. Therefore, the layman is advised not to choose friends and lovers with the aim of changing them. If the package is not acceptable the way it is, do not accept it. The major consequence of overestimating changeability of the other person is disappointment and failure in effecting the changes.

HOW TO CHANGE THE OTHER PERSON. The most effective and the most healthy way to produce wanted changes in the other person is *to behave toward him so he will want to change himself*. People have voluntary control over their reaction patterns to a surprising extent. It is true that people can, within limits, act as they want to act. If another person's behavior is unsatisfactory to himself, he can usually modify his own behavior so it becomes satisfactory.

If one's behavior is unsatisfactory to another person, one can usually alter the behavior so it will satisfy the other person. Naturally, it may not always be easy to alter modal reaction patterns, either for oneself or for another person, but it is surprisingly possible to achieve. From this it follows that for one person to induce stable changes in the reaction patterns of another, the most effective way is to somehow *induce the desire to change* in the other person.

The precise means of achieving this goal—the desire in the other person to act in ways desired by the first—will of course vary. In fact, there are no valid general rules which could be said to hold for all cases. There is this general proposition which can be announced, however, without too much error: If the relationship is one which provides satisfactions for both participants, where basic needs are being richly gratified, then each partner will want to please the other. Thus, the most effective means of inducing change in the other person is to behave toward him in ways which will satisfy his basic needs. Then, the wishes of the first person, within reason, and within limits set by reality and the other person's basic structure, will literally become the other person's willingly obeyed commands.

At first blush it would appear as if the person wanting the changes in the other person's behavior is "bribing" him with satisfactions. In a sense, this is true. But there is a difference between a cold, calculated attempt to bribe another person into conformity with one's wishes and a spontaneous wish that the other person, who is loved, will change. In the former instance, the one being bribed will eventually discover he is being manipulated. In the latter, the relationship is more likely to be one of mutual requests to change and mutual compliance with the other's wishes.

It should not be overlooked that we can change another person by force, by threats, or by "brainwashing" procedures. While change induced by threat, manipulation, or sanction may be effective in the short run, it will usually be achieved at the cost of resentment and hostility toward the person dictating the terms. The dictator or overbearing parent or teacher seldom takes into consideration, in his demands for conformity, the other needs and values of the subject. As these are violated and thwarted in consequence of the demanded change, hostility is mobilized. Whenever the subject becomes less dependent upon the other, he will rebel and terminate the relationship or inflict violence upon the would-be manipulator of his behavior.[20]

LIKING THE OTHER PERSON

In the opening section of this chapter, we asserted that one important characteristic of a healthy interpersonal relationship is the fact that each participant liked the other, or at least liked more of the other's characteristics than he disliked. Let us now inquire into the *liking response.*

THE NATURE OF LIKING

The experience of liking somebody or something refers to a feeling, or, in broader terms, an *affective* response to a stimulus. It is probable there are characteristic physiological concomitants to the liking response, but these are not clearly known or understood. We can recognize the characteristic "feel" of liking some one or something, however, without difficulty. Liking is a pleasurable feeling and is readily identified by most persons when it is present, unless the individual has repressed his feelings and emotions so successfully that he can recognize none. We may loosely define the liking response as *a pleasant feeling which is produced when the individual is confronted by some perceptible object, idea, memory, or situation associated with satisfaction.*

It is convenient and perhaps valid to think of the liking response as a conditioned response, or, more precisely, as the affective component of an expectancy. The object which induces the liking response has, in the past, produced satisfaction, or is related to something which produced satisfaction. The liking response is a sort of *preparatory set* for something satisfying to occur, just as anxiety is a preparatory set for something painful to occur.

THE CONDITIONS FOR LIKING

The crucial question for this section of our discussion is, "What will a person like, and why will he like it?" In answering these questions, it will become apparent that the answers are to be found in the past relationship between the person and the objects in question.

There are two separate but related factors which determine whether or not an individual will like something. The first of these is needs; the second is ideals or values.

NEEDS AND LIKING. Objects which an individual requires in order to produce satisfactions will be liked. In very general terms, we can assert that *a person likes what he needs to produce satisfactions.* When the need-tensions are operative, the thought or perception of the need-objects will be associated with feelings we can readily call liking responses. Naturally, people differ in their likes, and in addition, each person establishes a liking-hierarchy with respect to all the possible objects which could conceivably produce satisfaction.[21] Thus, a person likes edible things; but he likes steak better than ham and rare steak better than well-done steak. A man likes women, but he likes gentle women better than hot-tempered women and women his age better than women much older.

VALUES AS A DETERMINER OF LIKING. The values which a person has acquired, through assorted identifications with other people during the course of his development, will help to determine what he likes. In general, a person likes those things which have the characteristics specified by his ideals. Thus, a person likes horses which resemble his concept of the ideal thoroughbred; he likes women whose appearance and behavior correspond closely with his conception of the ideal woman. Jourard and Secord[22] showed that liking aspects of one's own body was a function of the discrepancy between the actual size of selected body parts and the subjective ideal which each subject held with respect to size. If a woman asserted that her desired hip-measurements were 35 inches and her actual hip-measurements were 42 inches, she reported she disliked her hips. We can thus regard a person's values, or ideals, as a kind of internal measuring device with which he always makes comparisons whenever he observes *anything*. Those things which conform closely with the ideal are liked; those things which deviate markedly from the ideals are disliked.

NEEDS, VALUES, AND LIKING THE OTHER PERSON. From the preceding sections, we can state that a person likes those aspects of another person—for example, his appearance and traits—which satisfy needs and which conform closely with values or ideals. Let us see how these factors operate as determiners of liking responses to another person.

The other person is a complex whole composed of many parts. It is true we can speak of the other-person-as-a-whole, and we can then say we like or dislike this totality; but we can also analyze the other person into parts and experience liking-disliking responses to those parts. In everyday experience, this part-liking and part disliking is very common. We must add, however, that we often generalize from the specific part of the person which we like or dislike to the entire personality. For example, the reader's room-mate may have one particularly annoying trait, for instance, the habit of leaving his clothing scattered around the room. If asked, the reader might say he dislikes him (all of him). What he is doing is generalizing his dislike-response from the *particular* disliked response to the *total behavior-repertoire* of the person; in short, to his entire personality.[23] Contrariwise, a girl may say she likes him (by implication, all of him), when in fact, all she has seen of him is some one response-pattern she likes. Psychologists have coined the term "halo-effect" to describe this tendency of generalizing a liking or disliking response from some particular aspect of a person to all of his traits.

In a friendship, or a marriage, or a parent-child relationship, each participant may be assumed to have assorted liking-disliking responses to assorted aspects of the other person. The healthier the relationship, the more detailed, accurate, and differentiated the concept (other-concept) each partner will have of the other. If the relationship is a healthy one, the liking responses, quantitatively, will be greater than the disliking-responses that are induced by the traits of the other. Practically, this means the other person behaves in more ways which produce satisfactions for the first than he behaves in frustrating ways. Further, it implies that more of the other's traits correspond with the first person's values and ideals than deviate from these ideals.

We have stated that in a healthy interpersonal relationship, each person likes more aspects of the other person than he dislikes for a specific reason. It is recognized that no one person can completely satisfy all the needs or conform with all the values of another person—at least not in all respects or for all times. For most healthy relationships, it is enough "cement" for the relationship if the ratio of like to dislike produces a preponderance of liking responses.

It is only in unhealthy relationships, where neither partner has an accurate other-concept, that we observe total, or global, liking and disliking. The young lover, enthusiastic over meeting the answer to his prayers and dreams, tells his mother, "She's *perfect;*

I like *everything* about her." It is only later, as he comes to know her better, that he discovers her imperfections (deviations from his values and ideals) and aspects of her appearance and behavior which produce deprivation and frustration instead of satisfaction.

It is only healthy to like a person-as-a-whole under special conditions: When an individual knows another person well and has quite differentiated likes and dislikes toward the other, in considering an *integrated* concept of the person as a whole, he concludes he likes the other person. This condition corresponds to Murphy's view of third-level cognition—where the object is perceived, not as an undifferentiated mass, and not as an aggregate of differentiated parts, but rather as an integration of parts which produces a whole with unique characteristics not reducible to parts.[24]

CONCERN FOR THE WELFARE AND GROWTH OF THE OTHER

An interpersonal relationship is healthy when there can be observed active concern on the part of each individual for the welfare, happiness, and growth of the other. What is meant by concern? Out of what conditions does it emerge? What do we mean by *active* concern?

It is difficult to define concern in precise, behavioral terms. Perhaps the most accurate way we can assert what is meant by the word is in the following terms: Concern means a person *wants* some valued end to be obtained—it matters to him, it makes a difference whether or not the valued end is obtained. Concern for the welfare, happiness and growth of the other person means that it *matters;* it is important whether or not the other person is well, happy, and growing. He wants the other person to be well, happy, and growing.

When we say active concern, we mean that the desire or wish for the happiness of the other is not *passively* longed for; rather, we mean that the concerned person acts. He engages in instrumental behavior, the aim of which is to produce happiness and growth, or at the very least provide the conditions for happiness and growth of the other person.[25] We shall turn to this point about active concern in a following section. For the present, we shall inquire further into the nature of concern.

A THEORY OF CONCERN

We generally like the other person because he behaves in ways which produce satisfactions for us. In a sense, the other person can be viewed as a supply-source of satisfactions. Experience shows us that the other person will behave in ways which satisfy us most richly *when he is himself satisfied.* Thus, we acquire a vested interest in his welfare, happiness, and growth. Concern for the happiness of the other person is a sort of insurance for one's own satisfactions. A workhorse cannot work for us when he is ill-treated. We use the horse's energy as a means for the attainment of our own goals. Thus, we have a vested interest in tending the horse's needs very carefully. We are, in short, concerned for the horse's happiness and growth, and we take active steps to promote his contentment and growth. In so doing, we insure that the horse will better be able to provide us with the means to important satisfactions.

It may offend the reader thus to be compared to a horse, yet the analogy is not farfetched. The other person, like the horse (though in different ways), provides us with behavior which produces important satisfactions and important need-objects. Thus, the other person may have skills which we need employed in our service. His affection-responses, or liking responses, may be important to us as means toward a sense of security or self-esteem. His very company may serve as a source of entertainment, diversion, and so on. In order for him to continue to be willing and able to provide us with satisfactions, it is important that he be happy. Therefore, each dissastisfaction of his promises a withdrawal of satisfactions from us. In order to avoid this eventuality, we learn to anticipate his wants and fulfill them. We help him when he asks for help. We help him to grow, because a mature partner is better able to provide us with satisfactions than an immature partner.

Thus, concern arises as a by-product of satisfaction, satisfaction provided us by the other person. Also, it may arise as a kind of calculated risk in cases where an individual becomes concerned with another person's happiness, but the other person is not yet a satisfier. It is only predicted that if one gets concerned, actively concerned with his happiness, he will in turn become concerned with yours and act toward that end.

Parents are concerned for the happiness and growth of their children for a number of reasons. Happy children are signs of success in child rearing, and this is an important condition for the self-esteem of parents. This also provides satisfactions for the parents—even security, for it is possible that the parents may need the future economic support of their children in old age.

A wife is concerned for the happiness and growth of her husband, because a happy and mature husband is a much richer source of satisfactions for her than a miserable, thwarted, and childish husband.

It should not be construed from the foregoing that all concern for others is an outgrowth of the calculated view that "if I take care of that person, then he will take care of me." A healthy personality is capable of a kind of disinterested concern for others; it simply gives him a feeling of fulfillment, or of abundance, to be able actively to care for another person. Thus, grandparents may delight in the growth of their grandchildren, whom they indulge and nurture, yet they get nothing else but the experience of fun and pleasure from watching the children's antics.

A further determiner of concern which must not be overlooked is the fact of *identification* with the other person. In a healthy interpersonal relationship, say, between spouses, one partner identifies very closely with the feelings and needs of the other. Where this has occurred, *the satisfactions of the other person are felt as deeply as satisfactions for the self.*

It appears, then, that concern for the other person is a kind of devious concern for one's own happiness and growth. This may appear offensive and selfish to the reader. Yet, with Fromm, we shall ask this question, "Why should we not be concerned about *our own* happiness and growth?" There is growing evidence to the effect that one can love another only if one loves oneself; that love and concern for the self and the other person are not mutually exclusive. Rather, they are correlated and derive from something else, a common factor which, for want of a better name, we shall call the "power to love."[26] In other words, only if one can be concerned for the self can one be concerned for the other.

People who appear to be totally unconcerned for themselves, and who instead make all manner of "sacrifices" in order to help another person (they are called "unselfish"), usually demand a terrible price in return and usually get this price—absolute conformity with their wishes. We are all familiar with the "unselfish" mother who sacrifices all her own chances at happiness in order to help her son get through school. Would it not be ungracious if the son then against his mother's "reasonable wishes," married a girl of *his* choice but not his mother's?[27]

We can see that knowledge, liking, and concern for the other person all interact as factors in a healthy interpersonal relationship. If one does not know the other person, how can one like him? If one does not know him, and like him, how can one get concerned about his happiness and growth? But concern, without knowledge, is blind. One can be concerned about the other's happiness, but if you don't know what he needs in order to be happy and to grow, how can you provide him with the appropriate need-objects?

BEHAVIOR WHICH PROMOTES HAPPINESS AND GROWTH IN THE OTHER PERSON

We have stated that a healthy interpersonal relationship is characterized by behavior on the part of each participant which promotes happiness and growth in the other. What is the nature of behavior which promotes happiness in the other? What kind of behavior promotes growth in the other?

INTERPERSONAL BEHAVIOR WHICH PROMOTES HAPPINESS. Happiness is the name we assign to the subjective feeling of satisfaction and to the feelings associated with the attainment of valued ends. In a healthy interpersonal relationship, one partner actively assists the other in obtaining satisfactions. The ability to behave in ways which promote happiness in the other, of course, is predicated on knowledge of the other person and concern for the other person. One can know what the other person needs in order to be happy, but this knowledge alone will not insure instrumental action toward securing the other's happiness. One can be concerned for the other's happiness and not know what is required in order to help the other to happiness.

In addition to knowledge and concern, however, there is one important factor which must not be overlooked in the quest for the other's happiness: The behavior patterns which are required of one partner in order to promote the happiness of the other must be *available*, or at least possible for the first person to perform. That is, the requisite behavior pattern must be within the behavior-repertoire of the first person; they must be consistent with the conscience of the first person; and finally, they must not be behavior patterns which will produce frustrations or important deprivations in the first person (except under conditions of a voluntary choice).

Let us illustrate. A wife may need her husband to behave in ways that will secure large sums of money so she can buy things which will make her happy. Let us suppose the husband knows what his wife needs and is actively concerned that she get it. It bothers him that she should be unhappy. But in his present circumstances he may not be able to acquire the skills necessary to earn more money. His present skill-repertoire will enable him to earn a certain limited income and no more. Thus he won't be able to satisfy his wife's need for more money. Let us suppose, however, that it would be possible for him to get more money by a little bit of forgery or theft. If he proceeds to engage in these activities, he may secure the money, but he may then be overwhelmed with guilt. Where this occurs we could not speak of a healthy interpersonal relationship, because the happiness of one partner is achieved at the cost of immense guilt on the part of the other.

Suppose the husband could supply his wife with the money she needs for her happiness but at the cost of depriving himself of many of the things he himself needs for satisfaction and happiness. Again, we could not speak of a healthy relationship unless the husband made a careful appraisal of his own values and freely decided that his wife's contentment was more important to him than his own immediate satisfactions.

We can see that in a healthy relationship each partner strives to act in ways which will provide satisfactions for the other person; but we cannot call the relationship healthy unless the necessary action is feasible, consistent with the value-system of each partner, and does not involve undue deprivation on the part of the active partner.

INTERPERSONAL BEHAVIOR WHICH PROMOTES GROWTH. Personality growth is defined as a *change in modal behavior and experience so* that:

1. *The individual displays the behavior and reactions which are appropriate to his age-role.*

2. *His self-structure changes correspondingly, so that the self-concept remains accurate, the self-ideal remains congruent with social mores and with actual behavior, and the various public selves remain accurate and mutually compatible* (*see Chapter 6*).

3. *The growing person becomes increasingly capable, through learning, of a broader repertoire of effective instrumental action.*

4. *His behavior is increasingly directed by his real self* (*see Chapter 6*).

How is growth promoted through interpersonal relations? It is theoretically possible for personality growth to occur in a social vacuum. As a solitary individual encountered problem after problem and solved them, learning new skills as a consequence, he would be manifesting one aspect of growth; namely, a diversification of his instrumental behavior-repertoire.

But nobody lives in a social vacuum; everyone is enmeshed in a number of interpersonal relationships. Some of these relationships may be quite neutral with respect to growth; others may be quite effective in producing regression, or growth in reverse, others may prevent growth, and still others may actively promote growth. Let us touch briefly upon those relationships which are neutral, regressive, and interfering, in their effect on growth, and then examine in greater detail the relationships which promote growth.

RELATIONSHIPS WHICH ARE NEUTRAL WITH RESPECT TO GROWTH. Any relationship with another person which does not produce enduring change in his behavior and personality structure is neutral with respect to growth. Into this category of "growth-neutral" relationships we would include all brief encounters with other people for specific purposes: the brief contact with a garage mechanic fixing your car; a person sitting beside you on a train, with whom you converse about assorted subjects, perhaps sharing a drink, but that is all; or socializing at a party and enjoying the company. We should not assume, however, that brevity is the sole characteristic which defines a "growth-neutral" relationship. Some relationships with others last for years, but neither partner changes his modal reaction patterns or his values one whit. Other relationships may last five minutes, but the partners may have been radically changed. Thus, a perfect stranger may say something to you which produces a marked change in your self-concept, a marked change in your values, or a marked change in modal behavior.

RELATIONSHIPS WHICH INDUCE REGRESSION. Students of personality development have developed crude norms which describe the appropriate, or expected, range of reaction patterns at each of several age levels. They have done no more than attempt to define the norms for expected behavior patterns which exist in each society for each age level. Thus, we can divide a total life history into infancy, early childhood, late childhood, adolescence, early adulthood, middle adulthood, late adulthood, old age, and senility. Different behavior patterns are expected in each society from persons falling into each age bracket. Sociologists speak of this kind of categorizing as *age-grading.* While growth means progressive change in behavior consistent with age norms, regression means growth in reverse.

Experimental psychologists have formulated the general proposition that frustration, or, more generally, *stress* is one of the factors which promotes regression.[28] A stressor is any factor which interferes with the ongoing course of value-pursuing activity. Thus, physical danger, illness, frustration, interference are all stressing agents and as such can induce regression, or growth in reverse. Adult persons will usually display childish behavior when they are ill, thwarted, or in danger.

There are some relationships which produce stresses resulting in permanent regression in one of the partners. Thus, one of the participants in the friendship, marriage, or boss-employee relationship may act in such a way that it literally "child-ifies" the other person, who otherwise can act in ways appropriate to his age. The wife may impose such impossible demands on her husband that in attempting to implement them he is obliged to act, or is forced by stress-tensions to act, in childish ways. A boss, perhaps an overweening and autocratic sort of person, may force his employees to behave like five-year-old children in order to avoid his wrath and protect their jobs. Bettelheim described the regressive behavior of concentration camp inmates, behavior which derived from the physical stresses of prison-camp life as well as from the arbitrary behavior of the guards.[29] Many of the prisoners were reduced to childlike levels of behavior.

Some teachers may transform students whose behavior was at first appropriate to their age into individuals who are much less mature.

We can generalize from these illustrations and assert that most dependency relationships tend to promote regression.

We must distinguish between situational regression and more generalized, or stabilized, regression. A person may display regressive behavior only in one kind of relationship while in all others he can act his age. A husband may behave in a quite childish manner with his wife (not much differently than the way he behaved as a child toward his mother); toward other women, he may act in mature fashion. Or, an employee may act like a grudgingly obedient child toward his boss and other authority figures, but toward his peers he acts his age.

A truly regression-producing relationship is one which produces *permanent* regression in the participant—regression which carries over to other relationships, so that other people are impressed by the juvenile or childish behavior of the individual. Such relationships reverse a slogan adopted by many schools: "Send us the boy, and we'll return a man." Instead, some people, by virtue of their demands and their power over anyone with whom they get involved, seem to say, "Send me a man, and I'll return a boy."

In this discussion, we have overlooked the very important fact that in a healthy relationship, the participants *can allow each other to regress;* they do not necessarily demand perpetual adultness from each other. This is an entirely different state of affairs from what we have been discussing above. There is a difference between a relationship which *enforces* regression and one which *permits* both regressive behavior and growthful behavior to occur. There is even reason to believe that genuine personality growth is not possible unless the individual is able to abandon his present modes of behaving, regressing for some time to a more infantile level of behaving and experiencing and then progressing to an even more adult level.

RELATIONSHIPS WHICH PREVENT GROWTH. There are some relationships which continue on the unspoken condition that neither partner will change, that is, grow. Thus, a man and woman marry. Each holds a certain concept of the other that they have deliberately constructed in the mind of the other (see Chapter 9, on public selves). At the time of the marriage, his concept of her personality was inaccurate and incomplete. She did not know him as he "really" was. However, he believed she was a person who possessed characteristics and traits which he needed in a wife. He believed she had all the traits of an ideal wife. If either behaved contrary to expectation then the other would be disappointed, would feel let down and deceived: "You are not the person I married or the kind of person I want to stay married to." In order to preserve their marriage (for whatever satisfactions it does provide), each partner would strive to remain unchanged; each partner might believe that a change in personality would result in the dissolution of the marriage—a consequence which is dreaded. Such a marriage prevents growth.

A bachelor, living with his parents long after his peers have been married, does not grow. His present behavior-repertoire may be acceptable to his parents; they are willing to support him, cook his meals, do his laundry, and they make no demands on him he cannot readily fulfill with long-rehearsed facility. For him, further growth is contingent upon his moving away, exposing himself to new challenges and to new people who make new demands upon him.

Some parents actively prevent growth in their children, either through ignorance because they do not place a value on their children attaining maturity, or because their own self-esteem is dependent upon playing the parental role. So long as their child is getting satisfactions out of the child role, he will not break away and expose himself to growth-promoting influences.

RELATIONSHIPS WHICH MAKE ONE SICK. When one is thrust into prolonged, intimate contact with other persons of a certain kind, the chances of illness—physical or personality illness—are increased. For example, if an individual is obliged to remain in close contact with someone on whom he is dependent for any reason, and this other person is obnoxious, depressing, overdemanding, or irritating, it can literally give rise to a "pain in the neck," headache, digestive upsets, and other by-products of suppressed emotion. The experience of personality therapists has amply shown that when parents make excessive or contradictory demands on their children, when they will not let their children be themselves, the children are likely to develop neurotic or psychotic disorders.[30]

Many physicians who have become alert to interpersonal sources of stress have been able to prove that for given patients, their symptoms of asthma, hemorrhoids, skin eruptions, hypertension, diarrhea, and so on, arose and lasted as long as the patient was inescapably involved with another person and disappeared as soon as the relationship was ended.

Probably there exist some few people with a special talent for spreading misery, who always depress or sicken, disorganize, and undermine the self-confidence of all they come in contact with. It is meaningful to regard such individuals as today's witches. The comic character Joe Btflsk, in Al Capp's strip *Li'l Abner,* is a fictional representative of the modern witch. In the comic strip, Joe always walks with a rain cloud over his head, and whenever he appears, expert workmen hit their thumbs with their hammers, hens do not lay, and the most robust people feel miserable. There is need for further study of those persons like Joe Btflsk who affect others in deleterious fashion.[31]

EXCESSIVE DEPENDENCY AND UNHEALTHY INTERPERSONAL RELATIONSHIPS. When a person is involved in a relationship with another person such that his growth is blocked and he is obliged to act in ways repugnant to him, we may ask, "Why is the relationship not terminated?"

We have touched on an answer to this question in a preceding section, where we pointed out that even though he may be frustrated in many ways and prevented from growing, the individual may be *dependent* upon the other person for important satisfactions. It is because the *individual believes he is unable to obtain satisfactions elsewhere* that he may submit to humiliating, frustrating, and growth-interfering relationships with another person.

Thus an employee unable to get a job elsewhere may put up with all kinds of degradation at the hands of a martinetlike boss; a lonely person, unable to find anyone else to like her, may put up with all kinds of misery-producing behavior from her friend so that she will not again face the awful prospect of loneliness.

In view of the unhealthy consequences of dependency, it will repay us to inquire into some of the factors which will minimize dependency and maximize the likelihood that healthy interpersonal relationships will be established.

PROPHYLACTICS AGAINST ENTERING UNHEALTHY INTERPERSONAL RELATIONSHIPS

SKILLS, KNOWLEDGE, AND COMPETENCE. If dependency increases the likelihood that unhealthy interpersonal relationships will be established, then it follows that competence, knowledge, and skill will decrease dependency upon others. The skilled individual is "independently secure," as Blatz[32] puts it. This does not mean his relationships with others will be healthy by axiom; but independent security will leave him much freer to dissolve any interpersonal relationships which do not give him enough satisfactions to make them worth while. His relationships with others will be entered into and maintained out of free choice. Humphrey Bogart, the late movie actor reputedly said, "The advantage of being rich is that you can tell any s.o.b. to go to hell." A similar advantage is possessed by the person who has so many skills as to be relatively autonomous. The autonomous person still needs other people for many of the satisfactions which make life worth living; but he can afford to be discriminating in his choice of friends, spouse, and bosses. He will not choose them simply because they possess what is desperately needed; rather, he will choose them because they have other characteristics in addition to those immediately needed.

Dependent persons are notoriously indiscriminate in their choice of friends and spouses.[33] Their urgent needs impel them to see in the other person only those traits which are relevant as objects for their needs. Consequently, they "fall in love" with persons who have what is needed; but the objects of their "love" (dependency) may demand an exorbitant price for giving it, and further, their other traits, less salient at first, will inevitably emerge from the background when the urgent needs of the dependent one are partially gratified. The dependent person may be literally shocked at what else came in this package of "need-objects" which he "bought" when he entered into the relationship.

A RICH GRATIFICATION HISTORY. If a person has enjoyed a life rich in satisfactions, it will be possible for him to choose his friends and lovers with more discrimination.[34] At the time of commencing some relationship, he is much less likely to be starved—for affection, approval, sex, material things. He will have been able to find gratification for many of these needs prior to commencing a permanent friendship or a marriage. Consequently, he is less likely to "fall for" the first person who has what he needs and seems willing to give it to him. Many a person is so starved for affection, appreciation, or sexuality that he will marry or befriend the first person who provides him with these, only to find as his need-tensions subside somewhat (allowing other needs and values to emerge into tension) that the other person lacks other important qualities.

It follows from this that nobody should establish long-term relationships in a state of starvation of any kind—whether it be affection-starvation, approval-starvation, hunger for status, and so on. Under those conditions, the starved person's judgments will be faulty. Other values and needs remain in the background, and all he can see in the other person is an opportunity for immediate gratification. The other person is a complex thing, made up of many parts. Even though these other aspects are not considered during the initial appraisal, yet they go along with the "package." One can liken many a marriage and friendship to the case of purchasing an automobile solely because it has a pretty color, without considering such additional values as comfort, durability, power, and so on.

AUTONOMOUS SELF-ESTEEM. By autonomous self-esteem is meant the fact that one's self-esteem is determined mostly by *one's own evaluations of one's behavior*. This kind of autonomy probably results from early relationships with parents which produced a healthy self-ideal, or conscience (see Chapter 11). A healthy self-ideal comprises "shoulds," self-expectations, and demands which are feasible and flexible; conformity with them produces and maintains self-esteem. If the parents are affectionate, consistent, reasonable in their demands on the child, and in addition provide the child with an "identification-model" which can be readily followed, the child will probably develop a healthy self-ideal.

A person with such a healthy self-ideal is much less dependent upon external sources for his self-esteem. He can accept himself, without requiring a continual flow of reassurance, appreciation, affection, and flattery from other persons. He is not starved for favorable attention, feeling depressed and unworthy when it is not forthcoming from others. He may enjoy being appreciated by others, but his self-esteem is not wholly dependent upon these outside appraisals. He is much less likely, then, to "fall" for the first person who seems to like him and who flatters him for his accomplishments. Further, he is much less likely to govern his behavior so that it will insure a continuous supply of external appreciation. He can, to a higher degree, do what he wants to do, rather than do what he must do in order to please others.

EFFECTIVE COMMUNICATION WITH THE OTHER

The ability to communicate effectively was pointed out earlier (in Chapter 1) as one of the criteria of healthy personality. According to one analysis of the communication process,[35] effective communication entails the ability to transmit intelligible messages and the ability to understand messages which have been sent by another. When communication is effective between two persons, maximum opportunity is afforded for mutual understanding and knowledge. Any factor which interferes with transmission, receipt, or decoding of messages between two persons will thus foster growing mutual misunderstanding and ignorance. The aspect of communication in which we are most directly concerned in the present context is the transmission of personal messages, or *self-disclosure.* Honest self-disclosure between persons is the most direct means by which they can come to know one another as distinct persons, but such disclosure is frequently blocked by fear. In a healthy interpersonal relationship, mutual self-disclosure will be untrammeled, free, and spontaneous. As two persons interact over a period of time, revealing their thoughts, feelings, beliefs, and needs to one another, they will of course come to know one another better. But beyond mutual knowledge, honest self-disclosure inevitably will produce *impasses* in the relationship. It is in the resolution of these impasses which inevitably arise in personal relationships that growth can be fostered.

IMPASSES AND THEIR RESOLUTION[36]

An impasse between two persons exists when one has a need, demand, or wish which, if fulfilled by the other, would promote satisfaction. The other person, however, either will not, or cannot, comply with this wish. Impasses may be open or covert. In the usual course of events, only open impasses can be resolved in growth-promoting ways. Covert or hidden impasses are likely to result in a gradual deterioration of the relationship.

The most obvious sign that an impasse has arisen in a relationship is conflict or open argument and debate. However, many impasses come into being before they are recognized as such, and they only manifest themselves indirectly, as in boredom, irritation, restlessness, dissatisfaction with the other, nagging, recurrent criticism, or recurrent anger. These symptoms indicate that one of the partners is being thwarted in the relationship but is unable or unwilling to specify in what precise ways the other person is failing to satisfy. In one marriage, for example, the wife found herself getting increasingly bored with her husband and overcritical of his appearance, eating habits, hobbies, and other minor matters. When he changed his grooming, eating habits, and abandoned his hobbies for the time, she still remained bored and irritated. She had not yet put her finger on the precise way in which her needs were being thwarted by her husband's behavior. It was only when he spontaneously lavished affection upon her that the impasse was resolved. She did not realize that this was what she had wanted.

The simplest case of an interpersonal impasse consists in one person's *expressing an open wish or demand* that the other person do something, or stop doing something, which the other person *refuses* openly. The simplest case of impasse-resolution consists in either (a) the person withdrawing the demand, (b) the other person complying with the demand, or (c) some compromise between (a) and (b).

A resolution to an impasse can be judged for its effect on growth. If it results in a valued change in the behavior-repertoire of the person, or if it results in a healthier self-structure (see Chapter 6), then we can regard the solution as a growth-producing one. If, on the other hand, the solution simply crystallizes the present behavior-repertoire and personality structure of either partner, or if it interferes with growth or involves regression, then we must adjudge the solution of the impasses as unhealthy.

The compulsive avoidance of impasses and compulsive avoidance of interpersonal conflict is unhealthy. A person may avoid impasses by refusing to make demands, or he may avoid them by compulsively acceding to the other's demands. Open conflict is always preferable to covert guerrilla warfare, because it can result in a more open and rationally considered solution, at least in the long run.

Thus, in a healthy relationship, each partner feels free to express his likes, dislikes, wants, wishes, feelings, impulses, and the other person feels free to react with like honesty to these. In such a relationship, there will be tears, laughter, sensuality, irritation and anger, fear, babylike behavior, and so on.

The range of behavior, feelings, and wishes which will be brought out into the open is not arbitrarily limited. In fact, one gauge to the health of a relationship is the *breadth of the topics of conversation, the range of feelings which are openly expressed*, and *the range of activities which are shared.* In each case, the broader the range, the healthier the relationship.

UNHEALTHY RELATIONSHIPS AND BEHAVIORAL RESTRICTION

In an unhealthy relationship, much is taboo. The relationship continues only on the premise that certain aspects of behavior will be excluded. Thus, a marriage may continue only so long as criticism of one partner by the other is avoided. Or a friendship may continue only so long as neither partner brings up certain topics of conversation, for example, sex, war, politics, family affairs, and so on. One gauge which psychotherapists use in order to determine whether or not their patients are approaching health is the freedom of expressiveness of the patient toward the therapist. Can he express affection? hostility? criticism? sexuality? boredom? dislike? Can he express these feelings and attitudes toward others and not be afraid to accept the consequences of so doing? Can he talk freely about anything under the sun to his therapist? If some topics promote tension, anxiety, or embarrassment, can he state in words that he is tense, anxious, and embarrassed?

Unhealthy communication-restriction may be found in many parent-child relationships. The personality hygienist might ask, "Can the individual admit there are some aspects of his mother or father which he despises as well as others which he likes? Or does he feel compelled to assert that his parents are perfect?"[37] The same with marriages. Can one spouse acknowledge to the other that there are some repugnant features in the other's behavior? Any factor which curbs the full and honest communication of feelings, thoughts, and demands is a factor which interferes with the attainment of a healthy relationship and encourages the development of an unhealthy one. The only exception to the above-mentioned general rule is the case where the partners have agreed, following past experiences, to impose voluntary restrictions on their own behavior and communication because they have found that when they do not impose these restrictions, more important values are jeopardized. Thus, a couple of friends may agree, following bitter and insurmountable arguments, that politics is an area which they cannot discuss; they agree to exclude this area of discussion from their relationship.

HOW DOES FULL COMMUNICATION PROMOTE GROWTH?

Growth in personality occurs as a consequence of meeting conflicts and impasses head-on and reconciling these. Interpersonal conflicts and impasses constitute *problems* which require solution so that a satisfying relationship may be maintained or started. Whenever a person encounters a problem in his everyday living, he is obliged to vary his behavior until he discovers some mode of responding which is successful in achieving a solution. With no conflicts, with no impasses, there would be no instigation to change one's modal behavior-repertoire—one would, in short, not learn. If a person had no need to keep afloat and move in water, he would never learn to swim. If he had no occasion to keep records or to communicate by letters, he would not learn to write. If nobody made open demands upon him, he would never learn ways of behaving which would please the other person.

In interpersonal relationships, it is only when there is an open and fully felt and recognized conflict between the participants that an occasion is provided for growth, for learning new, more adequate modes of behaving. *Interpersonal relationships, besides being a rich source of satisfactions for the participants, also provides a rich source of problems for each participant.* The solution of these problems results either in growth of personality toward health or away from health.

Conflicts and impasses are created in interpersonal relationships *only* when each participant acts fully in accordance with his own genuine wants, feelings, and values. Inevitably, as these are expressed and acted upon, they will come into conflict with the wants, feelings, and values of the other. *Accepting and recognizing the conflict is the necessary condition for its resolution.* Persons who strive to avoid interpersonal conflicts in a compulsive manner are actually doing all in their power to avoid growth and change.

Let us illustrate how full communication can create problems and provide the conditions for growth:

A husband, for years, has been acting in ways which annoy his wife. She has avoided mentioning her annoyance to him, though she feels it deeply enough. Since the husband does not know of her annoyance, he continues to act in those ways, thus continually provoking his wife. If the wife one day bursts into a rage and lets her husband know, through this full communication, how his behavior affects her, then at least the necessary conditions for growth are present. The husband may modify his behavior so as to please his wife more, and this may be adjudged growth. Or, he may with considerable vigor refuse to change; this refusal may require the wife to modify her demands, to accept her husband's idiosyncrasies, or to continue asserting her disapproval. At any event, the issue is now out in the open, and a greater opportunity for resolution is now available than when the issue was covert.

One by-product of full and honest communication between partners is *trust*.[38] When a person knows that his friend or spouse will always and immediately let him know what he thinks or feels about him, he acquires the concept of the other person as honest, and he will believe what the other person says. Most readers will agree that there is nothing more uncomfortable and anxiety-provoking than the situation of never knowing what the other person *really* thinks, feels, wants. Many a patient undergoing personality therapy reports he never knew whether his parents liked each other or him; that he can hardly believe it when someone says nice things to him. Instead, he feels anxiety and suspicion when someone says something nice. In fact, it is only in personality therapy that some persons have their first experience at full communication, when they relate *everything* which comes to mind to the therapist.

When one does not know the real structure of the physical world, one is naturally insecure and anxious. If we could never tell from moment to moment whether a flood, earthquake, or hurricane was going to occur, we would feel chronically anxious, and we would live a life hemmed in by precautions against these catastrophes. But climatology has been so well cultivated that "honest" signs of forthcoming catastrophes are readily available.

In the social world, and in interpersonal relationships, honest self-disclosure is the counterpart of natural "signs." If we believed that verbal expressions of feelings and demands from other people were *not* accurate statements of their feelings and forecasters of their behavior, we would always remain anxious and defensive. We may not like the honest communications of the other person, but it is only when these honest communications are present that we can find ways of acting which will save whatever is valued, including the relationship itself.

Full self-disclosure between the participants in an interpersonal relationship promotes growth, then, *by creating impasses and conflicts in the relationship*. It is in the resolution of the impasses that growth of personality occurs, but without the communication, there would never be sharply defined impasses.

SOME FACTORS IN FULL COMMUNICATION

Under what conditions will persons disclose themselves fully and in authenticity to others? One factor which seems related is perception of the other person as trustworthy and understanding. This places the onus upon the other individual to *be* trustworthy and understanding and to be able to communicate the reality of these traits so he will be seen as he *is*.

Another factor seems to be a considerable measure of security and self-acceptance or self-esteem. Individuals who are relatively unafraid of others and who regard themselves as acceptable will tend to be readier to let themselves be known than will insecure, dependent individuals.

Curiously enough, some individuals feel freest to disclose themselves to strangers, such as a casual companion on a train or plane, or a barber, hairdresser, or bartender. This freedom to disclose the self to strangers probably stems from the conviction that it does not matter what the other person thinks of one, because one is unlikely to encounter him in one's everyday life with "people who count": viz., parents, friends, and relatives. Now, let us discuss some of the barriers to full communication in personal relationships.

SOCIALLY DERIVED BARRIERS TO FULL COMMUNICATION

Although honesty in interpersonal communication is highly valued in our society, there is another socially defined value which is often more strongly affirmed than honesty. We are speaking here of the value which is placed on "saying nice things." There is an old slogan which describes this value succinctly: "If you can't say something nice about another person, don't say anything." When people conform with this semiformal rule for acceptable conduct, they impose a constant restriction over their own communicative behavior. In close relationships, such as marriage, friendships, teacher-pupil, parent-child, and so on, the recipient of "nice" evaluations can never know how his behavior really affects the other person. Further, the "nice" appraisals of him made by significant others will contribute to the formulation of an inaccurate self-concept. We have shown (in Chapter 6) that the judgments of oneself made by significant others are an important determiner of the self-concept. If these others have lied to you about your behavior, you will acquire beliefs about your personality which are inaccurate. Many a person, the recipient of uncritical praise from parents, friends, and teachers, has come to evaluate his talents erroneously. When he encounters impartial critics of his musical or artistic ability, he is undone and overwhelmed by such criticism. When one of the participants in an interpersonal relationship represses all those opinions, feelings, evaluations which are "not nice," he is contributing to unhealthy personality in the other, and he is developing an unhealthy relationship with the other.

Another socially derived precept holds that people should not be either demanding or complaining in a relationship. As they conform with this precept, they delimit their communication markedly. A wife who would lose self-esteem if she makes demands on her husband may refrain from so doing. Since he has no signs available that he is thwarting or depriving her of legitimate satisfactions, he will continue blithely to behave in his accustomed ways. The upshot will be that the wife will preserve her self-esteem, true enough, but the cost may be a long life of suffering and repressed resentment on her part. The same holds for complaints. Complaints are to an interpersonal relationship what pain or pus is to the body—a sign that something is wrong, a sign that something must be done in order to restore the valued state of affairs. If people were incapable of feeling pain, they would have little incentive to seek competent medical attention, and they might die long before their allotted three or four score of years. If complaints were not made by one participant in a relationship, the other person would have no indication that his behavior or omissions were producing dissatisfaction and unhappiness. Vigorous and honest complaints will at least create an impasse, which we have seen is the first and necessary step in the direction of adjustments. The author, in therapeutic and counseling work, has advised quietly martyred spouses to learn the art of complaining. This is not to say that complaining is valued per se; it may happen that a person complains on the basis of irrational and unrealistic needs and demands. In such cases it is to the other's advantage to rebut the complaints with as much vigor as they have been presented. This reaction insures that all sides of the issue are brought into the open where they can be more effectively resolved.

There are some needs which one or both participants may feel ashamed of, or condemn, because of social mores. Thus, a wife may be ashamed of her longings to be "fathered" by her husband from time to time. If she is ashamed of it, she will never ask her husband (subtly or openly) to behave toward her in a paternal fashion, and he will never learn of her need. The wife may then develop a strong hatred of her husband for not being a mind-reader and sensing her need, and she will be obliged to repress the hatred, too. This will produce an impasse which is insurmountable because it is covert. But the wife may be assuming without warrant that her husband would condemn her for longing to be an infant. Perhaps he feels unnecessary to his wife and would welcome the opportunity to act as she needs him to act. But because of assimilative projection, the wife presumes that if she were to ask him to cuddle her he would laugh at her and reject her. One ounce of reality-testing might correct this misconception.

DEPENDENCY. We have already touched on dependency in other contexts, but it warrants restatement in the present setting. A helpless person may dread full disclosure of self to the one upon whom he is dependent, because he fears the other will withdraw his support. The dependent employee doesn't tell his boss how he feels about him out of dread he will be discharged from a job he needs. The dependent wife doesn't tell her husband all her feelings, needs, thoughts, and opinions, because she fears he will leave her. The dependent friend doesn't tell his buddy what he thinks and feels, because he fears he will be abandoned. Any factor which promotes dependency and interferes with the attainment of independent security is a factor which interferes with full communication.

AN EXCESSIVELY STRICT CONSCIENCE. A conscience which is excessively strict may prevent a person from acknowledging his thoughts and feelings to himself as well as to the other person. If the individual with a strict conscience discloses himself to the other person, he may suffer not only agonies of anxiety concerning the reaction of the other person but also agonies of guilt and self-hate.

Thus, a student may condemn petting but yet experience a strong impulse toward just that kind of behavior. Merely to admit it openly to himself might be the occasion for profound guilt. To admit to his girl friend what he longed for would produce guilt, and dread that the girl would reject him. Yet, if he were able to bypass the defense of repression and express what he wanted despite his guilt and anxiety, he might find that (a) his girl friend would welcome a kiss from him and (b) upon open scrutiny and evaluation of the moral precept, it might be possible to revise or modify it, thus enabling acceptance of this aspect of his personality.

An excessively strict conscience can thus interfere with self-disclosure and with the opportunity to establish a healthy interpersonal relationship.

COMMUNICATION AND THE REAL SELF

The "real self" is a term which Horney used to refer to "that central inner force, common to all human beings, and yet unique in each, which is the deep source of growth . . ." (page 17). In another context, she speaks of the real self as "the most alive center of ourselves . . . it engenders the spontaneity of feelings. . . . It is also the source of spontaneous interests and energies . . . the capacity to wish and to will . . ." (page 157).[39]

We can redefine the *real self* in more clear-cut terms. By real self, first of all, we are referring to *subjective experience* which only the person himself can observe directly, since he is the one who is experiencing it. The immediate subjective experience which the term real self refers to comprises *feeling* (affection, anger, anxiety, guilt and so on) and *cognitive content* (memories, perceptions, or, more generally, thoughts). *Wants and wishes,* as these are consciously experienced, are also an integral component of the real self: a wish to hurt somebody, a longing to disagree with someone, or a desire to eat, sleep, make love, and so on.

Let us now raise the question, *how much of his real self is a person willing to disclose—through words and through action—to another person?*

In a healthy interpersonal relationship, an individual is willing and able to communicate *all* of his real self to the other person when it is appropriate to do so. It must not be forgotten that the real self refers to the subjective, or private, aspect of a person's behavioral repertoire. Anybody can see what a person *does*. Nobody, without the co-operation of the individual himself, can discover what a person is thinking, feeling, or wanting. The person himself must be willing to translate his thoughts, feelings, and wishes into words and/or actions before the other individual can have an accurate idea of the person's real self.

For that matter, the individual himself may strive to ignore, or to repress, his real self. Where this has been successfully accomplished, Horney speaks of *alienation from the* [real] *self*. She sees the process of neurotic development, or unhealthy personality development, as having its origin in active "moves away from the real self."[40]

Thus, a person may ignore his "real" feelings, wishes, and wants and try instead to feel what he is supposed to feel; want what he is supposed to want; think what he is supposed to think. By whom or what is he "supposed" to think, feel, and want? He feels compelled by his conscience, by "duty," or by the expectations and demands of other people to think, feel, and want in certain restricted ways. Failure to think, feel, and want what he is supposed to will produce guilt or anxiety. That is, if the individual confronts and acknowledges his real feelings, thoughts and wants, as these arise *spontaneously*, he will then experience self-loathing, guilt, or the dread that significant others will reject and despise him. The person who has become alienated from his self is a person who is afraid or ashamed of his real self. Discontented as he thus is with his real self, he strives to destroy it, bury it, change it, ignore it—in short, he does everything with his real self but recognize it, accept it, and act in accordance with its promptings. As Horney views it, psychotherapy, or personality therapy, has as its goal the undoing of the process of alienation from the self. The therapist tries to confront the patient with his real self and to help him accept it and to view it with compassion and concern rather than fear and revulsion.

Personality therapy is undertaken by means of communication between one person with an unhealthy personality who is called the patient and an expert called the personality therapist. The therapist tries to encourage his patient to disclose his real self to him. He avoids criticism, he avoids punishment, and he tries to minimize all of the common barriers to full communication. Freud introduced the technique of "free association" into the mechanics of therapy. He imposed a "fundamental rule" upon the patient; the patient was required to do one and only one thing—report *everything* which passed through his mind during a therapeutic hour. The reader is asked to try this. Pick someone who is close to you and start, with ruthless honesty, to report in uncensored fashion *everything* which enters your mind for one hour. You will find that you start off well enough, but soon, a resistance will be encountered. Your mind will go blank. Or something will come up which you would rather die than utter to another human being. Freud found that if each resistance was studied and interpreted to the patient, the process of free association would continue until the patient might just as well be pronounced cured, because he would have finally established a healthy relationship with his therapist. He would have experienced the process of disclosing his real self immediately—in statu nascendi (which may loosely be translated to mean expressing his private thoughts, feelings, and wishes the very instant they were "born"; i.e., the very instant they popped into the person's mind).

Whitaker and Malone accomplish the same aim—helping a patient discover his real self, accept it, communicate it, and love it—by encouraging the patient to *speak his fantasies aloud to the therapist.* The therapist may encourage this activity by speaking aloud his own fantasies which he experiences during the therapeutic hour with his patient.[41] It should be apparent that one's fantasies, determined as they are by needs and feelings (see Chapter 2), will reflect one's real self with utmost nakedness. Again, the reader is asked to select some friend and, in his presence, speak aloud all the fantasies or daydreams which he develops in the presence of his friend. Probably embarrassment and guilt will drastically limit the kinds of fantasies which the reader will alow himself to construct.

We can construct a rough scale for self-disclosure, a scale which ranges from statements that are easy to disclose to those which are increasingly difficult to utter. Thus, the following verbal communications from one person to another will illustrate:

Easy to disclose

↓

"It is now raining" (a reference to the "objective" world).

"I am hungry" (a reference to the "subjective" world and actually an honest statement of felt tensions).

"I wish that I could be a baby again."

"I hate you and wish that you were dead."

"I love you deeply and with passion."

Difficult to disclose

As a general rule, only *selected* aspects of the real self can be communicated to another person with comfort: those aspects which are consistent with (a) the self-concept, (b) the conscience, (c) the social mores, (d) the public self that has been constructed apropos the other person, and (e) the other person's actual concept of you. Messages which deviate from these restrictions will not be readily conveyed to the other person. There are some unhealthy personalities which are so repressed that the individual will communicate only *impersonal* messages to other people, and he will block or "clam up" if any question is directed at him concerning his personal feelings, wishes, opinions, and so on.

It should not be construed from all the preceding discussion that the sheer *amount* of self-disclosure that goes on between participants in a relationship is an index of the health of the relationship or of the persons. There are such factors as timing, interest of the other person, appropriateness, and effect of disclosures on either participant which must be considered in any such judgment. In one research study, it was found that of the two least liked and most maladjusted members of a work-setting, one was found to be the most secretive and undisclosing, and the other was the highest "discloser" in the group.[42] If a relationship exists between self-disclosure and factors of health, it is likely *curvilinear,* not linear; that is, too much disclosure and too little disclosure may be associated with unhealthy personality, while some intermediate amount, under appropriate conditions and settings, is indicative of healthier personality. However, as a general principle, it may be proposed that persons who feel obliged to lie to others about their inner being are making themselves sick. Honesty may yet prove to be the best policy—in this case, the best health insurance policy! And we may find that those who become sick most frequently—physically and mentally—have long been downright liars to others and to themselves.

REALISTIC AND FEASIBLE DEMANDS ON THE OTHER PERSON

In a healthy interpersonal relationship, the demands which each partner imposes on the other as conditions for the continuation of the relationship are realistic, mutually agreed upon, and consistent with the values and happiness of the other. What does this prescription imply? What is a realistic demand?

As we have seen, interpersonal relationships are entered into as a means toward the ends of happiness, satisfaction, and growth. Each partner needs the other to act in certain ways in order to attain those ends. In most friendships, or marriages, the participants are willing to accede to the requests, demands, and needs of the other. But it can happen that one of the partners has unusual needs—needs deriving from an atypical life history. That person needs the other to act in atypical or perhaps impossible ways in order to produce satisfactions. Where one partner has unusual needs, or where each has an inaccurate concept of what the other is capable of doing, the demands may be unrealistic and impossible of fulfillment. There is a distinction between a demand which is difficult to conform with and one which is impossible for the other to fulfill. In the case of difficult demands or challenges, efforts to fulfill these may well contribute to growth. In fact, challenges made by one person to the other may serve to motivate new efforts and creative achievements that would not have materialized without the challenge. In the case of impossible demands, they may either be physically impossible to fulfill or they may cost so much that other values would have to be sacrificed, thus making it not worth while.

Thus, a sweetheart may demand of her lover that he abandon his work in order to spend all of his time with her. Or, a mother may demand a straight "A" average from a child of below-average intelligence. In these instances, the demands cannot be met. Growth would not consist in one person conforming with the other's demands; rather, growth would be promoted if the individual refused to conform and strove instead to show that the demands were unrealistic. If these attempts were successful, and the demanding one accordingly adjusted his demands to bring them into reasonable limits, then we could assert that the one who modified his demands had grown.

A partner in a healthy relationship would not deliberately introduce a demand on the other which would result in his unhappiness. But in accordance with the principle of open communication, even unreasonable demands should be openly asserted so that the other can know of them and rebut them with vigor. It is only through the open expression of these demands that an opportunity is provided whereby the demands can be assessed against knowledge of the other person.

The personality hygienist can employ the demands which one participant makes of the other in their relationship, as an index of the personality health of the participants and as an index of the health of the relationship. As an impartial observer, he can compare the demands with the ability of each participant to fulfill them and make judgments about their realistic or unrealistic nature.

Insofar as possible, in a healthy relationship there will be a close congruence between the demands which one partner imposes on the other and the latter's self-demands. If the partners share many values in common, this will likely be the case.

RESPECT FOR THE OTHER'S AUTONOMY AND INDIVIDUALITY

AUTONOMY. Ours is a democratic society in which relative autonomy of the individual person is seen as a high value. Self-determination is a trait valued by the society at large and by personality hygienists. This emphasis upon the autonomy of the single person contrasts with concepts of the ideal man which are held in other societies. Thus, it could be said that in Nazi Germany, the ideal man could be described, not as the "autonomous man," but as the "obedient man," obedient to the leaders of the State. Nazi parents raised their children toward this goal of obedience; Nazi wives admired husbands who showed unflinching obedience to superiors and condemned those who were so "weak" and "selfish" as to put private interests above those of duty.

In a healthy interpersonal relationship, each partner will theoretically place a strong positive value on the autonomy of the other, and further, will value the goal of growth toward self-actualization of the other. When these values are clearly stated, it becomes apparent that many other values can readily conflict with them. In a marriage, for example, a husband may refuse his wife's request for a divorce because he values public opinion more than her growth. A parent may force unwilling compliance from the child so as to maintain self-esteem. In each case, we observe a lack of respect for the individual needs of the other person. This is a subtle point but one which warrants elucidation because of its importance.

In a healthy relationship, each partner wants the other partner to do *what he wants to do.* Certainly, friends or spouses choose one another because of similarities in values; i.e., similarities in what each wants to do. In our society, because of the high value placed on free will, few spouses would want the other to remain married unwillingly. What we are here saying is that a sign of a healthy relationship is present when each participant shows an active concern for the *preservation of the integrity and autonomy of the other,* even when this involves at some time the dissolution of the relationship. If a divorce, or the break-up of a friendship, or leaving the parent's home, or quitting a job, is an important means of promoting growth and increasing autonomy, then in a healthy relationship, the other person will want this to occur.

Very often a concern and respect for the other person's right to integrity and autonomy involves some pain. For that matter, to be concerned with *one's own autonomy* may often involve a good deal of social pressure—especially in those instances where one's wishes differ from those of the majority of people. The "nerve of failure" as Riesman and others have called it, is rare. By this is meant the courage to continue to assert one's difference from the mass of other people, despite economic and social pressure to conform.

INDIVIDUALITY. To respect and to value another's individuality means that one sees his unique qualities as something priceless and irreplaceable. His individuality includes not only those characteristics that are considered socially valuable but also traits that might be called faults. Yet, in a healthy interpersonal relationship, the participants seek to learn one another's unique and distinctly idiosyncratic qualities and seek moreover to affirm these.

Martin Buber,[43] the philosopher mentioned earlier, stated this appreciative view of the other person's idiosyncrasies in elegant terms: "The basis of man's life with man is twofold, and it is one—the wish of every man to be *confirmed as what he is,* even as what he can become, by men; and the innate capacity in man to *confirm* his fellow-men in this way." ". . . Genuine conversation . . . means acceptance of *otherness.* [Everything] depends, so far as human life is concerned, on whether each thinks of the other *as the one he is* [and] unreservedly accepts and confirms him in his being this man and in his being made in this particular way" (page 102, my italics).

"Man wishes to be confirmed in his being by man, and wishes to have a presence in the being of the other" (page 104).

The concept of *confirmation,* as employed by Buber in these passages, has a precise meaning, one which amplifies our assertion that respect for individuality of the other characterizes healthy interpersonal relationships. To "confirm another man in his being" means that one acknowledges that *he is what he is.* One may not necessarily like all that he is, but at least one acknowledges and respects the fact that *he is that very person,* with those very characteristics, and not someone else. This is the direct means of respecting another's individuality. Rogers referred to it as "unconditional positive regard," and he sees it as a necessary condition for helping others fulfill their individuality.[44]

SUMMARY

Interpersonal relationships differ from role-relationship in that in the former the participants are interested in the subjective and personal side of each other's lives. The capacity to establish and maintain satisfying personal relationships with others is regarded as an indicant of healthy personality. Interpersonal relationships that are most compatible with health have seven main characteristics:

1. Each partner knows—that is, has an accurate concept of—the other's idiosyncrasies.

2. Each partner likes more of the other's traits than he dislikes.

3. Each partner feels concern for the happiness and growth of the other.

4. Each partner behaves in ways which will promote the growth and happiness of the other.

5. Each partner can communicate effectively and can fully disclose himself to the other.

6. Each partner imposes feasible demands and expectations on the other.

7. Each partner respects the autonomy and individuality of the other.

An accurate concept of the other person's personality (accurate other-concepts) is achieved by accurate observation of the other person. First impressions of another person are generally inaccurate, in consequence of projection, attribution, needs, and social factors, such as pressure to conform with others.

People are changeable. Underestimating and overestimating the changeability of others can impair interpersonal relationships. Another person can be encouraged to change by so gratifying his basic needs that he will want to change.

The liking response—liking aspects of the other person—is a function of needs and values. We tend to like those aspects of another person which gratify our needs and which accord with our values and ideals.

Concern for the other person's happiness and growth is a by-product of concern for the self; a happy and mature partner can more fully gratify us than one who is dissatisfied and immature.

Behavior which promotes happiness in the other person is predicated on knowledge of and concern for the other person. The behavior which promotes growth includes *full honest communication. Some relationships are* neutral *with respect to growth, others* induce regression, *some* prevent growth. Excessive dependency *is seen as a factor which promotes unhealthy interpersonal relationships.* Skills, a rich gratification history, *and* autonomous self-esteem *are seen as factors which promote the development of healthy interpersonal relationships.*

Full and honest communication, so important to promoting growth, leads to impasses. *An impasse exists when one person needs something from the other which the latter cannot or will not provide.*

Impasses are resolved when the "needy" one

withdraws his demands or when the other person accedes to these demands.

In unhealthy relationships, not only is communication restricted, but so also is behavior of all kinds restricted. Dependency and an excessively strict conscience are seen as barriers to full communication, along with certain socially determined barriers. In a healthy relationship, the "real self" of each partner is made known by each to the other.

In healthy interpersonal relationships, the demands *which each makes on the other are* open, reasonable, and compatible with the health and happiness of the other.

Each participant in a healthy interpersonal relationship respects the autonomy and individuality of the other.

NOTES AND REFERENCES

Excellent supplementary reading will be provided by those references marked with an asterisk (*).

1. The distinction between "persons" and "personages" (role-players) is drawn by Tournier. See Tournier, P., *The Meaning of Persons* (New York: Harper, 1957), especially pp. 11–27. The distinction between interrole and interpersonal relationships is elaborated in Jourard, S. M., "Healthy Personality and Self-Disclosure," *Ment. Hyg., 43,* 499–507 (1959).

2. This interest in the systematic study of interpersonal relationships is commonly attributed to Harry Stack Sullivan, who defined psychiatry, not as the study of mental disease, but rather as the study of interpersonal relations. For the most recent statement of his viewpoints, see Sullivan, H. S., *The Interpersonal Theory of Psychiatry* (New York: Norton, 1953). It should be asserted, however, that Moreno, with his "sociometric" methods of studying groups, long anticipated Sullivan as a formal student of interpersonal relationships. See

Moreno, J. L., *Who Shall Survive?* (Washington, D.C.: Nerv. Ment. Dis. Publ. Co., 1934).

*3. These criteria borrow heavily from Fromm's characterization of "productive love," which includes the attributes of knowledge, care, responsibility, and respect. See Fromm, E., *Man for Himself* (New York: Rinehart, 1947), pp. 96–101. Ackerman has developed some specific criteria for determining whether or not a marital relationship is healthy. Ackerman, N. W., "The Diagnosis of Neurotic Marital Interaction," *Social Caswk.*, April 1954.

4. See Newcomb, T., *The Acquaintance Process* (New York: Holt, 1961), for a more extended analysis. See also Maslow, A. H., *Toward a Psychology of Being* (Princeton, N.J.: Van Nostrand, 1962), pp. 33–34; and ch. 9.

*5. Asch, S. D., "Forming Impressions of Personality," *J. Abn. Soc. Psychol.*, *41*, 258–290 (1946). See also Gollin, E. S., "Forming Impressions of Personality," *J. Pers.*, *23*, 65–76 (1954); Heider, F., *The Psychology of Interpersonal Relations* (New York: Wiley, 1958), pp. 59–78, for a discussion of "being seen."

6. Secord, however, found that facial features (physiognomy) were more important determiners of trait-ascription than occupational stereotypes. In one experiment, he showed a group of subjects several facial photographs, and the supposed occupation of each person's face was indicated, e.g., banker, minister, and so on. He expected that as he switched occupational labels, the traits which were ascribed to each person would be changed. Instead, he found that his subjects were rating personality traits on the basis of facial features rather than on the basis of occupational labels. On pursuing this line further, he conducted some highly original studies of the facial characteristics which induce subjects to agree in assigning personality traits to persons on the basis of facial apppearance. See Secord, P. F., Bevan, W., Jr., and Dukes, W. F., "Occupational and Physiognomic Stereotypes in the Perception of Photographs," *J. Soc. Psychol.*, *37*, 261–270 (1953). Also, by the same authors, "Personalities in Faces, I. An Experiment in Social Perceiving," *Genet. Psychol. Monogr.*, *49*, 231–279 (1954). Secord has continued this program with a number of collaborators and has published, to date, about nine separate studies.

7. Cameron, N. and Magaret, Ann, *Behavior Pathology* (New York: Houghton, 1951), pp. 381–387. See Lundy, R. M., "Assimilative Projection and Accuracy of Prediction in Interpersonal Perceptions," *J. Abn. Soc. Psychol.*, *52*, 33–38 (1956), for an empirical study which is related to our discussion of assimilative projection.

8. See pp. 208–210 of this volume.

9. In 1954, a Negro male was brought to trial on the testimony of a white woman that he looked at her with the apparent "intent to rape"—she displayed disowning projection.

10. Rogers, C. R. and Dymond, Rosalind F. (eds.), *Psychotherapy and Personality Change* (Chicago: U. of Chicago, 1954), pp. 90, 98.

11. Sullivan, H. S., *op. cit.*, 28–30 (footnote).

12. Secord, P. F. and Jourard, S. M., "Mother-Concepts and Judgments of Young Women's Faces," *J. Abn. Soc. Psychol., 52,* 246–250 (1956).

*13. "Social perception" is an area of intense investigation at the present time. A convenient summary is available to the serious student in Lindzey, G. (ed.), *Handbook of Social Psychology* (Cambridge, Mass.: Addison-Wesley, 1954), II, ch. 17: "The Perception of People" (by Bruner, J. S. and Tagiuri, R.).

*14. Murray's early experiment with young girls illustrates this. He asked girls to describe the picture of a man before and after they had played a very spooky children's game called "murder." The subjects saw more scary and evil characteristics in the man after the game than they did before. Murray, H. A., "The Effect of Fear upon Estimates of Maliciousness of Other Personalities," *J. Soc. Psychol., 4,* 310–329 (1933). Krech and Crutchfield provide many examples of the influence of needs and emotions on the concept of other persons. See Krech, D. and Crutchfield, R. S. *Theory and Problems of Social Psychology* (New York: McGraw, 1948), pp. 88–94. Chs. 5, 6, which provide fundamental information on beliefs, will make this section more meaningful for the serious student. Compare such need-motivated perception of a person with Maslow's account of the "B-cognition" of another: desireless contemplation of his whole "being," of his uniqueness, as opposed to scrutinizing him as a source of frustration or gratification. See Maslow, A. H., *op. cit.*

15. The influence of other people's opinions upon our own judgments and other-concepts is a special case of the more general phenomena of suggestion, hypnosis, and propaganda. See Krech and Crutchfield, *op. cit.*, for an intelligent discussion of suggestion and propaganda, and Gill, M. M. and Brenman, M., *Hypnosis and Related States* (New York: International Universities Press, 1961), for a discussion of hypnosis.

*16. Crutchfield, R. S., "Conformity and Character," *Amer. Psychologist, 10,* 191–198 (1955).

17. Dewey, J., *Logic: The Theory of Inquiry* (New York: Holt, 1938), chs. 4, 6. These two chapters outline clearly, although in rather turgid prose, the fundamentals of scientific inquiry as these are applied to everyday living as well as in the laboratory. See also ch. 3 of this book, on reality testing.

18. But not too readily. G. Brock Chisholm stirred up public furor with an address which he delivered as a William Alanson White Memorial speech, in which he was deploring the fact that parents will lie to children about such things as birth and Santa Claus. Newspapers all over the country and Canada picked up his remarks about the Santa Claus myth, and the public berated him for trying to destroy a happy illusion. See Chisholm, G. B., "The Psychiatry of Enduring Peace and Social Progress," *Psychiatry, 9,* 1–36 (1946), for his actual remarks.

19. Jourard, S. M., *op. cit.*, footnote 1.

20. See Secord, P. F. and Backman, C. W., "Personality Theory and the Problem of Stability and Change in Individual Behavior," *Psychol. Rev., 68,* 21–32 (1961), for a recent attempt to delineate variables in personal change.

For comments on manipulation, see Jourard, S. M., "On the Problem of Reinforcement by the Psychotherapist of Healthy Behavior in the Patient." In Shaw, F. J. (ed.), *Behavioristic Approaches to Counseling and Psychotherapy* (Tuscaloosa, Ala.: U. of Ala. Studies No. 13, 1961), pp. 8–19.

21. Clyde Coombs has developed some highly sophisticated methods for determining and measuring liking-hierarchies. See his chapter 11 in Festinger, L. and Katz, D., *Research Methods in the Behavioral Sciences* (New York: Dryden, 1953), pp. 491–492.

22. Jourard, S. M. and Secord, P. F., "Body-Cathexis and the Ideal Female Figure," *J. Abn. Soc. Psychol., 50,* 243–246 (1955). See also, by the same authors, "Body-Cathexis and Personality," *Brit. J. Psychol., 46,* 130–138 (1955), for a more extensive discussion of these themes. In these technical papers, the words "cathexis-response" may be understood as synonymous with "liking-disliking"; thus, "positive cathexis" means liking and "negative cathexis" means disliking.

23. This tendency (generalizing from some aspect of a person's behavior-repertoire to the entire personality) is very much like one of the primitive ways of thinking and explaining—the so-called "law of *pars pro toto.*" See Werner, H., *The Comparative Psychology of Mental Development* (Chicago: Follett, 1948), p. 423.

*24. The serious student should read carefully the section of Murphy's text which deals with the "levels" of cognitive activity. See Murphy, G., *Personality: A Biosocial Approach to Origins and Structure* (New York: Harper, 1947), pp. 342–346.

*25. This section draws heavily from Fromm's discussion of "productive love." Fromm, E., *op. cit.,* pp. 96–101.

*26. Fromm, E., *op. cit.,* pp. 129–141. Fromm's discussion of "selfishness, self-love, and self-interest" is a classic which the student should read in entirety.

*27. Howard, S., *The Silver Cord.* This play should be read by all students as part of a liberal education. It treats of "Mom" before Philip Wylie and E. Strecker handled this theme.

28. Mowrer provides an astute analysis of the concept of regression and cites one of his rat studies to illustrate some of the conditions under which regression occurs. See Mowrer, O. H., *Learning Theory and Personality Dynamics* (New York: Ronald, 1950), ch. 13.

*29. Bettelheim, B., "Individual and Mass Behavior in Extreme Situations," *J. Abn. Soc. Psychol., 38,* 417–452 (1943). Also his book, *The Informed Heart* (Glencoe, Ill.: Free Press, 1961).

30. *Cf.* Bateson, G. *et al.,* "Toward a Theory of Schizophrenia," *Behav. Sci., 1,* 251–264 (1956). Bateson has proposed that parents who create "double-bind" conflicts for their children contribute to the development of schizophrenia. An example of a double-bind is a mother who complains that her son does not

love her. If he then hugs her, she pushes him away because she does not like to be touched.

31. This theme is further expounded in Jourard, S. M., "The Role of Spirit and Inspiritation in Human Wellness," *J. Existent. Psychiat.* (in press) (1963). Any of the research into characteristics of parents and relatives of the mentally ill provides some information about characteristics of "illness-fostering" people. See, for example, Spiegel, J. P. and Bell, N. W., "The Family of the Psychiatric Patient," ch. 5, in Arieti, S. (ed.), *American Handbook of Psychiatry,* I (New York: Basic Books, 1959).

32. Blatz, W., *Understanding the Young Child* (Toronto: Clarke, Irwin, 1944), ch. 9.

*33. See Horney's descriptions of the person who "moves toward" people and her discussion of the "self-effacing solution" in, respectively, Horney, K., *Our Inner Conflicts* (New York: Norton, 1945), ch. 3; and Horney, K., *Neurosis and Human Growth* (New York: Norton, 1950), ch. 9. These chapters provide excellent illustrations of dependency.

*34. This discussion borrows heavily from Maslow's concept of "gratification-health." See Maslow, A. H., *Motivation and Personality* (New York: Harper, 1954), pp. 115–117.

35. Liberally paraphrased and condensed from Ruesch, J. and Bateson, G., *Communication, the Social Matrix of Psychiatry* (New York: Norton, 1951), pp. 15–20. See also Ruesch, J., *Disturbed Communication* (New York: Norton, 1957), pp. 34–40.

36. The discussion of impasses is based on the recent work of Whitaker and his co-workers. See Whitaker, C. A. and Malone, T. P., *The Roots of Psychotherapy* (New York: Blakiston, 1953); Whitaker, C. A., Warkentin, J., and Johnson, Nan, "The Psychotherapeutic Impasse," *Amer. J. Orthopsychiat., 20,* 641–647 (1950).

37. The present writer showed that those subjects who were least able to admit any dislike or criticism of their parents showed the highest degree of moral indignation. Jourard, S. M., "Moral Indignation: A Correlate of Denied Dislike of Parents' Traits," *J. Consult. Psychol., 18,* 59–60 (1954).

38. Inability to trust others is seen as a factor leading to serious personality disorder. See Erikson, E. H., *Childhood and Society* (New York: Norton, 1950), pp. 219–222.

39. Horney, K., *Neurosis and Human Growth* (New York: Norton, 1950).

40. Horney, K., *op. cit.,* ch. 6.

41. Whitaker, C. A. and Malone, T. P., *op. cit.,* pp. 202 ff.

42. Jourard, S. M., "Self-Disclosure and Other-Cathexis," *J. Abnorm. Soc. Psychol., 59,* 428–431 (1959).

*43. Buber, M., "Distance and Relation," *Psychiatry, 20,* 97–104 (1957).

*44. Rogers, C. R., "The Necessary and Sufficient Conditions of Therapeutic Personality Change," *J. Consult. Psychol., 21,* 95–103 (1957).

CHAPTER *11*
LOVE AND HEALTHY PERSONALITY

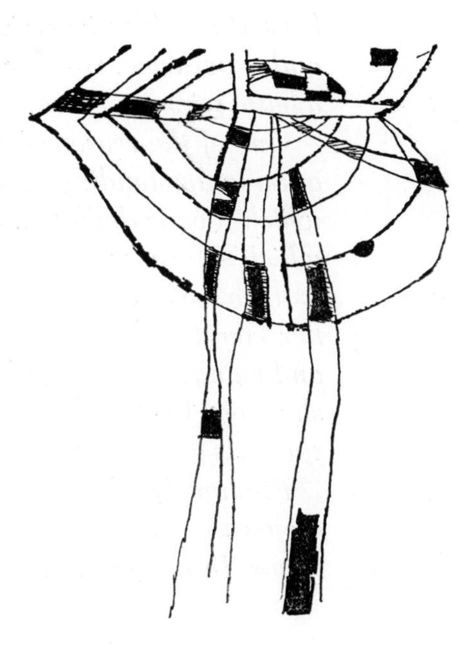

INTRODUCTION

Love is a phenomenon of crucial interest and concern to the personality hygienist. Freud once remarked that lieben und arbeiten, *loving and working, were the crucial signs that personality health had been achieved, through growth or through therapy. Loss of the capacity to love, or failure to develop it on the other hand, is one of the most universally agreed-upon signs that personality health is impaired. Yet love is among the least understood of all human phenomena and is the least studied by investigators of human behavior and experience. We do not yet have an applied or a basic science of love.*

One of the reasons for the difficulty in arriving at an understanding of love is the ambiguity with which love is defined and the diversified ways in which the concept love is employed in speech. A woman loves her fiancé, her mother and father, her country, fudge, swimming, bone chinaware, and many other things besides. She "falls" in love, she longs for *love, she* gives *love, she* makes *love, she* feels *love, and so on.*

Fromm[1] *has been almost singular among writers on the subject by defining love in behavioral terms. In his work, love is not a passion or emo-*

tion; rather, it is a way of behaving *toward the loved one. A love relationship exists when a person behaves toward the object of his love in ways that convince an objective observer that the lover* knows, cares for, respects, *and* feels responsibility for *the other. Unless there is knowledge, care, respect, and responsibility, there is no love.*

This is a definition of love which encompasses the common-sense meanings of love and yet permits more precise study of the behavior of lover and its conditions.

THE DEFINITION OF LOVING-BEHAVIOR

Let us modify Fromm's definition of love in a way which will conform more closely with the concepts already employed in the present volume. For us, love is an *adjective* which describes behavior, as it does for Fromm. We shall speak of *loving-behavior.* Loving-behavior is distinguished from other kinds of instrumental behavior by its *motives* and by its *consequences.* We can speak, with Fromm, of the "power," or capacity, to love. It should be possible to determine whether loving-behavior is *effective* in achieving its aims, and it should be possible to study the relationships between loving-behavior and the health of personality.

Loving-behavior refers to all action which a person undertakes to promote the happiness and growth of the being he loves.

It is not enough, however, that the lover wants to promote happiness and growth; he must want to promote these values in his object for their own sake, as *ends in themselves.* We make this point because it is possible for a person to perform in ways which look like loving-behavior, but the reasons for so behaving are ulterior—the person wants to impress the other favorably, or use him. Loving-behavior cannot be defined as such unless the lover does freely whatever is necessary to make his object happy. A near synonym for loving is *giving*.

Probably love begins as a feeling or as a commitment—both *subjective* reactions. But if these feelings or the commitment to another's well-being are real, they will inevitably become manifest in loving-behavior.

EMOTIONS, MOTIVES, AND LOVING-BEHAVIOR

When love is defined as behavior, we can inquire into its motives. As we have seen, the motive basic to love is a desire to give, to do whatever will be effective in promoting happiness and growth in the object; where the very act of giving and doing is free from other, ulterior motives. It is giving for the sake of the loved one. There is no compulsion or duty in love. Loving-behavior cannot be commanded or ordered; the lover is not doing his duty to his object under threat of punishment or guilt. He is, par excellence, doing what he *wants* to do when he loves. The loving act may be regarded almost as the acme of free choice.[2]

But we think immediately of powerful emotions when we speak of love: affection, lust, longing, tenderness, romance. What is the relationship between such emotional responses and love?

EMOTIONAL RESPONSES AND LOVING-BEHAVIOR

When we love another person (or an animal, or our country), we *identify* ourselves with him.[3] Since the lover is very concerned with the happiness and growth of the other, he will *feel* the pleasures and pains, the dangers to and the happinesses of his loved one *as if they were his own*. It is as if he had extended the "contact-surface" of his mechanisms for feeling and experiencing. He reacts emotionally to the events which affect his loved one as well as to the events which affect him personally.

Just as the lover becomes angry when someone hurts or insults him, so he becomes angry when something hurts the being he loves. Just as he is happy at his own successes and rich need-gratifications, so is he affected by the successes and gratifications of his loved one. Just as he is concerned about his own growth, so is he concerned for the growth of the other. *Identification, empathy* and *sympathy* are thus all involved in loving. Empathy involves the correct interpretation of cues which reflect the feelings and wishes of the object.[4] Identification—becoming like the other, in imagination, for longer or shorter intervals of time—makes sympathy (literally, feeling *with* the object) possible.

Experiences which affect the object provoke emotions in the lover. These, in turn, serve as important *motives* for loving-behavior. Under the impetus of emotional tensions provoked by whatever has affected the loved one, the lover strives to do those things which will promote happiness and reduce unhappiness in the one he loves.

SEX IN LOVE

Sexual behavior is a rich source of happiness and gratification for the self as well as for the object. There are many love relationships, of course, where sex is out of place: in the love of parents for their children or in the love of a woman for her close girl friend. But in a love relationship where sexuality is socially and personally sanctioned, for instance in marriage, sexual behavior can be regarded as one of the patterns of loving-behavior—it is indeed behavior which makes the other person (and the self) happy. Sociologists interpret the sexual act as a *ritual,* not unlike religious behavior; it has the function and consequence of cementing the "solidarity" of a small group—the married couple.[5]

It should be pointed out that there can be sexuality without love, and there can be love without sexualiy. We would not call sexual intercourse which was desired by one partner but not by the other an expression of loving-behavior. And we could call it a love relationship between a man and his friend, male or female, when there was active concern for happiness and growth but no sexuality in the relationship. We will discuss sex more fully in the next chapter.

CHOICE IN LOVE

We have seen in what loving-behavior consists; we can assume that any human has the *capacity* to love someone or some thing if he is capable of behaving at all. But there remains the question of the *choice*[6] of an object toward whom a person will devote his power to love, i.e., his power to satisfy, make happy, and help grow.

In principle, a person can choose almost anything or anyone as the object of his loving-behavior, if he wants to love at all. But it is well known that when choices are made from among a variety of possible alternatives, the motivations for the choice may be very complex and sometimes unconscious. As the psychoanalysts say, choices are "overdetermined."

A person may choose another person as the object of his freely given loving-behavior on the basis of certain estimable characteristics of that person. Or, he may choose someone whom he thinks will give him much love. Let us explore some of the more common bases for choice in love. A person acquires preferences[7] for possible love-objects in advance of his actually finding them and then loving them.

SOME COMMON CRITERIA FOR CHOICE OF A LOVE-OBJECT

HELPLESSNESS AND NEED. One may be moved to love another because the other seems to be helpless and in need of loving-behavior. Thus, most people find that it is easy for them to love small children or helpless animals without necessarily expecting anything in return.

CONFORMITY WITH THE LOVER'S IDEALS. A potential lover may have constructed certain ideals of appearance, personality, and behavior with which the other must conform before love will be offered. The concepts of the "ideal wife" and "ideal husband" may be decisive factors in determining whom a young man or woman will select to "fall in love with." The young adult observes the "passing parade" of potential spouses, and when he observes someone who accords with his ideals, he may then pursue this person as the object of his present and future loving-behavior. There is considerable cultural stereotypy in the characteristics which define the beautiful and/or ideal person who will be one's love-object, but there may be much individual variability as well. Langhorne and Secord,[8] in one study, showed that unmarried college males sought a "pleasing personality," tenderness and consideration, moral uprightness, and a complex trait which included health, emotional maturity, stability, and intelligence. Any personality therapist will be familiar with various deviations from the more usual bases for choosing someone to love. Freud described a class of men who were most attracted to women who were the "property" of another man, or whose fidelity and sexual propriety were questionable. The author knows of men who can love, or who seek to love, only women who are much older or much younger. A sociologist gathered evidence to show that many persons select mates on the basis of complementary needs: viz., dominant men choose passive women, and so on.[9] Some men may choose women who will not make them feel inferior, e.g., someone less intelligent, or from a lower socioeconomic status. The range of possible variability in object-choice is remarkable. The reasons for this variability probably stem from life-history experiences which deviate somewhat from the modal life-history of the average male and female. Thus, the man whom one woman is attracted to as a potential love-object may be repugnant to another and fear-inspiring to still others.

ABILITY OF THE LOVED ONE TO RECIPROCATE LOVE. A person may not experience the desire to love another person *until and unless* the other person shows clear signs of a desire to love first. In other words, the person can be moved to love if and only if he has been first assured that he is loved. It is almost as if the would-be lover is afraid to risk possible rejection of his or her loving-behavior or else is not willing to love unless there is some guarantee that the love will be returned.

RATIONAL CHOICE OF SOMEONE TO LOVE

The following discussion applies mainly to marriage, where mutuality of love is almost a *sine qua non* of a successful and happy marriage. In our culture, the custom obtains that would-be spouses must first "fall in love" with each other, before they consider marriage. The process of falling in love is itself a nonrational phenomenon, probably based on strong need-deprivation of a sexual sort. When a person in our culture is in love, he or she display most of the characteristics associated with deprivation: viz., preoccupation with the need-object, "overestimation"[10] of the value of the object, a desire to possess and "consume" the object so as to appease the hunger, and so on. In fact, what is called romantic love sometimes resembles the effects of a special variety of hunger, for it is not love. Romantic love becomes active loving when the lovers actually behave in ways which will produce mutual gratifications and happiness and which will promote growth in each other. The hunger to "be loved" may serve as a factor which brings people together. But whether or not love can emerge from romantic love depends on the actual loving capacity of each partner and the *actual* suitability of each person's traits for promoting happiness and growth in the other.

The person who would choose wisely for marriage should soberly ask himself the question, at some time prior to marriage, "Can I make this person happy, and can I help her to grow?" Obviously, the more reality-based the answers are to these questions, the more likely it is that a rational choice will be made.

Whether or not a given choice of a spouse has been suitable can be determined only by observation of the subsequent relationship through time; "time will tell." It is possible, however, to make a choice of a spouse in ways that will increase the probability of the relationship moving in a healthy direction. The guiding philosophy of choice would be to state, as clearly as possible, (a) the needs and values of the choosing person and (b) the traits of the person being chosen in as detailed a fashion as is practicable. If choices are predicated on such a broad base, the chances are greater that they will be fortunate choices. Naturally, though, there are many purely technical problems involved in specifying the needs and values of the chooser and in describing accurately the traits of the person being chosen. Since these are psychological problems, or problems within the professional realm of the psychologist, one can sometimes obtain professional help in making a judicious choice of a partner in such important interpersonal relationships. Thus, to an increasing degree, engaged couples consult professional marriage counselors to assist them in clearing up misconceptions about each other and about marriage.

In a less technical setting, one's family and present friends can serve as a kind of investigating committee to examine and pass judgment on a lover's choice of a spouse. "Lovers are blind," it is assumed with some validity; and so the well-intentioned family and friends try to examine all the fiancée's traits which have been ignored as "unimportant" by the love-blinded youth. He may have fallen in love because of some one need-related trait, and ignores all the rest of her characteristics. The uninvolved others look the girl over from many other standpoints, looking at such things as her health, her income, her religion, her attitudes and values, her tastes, and so on. If these judges know the over-all needs and value-hierarchy of the young lover, they may be able to see she has attributes which make her unsuited to him. He may or may not pay attention to their advice.

FACTORS WHICH PROMOTE UNWISE CHOICES IN LOVE

Let us consider some of the factors which will impair the capacity of a person to make a suitable choice of someone to love.

CHRONIC NEEDS. An individual with strong, unsatisfied needs will be likely to perceive other persons in an autistic fashion.[11] He will seek satisfaction of his immediate needs and ignore other traits of the object that are important to his growth and *over-all* happiness. In consequence, he might choose a person for a love-object who can gratify this need. He doesn't realize he has other needs and values that will emerge into importance when the present needs have been satisfied.

Thus, the inadequate man who needs to be taken care of and to have decisions made for him may fall in love with a dominant woman. Eventually, he may outgrow his need for dominance and require other modes of behavior from the woman. If she cannot change her ways of behaving toward him, an impasse may arise which will result in termination of the relationship.

Or, a man may be attracted only to women who are "owned" by another man—the fact of being the property of another man constitutes their appeal.[12] And so he pursues and wins such a woman. Once he has won her, he then might "look her over," as it were, and find that she doesn't have what it takes to make him happy. His need, if it can be called such, is to prove himself a better man than others—and if the psychoanalysts are correct, it may be an outgrowth of an unresolved "Oedipus complex."

LACK OF SELF-KNOWLEDGE. The person who is alienated from his real self, whose self-concept is inaccurate, may be said not to know what he needs from another person to make him happy or to help him grow. Since his choice of a love-object is not based upon consideration of these important factors, it will be based on other criteria which are irrelevant to growth and happiness. Thus, he might choose a possible wife just on the basis of appearance alone —because other people regard the woman as desirable. He doesn't know if he really desires the woman; rather, he wants her because he believes he ought to. This would be the case with the other-directed character described by Riesman. Or, he may choose a woman as a possible mate because his parents, or his conscience, demand he make that choice.[13] Again, he is ignoring, or is ignorant of, his own needs and wants. It is not rare for a person to fall in love, court, and marry someone, and then, much later, come face to face with his real self and wonder, "How did I ever get joined to this person?"

LACK OF KNOWLEDGE OF THE LOVED ONE. It was pointed out earlier[14] that there is only one way to acquire an accurate other-concept: that is, to observe, to come to tentative conclusions, and then continuously to modify these conclusions as more observations are made. This calls for time to make many observations of the behavior of the object in a wide range of life situations.

When this procedure has not been adopted by the would-be lover, then it follows that his concept of the other will be autistic, or inaccurate. That is, it will be based on need-selective observation, attribution, disowning or assimilative projection, hearsay, or other mechanisms which guarantee inaccurate other-concepts.[15]

Optimally, of course, in anything so intimate as marriage, the couple should explore each other, perhaps for a long time, so that each will come to know the other's traits before they become legally committed to one another. This is unromantic, however, and seldom done; the longer-range consequence is either divorce or a long life of tortured martyrdom. But even more, each person may strive to *hide* many of his characteristics from the scrutiny of the other because he needs the other person and is afraid he will be rejected should the other person find out these traits. And so a courtship, instead of being a period of mutual real-self exposure and study of the other, becomes a period of mutual deception and construction of false public selves. Many a person has experienced tragic disillusionment with his spouse when once the ceremony has been completed and the marriage begun. Even more tragic, however, is a longer-run consequence—that of striving to conform with a false public self which has been constructed during the courtship. The "perfect lovers" in the *Chocolate Soldier* found their relationship too idealistic, too perfect—it was a strain; and so the nobleman married the maid, with whom he could be himself, and the girl of high degree married the bourgeois chocolate soldier-innkeeper for the same reason.

LOVE AND PERSONALITY HYGIENE

We have stated that the ability to love *actively* is a personality-hygiene value and that the person who cannot love is "sick" in basic ways. By the same token, the person who is afraid or unable to *accept* love may be regarded as sick. Since incapacity at loving and at accepting love is regarded as a psychiatric symptom, let us inquire into some of the conditions of loving.

THE NEED TO LOVE AND TO BE LOVED

We are born helpless, and so we need to be loved by our parents if we are to survive in the physical sense. There is evidence that we need to be loved in order to grow in a psychological sense as well. Good physical care is not enough to insure healthy personality growth. Unless the child has received loving care, including emotional displays of affection and attention to his idiosyncratic needs, he is likely to grow in deviant ways. Spitz,[16] for example, showed that children raised from birth in a foundling home, with adequate physical care but no personalized attention from a mother figure, were retarded in physical growth, were less resistant to disease, and were retarded in their over-all "developmental quotients," compared to infants raised by their own mothers. Goldfarb[17] showed that institution-raised children, by the time they reached adolescence, were severely handicapped in their ability to relate to others on an emotional and loving basis. Ribble[18] saw a lack of "adequate mothering" as a causal factor in the development of infantile *marasmus*—a rare disease in which the infant literally wastes away. And Spitz showed that depression in infants was the by-product of separation from the mother. It would appear to be definitely established that in infancy and early childhood, passive love is needed both for physical growth and for optimum personality growth toward health.

One experimental psychologist was able to demonstrate that infant monkeys who were denied access to a mother during their earliest days but were instead reared with a "mother" constructed out of terry cloth or wire reached maturity with impaired ability to mate.[19]

It is doubtful if anyone ever completely loses the need to be loved. The strength of the conscious longings for love, however, is probably related to the amount of love-indulgence which a person has experienced. If from early infancy, a child has had no love, he may grow into a psychopath who is incapable of active loving and who experiences no conscious longings for love. If, on the other hand, the child has had a "taste" of love, just enough to learn that it feels good but not enough to satisfy, then he may develop what Levy called "primary affect hunger"[20] and pursue love for the rest of his life at any cost.

It seems likely that the ability to love actively is an outgrowth of having one's love-needs gratified earlier in life. There is a logical basis for such a statement, as well as empirical grounding. A person whose needs are greatly thwarted is a "hungry" person, seeking to be filled. When one is empty, one can hardly give. Active love seems to rest on the "economics of plenty" rather than on "scarcity economics."[21] The healthy lover is as one who is "filled," and who gives freely to his objects, not only because of the object's need, but because of the lover's abundance. He gives out of the joys of giving with no preconceived notion of getting something in return.

No one, however, is so "full" that he can love endlessly without receiving loving-behavior in return. In relationships of mutual love, where the partners have chosen wisely, each can give freely what the other needs, and each receives in return, freely given, what is needed for happiness and growth. Thus, it is doubtful if a parent could actively love young children without receiving love from the spouse, or from the children, or from some source. It is doubtful if a personality therapist could meet the needs of his patients if he was not receiving love from his spouse or friends.

But once a person has approached mature years, society expects him or her to have the capacity and the desire to become an active lover. If the person has been sufficiently loved in the past, the likelihood will be increased that he will be able to establish a mutual loving-relationship with another person, rather than a relationship of continued passivity and dependency.

Let us try to highlight some of the factors which appear to promote the capacity to love actively as well as the ability freely to accept the loving-behavior of another.

SOME DETERMINERS OF THE CAPACITY FOR ACTIVE LOVE

GRATIFICATION OF BASIC NEEDS.[22] As a general rule, the person who has experienced rich need-gratification will be in a position to become an active lover. He is not obliged to devote all of his energies to personal need-satisfaction. He can afford to use some of his time, skills, and energies for other people's happiness and growth.

AFFIRMATION OF THE VALUE OF LOVE. If a person has acquired a strong sense of the worth and value of love in and for itself, then he will undoubtedly seek out opportunities to love. His self-esteem will be based, at least in part, on his ability to love actively. In other words, unless he is involved in an active loving-relationship, he may feel less than whole and fully "actualized"—less than a whole person.

HIGH FRUSTRATION TOLERANCE. Loving another person often involves deprivation of some of one's own needs. The more fully developed is the lover's ability to tolerate periods of privation, the better able will he be to love his object.

SELF-LOVE. Fromm has pointed out, in an important essay,[23] that love of self and love of some other person are not mutually exclusive, as was long believed. He states emphatically that one can love another only if one loves oneself. "Love of self and love of other are conjunctive, not exclusive." The rationale behind this precept may be stated in these terms: To love oneself means that one will be concerned with his own growth and happiness and will behave in ways which implement these values. Self-loving, in a real sense, gives one actual practice in loving; to the extent that others are similar to the self, then these ways of acting which constitute self-love will make another person happy if they are directed to that person. Self-love makes one attentive to one's own needs and probably increases one's sensitivity to the needs of others; if one has experienced needs and gratifications, one can visualize more vividly what the partner's needs and gratifications feel like.

It should also be pointed out that healthy self-love is an outgrowth of having been loved, by parents and other significant persons;[24] and we have shown that the experience of having been loved promotes one's active-love capacity.

When one ignores or hates oneself, one is less likely to be able to love others. The self-hater is unable to love others because he usually claims total obedience from those for whom he has "sacrificed" so much. The mother described by Sidney Howard in *The Silver Cord*[25] was such a martyr, who "loved" her sons more than she did herself—she sacrificed her own happiness on their (unasked) behalf. All she wanted in return was complete conformity with her wishes and demands, which is incompatible with genuine love. It is a subtle form of dictatorship rather than love.

Indeed, psychoanalysts regard excessive "unselfishness" as a neurotic trait, while such personality hygienists as Maslow[26] and Fromm[27] place a positive value on "healthy" selfishness. This is no more than a recognition on the basis of clinical experience and careful observation that the person who is concerned for his own growth and happiness will have acted so as to promote it; in consequence, he is a better person and better able to give. He has more to give in active love, more "self." And since "self" is, in the last analysis, all that is or can be given in love, it follows that the more self one has to give, the more gratification the recipient will receive from such a gift.

SKILLS. The more skills a lover has, *the more diversified will be the kinds of needs of the object which he can gratify through his loving-behavior.* This presumes, of course, that the individual has few inner barriers, such as an unhealthy self-structure, to the full use of his entire behavior-repertoire. If he has, then he will experience threat whenever he is about to behave in a loving manner, and so he will suppress the loving-behavior.

HEALTHY SELF-STRUCTURE.[28] If the lover has a self-concept, a self-ideal, and public selves which permit him to function at the real-self level, then his loving capacity will be promoted (see Chapter 9). In other words, the lover will have access to all of his behavior potential. He will not be obliged to exclude some ways of behaving in his love relationships because of the need to defend an unrealistic self-concept or to conform with a false public self or an excessively strict self-ideal and conscience.

Thus if the object wants tenderness, affection, domination, and so on, the healthy lover will be able to sense these needs and behave in a gratifying way without a sense of forcing, faking, or threatening himself. Indeed, if the healthy personality is defined as the individual who can gratify his needs by behavior which is personally and socially acceptable, then *the healthy lover can be defined as the one who can gratify the needs of the one he loves by means of behavior which is personally and socially acceptable.*

In principle, the more diversified the personality structure of an individual and the healthier his self-structure, the broader the range of persons whom he can effectively love. Practically, however, the healthy lover probably prefers to seek an object who has an equally diversified personality and healthy self-structure, since his needs may require just such a person to love him. Anyone with a less differentiated personality would be less able to meet his needs.

REALITY-CONTACT. It takes accurate knowledge of the loved one to be able to love effectively; the person with autistic other-concepts will generally be unable to love in a way which meets the needs of the object. As Fromm has pointed out, the lover must *know* whom he loves. Very often, a person may suffer a handicap in love because he cannot interpret accurately what his loved one needs, in spite of his willingness to provide it if able.

SECURITY. Probably fear and anxiety are among the factors most responsible for impairment of the capacity to love. The fearful person is much more likely to be dependent to a morbid degree on the one he loves; he may give, not out of love, but out of fear of being ridiculed or rejected. The more secure a person, the more likely will he be able to employ his whole self in loving.

A person may withhold much loving-behavior because of unwarranted fears. Thus the author has observed a man who would not display signs of affection to his wife on the assumption she would scorn him as a weakling. In the past, he had learned to suppress and to repress open affection as a means of being safe. He expected women to interpret open affection as a sign the man was weak and easily exploited. In truth, his wife was yearning for affection from him.

REASONABLE IDEALS. A person may construct such impossible ideals and expectations as conditions for expressing his own love that no human could ever hope to qualify. He may then engage in an endless and fruitless quest for the "worthy" and "perfect" recipient of his love. Of course, he will never find this paragon, or else he will experience perpetual disillusionment. If it happens that a person has married on grounds other than love, he may place such stringent conditions on his love that it is never given. The spouse doesn't "deserve" his love and must meet his impossible demands for perfection before it will be given. Sometimes a person who has only limited capacity to bestow affection will show remarkable skill in finding out what his mate *cannot* do; once he discovers these inadequacies, he uses them as the reason for not loving the other.

It becomes apparent that one can love only if one's demands and ideals with respect to the other are within the latter's capacity to conform. Reasonable demands and ideals apropos the other are likely to be held by a person who holds reasonable demands and expectations of himself.

EMANCIPATION FROM PARENTS. When a person cannot direct his behavior in accordance with his real self, his capacity to love another may be impaired. A person who is not alienated from his real self will be better able to govern his loving-behavior in accordance with the needs and wishes of his loved one and with his own real feelings and wishes. But if the person behaves only so as to please his parents in opposition to his own true feelings, his capacity to love may be reduced markedly. The reason for this lies in the fact that much of the behavior which might be necessary to promote happiness in the spouse may be tabooed or condemned by the parents, and the individual does not dare to displease his parents. The psychoanalysts have shown that much of the sexual difficulty in marriage, that is, impotence and frigidity, derives from a failure to emancipate the self from parental control and a failure to withdraw unconscious sexual interest in the parents. It is as if the spouse cannot devote love and sex to the partner because unconsciously love and sex "belong" to the opposite-sexed parent.

SOME DETERMINERS OF ABILITY TO ACCEPT LOVE

It may seem surprising to the reader that some individuals find it hard, if not impossible, to accept love which is freely given by others; yet such is the case, as any personality therapist can attest.

Some persons cannot accept the deepest expressions of the real self of another person who loves them. They find such expression cloying, or threatening, or embarrassing. When someone loves them, they become suspicious of the lover—the lover may be just pretending to love in order to disarm him and make him vulnerable. Or the lover may be trying to get the individual to do something. The person who cannot accept love may hold the false assumption that to accept love implies that one needs love and to need love means one is weak.

We may generalize and suggest that the factors which might prevent a person from accepting authentic love from others include (a) *inaccurate other-concepts* and (b) *repression of the need to be loved.*

INACCURATE OTHER-CONCEPTS. Because of past experiences with

people, the individual may project or attribute motives to others which they do not in fact possess. He may assume they do not, or cannot, love him. If he believes this, then he will probably misinterpret loving-behavior from others; he will believe their behavior toward him is motivated by sentiments other than active and unselfish concern for his own welfare and happiness.

REPRESSION OF THE NEED TO BE LOVED. In the past, the individual's longings for love may have been thwarted, or he may have been deeply hurt in his quest for gratification of his need to be loved. The consequence may be that he represses his need for passive love; he may, indeed, develop *reaction-formations* against his love-needs and make loud protestations of his independence from others: "I don't need anybody for anything." Such a person may actually strive to prevent other people from loving him, with considerable success in such efforts.

The healthy personality is able to accept freely given love just as he is able to give love freely. He does not demand love from his lover as a duty for his partner to fulfill. Rather, he assumes that if he is loved, the lover is giving out of free will, with no strings attached, and so he can accept it without guilt or fear.[29]

LOVE AND DEPENDENCY

Although we have placed a positive valuation upon autonomy and self-sufficiency, this is a relative matter. In the first place, it is impossible for a person to be completely self-sufficient; indeed, attempts directed toward complete independence of everyone may be regarded as pathological, since they are likely to be predicated on a profound irrational distrust of all people.

In the second place, it is undersirable for a person not to need people for some things. People *want* to feel needed by those to whom they feel close. Thus, it can be said that there are occasions where actual dependency upon another person is an expression of active loving, for it implies trust and accords dignity and worthwhileness to the one who is needed and depended upon.

A healthy love relationship probably involves two persons who are relatively self-sufficient in most ways but who are mutually dependent one on the other for important gratifications. The love relationship thus involves mutual giving and mutual taking, mutual needing and mutual willingness to provide what is needed.

The lover, in an important sense, needs or is dependent upon his loved one, in spite of marked self-sufficiency in many areas. He needs the relationship with his loved one in order to enrich his own gratification-experiences; he needs his partner and the relationship to promote his own growth; he needs the relationship so as to enrich self-esteem.

Dependency in a love relationship is compatible with personality health when it does not involve undue suppression of the real self in either partner and when each partner does not use the other's dependency as a means of controlling his life.

It may happen in a marriage, for example, that one spouse may use sex as a means of controlling the behavior of the other. A wife whose sexual needs were apparently less frequent or urgent than her husband's used sexual compliance almost as a club to force her spouse to do her will. We could hardly call this relationship a love relationship. Because of the social mores, the husband was dependent upon his wife for sexual gratification, as she was upon him; but she was content with the frequency of coitus while he was not. She took advantage of his dependency and discontent to regulate his life in accordance with her often unreasonable wishes.

HOW MANY PEOPLE CAN AN INDIVIDUAL LOVE?

Love is activity, and there are limits upon how many things a person can do. If one devotes more time and attention to one sphere of activity, then other spheres of possible activity will suffer relative neglect. Consider an analogy. A farmer has numerous fields, livestock, and buildings to maintain and a family to look after. If he spends all of his time and skill at cultivating his cornfields, then his wheatfields and vegetable plots will become overrun with weeds; his farm buildings will begin to deteriorate from neglect, and his livestock may fall victim to diseases owing to lack of prophylactic measures. In order to be an adequate farmer, he has got to apportion his time so that everything is attended to according to its requirements.

Now, a grown-up man or woman has many things to attend to, not the least in importance being the needs of the people whom he loves. Thus, the husband must earn a living and satisfy his own urges toward productivity and status, but he also wants to promote the growth and happiness of his wife and children. Often, there will be sharp and poignant conflicts experienced by the man with respect to how he will divide himself. How much of himself should he give to his work and how much to his wife and children? His friends? His parents? Is there room in his life for other loves in addition to his wife and children?

There is no simple answer to these questions. The needs of the lover, and the needs of other persons, have to be taken into consideration. In addition, there will be broad individual differences from love relationship to love relationship with respect to the "amount of self" which must be invested.

In some marriages, for example, the wife is quite happy and able to grow with only occasional contacts with the husband, who may be immersed in a career or traveling at his occupation. In others, the wife may receive the loving attention of her spouse for all of his time away from his work, and it is yet not enough to make her happy.

Since there is a limit on how many things a person can *do,* there is thus a limit on the number of people a person can *love.*

Many a wife has complained her husband loves his work or his hobbies more than he loves her. If he devotes more of his undivided attention to these than he does to her needs, then to that extent she is correct.

The healthy personality is able, like the good farmer, to apportion his time and his instrumental behavior, so that he is able to harmonize his own needs with the growth and happiness of his loved ones. This is not a simple task but one which requires continuous reassessment, readjustment, and vigilance.

In cases where a wife or husband loves some other person more than the spouse, for example, a parent or a child, and the ignored spouse does not complain, then it signifies the needs of the ignored one are not very intense or diversified, since they are so readily gratified. Usually, however, a spouse needs all of the partner's love which is available and is willing to share this loving-behavior only with the children.

We may now provide an answer to the question, "How many people can an individual love?" *A healthy personality actively loves as many people as he can, without doing violence to his own growth and happiness and the growth and happiness of his loved ones.*

This answer is sufficiently flexible to allow for individual differences in the capacity of the individual to love and in the needs of objects, differences which occur between persons, and in the same individual at different stages in his life.

Thus, a healthy personality may be able to love his wife and his children and nobody else. He may *like* many people and have many friends, but if he is to avoid spreading himself too thin, he is obliged to limit his loving-behavior to his wife and children. If he has a choice between meeting the needs of a friend and those of his family, he will select his family as the object of his loving-behavior. If, on the other hand, his family can "afford" to allow him to "spend" himself on friends (at the time his family is not in need), then he will be able to work for the growth and happiness of his friends.

When a person's own growth and happiness are in jeopardy, his ability to love others actively is impaired. Since he can love actively only when he is happy and growing, then he will be in accord with personality-hygiene precepts if he attends to his own needs before those of others. While this may sound selfish[30], yet it may be seen that he cannot love actively and effectively when he is less than a whole and fully functioning person. An individual with an unhealthy personality may devote his time, attention, and money to personality therapy, the while ignoring the needs of people who are close to him. This is desirable, since he will be a more effective lover *after* he has taken care of his own growth.

ATTRACTING LOVE FROM OTHERS

It commonly occurs that an individual believes no one could ever love him and that he is powerless to induce someone to love him.

This belief may stem from a childhood which was devoid of parental love and an adolescence devoid of friendship and peer-acceptance.

How does one induce others to love him? Ignoring for the time being such factors as attractive appearance, we can assert that *love begets love.* Active concern for the needs of another individual will in general, tend to motivate the other person to become actively concerned for the growth and happiness of the giver. Unfortunately, a vicious circle often appears. The unhappy person who believes no one can love him is usually in such a chronic condition of need-deprivation that he cannot give to others freely and unstintingly. Hence, while he may be pitied by others, he is unlikely to be loved by them. How can one break this vicious circle? How can one arrange it so that the person who "hath not" love will be given love? The biblical precept "To him that hath shall be given" seems to hold true for love.

In our society, the love-deprived individual may be able to reach a stage wherein he becomes able to love only through effective personality therapy. The professional personality therapist is, in a sense, a source of love for the deprived individual.[31] The therapist behaves toward his patient in ways which will promote growth and happiness—and this is love, albeit without romance. Through successful therapy, an individual may acquire the capacity to love others and thus make it possible to induce others to love him.

LOVE AND THE SELF-STRUCTURE

We have alluded several times to the fact that a person's capacity to love is influenced by the nature of his self-structure. Let us see more directly some of the ways in which the self-structure imposes limits on love.

THE SELF-CONCEPT AND LOVE. The self-concept refers to the system of beliefs which an individual holds with respect to his personality (see Chapter 7). In general, a person strives to delimit his behavior to the framework of these beliefs. Behavior which conflicts with these beliefs generates threat, and the threat impels the individual to exclude that behavior from his repertoire if he is to defend his self-concept. Now, love is behavior. In order to gratify the needs of the partner, the lover is obliged to act in many and diverse ways. Not all of these modes of behavior will be in accord with the lover's self-concept, and they will hence generate threat. What should the lover do when he faces a conflict between preserving his present self-concept and meeting the needs of his loved one? The general answer is this: If to love the other threatens his self-concept, and if the requisite change of the self-concept is in the direction of a healthier self-strucure, then he should act in the way required by his partner and strive to alter his self-concept. If, on the other hand, to gratify his loved one would move him further away from personality health, then he must ignore that person's needs.

An example will clarify this point. Let us suppose that a lover believes he is inadequate and lacks the ability to do certain things, for instance, change occupations. He may not be abjectly miserable in his present occupation, but he would like to change to another. The reason he does not is because he believes he does not have the capacity to learn new skills. His wife wants him to change occupations for assorted reasons, and he wants to please his wife. He may make the change and discover in fact he does have the capacity to learn his new vocation. Thus he has altered his self-concept and met the needs of his wife.

On the other hand, a husband may need his wife to be subservient to him, in order to warrant a component belief of his self-concept that he is strong and dominant. His wife, on the other hand, has come to realize she no longer is helpless and subservient but rather a fairly self-reliant person. She has to choose between her own growth and keeping her husband free of threat. Her choice, if it is to accord with personality-hygiene precepts, must be as follows: She must eliminate the subservient behavior from her repertoire and *be herself*, that is, act in accord with her healthier self-concept. Thus she has moved closer to personality health, but she has threatened her husband's self-concept. This throws the responsibility back to her husband as to whether he will handle the threat in a healthy way or in a defensive and unhealthy way.

THE SELF-IDEAL AND LOVE. The self-ideal refers to the individual's conscience: the ideals, values, and taboos with which he strives to conform and which he strives to approach. It will be recalled that self-esteem is a function of the extent to which a person's actual behavior conforms with his self-ideal. Failure to conform with the self-ideal produces guilt, self-hate, inferiority feelings or hurt pride.

In order to love effectively and in healthy fashion, a person must have a fairly broad repertoire of behavior patterns and roles at his disposal. The reason for this has been pointed out earlier. As the needs of his loved one vary, so must his loving-behavior if he is to promote the happiness and growth in the other. But if some of the behavior objectively required (in order to keep the other person growing and happy) is in conflict with the self-ideal, then again the lover faces a rather sharp value-conflict. *Which is more important, the happiness of his partner or the maintenance of self-esteem?*

Again, we can provide a principle which would enable us to assess a given solution to such a conflict, but there are obviously no recipes which we could offer to resolve the conflict when it arises with two given persons.

In principle, the conflict may be resolved by a decision as to which is the most productive of growth and happiness in both the lover and his partner.

Thus, if the lover's conscience, or self-ideal is *excessively restrictive,* he may be obliged to take whatever steps might be necessary to alter his self-ideal if he is to grow and at the same time maintain his love-relationship with the other. However, he may discover he cannot meet his partner's needs without losing self-esteem. Since he believes he has a healthy conscience, he decides to affirm his values and ignore his partner's needs.

In every relationship, a conflict will at some time arise between the maintenance of pride, or self-esteem (conforming with the self-ideal), and acting in ways which will please or satisfy the other. The individuals involved in the relationship may not always be able to formulate the nature of the conflict very clearly or understand it. All that each might realize is that in pleasing the object, he "doesn't feel right about it," or he feels vaguely uneasy, or he is "being untrue to himself."

When a person habitually neglects his real self in this way (his values are part of his real self, as are the feelings of uneasiness which he might vaguely experience when he conforms with his partner's demands or needs), the relationship is almost by definition unhealthy (see Chapter 7). A conflict between a person's self-ideal and the needs of the other is one kind of impasse, and we have seen that it is not healthy to avoid an impasse by repressing one or the other aspect of it. Continuous conforming with the partner's demands while ignoring one's own pride or values is an active move away from the real self, as Horney would put it, and is productive of unhappiness and the reverse of growth.

The only healthy way to resolve a conflict between the self-ideal of a lover and the needs of his loved one is to sharpen the conflict as much and as openly as possible, so that an autonomous and responsible decision can be made by either partner, a decision which will be acted upon and in which the decider is willing to accept the consequences. The person may withdraw the demand or seek to satisfy the need in other ways. The lover may strive to alter his self-ideal in order to be able to satisfy his loved one without inner conflict. Or, he may elect to avoid satisfying the other and face the consequences of an abrupt end to the relationship. Whatever the outcome, if the impasse is openly faced and resolved in the manner suggested above, it is compatible with the precepts of personality hygiene.

LOVE AND THE REAL SELF. It is more important in love than in any other kind of relationship that the participants act at a real-self level, rather than in accord with other determiners of actions: e.g., an unhealthy conscience, the expectations of others, an unhealthy self-concept, a formal role, and so on. To act at the real-self level implies each partner is willing and able to announce and express unequivocally what he feels, needs, wants, expects, thinks, and is willing, in addition, to face the consequences of so acting. When such mutual authenticity is missing, the relationship cannot be called a love relationship but instead must be called a friendship, a habitual companionship, or something of the sort.

The loved person makes his needs known by full disclosure of his real self to the lover. The lover will know whether he honestly wants to meet these needs only if he can experience his own real self fully.

When the participants in a relationship simply enact a social role, the role of husband, wife, or teacher, without regard to their own feelings, then the relationship loses the vital and often intensely felt quality of a love relationship.

If a wife and husband have been constructing false public selves in relation to the spouse, then their behavior will not express their real selves; instead it will aim at consistency with their respective public selves. The consequence will be that neither person will come to know the other, and this mutual ignorance about each other's needs will lead to irreconcilable impasses.

LOVE, MARRIAGE, AND DIVORCE

When and whom should a person marry? When should a divorce occur? In this day and age, when almost one marriage in three terminates in divorce, and when the persons who remain married often feel quite trapped or unhappy in the relationship, the questions above become crucial. It is difficult to proffer answers of a helpful sort to these questions, however, since there are many values at stake in a marriage.

The reasons for undertaking marriage in the first place are numerous and varied. Young couples enter marriage for companionship, for an opportunity to raise a family, for sexual gratification, to change their status in the eyes of the community, or, in a more general sense, they enter marriage on the premise that they will find greater happiness in the married state than in the single state. While many achieve these desirable outcomes, others are, unfortunately, often dismally wrong, as the divorce rates attest.

In Chapter 10 we provided some criteria for assessing whether a relationship such as marriage is healthy. When a marriage relationship deviates strikingly from these criteria, the participants experience the marriage as flat, dead, devoid of meaning or satisfactions, or, more emphatically, they may experience the marriage as positively agonizing, stifling to the self and partner. When this state of affairs arises, action is called for, unless the participants are of the unhealthy type which seeks or needs punishment (unconscious guilt, masochism). When there are children in the family, an additional problem is presented, since the children will require some care that will help them attain maturity and personality health.

If the partners are unable to face and work through interpersonal impasses themselves, in a growth-productive manner, then ideally each or both together should consult a personality therapist. With expert outside assistance, each partner can often be helped to grow, so that an autonomous, responsible, and mutually agreed-upon reconciliation, or divorce, can be arrived at. When the partners will not avail themselves of such help, or seek it out, then the probability is high that whatever decision they make will be incompatible with their own personality health and the personality health of the children. It is an open question whether children are better off, from a personality-hygiene point of view, living with two unhealthy parents enmeshed in an unhealthy marital relationship. A strong case could be constructed to show that children raised by one parent who is divorced from the other, where the divorce was a healthy one, have a greater chance of attaining personality health than the children raised in a miserable marriage.

WHEN IS A DIVORCE HEALTHY? A divorce is healthy when it becomes apparent that the changes necessary to "healthify" the marriage are just not practicable. There are limits to how much a person can change his personality structure in order to meet the needs of a partner; and often the changes which would be required to keep a marriage going would be personality changes in a direction away from health. Thus, one partner may need the other to be an absolute paragon of perfection in a moral sense in order to be happy. No amount of feasible change could make the partner attain those ideals. Further, no amount of personality therapy is successful in altering the needs of the spouse who demands perfection. They may be too deeply rooted. Perhaps, in such an impasse, the best that can happen is divorce, in the fervent hope that each will be better able to grow when separated from the other (something which happens quite often) or that if they don't grow, and still want to marry, they will find a spouse with an unhealthy personality which complements their own.

The author has observed several instances where a marriage went "stale" and where insurmountable impasses existed between the partners. Each needed the other to be different but neither partner could comply, or wanted to comply, with the other's demands and needs. A personality hygienist could ascertain quite readily in observing the unhappy partners that neither of them came very close to the traits of a healthy personality. When a divorce finally occurred, each partner became, almost like magic, the embodiment of the desires and needs of the former spouse (perhaps out of unconscious or conscious hostility?). Then after some time, the partners would (with or without the aid of a personality therapist) move in the direction of a healthy personality. It seemed, then, that their prior relationship was a factor which blocked growth, rather than promoted it. The traits which drew the couple together into marriage in the beginning later became obstacles to growth.

In one marriage, the man "fell in love" with his wife because of her cute, childish innocence, dependency, a lisping manner of speech, and so on. He evidently needed to enact a fatherlike role for assorted reasons, and she needed to be fathered. As time proceeded, he began to feel the need of an adult peer in his marriage, and he made this need known to his wife. She reacted always with tears and the assertion "You don't love me any more." She could not change her interpersonal behavior. He divorced her and remarried. She suffered considerably through the divorce, sought therapeutic help, and eventually achieved an understanding of the reasons for her infantile characteristics; she was assisted in growing to a healthier level. She remarried, and the new marriage appeared to be a healthier one.

THE POWER TO LOVE AND HEALTHY PERSONALITY

In the last analysis, love may be regarded as a gift, freely and spontaneously given by the lover to his loved one. The being who is loved may be the self, a spouse, a child, a friend, and so on. The gift which is proffered to the loved one is the *real self* of the lover. He gives of himself—he focuses his "powers" on the object—so that the loved one may be happier and may better actualize his potentialities. The criterion of the success of loving-behavior, which gives the lover rich satisfaction, is *perceptible evidence of happiness and growth in the loved one.*

From our preceding discussion, it should be apparent to the reader that love, or the capacity to love, is very important as an indication of personality health, and it is also the means by which personality health is promoted, maintained, and even achieved, in the self and in others. Any factors which hinder or prevent a person from loving are thus factors which jeopardize personality health in him and in all of the other people with whom the handicapped individual comes into contact.

Since the real self is the "ingredient" of love—in loving-relationships, it is the real self which is given to the object—then any factor which prevents a person from knowing and expressing his real self is thus a factor which prevents love. The individual who is alienated from his real self cannot love. He cannot even love himself, since he lacks knowledge of what his real self is. The individual with a personality illness—neurosis, psychosis, or character disorder—is fundamentally a person who cannot love. Many patients who have undergone personality therapy report they have had restored to them, or else they have acquired for the first time in their lives, the power to love themselves and others. Probably what the psychoanalysts refer to as "genitality" or as "orgastic potency" refers to more than sexual adequacy; it may be interpreted as the power to love in the broader sense in which we have interpreted the word love; the neurotic who does not "command" his sexual functions, who is "alienated" from control of his own sexuality, may be viewed as a person in whom sexuality is symbolic of all that is summed up by the term "real self." Just as he cannot give (or take) sexuality to his object, so can he not give (and take) his real self.[32]

SUMMARY

Loving-behavior is defined as any action freely undertaken by a person with the conscious aim of promoting happiness and growth in the loved one.

The motive which is most basic to loving-behavior is the desire for the object's growth and happiness. Identification *with the loved one is probably responsible for much of the emotion which a lover experiences; he feels the pleasures and pains of his partner.* Empathy *and* sympathy *both are involved in loving.* Sexuality *may be involved in loving, but love relationships can exist where there is no sexuality, and sexual behavior can occur in nonloving-relationships.*

People choose someone to love on the basis of many criteria, e.g., helplessness, conformity of the partner with the lover's ideals, the ability of the other to reciprocate love, and so on. A suitable *choice of a loved one has been made when the person chooses someone whom he* can *love and who can act in loving ways toward him.* Unhealthy choices *are likely to be made when the chooser is under the tension of very* strong needs, *when he* lacks self-knowledge, *and when he* lacks accurate knowledg of the personality and needs of the other.

Humans need to be loved, *and they need* to love actively *if they are to become and remain healthy personalities. Some of the factors which promote the ability to love actively include* rich gratifications of needs *in the past,* affirmation of the value of love, *high* frustration-tolerance, self-love, *a* diversified personality structure, *a* healthy self-structure, reality-contact, security, reasonable ideals *for the love-object,* emancipation from parental direction, *and* emanicipation from inner-direction.

The ability to accept love from others may be prevented if a person has repressed his need for love and if he has inaccurate concepts of the other person.

While excessive dependency may interfere with the establishment of a healthy love relationship, dependency per se is quite compatible with love. In fact, without mutual dependency, there could be no love relationships. A person can love adequately only a limited number of others. If he attempts actively to love more than he is able to, then either he will suffer, or the happiness and growth of the others may suffer. Love from *others appears to be promoted most directly by the fact of* loving them.

The self-structure *of an individual may impose limits on the range of behavior which he can include in his loving-behavior repertoire. The more the self-structure is congruent with the person's real self, the more effective will he be in loving.*

Impasses *will arise in marriage. If a couple cannot resolve these impasses in a health-promoting way, then they should seek professional help before undertaking divorce. There are some instances where a* divorce *may be necessary in order to preserve or promote personality health in one or both of the partners.*

The power to love *is regarded as an index of over-all personality health.*

NOTES AND REFERENCES

Excellent supplementary reading will be provided by those references marked with an asterisk (*).

*1. The author was strongly influenced by Fromm's views on love as activity. The reader is encouraged to see Fromm's remarks in Fromm, E., *Man for Himself* (New York: Rinehart, 1947), pp. 96–101. Also his more recent book, *The Art of Loving* (New York: Harper, 1956). See also Sorokin, P., *The Ways and Power of Love; Types, Factors, and Techniques of Moral Transformation* (Boston: Beacon, 1954).

*2. Compare with Benda, C. E., *The Image of Love* (Glencoe, Ill.: Free Press, 1961), pp. 1–28.

3. The psychoanalysts regard identification as a more primitive mode of relating to another person than love. We would state that identification plays some role in love, even at mature levels of development, for reasons which are brought out in the text *Cf.* Fenichel, O., *The Psychoanalytic Theory of Neurosis* (New York: Norton, 1945), pp. 83–84.

4. *Cf.* Dymond, Rosalind, "Personality and Empathy," *J. Consult. Psychol., 14,* 343–350 (1950), for an empirical study of empathy. See also Stewart, D. A., *Preface to Empathy* (New York: Philosophical Library, 1956); and Foote, N. N. and Cottrell, L. S., *Identity and Interpersonal Competence* (Chicago: U. of Chicago, 1955).

5. Parsons, T. and Bales, R. F., *Family, Socialization and Interaction Process* (Glencoe, Ill.: Free Press, 1955), p. 21. The authors state, " . . . genital sexuality . . . the primary 'ritual' of marital solidarity. . . . " Compare also Benda, C. E., *op. cit.,* pp. 1–28.

6. See Fenichel, O., *op. cit.,* pp. 98–99. He distinguished, as did Freud, between *anaclitic* and *narcissistic* types of object-choice. In the former, an object is chosen because it provokes associations about another original object of the past, usually the parent of the opposite sex. In the latter, the person is chosen because he represents some characteristic of the person's own personality. See also, Freud, S., "On Narcissism: An Introduction." In Freud, S., *Collected Papers,* IV (London: Hogarth, 1953).

*7. See Murphy, G., *Personality: A Biosocial Approach to Origins and Structure* (New York: Harper, 1947), ch. 8.

8. Langhorne, M. C. and Secord, P. F., "Variations in Marital Needs with Age, Sex, Marital Status, and Regional Location," *J. Soc. Psychol. 41,* 19–37 (1955).

*9. Freud, S., "Contributions to the Psychology of Love. A Special Type of Choice of Object Made by Men," in Freud, S., *op. cit.,* ch. 11; Winch, R. F., *Mate-Selection* (New York; Harper, 1958).

10. Fenichel states, "When a person in love estimates his partner's virtues,

he usually is not very realistic; by his projection of all of his ideals onto the partner's personality, the reunion with him becomes all the more enjoyable." Fenichel, O., *op. cit.*, p. 86.

11. See chapter 2 for a discussion of autism.
12. Freud, S., *op. cit.* note 9.
13. When a person does not choose a spouse on the basis of his own needs and feelings, he is much more likely to choose on the basis of these other criteria. See Riesman, D., *The Lonely Crowd* (New Haven, Conn.: Yale, 1950), for a discussion of behavior which is directed by the conscience, or by others' demands, in contrast with autonomously directed behavior.
14. *Cf.* chapter 10.
15. *Cf.* chapter 10.
16. Spitz, R. A., "Hospitalism: An Inquiry into the Genesis of Psychiatric Conditions in Early Childhood," *Psychoanalytic Study of the Child,* I (New York: International Universities Press, 1945).

*17. *Cf.* Goldfarb, W., in Hoch, P. and Zubin, J. (eds.), *Psychopathology of Childhood* (New York: Grune, 1956), pp. 105–119.

18. Ribble, M. A., *The Rights of Infants* (New York: Columbia U. P., 1943).
19. Spitz, R. A., *op. cit.*, II; Harlow, H., "The Heterosexual Affection System in Monkeys," *Amer. Psychol., 17,* 1–9 (1962).
20. Levy, D. M., "Primary Affection-Hunger," *Amer. J. Orthopsychiat., 94,* 643–652 (1937).

*21. This point is well brought out in various writings of Maslow. See, for example, "Love in Self-Actualizing People," in Maslow, A. H., *Motivation and Personality* (New York: Harper, 1954).

22. *Cf.* Maslow, A. H., *op. cit.*
23. Fromm E., *op. cit.*, pp. 119–140
24. See Sullivan, H. S., *Conceptions of Modern Psychiatry* (Washington, D.C.: William Alanson White Psychiatric Foundation, 1947), p. 10. Murphy, G., *op. cit.*, p. 522. For an empirical study, see Jourard, S. M. and Remy, R. M., "Perceived Parental Attitudes, the Self, and Security," *J. Consult. Psychol., 19,* 364–366 (1955).

*25. Howard, S., *The Silver Cord.* See also, for an indictment of "Mom," Strecker, E., *Their Mothers' Sons* (Philadelphia: Lippincott, 1946).

26. Maslow, A. H., *op. cit.*
27. Fromm, E., *op. cit.*
28. See chapter 6 for a discussion of the healthy self-structure.
29. So-called "psychopathic personalities" appear to have repressed their needs to be loved.
30. Fromm, E., *op. cit.*
31. Maslow makes this point. See Maslow, A. H., *op. cit.*, pp. 305–334.
32. Compare with Benda, C. E., *op. cit.*

CHAPTER *12*
SEX AND HEALTHY PERSONALITY

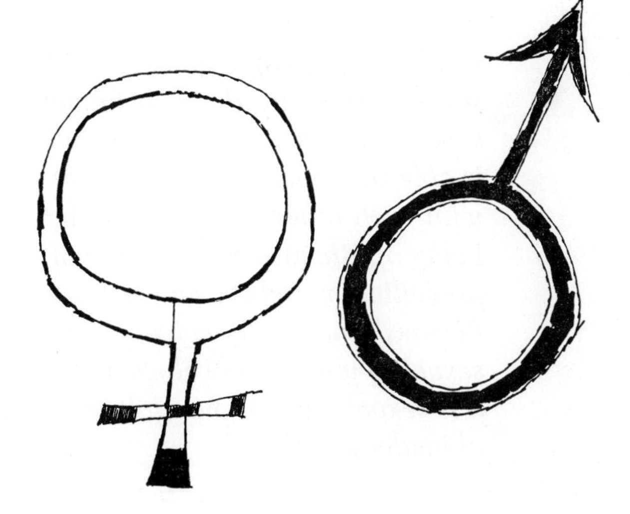

INTRODUCTION

The sexual relationship can provide some of the richest delights in life, and it is through the sexual relationship that the deepest love can be expressed between man and woman. Yet sex is a problem to many people in our society. The problem stems, in part, from the obvious fact that children are conceived through the sexual relationship. Every society imposes some restriction on sexual behavior, probably to insure that when children are born, they will be born to parents who are willing and qualified to assume responsibility for their upbringing. Our society, perhaps, has been overzealous in seeking to instill a sense of caution and responsibility regarding sex; as a result, many people grow to adult years regarding sex as dangerous, dirty, or immoral. Healthy personality is difficult to achieve unless the individual is able to reconcile fulfillment of his sexual needs with such other values as the integrity and well-being of others, some measure of conformity with prevailing morality, and a sense of self-esteem. Persons unable to achieve such integration of sexuality with other values will likely suffer needless sexual frustration, guilt, or profound feelings of inadequacy.

Despite the strict moral limits which our society imposes on sexual behavior, the limits are transgressed by many, as Kinsey's studies have shown. Many personality hygienists assert that our official sexual morality must be changed in fundamental ways because its strictness contributes to unnecessary repression, misery, and even to the development of various perversions. Such a change in morality, however, is a complicated social problem, and it is difficult to foresee in what ways and by what means such change might be carried out. Among the Western nations, Sweden has achieved a sweeping revolution in sexual morality, such that premarital sexual affairs are widespread, and unmarried mothers are not penalized by social censure or ostracism. Yet Sweden is not without problems, as evidenced by a relatively high incidence of suicide and alcoholism among its citizenry. So long as we live in America and so long as our sexual mores continue to condemn all sexuality save that which occurs within marriage, then all will be obliged to grope for a solution to the conflict between their sexual needs and their wishes to be free of guilt and shame.[1]

Before examining sex in relation to healthy personality, it will repay us to review the psychoanalysts' contribution to our understanding of this important topic. Freud was the first of the modern psychologists to attempt to trace the changing patterns of sexuality all the way from infancy to adulthood.

PSYCHOANALYTIC VIEW OF SEXUAL DEVELOPMENT[2]

Freud devoted considerable attention to the study of the sexual side of his patients' lives, correctly recognizing that in his time also people were prudish about sexual matters and that such excessive prudery might have played some part in the development of their neurotic disorders. He postulated that early in infancy, sensual gratification centered around the child's mouth, in sucking behavior especially. He termed this period the *oral stage* of "psychosexual development," and it was considered to last up until about the second year of life. During the second year and up until about the third or fourth year, Freud claimed that the most important bodily focus of sensory pleasure shifted from the mouth to the excretary organs, especially the organs of defecation. He termed this phase the *anal stage*. Readers of his writings at the time were digusted at this notion, that pleasure might be associated with bowel evacuation. Many contemporary readers may share this disgust. That Freud had some empirical warrant for his assertions can be readily attested by candid observation of small children or upon frank self-examination.

By about the fourth or fifth years of a child's life, the zone of the body directly concerned with pleasure appeared to shift to the genital organs. Freud termed this phase the *phallic stage*, applying the term to girls as well as to boys. The main source of pleasure for children in this stage, he claimed, was direct manipulation of the genital organs, as in masturbation. During this stage, too, the child of either sex typically becomes involved in the so-called Oedipus situation. This term, "Oedipus situation," was used by Freud to describe a very common type of infantile fantasy. The little boy wishes, in his imagination, to possess his mother and to exclude the father from her attentions and affection. The little girl wants to own or marry her Daddy and be done with Mother. Yet, each child has positive feelings toward the rejected parent, and to make matters more complicated, each child fears some kind of retaliation from the rejected parent—retaliation for secret wishes that the rival parent would die. It may be seen that the period of the Oedipus "complex," as it was termed, is fraught with acute conflicts. Freud claimed that the conflicts were commonly resolved in the following manner: The child would give up his wish for exclusive possession of the parent of the opposite sex. Further, he would "identify with," or strive to become like, the parent of the same sex. This solution, if successful, would permit ongoing psychological growth to resume. The child was then said to enter the *latency period*.

The latency period was said to last from about the age of five to 12 or 13, when puberty brings it to a close. Sex play during this time is not united with romantic or Oedipal fantasies but is instead pursued out of curiosity or for the excitement and pleasure it yields. As the child enters adolescence, however, he has begun the process of rapid physiological maturation, with its attendant strong sexual urges. The adolescent may participate in solitary or in shared sexual play, but by this time, the real or imagined partners become increasingly suitable as possible marriage partners. That is, they are of appropriate age and sex as contrasted with the fantasied partners of the Oedipal period. Unless earlier conflicts have prevented growth, the adolescent gradually enters what Freud called the *genital stage* of psychosexual development. By the time he reaches his adult years, he is ready to integrate his quest for sexual pleasure with other values, such as love and respect for the partner. He is increasingly ready for marriage.

Persons who have successfully passed through the "pregenital stages," claimed Freud and his followers, were said to have then become *genital characters*.[3] Again, this term may seem somewhat outrageous to the thoughtful student, but it is a term that derives its meaning from the complex theory of development that has been sketched out above.

For the psychoanalysts, the genital character is the healthy personality. Adults who have successfully become genital characters have been described as follows: They are able to love and work effectively. They are not hampered by unresolved conflicts with their parents, conflicts arising from earlier childhood. They are not obligated, by guilt or anxiety, to repress their imaginations or their feelings. They can reconcile their sexual feelings toward a partner with feelings of tenderness and esteem. Hence, they can be affectionate, spontaneous, creative, playful, able to work productively, and to love other people.

FACTORS IN SEXUAL BEHAVIOR

The previous outline of Freud's views shows us that experiences in childhood can have a decisive effect upon the sexual life of the adult. Frightening experiences relating to sex and prudish attitudes on the part of the parents fostering guilt in the child can make it difficult to achieve a healthy pattern of sexual behavior.[4] Let us examine sexuality as it may be observed in the adult and seek to enrich our understanding of the conditions which foster the healthy and the unhealthy patterns.

MOTIVES FOR SEXUAL BEHAVIOR

HEALTHY MOTIVES. One purpose for which sexual behavior is commonly undertaken is to achieve *pleasure*. This holds true for children and adults alike. The sexual climax, or orgasm, is probably among the most intense pleasures that humans can experience, and so it is no wonder that it is sought even into advanced years as long as persons are in reasonably good health. Contrary to common expectation, not only do very young children have a rudimentary sex life, but old persons as well, up to their eighties and nineties are known to maintain their sexual activity at a level compatible with their physical health.[5]

Pleasure, however, is not the sole motive for which healthy personalities will engage in sexual behavior. Sex is heavily freighted with symbolic meaning, and in our society it is generally regarded as a *symbol of love*. In fact, it is probably only within the context of an authentic loving-relationship, where both partners feel free to express themselves fully, that sexual experience is the source of the richest and most meaningful pleasure.

Married couples will engage in the sexual relationship not only for love and for pleasure but also *to conceive children*. We live in an age when the means of preventing conception have been developed to a high degree so that, in principle, married couples can have more freedom to choose the time that they will have children in, as well as choose the size of their families. It should be recognized that interference with conception is forbidden in some religious groups, such as among the Catholics. Whether or not contraceptive practices are compatible with the over-all health of personality is a complex question for persons with such religious commitments and cannot be discussed here. Where contraception is not a transgression of one's moral views, the practice is quite compatible with personality health, since it affords an opportunity to exercise responsible choice in the matter of bringing children into the world.

Thus, the attainment of pleasure, the expression of love, and the conception of children are all motives for sexual behavior which fall within the healthy range. Now, let us explore some motives which are less healthy.

SOME UNHEALTHY MOTIVES FOR SEXUAL BEHAVIOR. We shall select for discussion the following: (a) sexual behavior *as reassurance*, (b) sexual behavior as an *opiate*, and (c) sexual behavior as an *exchange commodity*.

Sex As Reassurance. It is not uncommon for males in our society to have grave doubts concerning their adequacy, sexual potency, or general competence as men. Sexual behavior is a primitive and basic proof of one's masculinity, and so a man might seek numerous sexual experiences to demonstrate his prowess to himself. So long as he is able to continue his "conquests," he can maintain his self-esteem; if any factor such as illness or enforced abstinence prevents him from maintaining a certain level of sexual activity, he is likely to undergo feelings of depression, inferiority, or anxiety.

A woman might have grave doubts concerning her attractiveness to males and her "womanliness." Where this is the case, she might become promiscuous in her sexual behavior with the aim of reassuring herself that she is indeed attractive and desirable.

The use of sexual behavior as reassurance is deemed unhealthy in these cases because it does not get to the root of the feelings of inadequacy which motivate the need for reassurance.

Sex As an Opiate. Sexual gratification is a fundamental pleasure. For many persons, everyday life may be quite "gray" and devoid of many meaningful satisfactions. Their work may be boring and their relationships with people superficial and unsatisfying. Under such conditions, a person might engage in very frequent sexual relations or masturbation as a kind of compensation for the emptiness of everyday life. Again, such a use or aim of sexual behavior is unhealthy because it does not get to the root of the difficulty. Instead, the sexual pleasures may so "tranquilize" the person that he loses some of the impetus for efforts that could change the circumstances responsible for the suffering, boredom, and emptiness in his life.

Sex As Exchange Commodity. A person might engage in sexual behavior as a means of getting things he believes cannot be gotten in any other way.

The most obvious example of sexuality as an exchange commodity is provided by the practice of prostitution. The prostitute sells sexuality for money.

Less obvious examples, but apparently quite common ones, may be provided through the study of many marriages. A wife "starved" for affection and tenderness may engage in sexual relationships with her husband when she does not really want to because she feels it is only through such submission that she can gain her husband's affection.

In one case (mentioned later in this chapter), a frigid wife would abstain from sexual intercourse with her husband whenever she wanted to force him to comply with her wishes for a major household purchase, a trip, and so on. She would "submit" only after her husband came around to her point of view.

The use of sex as an exchange commodity runs counter to our social mores. More important, it implies that the "vendor" is treating herself as an object or thing. When she does this, she is also relating to her partner, not on a loving basis (see Chapter 11), but rather as an impersonal source of satisfactions.

HEALTHY CONDITIONS FOR SEXUAL AROUSAL

A man in our culture is likely to become at least mildly aroused or sexually interested whenever he looks at an attractive, shapely woman clad, partially clothed, or nude. Part of the reason for his arousal may stem from the fact that women seek to dress, speak, and move in ways that are subtly inviting. For the man to respond with interest probably signifies that he is "getting the message"; that is, he is in good health and in contact with reality.

Women, typically, can be aroused by expressions of love, tenderness, and by caresses. By their manner of dress, their gait, and glancing, they may give off signals meaning they would welcome advances from a man, but whether they will respond to these advances depends upon many other conditions being met. These conditions include reassurances of the love and esteem in which they are held by the other, safety, and the degree to which ethical precepts are being observed.

In a socially sanctioned relationship like marriage, many of the barriers which ordinarily might block full sexual arousal will be absent. If the couple truly love one another, they will learn the idiosyncratic conditions for full mutual arousal, and they will find little difficulty in providing these for one another, e.g., tenderness, expressions of endearment, caressing, and the like. Now, let us consider some of the unhealthy conditions for arousal.

UNHEALTHY CONDITIONS FOR SEXUAL AROUSAL

A failure to respond sexually to the usual symbolic or direct forms of sexual stimulation is generally referred to as *frigidity* in a woman and *impotence* in a male. The most common psychological causes of these conditions are emotions incompatible with sexual responsiveness, such as guilt, anxiety, or disgust. Thus, a woman may have many irrational fears associated with sexuality. The stimuli which would arouse a healthy person serve only to induce guilt, anxiety, or disgust in this woman. Likewise, a male may have various irrational fears pertaining to sexuality which preclude his becoming aroused even under conditions where there is no rational basis for these fears. Such fears usually stem from early training and experiences with sex, and they may be read about in almost any treatise concerned with neurosis or personality therapy. For such persons to become capable of sexual responsiveness, it is necessary that the incompatible emotional responses to sexual stimuli be removed by some means.

Some persons will respond sexually to stimuli not generally regarded as sexual symbols in our society. The homosexual, for example, is a person who fears, is repelled by, or is indifferent to persons of the opposite sex; he can only be aroused by members of the same sex. The fetishist is aroused by the objects of his fetish and not by a receptive partner of the opposite sex. The sources of these deviations are to be found in an intensive study of the life history of the persons who suffer from them. There is no evidence that deviant sexuality is innate or caused by endocrine disturbances except in rare cases.

SACRED AND PROFANE LOVE

Many persons, because of overly strict sexual training, are unable to fuse the tender and sexual aspects of love.[6] They are unable to respect and care for the same person toward whom they experience sexual feelings. Thus, a man may marry a woman because she has many exemplary traits of personality and character but finds himself unable to become sexually aroused with her. He may be quite potent with other women whom he does not respect. Similarly, a woman may admire and respect her husband but not be able to respond sexually to him; with a lover (who is quite unsuitable as a marriage partner), she may find herself sexually responsive.

This state of affairs is quite common in our society. Freud thought it was a derivative of an "unresolved Oedipus complex." That is, a man might choose as a spouse some woman who bears certain resemblances to his mother. Sexual feelings are tabooed toward the mother; it is as if the man tranferred many of the same feelings and attitudes from his mother to his wife. The woman might likewise transfer many of her attitudes and feelings from her father to her husband.

Although the Oedipus complex may in part account for the inability of many persons to be sexually responsive to a person whom they admire and respect, another factor may be the belief that sex is a basically degraded kind of activity. This is a conception many persons acquire during the process of being socialized. They feel that sexual intercourse degrades both themselves and their partners. Consequently, they can be responsive and sexually competent only with a person whom they believe to be morally or socially inferior to themselves. In their marriage, they may display marked sexual maladjustment and discontent.

HEALTHY SEXUAL BEHAVIOR

Sexual behavior is healthy when it is effective in achieving a healthy sexual aim yet is in accord with the social mores and the self-structure of the individual. If the aim is to achieve a climax for the self and the partner, the healthy personality will display the capacity to achieve these ends. If the aim is to express love and esteem for the partner, the healthy personality will behave sexually in ways which convey these sentiments. Among healthy personalities, sex is a source of much satisfaction and enjoyment with considerable freedom in the choice of modes of sexual behavior.[7]

Among some persons, the conscience may impose certain restrictions on the varieties of sexual behavior which are theoretically available. Thus, certain modes of sexual stimulation, caressing, and sexual intercourse may be deemed desirable by one partner in a marriage and distasteful or ugly by another. Such incompatibilities in values and ideals may produce dissatisfaction with the sexual relationship between the spouses. It becomes apparent we cannot consider sexual behavior apart from the self-structure of the individual. We are obliged to state that healthy sexual behavior more or less presumes a healthy self-structure in the individual and, of course, a loving-relationship between the partners.

With respect to modes of undertaking sexual intercourse, it is compatible with personality-hygiene principles to assert that any sexual behavior mutually acceptable to both partners may be deemed healthy. Some spouses find their sexual relations become rather boring but fear if they change their mode of intercourse they will be doing something perverse. Most experts in the field of sex would agree that varying the styles of intercourse is quite compatible with personality health and social normality.

Freedom and spontaneity in sexual love-making is most likely to be possible when the couple have established a loving-relationship within which they have learned to know, respect, and trust one another. In the love-making of such couples, "anything goes."

SOCIALLY UNACCEPTABLE PATTERNS OF SEXUAL BEHAVIOR

Let us discuss some patterns of sexual behavior which deviate from the social ideals. These patterns are not necessarily unhealthy, however. Whether they influence the health of personality in adverse ways can only be ascertained after careful study.

MASTURBATION. The practice of masturbation is well-nigh universal among members of our society, and yet it runs counter to the social mores. This implies many persons undergo acute moral conflicts at some time during their lives because they masturbate. The personality hygienist is not in a position to make moral judgments about masturbation, but he can offer some natural-scientific comments about it.

Many parents will instill erroneous beliefs into their children's minds concerning the supposed effects of masturbation. The child may be told that this practice will weaken him, will destroy his mind, make him insane, or render him impotent later in life. So far, there is no evidence to support these beliefs. Some parents even make dire personal threats to their children in connection with "self-abuse."[8]

Children with strict training in regard to masturbation will have severe guilt feelings because they cannot withstand the impulse to masturbate. These guilt feelings often produce undesirable consequences in the form of feelings of inferiority and worthlessness. Some children become so threatened by the supposed consequences of masturbation that they completely repress sexuality. Such a means of handling sexual feelings can lead to serious personality illnesses.

In time, the sternness with which masturbation is condemned will likely be mitigated. More and more parents are beginning to regard masturbation as a rather natural part of growing up; they may attempt to discourage their children from masturbating, but they no longer punish it with severity. Some parents even overlook it completely.

PREMARITAL INTERCOURSE. Strict taboos are directed toward this pattern of sexual behavior. The reasons behind the taboo are partly moral and partly practical, e.g., the possibility of pregnancy, venereal disease, and so on. Almost everyone in our culture has been raised to regard premarital sexual relations as morally wrong. Yet there is increasing evidence that the taboo is being bypassed by a steadily growing number of young people. Among some teen-age groups, the fact of virginity is even regarded as a sign of inferiority.

Again, the personality hygienist cannot comment on the moral issues that are at stake. He can only observe the consequences of conformity or nonconformity with the mores for over-all personality health. Many of the practical reasons for avoiding premarital relationships are less pressing than they were at an earlier stage in history. Methods of avoiding conception are becoming increasingly known and understood, both by married and unmarried persons. These methods do not guarantee one-hundred per cent effectiveness, but they reduce the probability of conception following sexual intercourse. Venereal disease is becoming less common than it once was, and so this reason for premarital continence is becoming less urgent.

These observations mean that spokesmen for premarital chastity must find other reasons besides moral precepts to support their position. There are many such reasons that can be considered. For example, premarital sexual intercourse, because it is tabooed, must usually be carried out in secrecy in circumstances that are not conducive to relaxed and mutually satisfactory love-making. Guilt and fear of being discovered can readily hamper or destroy the enjoyment of sex. Furthermore, many authentic objections to premarital sex may be suppressed during the entire episode only to become fully conscious in the "cold light of day." Such regrets and afterthoughts can create problems in the ongoing relationship between the partners. Perhaps the best advice that can be offered from the standpoint of personality hygiene is that unmarried sex, while it may be a delight, frequently involves some cost. The unmarried partners should be cognizant of possible consequences and be prepared to face these in responsible fashion.

SADISM, MASOCHISM, VOYEURISM, AND OTHER PERVERSIONS. As a consequence of various life-history events, some persons are incapable of achieving sexual gratification in the accepted ways but can attain a climax only through inflicting pain, receiving pain, peeping, and other deviant means.[9] Such individuals are generally found to display *other aspects of unhealthy personality* besides unhealthy sexuality.

RECOGNIZING HEALTHY SEXUALITY

When would a personality hygienist evaluate a person's sexual behavior as healthy? Let us present what appear to be the most salient attributes of healthy sexuality.

ACCURATE KNOWLEDGE ABOUT SEX. A person with reasonably accurate beliefs about sex—its anatomy, physiology, relationship with reproduction, and so on—will be more likely to achieve healthy sexuality than an ignorant person. Accurate information is readily obtained from books, from parents, teachers, and physicians; yet there are many persons who have not availed themselves of even rudimentary knowledge pertaining to sexuality because of shame or guilt. Unfortunately if a person does not have accurate knowledge, he will probably have an assortment of false beliefs concerning sexuality. These can only lead to difficulties in sexual adjustment.

AN ATTITUDE OF ACCEPTANCE. A person who regards sexuality as a natural and healthy part of living is more likely to achieve healthy sexuality than a person who views it as basically evil. The healthy personality is neither ashamed nor afraid of his sexual tensions; he may exercise self-control by suppressing any sexual behavior which violates his ethical system, but he does not try to exclude sexuality from his life as a dangerous or nasty phenomenon.[10]

INTEGRATION OF SEX WITH OTHER VALUES. The healthy personality views sexual gratification as an important condition for happiness, but sex is integrated in a harmonious way with other values. Although sexual gratification is not deemed to be the most important condition for happiness, it is not relegated by a healthy individual to the realm of the unimportant. For the healthy personality, sex can contribute richly to his over-all happiness and effectiveness in living; he would not regard sexual gratification as more important, however, than personal integrity or the integrity of his relationship with someone he loves.

EVALUATING SEXUAL BEHAVIOR IN SELF AND OTHERS

There are no absolute health standards for sex, but some useful general guidelines are available. Let us consider sexuality as it may appear in the infant, the child, the adolescent, and the young unmarried adult.

SEXUALITY IN INFANCY.[11] Young infants (two years of age and younger) can sometimes be observed exploring and manipulating their genitalia. Their parents may become anxious when they observe this. It can be asserted there is little ground for alarm in connection with such activities; the most general interpretation that may be made is that the infant is in process of discovering his body.

SEXUALITY IN CHILDHOOD. Children from about three onward will touch or manipulate their genitalia when resting in bed or occasionally when they are at play with other children. The most relevant interpretation is that the children have discovered the pleasurable sensations which self-manipulation can produce, and they tend to seek this pleasure from time to time.

Unless such activity is excessive, the parent is advised to avoid making an emotional issue out of it. If the child shows many signs of unhealthy personality, such as inability to get satisfactions out of his relationships with his family and friends, then it may be that masturbation is serving as a compensatory mechanism. Under these circumstances, the parent is advised to seek professional advice from a pediatrician or a child psychologist.

SEXUALITY IN ADOLESCENCE. Sexual tensions are very strong during adolescence, and sex poses intense problems to the average adolescent. He will generally experience acute conflicts between his desire to conform with the morals pertaining to sexuality and his intense desires for relief from sexual tensions.[12]

Many adolescents are able to resolve the conflict by engaging in masturbation, regarding it as a sort of necessity. Masturbation is not entirely guilt-free for them, yet their guilt-reactions are not too intense or burdensome. Others find they cannot accept themselves if they masturbate and can maintain self-esteem only if they abstain entirely.

SEXUALITY IN THE UNMARRIED ADULT. Marriage is seldom possible in our culture before the late teens or early twenties, and so many young adults have problems connected with their sexual tensions. Again, since moral issues are at stake, the personality hygienist cannot offer advice very authoritatively. The moral precepts of our society may be restrictive from a cross-cultural point of view, but they represent one of the realities with which all of us have to come to terms.

Young adults are quite sexually responsive, and it troubles them as to what they should do—should they seek relief through masturbation, should they engage in premarital sexual intercourse, or should they strive to abstain? The personality hygienist can assert there is nothing unhealthy about experiencing sexual arousal; the person's sexual behavior cannot be judged healthy or unhealthy in isolation. However, what he does (or avoids doing) must be assessed with respect to over-all consequences for personality as a whole, physical health, and other values.

VARIOUS RESPONSES TO SEXUAL TENSIONS

Let us examine some of the ways in which a person can respond to sexual feelings once they have arisen. First, we will discuss the healthy pattern and then comment upon some of the less healthy responses.

THE HEALTHY PATTERN: SELECTIVE SUPPRESSION AND RELEASE

The healthy personality will have formed a set of ethical interpersonal and perhaps aesthetic conditions under which he will feel free to express his sexual feelings in behavior. He will be fully aware of sexual feelings whenever they arise, even under conditions that for him are inappropriate. He does not feel threatened by his own feelings and hence does not need to deny their existence through repression. When the above-mentioned conditions have not been met, however, he will have the ability to suppress his sexual feelings and refrain from sexual behavior. The reason for such suppression, fundamentally, is that sexual intercourse when the conditions are not right is not satisfying. We may call this pattern selective suppression and release.

SOME UNHEALTHY PATTERNS

IMMEDIATE RELEASE OF SEXUAL TENSIONS. A person may find it impossible to delay or to postpone sexual gratification, so intense or urgent do his tensions and desires feel. Consequently, he may seek release in any way which is immediately available to him. The quest for immediate release reflects an inability on the part of the person to impose voluntary control over his impulses. This inability to impose control is likely to result in sexual behavior which may jeopardize many important values. If the person seeks sexual release with a partner, he may choose that partner only on the basis of immediate availability, ignoring other important criteria for the choice of a sex-object. Thus, the person chosen may be quite unsuitable because of age differences, ill-health, intelligence level, or social class. Probably many unwanted pregnancies, instances of venereal disease, hasty marriages, rapes, and other undesirable occurrences derive from the inability to tolerate delay in the attainment of sexual gratification.

If the person seeks relief from urgent sexual tensions through masturbation, and if he has strong taboos with respect to this practice, he will probably experience intense guilt feelings and feelings of inferiority. His life becomes something of a vicious circle of sexual arousal, masturbation, self-hate, dissatisfaction with his everyday life and relationships with people, compensatory sexual desire, and so on.

In an adult, the inability to tolerate delay in sexual gratification, so that the sexual behavior conflicts with other values is often an indicator of unhealthy personality. It is probable that with more permissive sexual mores or with a change in the social conditions responsible for delaying marriage, some of the problems associated with immediate sexual release would disappear.

REPRESSION. Repression of sexual tensions is likely to occur in persons who have excessively strict consciences with respect to sexuality and in persons who have come to fear sexuality in general. Repression of sexuality manifests itself in various ways, for instance in (a) an absence of any conscious sexual wishes or desires or (b) a denial of any sexual intent. All of us repress sexuality at various times and in various situations because we have been trained to observe and accord with certain taboos, e.g., the incest taboo. Most of us would become quite upset or threatened if we became sexually aroused by members of our immediate family. Yet psychoanalysts have shown that such feelings have occurred at one time or another in all our lives; however, we found this so threatening to self-esteem and security that we repressed sex within the family circle.

Repression of sexual desire in the right times and places is compatible with personality health provided the repression is not too general. Social living would be impossible if persons were chronically aroused sexually by unsuitable sex-objects. Imagine being sexually aroused all day, every day, every year! It would interfere with other pursuits, to say the least! But if sexuality has been totally repressed, many unhealthy consequences ensue. The represser carries a virtual "well" of unconscious sexual desire, manifested in unpredictable and uncontrollable ways, in accidents, gestures, unwitting sexualization of interpersonal relationships, and so on. Chronic unconscious sexuality disturbs the person's capacity to work effectively, and it disturbs his relationships with people by making him unduly defensive or autistic. The psychoanalysts assert that repressed sexuality contributes to the development of neurosis and other patterns of unhealthy personality.

The worst danger associated with a total repression of sexuality is the fact that from time to time the repression may be overcome in explosive fashion. This may occur when the sexual tensions become too strong or when the energy required to maintain the repression is decreased, e.g., in fatigue or intoxication. On such occasions, the represser may engage in impulsive sexual behavior or he may become overwhelmed with guilt and anxiety without really understanding why.

CHRONIC SUPPRESSION. A person can be fully aware of his sexual tensions but suppress sexual behavior for a number of reasons: fear of disease, pregnancies, guilt, ideals, and other causes. Chronic suppression sets the stage for unremitting sexual tension.[13]

Chronic sexual tension will produce many undesirable effects. The most obvious is unhappiness and a sense of frustration. In addition, the suppresser will be plagued by chronic sexual fantasies so that he cannot concentrate on his work. His relationships with people will be impaired for a number of reasons: viz., he may not be able to appraise the feelings of others with accuracy, or he may be irritable and short-tempered.

Suppression of sexual behavior is unhealthy *when the consequences to which it leads are unhealthy* and when the reasons for the suppression are unrealistic and unwarranted. The ability to suppress, however, is a desirable ability, as we shall see in the next section.

SOME DETERMINERS OF HEALTHY SEXUALITY

Healthy sexuality in an adult is no accident, nor is it a natural phenomenon. It is rather a product of determining factors. Some of the factors likely to play a role in determining sexual health are (a) the nature of sexual instruction and training, (b) early sexual experiences and their consequences, (c) the self-structure, (d) availability of suitable sex-objects, (e) a wide repertoire of other satisfactions, and (f) the capacity to establish love relationships.

Unlike many of the lower forms of animal life, humans have to learn how to behave sexually, and they have to learn when it is socially appropriate to become sexually aroused. Some of this learning results from deliberate parental instruction of children. Much of this instruction in our society is negative; it consists in admonishments about what is taboo. Children are told not to masturbate, not to display their bodies; in fact from an early age many children are actively trained to be ashamed and afraid of things pertaining to sex. Because many parents are embarrassed or tense about sexual matters, their children may be afraid to ask questions about their sex organs or about reproduction. The children may then acquire many false beliefs concerning these matters.

Healthy sexuality is most likely to be promoted if the sexual instruction which the children receive is matter-of-fact, accurate, and in response to the children's spontaneous curiosity.

NATURE OF EARLY EXPERIENCES WITH SEX. Healthy adult sexuality is most likely to be achieved against a background relatively free of fears and guilts pertaining to sex. Many children have undergone severe punishments for childhood masturbation or sexual experimentation.[14] These punishments have made sexual situations a stimulus for emotions incompatible with healthy sexuality. The severely punished child may, if other contributing factors are present, develop impotence, frigidity, various perversions, and other unhealthy patterns. Healthy sexuality will be promoted if the parents handle the children's deviations from their own sexual ethics with kindness, understanding, and with explanations which the child can understand.

Thus, if a child is observed to be masturbating, the parents should let the child know why they do not want him to continue this activity if they don't like it. They should not tell lies about the results of masturbation; if need be, they can just say that it is not nice, and they would like him to stop. If the relationship between the parents and the child is a healthy one, the child will gradually acquire the standards and ideals which the parents would like him to have. Failures to accord with these ideals should be viewed as signs of immaturity in the child or as evidence of an unsatisfactory relationship between parent and child, not as signs of moral turpitude and worthlessness.

HEALTHY SELF-STRUCTURE. Healthy sexuality is prevented by an unhealthy self-structure. An individual may acquire a self-ideal which deplores and condemns sexuality. In order to maintain self-esteem, such a person develops a self-concept that includes the assertion, "I am a person who does not have sexual feelings." For him, sexual arousal would constitute a threat. To avoid or remove threat, the individual is obliged to repress his sexual feelings.

If a person has been able to acquire and maintain a healthy self-structure, he will recognize and accept his sexual feelings when they are aroused. In addition, his self-ideal is not so restrictive that it precludes the possibility of guilt-free sexual behavior. As a general rule, it can be said that any factors which promote the development of a healthy self-structure will also promote the development of healthy sexuality.

AVAILABILITY OF SUITABLE PARTNERS. When partners appropriate to a person's age and status are not available, he may make a *deviant* object-choice in his quest for sexual gratification. It is not uncommon for homosexuality to occur among students in an all-male or all-female school, among prisoners in jails, camps, and penitentiaries, among sailors. In rural areas, where the population is scanty and the opportunities for marriage are limited, sexual contacts with animals may occur.

The incidence of deviant object-choices could be reduced if appropriate sex-objects were available to persons living under these conditions. It should be asserted, however, that not all cases of perversions stem from the lack of availability of more socially appropriate sex-objects, and, further, not all persons living under such conditions develop these perversions.

A GENERALLY SATISFYING LIFE. The probability of attaining and maintaining healthy sexuality is increased if a person is gaining many satisfactions in the other realms of life. Adequate sexual relationships will promote a person's ability to function satisfactorily in his work, his leisure, and in his nonsexual relationships with people. The reverse also appears to be true: If a person is able to derive satisfaction from his work, his leisure, and his relationships with people, he is likely to be better able to achieve healthy sexuality. A person filled with unresolved need-tensions arising from other areas of his life may try to compensate for his other frustrations by means of sexual activity. He may be demanding more of sexuality than it can deliver. And further, the burden of nonsexual tensions which he is carrying may prevent him from performing adequately in a sexual situation. A tense, thwarted person can't be a relaxed, effective sexual lover.

LOVE FOR THE PARTNER. Many barriers to healthy sexuality will not arise in a healthy love relationship. If a person has the capacity to love another person, he will doubtless have the capacity to achieve healthy sexuality within the context of that love relationship. Loving involves knowing the object, caring for the object, behaving in ways which will promote the growth and happiness of the object, and making the self known to the object. If a couple have been able to establish such a relationship, then neither will be afraid or ashamed to make needs and desires known to the other. Each wants to please the other and to promote the happiness of the other. At the outset of marriage a loving couple may not achieve full harmony and mutual satisfaction in sexual relationships, but in time they should be able to accommodate to each others' changing needs and wishes.

If they are afraid or ashamed to convey their deepest feelings, needs, and desires to each other, it is easy to see how dissatisfactions will soon arise; and the dissatisfactions will not be brought out in the open and discussed. It might be said that the richest sexual satisfactions can only occur in the context of a love relationship, where the communication barriers between the partners are reduced to a minimum.

THERAPY FOR UNHEALTHY SEXUALITY

The individual with unhealthy sexuality generally suffers. The nature of the suffering will of course vary with the nature of the sexual deviation from health. The sexual represser and suppresser suffers from prolonged sexual privation, from guilts and anxieties. The person with deviant sexual behavior may suffer from fear of punishment and possibly losses of self-esteem. The impotent husband and the frigid wife suffer from disturbances in the over-all relationships with the spouse.

As a consequence of their suffering, persons with unhealthy sexuality may be motivated to seek professional personality therapy. While assistance cannot always be guaranteed, yet often guidance, instruction, or more intensive personality therapy may be effective in removing some of the obstacles to healthy sexuality.

A woman undertook therapy because of marked difficulties in her relationship with one of her children. During the course of therapy, it was discovered she could not be sexually responsive to her husband. She merely endured the sexual aspects of marriage. Indeed, she used sexual compliance as a means of controlling her husband. It was soon discovered her lack of responsiveness derived largely from attitudes acquired from her mother. Her mother had instructed the patient to view sex as dirty. The patient, when she became aware of the origins of her attitudes, came to see them as silly. Her lack of responsiveness vanished, and with it vanished also a lack of zest in the marriage, a lot of tension, and finally, the difficulties in her relationship with her child.

OUR MORES AND HEALTHY SEXUALITY

Most persons in our society have been socialized in ways which impel them to espouse our current sexual mores. Yet Kinsey showed that most of the subjects whom he interviewed had violated, or were violating the mores with respect to sexuality. It is possible that a certain proportion of those who conformed to the mores strictly were not obtaining enough sexual gratification to make them happy. Could we conclude from this line of reasoning that healthy sexuality is a rarity, and that normal or typical sexuality either is out of line with the mores or else fails to bring happiness to the individual?[15]

Sexual mores are a social necessity. There is no society which does not impose some form of restriction on the sexual behavior of its members. But there are some societies where guilts and anxieties pertaining to sexuality do not appear, where sex is not a problem. Some extremists have suggested that our society needs a "sexual revolution"[16]—that the solution to man's ills and unhappiness is to overthrow the sexual mores and to substitute absolute freedom in sexual behavior. This is impossible, and it is not known what undesirable consequences would follow from such license anyway. A more sensible view would appear to be somewhat as follows: Gradually, with the passage of time, our mores may change, bringing them more into accord with human practice. Certainly we have come a long way in the past fifty years in that sexuality is no longer a taboo subject for study or discussion. As more is learned about sexuality and its role in personality health and illness, socialization practices with respect to sexuality may be expected to change, and with these changes there may be expected the gradual modification of the sexual mores.

SUMMARY

Every society imposes strict taboos and restrictions on sexuality. In our society, almost all forms of sexual behavior are prohibited except actual sexual intercourse between married couples.

Healthy sexual behavior *is behavior which is effective in securing sexual gratification for the individual and which accords with the social mores and the individual's self-structure.* Healthy sexual motives *include the giving and receiving of pleasure, the expression of affection for the partner, the conception of children. Examples of* unhealthy sexual motives *include reassurance, compensation for other frustrations, and the use of sexual behavior as a means of getting other valued objects.*

A person is said to display healthy conditions for arousal *when he or she is sexually responsive to the typical forms of sexual stimulation, that is, stroking of erogenous zones, terms of endearment, and so on. Persons who are unresponsive to typical methods of stimulation are generally regarded as frigid (if female) or impotent (if male).*

Quite commonly in our society, persons are un-

able to express respect and affection for the same person to whom they are sexually responsive. Thus, they may respect their spouses but be sexually inadequate with them; they can be sexually effective only with a person whom they do not admire or respect.

Healthy sexual behavior *is any kind of sexual activity which is mutually acceptable to the partners and which achieves the various sexual aims. Many sorts of sexual behavior which would be viewed as perverse if they were an end in themselves are regarded as healthy and acceptable within the context of a healthy love-relationship.*

A number of patterns of sexual behavior are regarded as socially undesirable, although they are quite common in our society. These include masturbation and premarital sexual intercourse. At one time these activities were tabooed for apparently scientific reasons; masturbation was thought to lead to insanity and premarital sexual relationships actually did lead to many unwanted pregnancies and venereal disease. At the present time, these reasons for taboo have lessened in urgency. Therefore, the main reasons for enjoining these practices are moral ones. Other patterns of sexual behavior more universally regarded as unhealthy are sadism, masochism, voyeurism, and other perversions.

Some signs of healthy sexuality *in a person include* accurate knowledge about sex, *an* accepting attitude toward sex, *and* the ability to integrate sexuality with the over-all value-system of the person.

Sexuality in infancy and childhood are to be regarded as natural and not to be severely punished. If sexual behavior is excessive during these stages, the parents are advised to seek professional guidance. Problems relating to sex during adolescence and young adulthood, and their solutions, must be evaluated with respect to their consequences for over-all personality health.

Immediate release, repression, *and* chronic suppression *of sexual tensions are all unhealthy means for the management of sexual tensions. Selective suppression and release are healthy modes of control.*

Personality therapy is recommended for cases displaying unhealthy sexuality. Our current sexual mores are factors contributing to unhealthy patterns of sexuality.

NOTES AND REFERENCES

Excellent supplementary reading will be provided by those references marked with an asterisk (*).

*1. An interesting contrast in approaches to the study of sex is provided by comparison of the following: Freud, S., *Three Contributions to the Theory of Sex,* in Brill, A. A., *The Basic Writings of Sigmund Freud* (New York, Modern Library, 1938), pp. 553–629; Kinsey, A. C., Pomeroy, W. B., and Martin, C. E., *Sexual Behavior in the Human Male* (Philadelphia: Saunders, 1948). Also, Kinsey, A. C., Pomeroy, W. B., Martin, C. E., and Gebhard, P. H., *Sexual Behavior in the Human Female* (Philadelphia: Saunders, 1953), and Benda, C. E., *The Image of Love* (Glencoe, Ill.: Free Press, 1961, pp. 11–28.

2. *Cf.* Freud, S., *op. cit.*, also Brown, J. F., *Psychodynamics of Abnormal Behavior* (New York: McGraw, 1940), pp. 178–237.

3. One psychoanalyst regarded the capacity to experience a fully consummating sexual climax as a gauge which attested the attainment of the genital stage. He referred to this capacity as "orgastic potency." See Reich, W., *Character Analysis* (New York, Orgone Institute Press, 1948, p. 300.

4. *Cf.* Freud, S., *op. cit.* Also see the comparison of socializing practices with regard to sexuality in Whiting, J. W. M. and Child, I. L., *Child Training and Personality* (New Haven, Conn.: Yale, 1953), pp. 77–91. In a survey of 34 societies, they found only two other societies with more severe sexual training practices than their American sample.

5. Newman, G. and Nichols, C. R., "Sexual Activities and Attitudes in Older Persons," *J. Amer. Med. Assoc.*, *173*, 33–35 (1960).

*6. An elaboration of this and other related points may be found in Freud's "Contributions to the Psychology of Love." See Freud, S., *Collected Papers*, IV (London: Hogarth, 1953), pp. 192–235. Compare also Benda, C. E., *op. cit.*, and Watts, A. W., *Nature, Man and Woman* (New York: Mentor, 1960), pp. 136–155.

*7. Maslow has described sexuality as it occurs among "self-actualizing people." See Maslow, A. H., *Motivation and Personality* (New York: Harper, 1954), ch. 13. See also Jourard, S. M., "Sex in Marriage," *J. Humanist. Psychol.*, *1*, 23–29 (1961).

8. Huschka compiled a number of parental reactions to their children's masturbation. Many of these reactions were quite brutal and sadistic. See Huschka, M., "The Incidence and Character of Masturbation Threats in a Group of Problem Children," *Psychoanalyt. Quart.*, *7*, 338–355 (1938).

9. A classic catalogue of sexual deviations is von Krafft-Ebing, R., *Psychopathia Sexualis* (12th ed.; New York: Pioneer Publications, 1947). A more recent effort to compile an exhaustive overview of sexual behavior is Ellis, A. and Abarnel, A., *The Encyclopedia of Sexual Behavior* (New York: Hawthorn, 1961).

10. Reich speaks of a "sex-affirmative" superego in the genital character. Reich, W., *op. cit.*, p. 167.

11. See the empirical studies of Spitz with regard to infantile sexual behavior. Spitz, R. A. and Wolf, Katherine M., "Autoerotism. Some Empirical Findings and Hypotheses on Three of its Manifestations in the First Year of Life," *Psychoanalyt. Stud. Child*, III–IV, 85–120 (1949).

12. Mead showed that a sexually conflicted adolescence is not innate, as was once believed, but is rather a by-product of the culture. See Mead, M., *Coming of Age in Samoa* (New York: Morrow, 1928).

13. The psychoanalysts regard sexual suppression as a causal factor in the "actual neuroses." See Fenichel, O., *The Psychoanalytic Theory of Neurosis* (New York: Norton, 1945).

14. See Whiting, J. W. M. and Child, I. L., *op. cit.*

15. Freud's opinion was that adherence to the sexual morality of his time

contributed to "nervousness." See Freud, S., "Civilized Sexual Morality and Modern Nervousness." In Freud, S., *op. cit.*, II, pp. 76–99.

16. Reich, W., *The Sexual Revolution* (New York: Orgone Institute Press, 1945). See also Ellis, A., *Sex Without Guilt* (New York: Lyle Stuart, 1958).

CHAPTER *13*

PROMOTING HEALTHY PERSONALITY THROUGH THERAPY

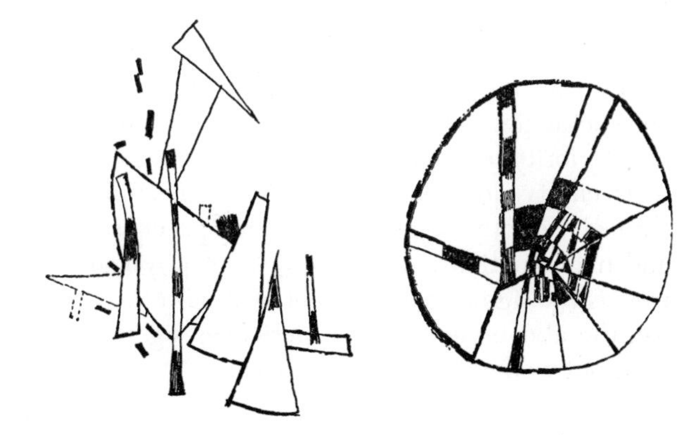

INTRODUCTION

A person can do much, without assistance, to foster his own personality growth; yet, many persons may find themselves plagued with minor difficulties in living that they cannot master. They are not "unhealthy personalities," but they may find their lives lacking in zest and meaning because of the persistent difficulties. For such persons, some form of professional therapy may prove invaluable. Fortunately, professional counselors and therapists of personality are available at most colleges. In the present chapter, we shall explore the process of therapy from various points of view in order to increase understanding of the manner in which it can be helpful.

TREATMENT OF SYMPTOMS

The individual with difficulties in living usually suffers. The name which psychologists give to the suffering varies. Some people suffer chronic anxiety and fear. Others are afflicted with guilt or feelings of inferiority and worthlessness. Still others complain that their life feels empty, joyless, and devoid of meaning.[1] Some manifest the clinical symptoms of neurosis and psychosis: phobias, obsessions, and hallucinations. As in the field of physical medicine, where distress is the signal that all is not well with the body, so with personality; the above-mentioned experiences signify to the individual that all is not well with his personality.

When a person suffers physical pain associated with wounds or infections, he generally strives to alleviate the symptomatic pain with palliatives: viz., aspirin and other drugs; or else he seeks treatment that will combat the causes of his suffering.

When a person suffers "psychological pain,"[2] he can seek temporary relief by means of assorted palliative measures or else seek to alter the basic conditions which have been responsible for his suffering. Naturally, the personality hygienist values most highly those attempts at treatment which will remove the causes of the psychological suffering. In general, such basic treatment calls for either some alteration of personality or some alteration of the environment, or both. The temporary treatment may be designated "symptom-treatment," or psychological first aid, since its aim is to relieve the patient from the immediate experience of suffering.

SELF-TREATMENT OF SYMPTOMS

Let us suppose a person is suffering chronic anxiety. His anxiety takes the form of specific worries about health, money, and career. If the person attempts to treat himself for these symptoms, he may *drink* each time his worries become too intense. While intoxicated, he may think about ill-health and the lack of money, but the unpleasant emotional tensions will likely be mitigated. Unfortunately, the cure of the symptoms in this case lasts only as long as the effects of the alcohol. Upon sobering up, the person will again find himself plagued with the chronically recurrent worries.

Another type of symptom-treatment to which a person might resort is *repression*, the refusal to think about the objects of his worry. Each time the themes of health, money, and career present themselves to his thoughts, or arise in conversation, he changes the subject and thinks or talks about something more pleasant. Unfortunately, the unwanted thoughts, with their concomitant feelings, will tend to sneak into his mind when he least expects them: viz., when he is at the point of falling asleep or when his attention wanders from some task at which he is engaged. In fact, the repressed thoughts *make* his attention wander; the represser may find it difficult to concentrate on his job. Furthermore, though the person may succeed in repressing his own thinking about the unwanted subjects, he cannot very well control the conversation of other people in his life. They may introduce the unwanted themes into discussion from time to time, thus forcing the person to think about and feel the emotion associated with the undesirable themes.

Still another common method for the alleviation of symptoms is the *quest for reassurance* from other people. The anxious individual may induce others, subtly or openly, to persuade and reassure him there is no reasonable ground for worry. They tell him his body is in A-1 shape, his funds are adequate for most usual needs, and his employer really thinks highly of his abilities and his contributions to the firm. If the reassurer is eloquent, he may succeed in alleviating the experience of anxiety as long as he is with the anxious person. Yet when the unhealthy one is alone or away from the uplifting influence of his reassuring friend, he will again find himself faced with his recurring worries.

The unhealthy personality may avail himself of *assorted defense mechanisms* in addition to repression in his quest to relieve himself of psychological pain. He may think about health, money, and work, but in a highly intellectualized way, thus relieving his anxiety through verbal reformulation. Or, he may resort to disowning projection: "It is not I who am worried, but others." He would then display a perhaps compulsive concern for the health, finances, and career of all of his friends, while showing no apparent concern over these aspects of his own life. All of the mechanisms of defense which were mentioned in Chapter 7 may be viewed in one sense as automatic attempts on the part of an individual to relieve himself of the symptoms of his unhealthy personality.

One way a person might adopt for the avoidance or reduction of psychological suffering is a *specialized arrangement of his social environment.* This arrangement might involve keeping people at a distance or keeping oneself surrounded by admirers or helpers. So long as this arrangement is maintained, the person may be able to work and avoid personality disorganization. But if any alteration is introduced into this environmental arrangement, the person becomes disorganized and suffers acute anxiety. In fact, one way in which unhealthy personality manifests itself is the relatively narrow range of environmental variation within which the person can get satisfactions, perform responsibilities, and avoid anxiety. The healthier the personality, the broader will be the range of environmental variation within which satisfactions can be gained and responsibilities performed.

MEDICAL AND PSYCHOLOGICAL SYMPTOM-TREATMENT

Physicians, psychiatrists, and clinical psychologists may be obliged to treat symptoms in cases where a full understanding of the causes of the suffering is not available or when causal treatment is inadvisable because of expense or the possibility of precipitating severe psychosis.

Some examples of *medical and psychiatric* symptom-treatment include the various forms of shock therapies—electroshock, insulin shock, and so on; the prescription of tranquilizing drugs such as thorazine or Miltown.

Psychological symptom-treatment includes such procedures as reassurance, inspiration, and striving to strengthen the sufferer's defenses rather than trying to help him do without them.

COMMENTS ABOUT SYMPTOM-TREATMENT

We can make some general summary statements about the limited value of symptom-treatment for unhealthy personality, whether this treatment is attempted by the individual himself or by other persons with good intentions.

The symptoms which produce suffering, or which are the suffering, arise as a by-product of the patient's way of life. His way of life, his stable and recurring modes of relating to the world and people, is mediated by his personality structure. This structure includes his modes of perceiving and interpreting the world and his self-structure. *So long as the personality structure remains unaltered, then the conditions responsible for the symptoms remain continually present.* The devices mentioned above for the relief of symptoms then serve somewhat the same function aspirin does for physical pain. A headache may be caused actually by some circulatory defect;

while the aspirin relieves the pain for a while, it does nothing to remedy the circulatory defect. The headaches will recur as long as the cause is operative. So with psychological suffering. It will recur so long as its causal conditions remain in existence. The attempts at symptom-treatment can at best provide only temporary and conditional relief from suffering.

It should not be assumed from what has been written above that there is no place for symptom-treatment in medicine or in psychiatry. When it is impossible or impracticable to discern the root causes of suffering, or to remove these causes, then symptom-treatment becomes a must. Furthermore, in personality problems, anxiety may be so intense as to prevent the person from communicating with the very therapist who is trying to help him. In instances such as these, the use of sedation and tranquilizing drugs may be strongly indicated. They reduce anxiety to the point where the patient can begin to co-operate with his therapist, and they may permit the patient to carry out his daily round of responsibilities without being hospitalized.

One danger may be noted, however, about the use of such symptom-treatments as tranquilizing drugs. In eliminating emotional stress, they may produce such a sense of well-being that the patient loses all incentive for treatment of the causes of his difficulties. He may become overly dependent on his drugs, since these causes persist. A prospective patient for personality therapy has to feel his suffering acutely in order to have the motivation to go through the often lengthy and distressing period that therapy entails.

TREATING CAUSES OF PSYCHOLOGICAL SUFFERING

The suffering of anxiety, deprivations, and guilt all signify some lack of adjustment to the world, especially to other people. Adjustment implies changes in the person, or changes in the world, which must occur before the suffering disappears and is replaced by happiness or satisfaction.

Now, both healthy and unhealthy personalities fall heir to psychological suffering. They differ, however, in the adjustments which they undertake in order to remove the suffering. The unhealthy personality generally adjusts in ways which are at best stopgaps: he treats symptoms. The healthy personality strives for *cure,* for alteration of the basic conditions responsible for the suffering. Oftentimes it would appear to the onlooker that the efforts of the healthy personality at cure are indirect, or roundabout. Yet this is only appearance. For often the causes of suffering are not readily observed; the symptoms only are detectable. The causes have to be discovered by means of directed inquiry.

Suppose a student finds himself in a class where he must give a weekly oral report on various topics. Each time that he confronts the class, he becomes so anxious that his mind goes blank, and he can only stammer a few half coherent sentences, in spite of the fact that he has read the material on which he must report. His anxiety in the presence of his teacher and classmates may be regarded as his most salient symptom.

If he seeks only to eliminate the symptom, he might try to relieve his anxiety by taking tranquilizing pills just before he goes to that class, or he might seek reassurance from his friends. These efforts at symptomatic relief may be temporarily effective, but they do nothing to eliminate the causes, which may lie in some area of his life that is quite remote from the classroom.

A more direct attempt to cure the symptom of crippling anxiety that arises in the classroom would entail a thorough examination of the student's entire life situation. It might be found, for example, that the student had chosen a field of specialization that he did not particularly want to enter, but he did so to please his parents. He may have found the work lacking in interest, but he feared the anger or disappointment of his parents if he openly disagreed with their choice of his vocation. Through discussion with some helpful person, such as a teacher or counselor, the student might realize the extent of his suppressed anger at his parents, and he might come to see his failure in classroom speaking as a disguised expression of that anger —by doing poorly, he is "acting out" his disagreement with his parents without having to face them in open disobedience. The outcome might be that the student finds the courage to discuss his own preferences about a course of study with his parents and make a change that is mutually agreeable.

We can use the term *healthy adjustment* to refer to those efforts on the part of a person to effect a basic cure of psychological suffering. In principle, there are two broad modes of adjustment possible to the individual: changing one's usual modes of behavior and changing the environment. The former is referred to as *autoplastic* adjustment, while the latter is *alloplastic* adjustment. We can speak now of healthy and unhealthy autoplastic and alloplastic adjustment.

AUTOPLASTIC ADJUSTMENT

Autoplastic adjustment is healthy when the individual alters his patterns of behavior in the direction of healthy personality. It is unhealthy when the personality changes move the individual further away from personality health.

HEALTHY AUTOPLASTIC ADJUSTMENT. Let us suppose that suffering occurs as a consequence of an inaccurate self-concept. The individual believes that he is inferior to others, that he is a sinner, unlovable, and so on. If he is able to examine, in a broad perspective, all of his past feelings and actions, as well as all of his present feelings and actions, he might emerge from the study with a more empirically based concept of his personality, with a self-concept which is more in accord with evidence. As we have seen, an accurate self-concept is one of the defining characteristics of healthy personality. Autoplastic adjustment of this sort—which removes the suffering and at the same time changes the personality in the direction of health—is healthy autoplastic adjustment.

UNHEALTHY AUTOPLASTIC ADJUSTMENT. Let us suppose a person is suffering because he does not receive the love and affection of his mother. As a consequence, he feels anxious and worthless. His mother may herself possess an unhealthy personality. Before she can bestow her affection on her son, he must conform with certain of her demands. These demands include a renunciation of self-assertion, repression of hostility, and pursuit of a vocation of her choice. The son then complies with these demands. The very act of compliance changes his personality in an unhealthy direction. Furthermore, the consequences of compliance actually produce a number of new symptoms of unhealthy personality. We should be obliged to regard the foregoing as a case of unhealthy autoplastic adjustment.

ALLOPLASTIC ADJUSTMENT

In alloplastic adjustment, the personality remains unchanged; instead, the suffering person strives to modify his environment, including the behavior of other persons, so that his needs will be satisfied and his suffering relieved. In order to make judgments about the health or lack of health in alloplastic adjustment, we must have knowledge of the present personality health of the individual, and we must also be able to observe the consequences to his personality of his attempts at alloplastic adjustment.

HEALTHY ALLOPLASTIC ADJUSTMENT. An individual may already possess most of the traits of a healthy personality, namely, reality-contact, accuracy of the self-concept, healthy emotionality, and so on. He encounters a situation where he suffers: A person is condemning him for certain kinds of behavior, and he experiences a sharp loss of self-esteem and of security in consequence. He may strive to convince and persuade the other person of the injustice of his condemnation, by arguments and by debate. If he is successful, then the suffering is relieved. If he has done everything at his disposal to achieve this and still fails, then he might assert with some validity that his suffering is unwarranted. It is not he who is sick or wrong, but rather his condemner. And so he may cut that person out of his life.

Or, a person may find himself suffering because of the way in which his work environment is set up. He does not like the physical or the social arrangements in his work situation. He may devote his skills and efforts to altering these arrangements; if these fail, then he might seek another position where work can be accomplished at a lesser sacrifice of ease, productivity, and comfort and where an unhealthy change in the self is not required.

UNHEALTHY ALLOPLASTIC ADJUSTMENT. The mode of adjustment attempted by the individual with an unhealthy personality is to strive to modify the entire world so it will accommodate his perculiar set of needs. Thus, if he can feel safe only so long as people report that they love him, he will engage in a continual campaign to solicit people's affection. If he can experience self-esteem only when people praise him, he will constantly seek a praising environment at any cost or else attempt to beguile or force people to praise him. The neurotic mother who strives to keep her children dependent upon her—she dreads being abandoned by them and can find satisfactions in life only in the performance of the role of mother—illustrates unhealthy alloplastic adjustment.

WHEN SHOULD ONE SEEK HELP IN ACHIEVING HEALTHIER PERSONALITY?

The answer to the question of when one should seek help in achieving healthier personality should be perfectly obvious. When one suffers from physical pain, and one's own attempts at treatment and cure fail, then one consults a professional person, the physician. When one suffers from psychological pain, and one's attempts at self-treatment fail, either at a symptomatic or a causal level, then one should consult a professional personality therapist.

The professional therapist of personality may be a psychiatrist, a clinical psychologist, a counseling psychologist, a social caseworker or certain ministers who have been trained as pastoral counselors. These workers have been schooled in the science of personality, and know in general the varieties of unhealthy personality, the causes of personality illness, and the basic principles for effecting personality changes in the direction of health.

PERSONALITY THERAPY

INTRODUCTORY COMMENTS. A distinction is often drawn between *personality counseling* and *intensive personality therapy*. In counseling, some one specific life problem is the chief focus of the therapist's and patient's attention. The aim is to so release the patient's problem-solving powers that he will be able to resolve the problem by himself, without giving up any of his autonomy as a person.[3] With therapy, the aim is to achieve more basic changes in the patient's modes of relating to his social environment and to his real self. Thus, we might speak of vocational counseling, marital counseling, counseling of parent-child problems, and so on. Personality therapy is a more intensive procedure, with more radical aims, namely, the quest for changes in basic personality structure.

A psychiatrist may select a broader range of aims for the treatment of patients than problem-counseling or intensive personality therapy. Because he is a physician, he is qualified to administer treatment procedures which the psychologist is not trained to employ. And so, with a given patient, the psychiatrist might seek to relieve symptoms by means of various drugs, without effecting any changes in basic personality structure. Or, he might strive to eliminate certain psychotic symptoms by means of electric shock therapy, with the aim of getting the patient out of a state hospital. But it should not be assumed that such procedures constitute a "cure" of the patient; he probably still retains the modes of relating to the world which were contributing to the development of his psychosis in the first place. It is only in special cases that the therapist will select as a practicable aim the alteration of the total personality in the direction of health.

A good question to ask in connection with any therapist's aims is, "Should the therapist aim at restoring the patient to normal, that is, to the way he was before he began to suffer? Or should he strive to help the patient attain a condition closer to optimum personality health than prior to the development of the symptoms?" If we regard the patient's presymptomatic personality structure as a *symptom-producing structure,* it becomes apparent that simply removing symptoms will not be a causal treatment. The optimum aim should be to so change the personality that the individual will no longer react to life situations in ways which encourage the development of symptoms.

SOME INTERPRETATIONS OF SUFFERING; RELATED THERAPEUTIC AIMS

While it may seem academic and unimportant, yet *the point of view from which a person regards psychological suffering will strongly influence his attempts to treat it.*

SIN AND REDEMPTION. If one interprets suffering as a by-product of "sin," then efforts at cure will be directed toward eliminating the evil, and perhaps directing the "sinner" in the paths of "righteousness."[4]

STRENGTHENING THE WILL. If suffering is thought to derive from "weak willpower," then treatment will consist in efforts designed to inspire the patient to "strengthen his will." This is the view espoused by many suffering laymen and their friends who try to help them.

MENTAL DISEASE AND TREATMENT. If suffering is regarded as evidence of "mental disease," then one will seek to find the "cause," remove it, and thus restore the patient to "normal"—the way he was before he became "sick." This has long been the view in psychiatry, but it is gradually being abandoned. Many psychiatrists are gradually modifying their views along lines similar to those cited in the following sections.[5]

EGO-WEAKNESS AND STRENGTHENING. Another way of interpreting suffering and symptoms is to regard them as a by-product of a *weak ego.* It will be recalled that the ego is a hypothetical component of personality which is held to be the *agent* of *adaptation and adjustment.* If the ego is weak, the person is unable to tolerate suffering long enough to determine the most healthy means of reacting to threat, anxiety, and deprivation. Consequently, behavior is undertaken which reduces suffering in the short run but does not get at root causes. When unhealthy personality is viewed as evidence of a weak ego, then one way of interpreting rational personality therapy is to regard it as efforts aimed at *increasing ego-strength.* When we have been able to formulate a more complete understanding of the ego, its functions, and its strength, then of course therapy will be a more effective tool than it is at the present time.[6]

GROWTH-IMPASSES AND FOSTERING GROWTH. In more recent years, psychological suffering has come to be regarded by many psychiatrists and psychologists as evidence of an *impasse in personality growth*. In other words, they conceive of man as an organism with a fundamental tendency to grow toward health and full functioning —self-actualization.[7] Obstacles in the path of growth make themselves known by producing suffering. Suffering may signify the person has been striving to preserve his present growth-status and to avoid further growth or that some factors are blocking growth. When suffering is so interpreted, the efforts of the therapist are then aimed at identifying the aspects of personality and environment which impede growth and striving to alter these so that growth can resume.

INHIBITION OF LEARNING; FOSTERING NEW LEARNING. Some therapists see psychological suffering as a by-product of inhibitions and distortions of the learning process.[8] According to this view, maladjusted persons have learned interpersonal and emotional habits, attitudes, expectancies, and perceptions which are no longer appropriate to the situation in which the person presently finds himself. Humans have incredible learning capacity, and when environments change, they have it in their power to learn new modes of conduct which can insure their well-being and the gratification of their diverse needs. Individuals with various patterns of unhealthy personality, that is, neurosis or psychosis, are viewed as people who have not "extinguished" inefficient habits nor relearned more adaptive modes of behavior. Personality therapy is viewed as a learning process, with the therapist in the role of a specialized kind of teacher. His techniques of interacting with his patients are designed to promote the extinction of maladaptive habits and conditioned emotional responses and to foster learning new ways of behaving.

THE RELEASE OF BEING. Therapists with an "existentialist" orientation are inclined to regard excessive and chronic psychological suffering as an outcome of thwarted or blocked "being."[9] In this context, *being* refers to the ongoing process or flow of subjective experience—what we have termed "real self." The sufferer is seen as alienated from his real self, from his fellow man, and from his natural environment. The task for the therapist is to reactivate "authentic being" in patients. This means helping patients to recognize, to be, and to disclose their real self and to dispense with contrivance and phoniness in dealing with others.

DUALITY AND PROMOTION OF NONDUALITY. Still another view of psychological suffering has been introduced into the thinking of American and some European therapists from the Eastern philosophies of Taoism and Buddhism, and the integration of these ideologies, as in Zen Buddhism.[10] This is the view that man suffers in consequence of a "dualistic" view of the world. According to this frame of reference, man has gotten into difficulty with himself, his fellow man, and the natural world by identifying his entire being with just a part of it—the ego which controls behavior. In so doing, he has made a fallacy comparable to identifying or equating an entire heating system—furnace, ducts, and so on—with the thermostat which regulates it or equating a steam engine with the governor which regulates its speed of operation. The thermostat or the governor simply are *not* the entire heating system or motor; they are only part of the whole. When a man sees himself as an ego or a self which is *in control of* his body, his behavior, or his personality, then he experiences himself as *separate from,* or different from, his body, nature, and his fellow man. This separation is most graphically illustrated by the phenomenon of self-consciousness—a close synonym for the more difficult term "dual mode of being." When we are self-conscious, or self-aware, during our daily transactions with other people or when we are performing some task, such as playing the piano, our behavior is effortful, exhausting, and likely to be ineffective. Self-consciousness presumes that we are suppressing or repressing our spontaneous response tendencies. We suppress spontaneity because we distrust our organisms. The therapist influenced by Zen Buddhism seeks to "trick" or to invite his patient to produce spontaneous, unpremeditated behavior, in situations involving skill or in his transactions with other people, and to learn thereby that nothing dreadful will happen when he is thus "unthinking" and unself-conscious. This spontaneous, effortless, uncontrived mode of behaving is described as *nondual.* It corresponds with the experience of the swimmer who, when he is first learning the strokes, is very much aware of the placement of his arms and the rhythm with which he kicks his legs. At some point, however, the novice swimmer "lets go," "loses himself," and "lets swimming happen." If his training has in fact been adequate, his stroke will be smooth, rhythmic, and effortless.

Summary of Section. The preceding overview of causes and proposed cures of psychological suffering will give the student some idea of the ferment which continues to go on in the psychological healing professions. All of the interpretations that were cited have some truth value to them, but no one of them explains all cases of suffering or all cases of successful treatment of suffering. The quest for understanding goes on.

HOW THERAPISTS PROMOTE HEALTHIER PERSONALITY

When a patient arrives at a therapist's office, he can be regarded as a person whose growth toward self-actualization has been blocked by some factors. The "normal" personality as well (see Chapter 1) can be regarded as one whose growth toward fuller functioning has slowed or stopped, but perhaps he does not suffer sufficiently to motivate him to seek help in overcoming the barriers to growth.

The task of a therapist is to engage in those activities which will serve to release the patient's adaptive capacities and remove the barriers to further growth toward health.

The therapist may achieve these ends (a) by manipulating the environment of his patient directly, or behaving toward the patient so the latter will either alter his present environment or move to a newer, more health-provocative milieu, and (b) by so behaving toward the patient that the latter's personality will be altered in the direction of health, as a direct consequence of the therapist-patient relationship.

ENVIRONMENT-MANIPULATION

It may often happen that a patient's symptoms represent reactions to a social environment which produces the symptoms in an almost direct causal relationship. That is, the persons with whom the patient is required to interact daily place demands and restrictions on him which produce the symptoms. This is often the case with young children. Their parents relate to them in ways which are directly inductive of unhealthy personality. The therapist, in order to promote the personality health of his patient, may not be required to work directly with his patient. Instead, he may find it necessary to undertake counseling or therapy with the patient's intimate associates, with the goal of altering their impact on the patient.

In other instances, the therapist may urge the patient to move to a different milieu, to surround himself with persons who have personalities different from those which he finds in his present, pathology-producing environment. Thus, he may be advised to change jobs, or move to a different part of the country, and so on. Or, it may be necessary to place the patient in a special hospital which constitutes a growth-promoting milieu.[11] There are many times when a therapist can observe clearly that growth toward health is obstructed by a marriage, a certain friendship, or a certain relationship with an employer. Of course, the question arises, why does not the patient himself take the initiative and dissolve the pathology-producing relationship? The answer to this question is not always simple. It can generally be shown that the pathology-producing relationship is satisfying important needs in the patient, and he is reluctant to forego these satisfactions for the risk of starting anew.

When the patient strongly resists attempts to get him to change his milieu, the efforts of the therapist are generally directed toward an analysis of the needs which are being gratified in the present environment and toward an analysis of the anxieties concerning the projected changes in life setting. Frequently the patient is able to gain insight into the reasons for his remaining in the unhealthy milieu and thus becomes able to effect the moves at his own initiative. Or, he may discover some other means for behaving in his life situation which are more conducive to growth and health.

THERAPEUTIC INTERACTION

In the following sections, we shall be concerned with characteristics of professional therapists and of the relationships they establish with their patients in order to promote healthier personality in them. Before people seek professional help with difficulties in living, they have usually attempted to overcome these difficulties alone. When their unaided efforts failed to bring relief, they may have sought the advice of friends or relatives. Nearly everyone has some person in his life, perhaps a parent, minister, friend, or teacher, to whom he can confide his problems. It is when the difficulties have reached such a degree of gravity that these "social therapists"[12] can no longer be helpful that the individual may become motivated to seek professional aid. In fact, many persons seek professional consultation only after their relationship to the social therapist has been terminated. Let us consider in what ways a professional therapist differs from the social therapist, or friend-in-need.

SOME CHARACTERISTICS OF THERAPISTS[13]

Some of the characteristics of the therapist are as follows: In the first place, a professional therapist has generally been highly trained in the more technical aspects of therapeutic counseling. Secondly, he has been intensively schooled in theory and knowledge relating to personality development and functioning. This technical training, coupled usually with an experience at being a patient himself during his period of training, produces certain predictable outcomes. The therapist is unlikely to be shocked or surprised or critical of anything a patient says about himself. He will generally be more empathic and better able to understand the feelings and actions of his patient than a nonprofessional person would. He will have attained a broader perspective on human problems in consequence of his education and training, his examination of his own problems, and his observation of the problems presented to him by other patients.

He will have become something of an expert at initiating and maintaining an honest, openly communicative relationship with others. As a professional, he is committed to devoting his skills to the causal understanding and relief of psychological suffering, and he gets a satisfaction beyond the receipt of a fee for being successful in his work, namely, professional growth. His qualities, together with strong personal motivation to be a helpful individual, combine to make a professional therapist easy to talk to—at least easier to disclose some personal problems to than one's parents, friends, or kin.

Now we may ask what characterizes the therapeutic relationship. In the following discussion, we have abstracted from the reported experience of therapists in their relationships with patients and have selected several "common denominators" which appear in therapeutic relationships no matter in what special "school" of therapy the professional person trained.[14]

THERAPISTS LISTEN. The activity therapists engage in most as they work with patients is listening. They provide a receptive, permissive, empathic, and understanding audience for a troubled person, often the first such audience the patient has ever had in his life. In such a situation, motivated by the suffering which brought him to seek help, the patient generally talks. He tends to disclose more about himself to his therapist than he has ever revealed to any other person. Even with the reassurance of professional confidence, however, many patients are reluctant to trust the therapist utterly, and it is at the point where patients "block" or "resist" further disclosure that the tact and professional skill of the therapist is called upon. The therapist will seek the reasons for the reluctance at disclosure, and if he is successful in his quest for such understanding, the patient will generally get on with the business of revealing himself.

THERAPISTS REFLECT AND INTERPRET. An experienced therapist almost always responds in spontaneous honesty to the disclosures and emotional expressions of his patient, but his responses differ in important respects from the responses that might be expected from a friend or relative. Patients are generally surprised at the therapist's reactions to what has been said to him. In fact, this unpredictable but helpful responsiveness of the therapist is thought to be one of the factors which fosters the desirable changes that are sought in therapy.

Although most experienced therapists are remarkably free in their reactions to patients' revelations (within the bounds of ethics, however), yet it can be found that a high proportion of their responses are either reflections of what the patient has just uttered or else attempts to interpret the meaning or the causes of what has been said or done. "Reflection" here refers to the effort on the part of the therapist to restate the *feelings* that were implicit or explicit in the patient's last remark: viz., the patient may say, "I keep coming late to my job, and it makes me feel miserable." The therapist might remark, "You don't like to be late," to which the patient will reply, "That's right." Then, seeing that he is being heard and presumably understood, but not condemned, the patient goes on to further disclosures.[15] When the therapist "interprets" a remark, or series of episodes in the patient's life, he seeks to find patterns, connections between childhood patterns and present behavior, or similarities in the patient's behavior that appear in a wide variety of situations. It is believed that such interpretations foster increased insight in the patient, and encourage further disclosure.[16]

However, the responses of qualified therapists to their patients are by no means solely confined to reflections and interpretations. Therapists might laugh, become angry, tell jokes that have some point to them that bear on the patient's difficulties, bring up ideas for consideration—but all these responses have the characteristic that they will arise in the context of the ongoing dialogue that is gradually established between the patient and therapist.[17]

THERAPISTS REWARD HEALTHY BEHAVIOR. Although few therapists will actually seek to do so, the net effect of their responses to their patients as the relationship unfolds is that they encourage, elicit, and reward any behavior in the patient that moves him closer to personality health.[18] Sometimes the reward of such "healthy" behavior is no more than a case of *not punishing it when it appears.* Thus, a patient may have expected to be punished or rejected in everyday life if he said or expressed what he honestly thought or felt. In fact, this may have been true, and so the patient learned to suppress or repress his spontaneous and honest responses in everyday life. Instead, he would enact various roles in his dealings with others and never reveal his real self. During therapy, however, he may spontaneously utter what he truly thinks and feels, even about the therapist. He may expect censure from the therapist for such frankness, and when it is not forthcoming, it is as if his honest and spontaneous behavior has been rewarded, or "reinforced," that is, strengthened.

Therapists will frequently be quite direct in rewarding behavior that seems health-yielding. When the patients indicate that they have said or done something that took courage and that they bore the consequences of this action with fortitude, the therapist may praise them for a job well done. And as the patient begins to modify his behavior outside therapy in ways that signify greater maturity, integrity, and authenticity, the therapist will naturally be delighted, whereas it often happens that the patient's friends or relatives are threatened by his growth. It is as if the patient's intimate friends and family have had a vested interest in his remaining inadequate, immature, or sick. The therapist is, of course, not threatened by his patient's increments in wellness.

THERAPISTS DIRECTLY OR SYMBOLICALLY SATISFY MANY OF THE PATIENT'S NEEDS. The patient, when he comes in for therapy, has many needs unfulfilled. The therapist attempts to discern precisely what the patient needs in order to feel secure, trusting, accepted, and he may either provide these need-objects through his own behavior in the relationship[19] or attempt to aid the patient in his attempts to find satisfactions outside the relationship. It happens that many of the patient's needs are gratified in the relationship without any deliberate effort on the part of the therapist. This accidental gratification occurs through what the psychoanalysts call the *transference*.[20] The therapist in many ways represents an ambiguous stimulus, and as such, his personality may be autistically perceived by the patient, according to the latter's needs, emotions, and expectancies. Thus, the transference situation serves a number of therapeutic functions; it offers the patient an opportunity to satisfy his need for a father figure or a mother figure, and at the same time it provides for the therapist an invaluable source of hypotheses concerning the nature of persons who influenced the life history of the patient.

THE THERAPIST RESPECTS HIS PATIENT. For the patient, the relationship with the therapist is often the first time in his life that he experiences respect on the part of another for his uniqueness and individuality. The therapist manifests this respect by not pressuring his patient and by not putting conditions on his attention, affection, and interest in what the patient is saying. Simply being attentively listened to is often an invaluable means by which the patient's self-esteem is lifted from a low point to a more tolerable level.

THE THERAPIST DOES NOT "USE" THE PATIENT. In everyday life, the intimates of the patient may have been using him for ends of their own. Thus, they may have profited in their own quest for valued ends by his ineffectuality, or by his passivity, or by other unhealthy traits. The therapist, as a consequence of his training, and presumably higher degree of personality health, is able to resist using the patient's traits as a means for reaching personal and private ends. It was pointed out earlier (Chapters 9, 10) that certain interpersonal relationships can continue only so long as one or the other partner remains thwarted in his growth. In the therapy relationship, the therapist strives to act in ways which will provoke growth. If the patient expresses affection for him, or shows dependency, the therapist does not feed his own self-esteem with this helplessly loving behavior. Instead, he strives to understand and interpret the meaning of this behavior to the patient.

THE THERAPIST ENCOURAGES AND PERMITS FREE EMOTIONAL EXPRESSION. The freedom of the therapeutic situation is such that gradually the patient is able to vent fully all his feelings about all of the significant persons in his life, including the therapist. The therapist accepts the expression of feeling and tries to help the patient understand why such intense feelings were repressed originally and why they were not acknowledged earlier in life. In fact, if a therapist observes that his patient avoids expressing any feelings about anything, he will call it to his attention and explore with him some of the reasons for such avoidance of emotional expression.

THE THERAPIST TRIES TO UNDERSTAND THE PATIENT AND TO PROMOTE SELF-UNDERSTANDING IN THE PATIENT. The trained personality therapist may be expected to be something of an expert in the general field of personality. When he has learned enough about his patient, he has become an expert about his patient. One of his aims is to enable his patient to become an expert about himself—to understand how he came to be as he now is and to know how he now is. The therapist accomplishes these ends by means of well-timed interpretations which he communicates to the patient at selected stages of treatment.

THERAPISTS INSPIRE FAITH AND HOPE IN PATIENTS. A therapist is a professional person, and he is consulted in his office. The very setting as well as the decision to go to this setting seem to inspire in the patient a certain confidence or faith that help will be received, that there may be hope for a better life. These emotions and expectancies seem to be factors in the recovery of wellness. One of the puzzles that continues to vex researchers into health is the manner in which an attitude of hopelessness seems to foster illness, whereas the inspiration of hope and expectation of help seems to trigger off, or at least accompany, progress toward wellness. Patients sometimes seem to get well no matter what a therapist says or does, and researchers have likened personality therapy to the "placebo effect" which has long been observed in the field of medicine. Physicians will frequently prescribe medicines that come in large, colorful capsules, or which taste vile, but which actually are inert—e.g., sugar or colored, flavored water. Yet patients report that following the ingestion of these "placebos," their symptoms were relieved. It is thought that the relief from symptoms such as pain and the speed-up of the recovery process which follows the placebo derive from the following circumstances: Healing is a reflex process which can be interfered with by the person's thoughts and feelings. If a sick person will simply relax and let healing go on, it will proceed at a natural pace. If he worries and is afraid he might die, or if he has no reason to go on living, these attitudes, mediated by brain function, can impede the healing process. The placebo, seen by the patient as "powerful medicine," convinces him that he is in good hands. He then relaxes and permits healing to proceed by itself.

In personality therapy, the hopeless patient is confronted by a professional person who inspires confidence and trust and who offers hope that the patient can ultimately transcend his difficulties and get on with more effective living. This hope, if communicated, serves to keep the patient trying new approaches to his dilemmas until he discovers a mode of behavior that yields health instead of chronic misery.[21]

SOME SPECIFIC OUTCOMES OF EFFECTIVE THERAPY

INCREASED NEED-SATISFACTION. Part of the patient's suffering stems from the fact that he is failing to find satisfactions in living. This deprivation-suffering may derive either from the fact that the need-objects are not available in the patient's present milieu or else inner obstacles prevent the patient from availing himself of satisfactions which surround him on all sides. He is "starving in the midst of plenty."

Working from the premise that need-gratification is an important means toward personality health, as well as a sign that it has been achieved, the therapist strives to make it possible for his patient to satisfy more of his needs. He tries to identify just what it is his patient needs in order to experience satisfactions in living and then tries to ascertain precisely why these satisfactions have not been obtained. If it is a case of an impoverished environment, the therapist might help the patient make a move to one where gratifications are more readily obtained, without the requisite of radical changes in personality structure. Frequently all that is required is a little urging or encouragement on the part of the therapist, in order to overcome the patient's inertia or his fears at leaving a familiar environment.

The situation is different when the deprivations occur in a potentially gratification-rich environment. In this case, the barriers to gratification lie in the structure of the patient's personality. Thus, the patient may be starved for affection or for simple acceptance from other people. The question arises, what is preventing him from acting in ways that will secure these need-objects from the people with whom he lives? Investigation may disclose that the precise ways of acting which could be almost guaranteed in our culture to achieve the valued responses from other people are not available to the patient for some of the following reasons:

1. Past conditioning experiences have led him to expect rejection, scorn, ridicule, or punishment for any attempts on his part to elicit the wanted responses from other persons. He believes in advance that other people are basically cruel, rejecting, and malicious.

2. His conscience includes very stringent taboos which condemn as sinful the very satisfactions he so badly needs for happiness.

3. His self-concept includes the unwarranted belief that he does not have the capacity to learn effective ways of behaving in order to achieve satisfactions.

4. He has acquired other-concepts with respect to people which lead him to believe they should give him what he needs without any request or effort on his part. These other-concepts, however, are no longer accurate.

The therapist, after identifying these barriers to satisfaction, may direct his efforts toward their removal. Thus, he may urge the patient to test his predictions that efforts to get satisfaction will evoke rejection or punishment from others. Or he may explore with his patient the nature of the ideals which comprise his conscience, so the patient may be able to reformulate some of the ideals which are not rational or appropriate to his present age and status. Or he may strive to help the patient experience successes of varied sorts so that his self-concept can now include the assertion, "I am a competent and capable person." Or he may help the patient learn the art of testing the validity of his other-concepts. The results of these efforts quite likely will enable the patient to avail himself of satisfactions which are available in his environment, thus increasing his happiness in living.

MORE EFFICIENT REALITY-CONTACT. It can be assumed that the patient suffers from impaired reality-contact in various realms of life. His self-concept may be inaccurate; his other-concepts may be autistic; his expectancies fail to be in accord with objective or scientifically grounded estimates of probability. Yet his behavior is regulated by his perceptions, inaccurate though they be. While accurate cognition is not the sufficient condition for healthy behavior, it is a necessary condition. Thus, anything which the therapist can do that will increase the accuracy of the patient's perceptions and beliefs, and which strengthens the reality-testing habit, will move the patient closer to the ideal of personality health.

The patient, in talking to the therapist, will often give a statement of his reasons or motives for acting in certain ways. If the therapist points out other possible or plausible interpretations but of a less pride-enhancing nature, it may encourage the patient to be more honest in formulating his motives to himself and others. By verbalizing evaluations of the patient which differ from the patient's self-descriptions (by being more accurate) he may assist the patient in the task of formulating an accurate self-concept. By questioning the patient's other-concepts, he may guide the patient toward self-questioning when he makes statements and judgments about the motives and traits of other persons in his life. By correcting misinformation about matters for which reliable knowledge exists, physiology, psychology, embryology, anthropology, and so on, the therapist may promote in his patient the acquisition of accurate knowledge about the world. By correcting the patient's misinterpretations of his (the therapist's) thoughts, opinions, and judgments about the patient, the therapist will promote reality-contact in the immediate therapeutic situation.

All of these activities will tend to promote reality-contact and the acquisition of a fairly stable reality-testing habit in the patient —both of which are healthy traits.

HEALTHIER EMOTIONALITY. The patient will generally display some or all of the varieties of unhealthy emotionality which were described in Chapter 4. Most commonly, patients seeking personality therapy on a voluntary basis will be emotional repressers or chronic emotional suppressers. If they are repressers, then they typically will be uncognizant of their own emotional tensions when in fact these tensions have been provoked by life situations. The therapist will be skilled in identifying subtle signs of emotional tension when these exist, and he will suggest tactfully to the patient that perhaps he has these feelings, when the evidence for them is obvious in the therapeutic situation. Generally, the patient will deny that he feels the things which the therapist is suggesting; but he denies it for a number of reasons which gradually will evaporate as therapy proceeds. One reason for repressing is the dread that other persons will condemn or punish the individual when he has these feelings. The therapist fails to be punitive or rejecting of the patient, even when he knows what the patient is feeling. This may encourage the patient to avoid repressing, at least while in the therapy session. Another reason for repression is the nature of the self-structure; the person may think of himself, with some pride, as a nonemotional person; hence, he would experience emotional responses as threats to his sense of identity and to his self-esteem. As his self-structure gradually changes in the therapeutic relationship, he no longer needs to repress his feelings but is instead able to feel them and acknowledge to himself that they exist.

The patient who chronically suppresses his emotions does so because he fears the probable consequences of open expression. Through time, the patient will gradually acquire courage to test the reactions of the therapist to increasingly less-controlled emotional expressions. As he finds that the therapist does not reject or condemn him as he had anticipated, he will allow himself to express what he feels in more open ways.

As the patient's reality-contact improves, the frequency with which irrational affects occurs will diminish. It will be recalled that irrational affects are emotional responses occasioned by autistic interpretations of reality. The more the patient is able to achieve veridical cognition about himself and the outside world, the more rational and appropriate to the situation will become his emotional responses. This too is healthy.

In all likelihood, the more the patient moves in the direction of healthy emotionality, the more physically healthy will he become, since it has been shown that many physical disabilities derive from chronically suppressed emotional tension.

Finally, as the patient comes to be less and less alienated from his self, he will become increasingly autonomous and self-reliant. This implies that he will be less dependent upon others for important satisfactions in living. The upshot is that another powerful reason for emotional suppression and repression will have been removed, and the patient will be increasingly able to display selective suppression and release as his characteristic mode for controlling emotions.

HEALTHIER SEXUALITY. Many patients seeking personality therapy will be found to suffer from some form of unhealthy sexuality. They may not have been able to talk frankly and openly to another person about their sexual activities, anxieties, guilts, and so on. For many patients, the therapy relationship is the first time in their life they have disclosed their thinking and feelings and experiences apropos sexuality to another human being.

Where there have been unrealistic anxieties concerning sexual practices, and where there have been false beliefs with respect to the "facts of life," simply talking about sex to a trained therapist is itself conducive to achieving a healthier sexual adjustment. Misinformation can readily be corrected, and the anxieties attendant upon misinformation can be relieved, with almost immediate benefit to the patient.

As the patient talks about his life, it will become apparent to the therapist what functions (in addition to pleasure and the expression of love and esteem) sexuality is serving for the patient. As the patient comes to be aware of some of the irrelevant needs which sexuality is gratifying, it may become possible for him to experiment with other means of satisfying these needs in a more direct manner, thus releasing sexuality from some of the functions for which it is psychologically ill-suited. Thus, if he is using sex as an "opiate" for an unsatisfying interpersonal life, he may make direct efforts to improve his relationships with people. If he is using sexuality as a means of bolstering self-esteem and reassuring himself of his masculine prowess, he may be enabled after the insight to base his self-esteem on other kinds of valued achievement.

If he has been repressing sexual thoughts, it may be possible for him to alter his conscience to the extent where thinking sexy things is not deemed a sin or grounds for guilt.

CAPACITY FOR HEALTHIER INTERPERSONAL RELATIONSHIPS. It may be assumed without doubt that the patient's relationships with other people fall far short of the criteria of a healthy interpersonal relationship. The therapy relationship itself can be regarded as *an actual living experience in relating to another person, and to the self, on a healthy basis.* The therapist tries to promote self-knowledge, self-like, self-concern, activity which promotes growth and happiness for the self, honest communication with the self, reasonable demands upon the self, and self-respect in the patient. In relating to the patient, the therapist displays these attitudes toward himself and toward the patient. The latter will acquire some of these attitudes on a trial-and-error basis and others through identification with the therapist.

DECREASE IN DEFENSIVE REACTIONS TO THREAT; A HEALTHIER SELF-STRUCTURE. The patient may be regarded as a person struggling to defend an inaccurate or unhealthy self-structure against threat. To that extent, the patient is actively resisting pressures for him to grow; i.e., to keep modifying his self-structure so that it keeps pace with the changing facts of his real self.

Prior to seeking therapy, it can be assumed the patient was ashamed or afraid of his real self and strove to repress it as far as possible in order to keep intact an inaccurate self-concept.

The therapist strives continually to ferret out the patient's real self whenever he can discern it through the web and network of defenses, evasions, and distortions. By continually being alert to unconscious or disguised expressions of the patient's real self, and by continually communicating the observations about the real self to the patient, the latter gradually becomes more alerted to it. If the therapist is continually accepting of these real-self manifestations, it can be expected that the patient will identify with this accepting attitude of the therapist and come to recognize and accept his real self. Thus, the cancerous process of self-alienation which Horney described so vividly will be stopped, and genuine growth of the self-structure will become possible.

As the patient's self-concept becomes increasingly congruent with his real self, the occasions for threat will be reduced, and hence the necessity for defensive reactions to threat will be lessened. Further, the patient may actually learn that a threat may become a challenge to growth if it is rightly employed or viewed (see below, page 456).

In many ways, the therapist will indeed function as a teacher during the process of therapy. As he becomes alerted to the assorted defense mechanisms the patient is addicted to, he may point them out to the patient, thus making him aware, often for the first time, of the fact of self-deception and self-alienation. When once the patient has learned how defense mechanisms work in himself, it may become possible for him to choose between growth and defense each time a threat to the self-structure is experienced, instead of defending his self-structure automatically and compulsively.

A HEALTHIER CONSCIENCE. During the process of personality therapy the patient's conscience will very likely become a subject of joint scrutiny for the patient and the therapist. Possibly for the first time, the patient will become aware of the make-up of his conscience, its origins in his earlier life history, and the role it has played in the production of his misery. He may acquire the ability to reformulate some of his values and to conform with this revised conscience.

HEALTHIER RELATIONSHIP WITH THE BODY. Inevitably in therapy the patient's attitudes, beliefs, ideals, and practices with respect to his body will come to be examined and evaluated for their impact on over-all personality health. If therapy is effective, the patient should learn to live more comfortably with his body, to take rational care of it, and to respect its needs.

I have observed numerous patients who began therapy looking rather unattractive in dress and grooming and suffering frequently from digestive ailments, headaches, flabbiness or obesity, excessive thinness, and a record of frequent absences from work or school because of colds or the flu. At the end of therapy, these same patients had, quite on their own, taken many steps to improve their appearance, and the benefits of more integrated personal functioning and meaningful relationships with others seemed to increase their general resistance to minor ills. I have wondered whether a regime of appropriate physical exercise, including calisthenics as well as such sports as swimming, tennis, and handball, might not be a valuable contribution to the over-all program of therapy for persons suffering various types of personality illness.

THERAPEUTIC LIFE EXPERIENCES

Personality health is a goal of growth and change; it is the ideal which is visualized by the special class of professional utopians called personality hygienists. In Chapter 1, some of the tentative pictures of personality health were sketched, and these were given assorted names by their respective authors. Thus, the healthy personality has been called the genital character, the productive character, the self-actualizing person, the creative artist, the autonomous character, the integrated personality, and so on. Our more detailed concept, as it has been spelled out in various chapters, has borrowed richly from these overlapping portraits. It must again be asserted that these concepts are theoretical or fictional in nature; they are concepts of the possible. They embody the values and ideals for man of their respective authors.

Yet these ideals can be approached and approximated in actuality. We have suggested in this chapter some of the means by which the individual himself and the professional personality therapist strive to move the individual closer to the goal of growth.

Let us now consider some of the life experiences which are encountered by almost everyone *which can have growth-provocative consequences.* Perhaps from the samples given below, the reader might be able to deduce certain clues which will enable him to recognize opportunities for growth when they stare him in the face.

THREAT TO THE SELF-STRUCTURE: ANXIETY AND GUILT. Anxiety and guilt are experienced by most persons every day. As with pain, there is a short-range manner of treating these unpleasant affects, and there is, in principle, a growth-productive way of handling them. The short-run manner consists in assorted devices aimed at reducing the unpleasant affects immediately. The growth-provocative methods may compel the person to experience his pain for longer intervals, but this toleration of pain will pay dividends in the long run. If the person reacts to his anxiety and guilt by engaging in reality-testing, by attempting to discern why he is experiencing these affects, he will be able to make at least a serious attempt at effecting the alterations in the situation or in his self-structure and modal behavior-repertoire, which move him closer toward health. Thus, he may learn some new skills, or he may alter his conscience or his self-concept, or alter some of his modes of relating to other people after he has investigated the sources of his threat. In short, the healthy personality will view threat, not as something to be avoided like the plague, but rather as a welcome sign that growth is incipient.

NEW CHALLENGES AND RESPONSIBILITIES. The explorer of unknown lands is truly an intrepid character. When he goes to some uncharted place, there is a limit to the preparations he can make in anticipation of unforeseen exigencies. He must have considerable faith in his own resourcefulness, in his ability to improvise means for the solution of problems he could not have expected in advance. So it is with the research scientist who is undertaking an investigation of some completely new area. He does not know in advance what kinds of technical problems in measurement he will encounter. He has faith that as these come up, he will do the best he can. As he meets and masters these problems, he grows. He grows because he has extended his skill-repertoire.

Seen from a phylogenetic viewpoint, man has incredible adaptive and learning potential (potential ego-strength). In the healthy personality, this adaptive capacity and growth-potential is not curbed or hampered by fear, an unhealthy self-structure, or other barriers. In point of fact, the extent to which adaptive capacity is unimpaired in an individual is one of the useful indices of personality health which is available to the diagnostician. Challenges and new responsibilities often require radical alternations in the present personality structure of the individual if he is to meet and master them. It is because challenges and responsibilities evoke a person's adaptive capacity that the personality hygienist regards them as opportunities for growth. The unhealthy personality avoids challenges and novelty as being too threatening.

LOVE. Every person with whom one relates in loving fashion is unique. Although there are broad similarities among persons in a given culture, yet each single personality also represents a unique variation on the cultural theme. The more persons whom an individual loves, or at the least establishes meaningful friendships with or with whom he communicates at other than a superficial level, the more opportunity he will have to grow. For with each person he is obliged to learn new modes of relating, new modes of interpersonal behavior; he is obliged to modify many of his generalized other-concepts; in the process of relating, he becomes acquainted with new values and ideals, with some of which he might identify. He becomes acquainted with a broader range of possible modes of solving life problems, some of which he may adopt when the need arises. Perhaps most important, he "uses" a broader range of his real self. Thus, personalized interactions with many people provide an opportunity for growth. The unhealthy personality is likely to be less able to relate to others on an individualized basis. Rather, he practices long-rehearsed modes of interpersonal behavior with each person who is viewed, not as an individual, but rather as a member of some crude *class* of persons, e.g., men, women, children, foreigners, and so on. For each class, he has his interpersonal modes of relating, and he acts in those ways, despite the broad individual differences which may exist among members of these classes. He does not learn or grow in his interpersonal relationships.

ACUTE PSYCHOTIC AND NEUROTIC EPISODES (NERVOUS BREAKDOWNS). The psychiatrist is familiar with these phenomena, since it is part of his professional task to treat patients so afflicted. Nervous breakdowns can be viewed as growth crises. They signify, among other things, that the patient's personality is no longer an effective tool for solving life problems or for achieving valued ends in his present milieu. The acute and painful symptoms indicate that either the environment must be prevented from changing (which is usually impossible) or else the patient must extinguish his old habitual modes for handling the world and learn new ones. It is of crucial importance that the patient suffering a nervous breakdown seek a professional therapist who will attempt to do more than cure symptoms through rest, sedation, electroshock, change of scene, prescription of a holiday, and so on. None of these prescriptions will alter the basic personality of the patient unless they have been carefully chosen toward that end. If the nervous breakdown is to be a growth opportunity, then the patient or his therapist must take those steps necessary to promote the development of healthy traits. If this goal is effected, the likelihood of recurrence of the breakdown is reduced, and the patient's adaptive capacities will have been restored.

CRISES IN EXISTENCE. Many people report that after some extreme crisis, such as a nearly fatal illness, a near escape from death, such as surviving imprisonment in a concentration camp or being the sole survivor of an airplane accident, their life has undergone a change for the better.[22] They report that they have reorganized their values, and regard many of the goals they previously sought as trivial. Instead of pursuing fame, status, wealth, or other worldly symbols of success, they come more to appreciate nature, they love others more profoundly and with more of themselves, and they put an end to sham, duplicity, and superficiality in their transactions with others. Some people undergo a religious conversion following crises of this sort and pledge their lives to service within some church. Less formally religious individuals may not align themselves with any church, but the conduct of their lives following the crisis closely resembles the highest ideals of most religions. These outcomes to crisis or to disaster are so similar to the outcomes sought in personality therapy that one sociologist,[23] a student of the behavior of people in such disasters as floods, hurricanes, holocausts, and so on, was able to document in considerable detail the personal therapeutic benefits that accrued to the survivors of such disasters.

CONTACT WITH THERAPEUTIC PEOPLE. In the presence of some people, like certain friends, teachers, relatives, or employers—even a barber, bartender, or stranger on a train—an individual may feel more whole, more worth while, surer of himself, and perhaps unusually inspired with hope and self-confidence. Professional researchers in the field of personality hygiene are becoming interested in locating and studying these "health-engendering people"[24] on the premise that they represent a virtually untapped resource in society for the prevention of serious mental illness.

These therapeutic people may simply be good, sympathetic listeners. Or, they may be busy people, strongly committed to the pursuit of some goal, as for example artists, scientists, or politicians. Whatever their vocation, they tend to inspire hope and imagination in the persons around them, such that the latter feel more fully alive and strongly motivated to cope with problems outside themselves. They feel the better for having known these people.

PERSONALITY HEALTH AND UTOPIA

Man is a biological being of incredible plasticity. As he is found in nature and in society, his personality structure varies enormously, yet is compatible with relative longevity, energy, productivity, and even happiness. The science of personality, that branch of psychology which is concerned with the description, explanation, and control of individual behavior, is still in its infancy, but it carries with it a weighty responsibility. When we understand with greater clarity how personality is formed, then we can apply this knowledge to the task of *forming* the kinds of personality which are deemed healthy. Naturally, this raises the question, "Who will do the forming?" Aldous Huxley, in his *Brave New World* presents one answer to this question. In this novel written in the 1920's, the leaders of the world have absolute control over the growth and development of the members of society. They decide how many people of what kinds are needed to keep the society running. They actively produce so many idiots to perform menial tasks, so many persons trained to sheer love of other kinds of hard work, and so on. Everyone's physical needs are taken care of, and all people are conditioned so that they will *love doing* what the leaders decide *they have to do* in order to keep the society functioning.

In a personality-hygiene Utopia, the picture as the present writer visualizes it would be different from the monstrous "brave new world." In the first place, a *flexible concept* of personality health would have been formulated as the goal of growth. Second, tested knowledge would have been gathered by personality scientists with respect to the optimum means of achieving this goal. All the persons who had anything to do with personality molding—parents, teachers, employers, and so on—would be instructed, or at least have available effective advice, as to how to mold in the direction of health. Further, each individual person would come to place a positive value on growth toward health, and he would implement this value by the kinds of decisions he made. Stated another way, the individual would regard his integrity as among his most important values, to be sacrificed to nothing. With such a value so strongly affirmed, he would always strive to act in ways which expressed his integrity or, at the very least, did not undermine it. We can only wonder what the world would be like if the personality-hygiene Utopia were achieved. The present writer believes that it would be a happier world, and it has been with this faith that he has written this book as an attempt to move us closer to that end.[25]

SUMMARY

Suffering of some sort is the inevitable consequence of unhealthy personality. Psychologists describe this suffering in different ways, depending on its specific causes and quality: viz., anxiety, guilt, inferiority feelings, deprivation, and so on.

Just as a person seeks relief from physical pain, so does he seek respite from psychological suffering.

Attempts to relieve suffering fall into two major categories; these are called symptom-treatment *and* treatment of causes.

Examples of symptom-treatment for psychological suffering include drinking, repression, seeking reassurance, the use of defense mechanisms in addition to repression. Other persons may seek to relieve the sufferer by means of advice or medical treatment.

The main flaw in symptom-treatment lies in the fact that while in the short run it may be effective in relieving the suffering, it does not remove the causes of the suffering; hence, when the effects of the treatment wear off, the symptoms will recur.

Causal treatment of psychological suffering consists in the attempt to ascertain the nature of the conditions responsible for the suffering, followed by direct efforts to alter or remove these conditions and causes.

We use the term healthy adjustment *to describe those efforts on the part of the person to effect a causal cure for his own psychological suffering. There are two modes of adjustment available to the individual subjected to psychological suffering:* autoplastic *adjustment, or changing the self, and* alloplastic *adjustment, or changing the environment. Healthy and unhealthy patterns can be identified for both of these modes of adjustment.*

When a person's efforts at adjustment fail to effect a cure of his psychological suffering, he should seek the assistance of a trained personality therapist: a psychiatrist or qualified clinical psychologist.

A distinction is drawn between counseling and therapy. In the former, attention is focused upon some specific problem or problem area, whereas in therapy the goal is to produce more extensive alterations in personality.

Modern therapists view psychological suffering from various viewpoints, and these viewpoints help to define the therapeutic aims of the therapist; e.g., if suffering is thought to derive from growth-impasses, then therapy is seen as an attempt to foster growth.

Therapists seek to help their patients attain healthier personality both by environment manipulation and through a therapeutic interpersonal relationship.

A number of life experiences are encountered by every one which provide opportunities for growth toward personality health (if handled correctly). These include anxiety and guilt, new challenges and responsibilities, broad and deep interpersonal relationships, nervous breakdowns, existential crises, contact with therapeutic people, and successes.

Finally, in a personality-hygiene Utopia, reliable knowledge would be available for the guidance of parents, teachers, and others in their efforts to promote personality health in children; each person would strongly affirm the value of personality growth toward health and have knowledge of the kinds of decisions which he must make and act upon in order to reach and maintain personality health.

NOTES AND REFERENCES

Excellent supplementary reading will be provided by those references marked with an asterisk (*).

*1. Frankl has coined the term "nöogenic neurosis" to refer to those persons who find their lives meaningless and empty. He contrasts nöogenic neuroses with the more familiar "clinical neuroses": viz., hysteria, obsessions, phobias, and so on. See Frankl, V. E., *The Doctor and the Soul, An Introduction to Logotherapy* (New York: Knopf, 1955), p. xi.

2. Szasz has written two excellent analyses of the psychology of pain. See Szasz, T. S., "The Nature of Pain," *Arch. Neurol. & Psychiat.*, *74,* 174–181 (1955). Also, "The Ego, the Body, and Pain," *J. Amer. Psychoanalyt. Assoc.*, *3,* 177–200 (1955).

3. See, for example, Rogers, C. R., *Counseling and Psychotherapy* (Boston: Houghton, 1942), for an excellent discussion of the rationale for counseling. An effort to distinguish between counseling and therapy is Wolberg, L. R., *The Technique of Psychotherapy* (New York: Grune, 1954), pp. 3–13.

*4. Mowrer has addressed himself with great vigor to the problem of discerning the role played by sin and guilt in the onset of disturbed personality and in the parallels between forgiveness and therapeutic healing. See Mowrer, O. H.,

"Sin, the Lesser of Two Evils," *Amer. Psychol., 15,* 301–304 (1960); also his book, *The Crisis in Psychiatry and Religion* (Princeton, N.J.: Van Nostrand, 1961).

5. See Szasz, T. S., "The Myth of Mental Illness," *Amer. Psychol., 15,* 113–118 (1960).

6. *Cf.* Hartman, H., "Comments on the Psychoanalytic Theory of the Ego," in *The Psychoanalytic Study of the Child,* V, (New York: International Universities Press, 1950), pp. 24–96. See also Redl, F. and Wineman, D., *Children Who Hate* (Glencoe, Ill.: Free Press, 1951); and their companion volume, *Controls from Within* (Glencoe. Ill.: Free Press, 1952), for excellent discussions of treatment aimed at the strengthening of the ego.

7. The assumption that man has an innate tendency to growth toward health is widely held today, and may be found in the writings of Rogers, Horney, Goldstein, Maslow, Whitaker and Malone, and many others.

8. Compare Mowrer, O. H., "Learning Theory and the Neurotic Paradox," *Amer. J. Orthopsychiat., 18,* 571–610 (1948); Dollard, J. and Miller, N. E., *Personality and Psychotherapy, an Analysis in Terms of Learning, Thinking, and Culture* (New York: McGraw, 1950); Bandura, A., "Psychotherapy as a Learning Process," *Psychol. Bull., 58,* 143–159 (1961); Krasner, L., "The Therapist as a Social Reinforcement Machine," paper presented to 2nd Conference on Research in Psychotherapy, Chapel Hill, University of North Carolina, May 1961; Slack, C. W., "Experimenter-Subject Psychotherapy: A New Method of Introducing Intensive Office Treatment for Unreachable Cases," *Ment. Hyg., 44,* 238–256 (1960); Wolpe, J., *Psychotherapy by Reciprocal Inhibition* (Stanford, Cal.: Stanford U.P., 1958).

9. See any issue of the recently established *Journal of Existential Psychiatry.* The beginning student might also consult Pervin, L. A., "Existentialism, Psychology, and Psychotherapy," *Amer. Psychol., 15,* 305–309 (1960); and May, R. (ed.) *Existential Psychology* (New York: Random House, 1961).

*10. The best overview of this approach is Watts, A. W., *Psychotherapy East and West* (New York: Pantheon, 1961). Watts shows interesting parallels between the "tricks" of Zen Buddhist masters and the techniques commonly employed by psychotherapists.

*11. Redl and Bettelheim have vividly described environments which promote growth. See Redl, F. and Wineman, D., *op. cit.;* also Bettelheim, B., *Love Is Not Enough* (Glencoe, Ill.: Free Press, 1950); and Jones, M., *The Therapeutic Community. A New Treatment Method in Psychiatry* (New York: Basic Books, 1953).

12. *Cf.* Whitaker, C. A. and Malone, T. F., *The Roots of Psychotherapy* (New York: Blakiston, 1953), p. 233. I have slightly modified their definition of this term. Evidence is beginning to suggest that the *interruption* of a relationship with a friend, loved one, or "social therapist" may actually be a factor *which helps bring on* physical or mental illness! See, for example, Schmale, A.

H., "The Relation of Separation and Depression to Disease," *Psychosom. Med., 20,* 259–276 (1958); LeShan, L. and Worthington, R. E., "Some Recurrent Life History Patterns Observed in Patients with Malignant Disease," *J. Nerv. Ment. Dis., 124,* 460–465 (1956). These two articles discuss evidence relating to physical disease. Any text in psychiatry will discuss separation as a predisposing factor in the onset of various mental illnesses.

13. *Cf.* Whitaker, C. A. and Malone, T. F., *op. cit.,* pp. 141–164.

14. *Cf.* Fiedler, F. E., "A Comparison of Therapeutic Relationships in Psychoanalytic, Nondirective and Adlerian Therapy," *J. Consult. Psychol., 14,* 436–445 (1950). See also Frank, J. D., *Persuasion and Healing, A Comparative Study of Psychotherapy* (Baltimore: Johns Hopkins Press, 1961). Frank shows many interesting parallels between the therapist-patient relationship and the relationships established by shamans, brainwashers, religious healers, and so on.

15. *Cf.* Rogers, C. R., *op. cit.*

*16. See Colby, K. M., *A Primer for Psychotherapists* (New York: Ronald, 1951), pp. 82–95, for an excellent discussion of interpretation in personality therapy; and Colby, K. M., "On the Greater Amplifying Power of Causal-Correlative over Interrogative Inputs on Free Association in an Experimental Psychoanalytic Situation," *J. Nerv. Ment. Dis., 133,* 233–239 (1961). See also Wolberg, L. R., *The Technique of Psychotherapy* (New York: Grune, 1954), pp. 439–462; Braatøy, T., *Fundamentals of Psychoanalytic Technique* (New York: Wiley, 1954), chs. 10–11; Menninger, K., *Theory of Psychoanalytic Technique* (New York: Basic Books, 1958), pp. 124–150.

*17. *Cf.* Jourard, S. M., "I-Thou Relationship Versus Manipulation in Counseling and Psychotherapy," *J. Individ. Psychol., 15,* 174–179 (1959); and "The Phenomenon of Resistance in the Psychotherapist." Speech presented at the meetings of the Southeastern Psychological Association, Gatlinburg, Tennessee, 1961.

18. See the papers in Shaw, F. J. (ed.), *Behavioristic Approaches to Counseling and Psychotherapy* (Tuscaloosa, Ala.: U. of Ala., 1961); also Krasner, L., *op. cit.*

19. See Maslow, A. H., *Motivation and Personality* (New York: Harper, 1954), ch. 16, for a discussion of need-gratification in therapy.

20. Check index in references cited in note 16 for extended discussions of transference.

21. See Frank, J. D., *op. cit.,* pp. 65–74; 142–169; the comment about the function of medicines in convincing a patient he is in good hands and can relax and let healing go on is adapted from Watts, A. W., *op. cit.,* p. 56.

22. *Cf.* Frankl, V. E., *From Death Camp to Existentialism* (Boston: Beacon, 1955), especially pp. 69 ff.

23. Fritz, C., "Disaster and Community Therapy." In Chapman, D. W. and Baker, G. W., *Man and Society in Disaster* (New York: Basic Books, in press).

24. The term "health-engendering persons" was coined by James Alsobrook

in connection with some research he was doing for his doctoral dissertation. James Alsobrook (unpublished research, U. of Florida, 1962).

*25. Psychologists have begun to write about Utopias. See Skinner, B. F., *Walden Two* (New York: Macmillan, 1949); and Maslow, A. H., "Eupsychia—the Good Society," *J. Humanistic Psychol.*, 2, 1–11 (1961).

NAME INDEX

SUBJECT INDEX